Throwing Sheep in the Boardroom

How Online Social Networking Will Transform Your Life, Work and World

Matthew Fraser
Soumitra Dutta

A John Wiley & Sons, Ltd., Publication

Other Wiley Editorial Offices

John Wiley & Sons Inc., 111 River Street, Hoboken, NJ 07030, USA

Jossey-Bass, 989 Market Street, San Francisco, CA 94103-1741, USA

Wiley-VCH Verlag GmbH, Boschstr, 12, D-69469 Weinheim, Germany

John Wiley & Sons Australia Ltd, 42 McDougall Street, Milton, Queensland 4064, Australia

John Wiley & Sons (Asia) Pte Ltd, 2 Clementi Loop #02-01, Jin Xing Distripark, Singapore 129809

John Wiley & Sons Canada Ltd, 6045 Freemont Blvd, Mississauga, ONT, L5R 4J3, Canada

Wiley also publishes its books in a variety of electronic formats. Some content that appears in print may not be available in electronic books.

British Library Cataloguing in Publication Data

Fraser, Matthew.
  Throwing sheep in the boardroom : how online social networking will transform your life, work, and world / Matthew Fraser, Soumitra Dutta.
    p. cm.
  Includes bibliographical references and index.
  ISBN 978-0-470-74014-9
  1. Business enterprises—Computer networks.   2. Online social networks.   3. Internet.
I. Dutta, Soumitra.   II. Title.
  HD30.37.F73 2008
  302.30285—dc22   2008041507

A catalogue record for this book is available from the British Library

ISBN 978-0-470-74014-9 (HB)

Typeset in 11/13 pt Palatino by SNP Best-set Typesetter Ltd., Hong Kong
Printed and bound in Great Britain by TJ International Ltd, Padstow, Cornwall, UK

Contents

Foreword

Imagine that you have been given the task of designing a new restaurant. The owner of the restaurant is willing to adopt a radical new concept and wants to you dream big. You're given a completely blank slate. Not just the look and the theme, but everything about the processes and business model are open to you to change as you wish.

Maybe you think to yourself, "Hmm, this restaurant will be serving steak. And since it's serving steak, the customers will need to have access to knives. And one thing we know about people with knives is that they might stab people. Therefore, in order to make the restaurant safe, we'd better put a cage around every table in order to keep the customers from hurting each other."

We chuckle at this idea because, when designing a restaurant, it is patently absurd to think this way. Yes, of course it is true that from time to time people go crazy and stab others in restaurants, but we have chosen – correctly so – not to make the threat of bad behavior the central element in the design of our social institutions.

And yet, it is exactly this kind of erroneous and flawed thinking that so often seems to grip people's minds when they think about the design of software for social interactions. Rather than start with the default assumption that we all correctly have when we drive our cars, or walk the streets, or eat in restaurants – the default assumption that virtually everyone we meet means us no harm and is not going to hurt us – some web designers (and their managers) want to start social software projects with the premise that if everything isn't locked down under a very carefully designed permission-based model, if every piece of information is not tightly controlled, something dreadful is going to happen.

But this simply is not true, something horrific is not going to happen. As it turns out, most people are not lunatics or mean. Most people are reasonable and nice. And we should count on that and act accordingly.

A few years after Jimmy founded Wikipedia and it was becoming successful, he was invited by a major media corporation to come and advise them about wikis inside the company. Executives had noticed that, unlike some of the top-down, pseudo-revolutions that had flopped in knowledge management in the past, wikis were creeping steadily into the enterprise from the bottom-up. Employees were finding wikis immensely useful and started installing them on departmental servers themselves. And this was apparently quite scary.

In one meeting, someone from human resources suggested that if the employee handbook were placed in a wiki, perhaps someone might edit it to double the number of vacation days allowed. What could be done if that occurred? The answer is quite simple – if an employee pours coffee on a colleague in the lunch room, or participates in any number of other ridiculously unprofessional behaviors, he is reprimanded, and told to stop it immediately or risk termination. But in reality, with properly designed social software, one doesn't need to forbid such activities, because the inherent transparency and accountability built into the software makes it clear to people that such behavior would be quickly noticed, frowned upon, and censured.

What makes *Throwing Sheep in the Boardroom* a timely business book is that the authors Matthew Fraser and Soumitra Dutta recognize the deeply-embedded reluctance by some organizations to embrace Web 2.0. They explain why this cautionary approach must be tackled head-on in order to fully harness the benefits of collaborative environments encompassing information-sharing and problem-solving, and wisely state that "social interactions, like financial transactions, must be founded on some basic notion of mutual recognition and trust."

What also makes this book appealing is that the authors take a very balanced and reasoned approach in their analysis. By neither underplaying the challenges faced by individuals and organizations participating in the online space, nor by being sensationalistically effusive about the positive social and collaborative opportunities offered, Fraser and Dutta provide an honest interdisciplinary framework that successfully blends theory with real-world examples and case studies.

To their credit, Fraser and Dutta don't hold back in pointing out some of the questionable behavior one can observe online, such as the phenomenon of competitively collecting friends. But they also make the effort to explain that there is a deep-rooted sociological motivation behind such behavior, namely the recognition that throughout history, status is in part measured by the breadth of one's influence, and that the desire to solidify one's social capital has now migrated to the online world where it is hoped by many that a large circle of friends, albeit sometimes tenuous and fragile, translates into greater influence and power.

Ultimately, however, Fraser and Dutta are optimistic about the long-term benefits of social networking sites – and rightfully so. Approaching Web 2.0 adoption from a position of innovation and opportunity reaps benefits manifold.

Organizations that refuse to regard Web 2.0 implementation as some sort of disconcerting, free-for-all endeavor have correctly recognized the positive potential of embracing collective intelligence and collaboration on their employees, customers, clients, and business partners.

Simply put, the basic fact is that all societies, ranging from private corporate entities, to local communities, to nation states, and finally to the global community as a whole, are best served by vigorously employing openness and a free exchange of ideas unhampered by fear of negative repercussions or censorship. Only by creating safe environments for the expression of ideas, even occasionally controversial ones, can we hope that the most valuable ideas will rise to the top. A free marketplace of ideas, supported by the Internet and social networking tools, is what we are ultimately striving for. And this is certainly achievable if we all, as participants in this new hyper-connected world, act responsibly with personal accountability.

Jimmy Wales, Founder of Wikipedia
and Andrea Weckerle, Communications Consultant &
Entrepreneur
New York City, Autumn 2008

Preface

This book is about the power of online social networks – MySpace, Facebook, Bebo, Friendster, Orkut and countless others – and how they are transforming our lives. Online social networking is revolutionizing how we see ourselves, how we interact with others, how we work and how we participate in the wider society around us.

Social networking sites are a global phenomenon. For the hundreds of millions of people worldwide who belong to sites like MySpace and Facebook, social interaction in cyberspace has become an indispensible part of their daily lives. This book examines the powerful forces driving this social e-revolution. It also describes the equally powerful reactions to it, and makes predictions about its far-reaching consequences.

We are indeed living, thanks to the Internet, at an exciting turning point in history. As *The Economist* put it: "Society is in the early phases of what appears to be a media revolution on the scale of that launched by Gutenberg in 1448."[1] The Renaissance revolution, which brought the printed word to the masses, empowered collective action that triggered the Reformation and helped shape the conditions that led to the emergence of capitalism and modern nations. The printing press provided a powerful demonstration of how new communications systems, when leveraged socially, can topple once unassailable empires of received truths.

The underlying argument of this book is that the "Web 2.0" revolution represents an equally powerful rupture – which we call an *e-ruption* – in established forms of social organization. These cataclysmic changes are occurring at a time when many, empowered by new technologies, are questioning core assumptions and breaking with past practices. We are entering an era of liberating self-awareness and self-reliance. We no longer need to make personal choices and

organize our lives with deference to established values and institutions. Today, we are increasingly trusting our gut feelings and acting
on instinct and intimate conviction. We have grasped that crowds,
when their collective intelligence is harnessed, are frequently smarter
and wiser than the most exalted expert. We have realized that everything important in life is essentially miscellaneous, unplanned, unexpected. We have learned the value of cooperating with others. And
we have, above all, felt the liberating power of consumer sovereignty
and citizenship engagement.

We are, in short, living in an era that marks a rupture with values
based on deference to rational design, orderly markets and vertical
institutions. We are embracing the exhilarating uncertainty of delight-
ful randomness, creative destruction and horizontal networks. In a
word, we are celebrating our deepest *social* impulses.

What we are describing here has been boldly declared, loudly trumpeted and sometimes unequivocally condemned, by other authors in
a growing body of literature on the subject. If this book can make any
claim to originality, it resides in the breadth of its analytical scope.
Specifically, this book examines the impact of social networking sites
at three different levels: first, our informal personal interactions;
second, our formal relationships inside organizations; and third, our
behaviour as consumers and citizens.

These three forms of social interaction – personal, organizational
and consumer/civic – constitute the three parts of this book. They
also correspond to the book's triptych thematic structure, which we
have called "ISP" – *identity, status* and *power*.

At its most fundamental level, all social interaction is concerned
with questions related to our personal *identity*. We need to construct
our identities before we can meaningfully interact socially with others.
The first part of this book examines the impact of social networking
sites on personal identities.

Our place within organizations, and in society as a whole, is
significantly determined by notions of *status*. How we regard ourselves is frequently determined by how others look at us. The book's
second part focuses on the e-ruptive influence of sites like MySpace
and Facebook on the way social *status* is assigned, acquired, maintained and enhanced.

Finally, the third part of this book examines the role of social networking sites on the distribution and exercise of power – in social
relations, in organizations, in markets and in political institutions.

While this book, on the surface, is rich in anecdotes and case studies
about how social networking sites are affecting our daily lives, our

analysis never loses sight of the underlying theme of how they are transforming accepted notions of identity, status and power.

Who will want to read this book? This book is written for a wide readership. It will, we hope, appeal to experts and laymen alike, to the young and old, to Web aficionados and Internet novices.

If you have heard only vaguely about the Web 2.0 revolution – Facebook, YouTube, Wikipedia – but have never used online social sites, this book is for you.

If you are a parent concerned about the inordinate amount of time your children are spending on MySpace, iTunes, Bebo and other sites, this book is for you.

If you are a business professional who knows about social networking sites like LinkedIn but are uncertain about how they work and what advantages they offer, this book is for you.

If you are already a member of social networking sites and wish to gain a deeper understanding of their underlying dynamics, this book is for you.

If you work in a corporate environment where Facebook and other sites are being used by colleagues and you wish to learn more about the ramifications for the workplace, this book is for you.

If you work for a voluntary organization or government bureaucracy and you are wondering about the opportunities and challenges presented by social media, this book is for you.

If you are a corporate manager assessing how Web 2.0 tools can affect your company's performance, this book is for you.

Finally, if you are simply an intellectually curious reader who wishes to learn more about the global explosion of sites like MySpace, Facebook, YouTube, Bebo, Cyworld and Orkut, this book is for you too.

This book describes, assesses and analyses the dynamics of the Web 2.0 e-ruption and explains what it means for you – today, tomorrow and in the future.

Acknowledgements

This book was born during a brainstorming session between the authors at INSEAD in 2007. They would accordingly like to express their gratitude to INSEAD for providing a stimulating environment and excellent research resources.

Thanks, too, to literary agent Ashton Westwood of Westwood Creative Artists for taking care of business. And to Cristina Casanova for her excellent design work on the ThrowingSheep.com website; and to Ashwin Reddy for his expertise as the site's webmaster.

At our publisher Wiley, executive editor Rosemary Nixon and her team brought tremendous enthusiasm and creativity to the project and much is owed to their hard and inspiring work.

Matthew Fraser would like to thank his students in France who give him real-time feedback every day on Facebook; and also his stepson David Ham for pressuring him to join Facebook in the first place.

Soumitra Dutta would like to express his deep gratitude to his wife Lourdes Casanova for her unfailing support; and to their daughter Sara who, as a member of "Gen V", instinctively knows more about the Web 2.0 revolution than the authors could ever hope.

Introduction: social networking e-ruptions – identity, status, power

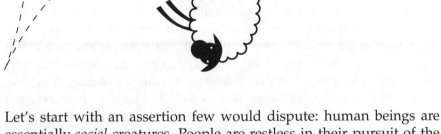

Let's start with an assertion few would dispute: human beings are essentially *social* creatures. People are restless in their pursuit of the satisfactions, reassurances and benefits procured by competitive advantages, conferred status and material gain. For most of us, these goals can only be achieved socially through *personal connections* with other people. In short, through linkages into social networks – contacts, connections, complicity, collaboration, conspiracies – which we are constantly creating, expanding and maintaining with those around us.

Yet there is a troubling paradox at the heart of these designs: our personal selves – or "true" identities – are usually banished from the organizations and institutions that formalize our relations with the world. Apart from genuine eccentrics, most of us instinctively keep in check our personal identity, which is concealed awkwardly behind a rigidly polite mask when we are interacting with strangers, conversing with colleagues and dealing with bureaucracies.

This tension between our *personal* and *institutional* selves is particularly acute at the office. No matter how sincere an employer may seem about creating a relaxed, convivial working ambiance – think "casual Fridays" – everyone except the pathologically naive is well-advised to keep their true self under psychological lock-and-key. At work, we put our institutional self forward. For reasons that remain inadequately explained, and yet instinctively understood, the spontaneous expression of our true identity is considered inappropriate in formal relations. Inside organizations, we repress our *social* selves as a matter of bureaucratic survival.

Why do *personal identities* collide so awkwardly with *institutional values*? The answer resides in the conflicting internal logic of social networks and institutional structures. Social networks are spontaneous, informal, horizontal, heterarchic, dynamic and shifting. Institutions, by contrast, are constructed, formal, vertical, hierarchic, static and rigid.

Grasping this fundamental tension – between *horizontal networks* and *vertical institutions* – will lay the conceptual groundwork for much of what follows in this book. We believe the inherent conflict between networks and institutions provides surprising insights into why social networking sites like Facebook have been so controversial. Web 2.0 social media are perceived as threatening because they challenge core assumptions – not only about social interaction, but about organizational behaviour, corporate management and democratic governance. In a word, *power*. Power is shifting, for better or worse, from institutions to networks, from vertical structures to horizontal systems, from hierarchies to heterarchies, from bureaucracies to individuals, from centre to periphery, from bordered territories to virtual cyberspace. This book examines that power shift.

Let's begin with a definition of terms. The term "Web 2.0" was coined in the aftermath of the dot-com meltdown in 2001 when disillusionment about high-tech tulip-mania was pervasive. In Silicon Valley, there was a widespread sense of defeat after the irrational exuberance of "Web 1.0" ended in meltdown. The Web had to be reinvented. Fortuitously, search engines like Google were emerging, phoenix-like, from the ashes of Web 1.0 and transforming the Internet into a *networked* platform. No longer a "push" medium to post information, send emails and sell books, the Web was being radically transformed into a dynamic network harnessing creativity and collective intelligence.

Most agree that the term "Web 2.0" was coined in 2004 at a San Francisco new media conference attended by a high-profile roster of Web entrepreneurs including Amazon's Jeff Bezos, Yahoo's Jerry Yang and Netscape founder Marc Andreessen.[1] This event was a catalyst for a wave of techno-optimism about the potential of an emergent *social* Web. On the vanguard of this Web 2.0 movement was the California geek subculture hovering around events like the annual Burning Man festival. Burning Man's survivalist ethos was based on ten founding principles: radical inclusion, gifting, decommodification, radical self-reliance, communal effort, civic responsibility, radical self-expression, leaving no trace, participation and immediacy. Among early Burning Man devotees were Google founders Larry Page and Sergey Brin, who in 1998 unveiled the company's famous logo (or "Google Doodle") at the summer solstice event in the Nevada desert. These counter-culture values were in the air at the 2004 conference where Silicon Valley heavyweights heralded the advent of a new Web 2.0 era in which "social computing" would transform corporations and business models.

The first wave of Web 2.0 hype took ideological inspiration from *The Cluetrain Manifesto*, which in 1999 had declared "the end of business as usual". *Cluetrain* contained "95 Theses" that were an unmistakable reference to Martin Luther's famous tract which, nailed to the door of the Wittenberg Castle Church in 1517, triggered the Protestant Reformation. The *Cluetrain* tract, rejecting a commercial vision of the Internet as a vast online shopping centre, conceptualized the Web as an ancient Greek agora, an essentially social place where people converge to trade goods and tell stories. *Cluetrain* was an unambiguous attack on the traditional vertically structured corporation burdened by the weight of the status quo. *Cluetrain* advocated flat, nonhierarchical organizations in which "respect for hands-on knowledge wins over respect for abstract authority". Thesis 51 asserted: "Command-and-control management styles both derive from and reinforce bureaucracy, power-tripping, and an overall culture of paranoia." For senior managers in big corporate bureaucracies, *Cluetrain* was revolutionary stuff.[2] Yet for the early Web 2.0 enthusiasts in Silicon Valley, *Cluetrain* was their bible.

Serendipitously, while *Cluetrain* was proclaiming a disruptive revolution for global capitalism, social networking sites like Friendster and MySpace were starting to take off in the United States and transforming the way people *socially* interacted. Thanks to the law of "network effects" – according to which networks become increasingly useful as they accumulate more members – social networking sites achieved phenomenal global growth in only a few years. MySpace reached 100 million users in 2006. Facebook, for its part, today counts more than 125 million users worldwide. While these figures may plateau one day, it has been almost impossible to keep up with the soaring growth rates of MySpace and Facebook, which have been adding between 250 000 and 300 000 new members every day. Today, their combined membership nearly equals the population of the United States – and may well surpass it by the time you are reading this. MySpace broke a record with 4.5 billion page views in a single day. Meanwhile, Friendster – one of the first social sites launched –

boasts 50 million members. Bebo, a social networking site popular in the UK, counts some 25 million users worldwide. Orkut, which enjoys a huge following in Brazil and India, counts roughly 70 million users. In South Korea, Cyworld has more than 20 million members. In Latin America, the hi5 site boasts roughly 50 million members. The Japanese social networking site, Mixi, has more than 10 million members. Many other social networking sites are, similarly, popular in specific regions: Skyrock (France), Mop (China), Badoo (Cuba), Grono (Poland), Hyves (Holland), iWiW (Hungary), LunarStorm (Sweden), Friendster (Indonesia) and Vkontakte (Russia).

The appeal of social networking sites cuts across national boundaries, aggregating networks representing every conceivable community. There are sites for business people: LinkedIn has 20 million members, Plaxo has 15 million and Xing has 4 million. BlackPlanet, a site for African-Americans, counts some 16 million members. There are also sites for doctors (Sermo), green activists (Care2), movie buffs (Flixster), photo-sharing (Flickr), book clubs (LibraryThing), car enthusiasts (CarDomain), dog lovers (Dogster) and gays (OUTevery-where). Friend and family reunion sites (Classmates.com, Reunion.com, FriendsReunited, MyYearbook) are massively popular worldwide. Other sites focus on highly targeted niche categories. Reuters news agency created a social networking site aimed at hedge-fund managers. Even the global celebrity jet-set has its own exclusive, invitation-only networking site, called aSmallWorld. Presumably, it's harder for the paparazzi to track you down in cyberspace. Other sites boast funky, alphabet-soup names like Xanga, Tickle, Fropper, Minglebox, Nexopia, Adoos, Cuspace, Tagged, 51.com, Ning, Passado, CafeMom, Jhoom, Yuku, Zorpia, Backwash and Fubar.

Social networking sites can, generally speaking, be put into five broad categories: *egocentric, community-based, opportunistic, passion-centric* and *media-sharing*.

First, *egocentric* networks. These are massively popular "profile" sites like MySpace and Facebook that serve as platforms for "friend" networks where members "poke" and "throw sheep" at others in their online social network. They also serve as virtual platforms for *identity* construction – frequently, as we shall see, the fabrication and management of multiple identities. Egocentric networks are also platforms for personal creativity and artistic expression – songs, videos, photos and so on.

Second, *community* networks. These sites aggregate members with strong identity linkages based on nation, race, religion, class, sexual orientation and so on. They generally replicate communities that already exist in the real world. Feelings of belonging on these sites are deeply embedded. A good example is the BlackPlanet site for African-Americans. Online neighbourhood sites furnish an example of micro-community social networks.

Third, *opportunistic* networks. These are socially organized sites like LinkedIn and Plaxo, whose members join for rational reasons such as business connections. They can also include vertically defined professional sites, such as Sermo for American doctors and sites for stockbrokers.

Fourth, *passion-centric* networks. These sites bring together people who share interests and hobbies. Also called "communities of interest", membership to these sites is horizontally defined according to "passions" (dogs, cats, cars, movies, etc.). Dogster and CarDomain are good examples of passion-centric sites.

Finally, *media-sharing* sites like YouTube and Flickr are defined not by their membership, but rather by their *content*. YouTube attracts people who share videos, while Flickr aggregates users who post photographs. People flock to these sites primarily to access content created by others.

Motivations for joining social networking sites are varied and complex. At risk of oversimplifying, we can classify motivations into two broad categories: *rational* and *nonrational*. Professionals who join sites like LinkedIn are primarily motivated by *rational* calculations related to career development. Teenagers who collect "friends" on MySpace, on the other hand, are not likely to be looking for career opportunities. Their social interaction is motivated primarily by a *nonrational* instinct to forge social bonds. The classic conceptual dichotomy for these two impulses comes to us from 19th century German sociologist Ferdinand Tonnies: *gemeinschaft* versus *gesellschaft*. Loosely translated, *gemeinschaft* describes "community" identification based on common values and close bonds. *Gesellschaft*, by contrast, describes rational forms of association based on self-interest. MySpace is a *gemeinschaft* site; LinkedIn is a *gesellschaft* site.

Since MySpace and Facebook first emerged globally circa 2005, social networking sites have quickly soared to the top of global Web rankings. According to the Alexa Global Traffic Rankings, the top ten most visited websites in 2005 were largely Web 1.0 destinations: Yahoo!, MSN, Google, eBay, Amazon, Microsoft, MySpace, Google (UK), AOL, Go.com. Only one, MySpace, was a bona fide social networking site. By 2007, the same Top 10 ranking had been completely shaken up: Yahoo!, Google, MSN, YouTube, Live.com, MySpace, Facebook, Orkut, Wikipedia, hi5. In only two years, there were suddenly *seven* Web 2.0 sites in the Top 10.

Looking closer at this Web 2.0 e-ruption, another pattern comes sharply into focus. In the same two-year period, new media sites were not overthrowing old media online destinations. The old media players – Disney, CNN, ESPN, USA Today, MSNBC – had already been knocked out of the rankings. They were history. The e-ruption that took place between 2005 and 2007 revealed a volatile process of creative destruction among new media players. What's more, the three non-Web 2.0 sites in the 2007 ranking – Yahoo!, Google and Microsoft – were already investing in Web 2.0 sites to catch up. Yahoo! owned Flickr; Microsoft owned Live.com and a piece of Facebook; and Google owned YouTube and Orkut among other sites. The message for the two sites that got booted off the Top 10 list in 2007 – Amazon and eBay – was unequivocal: build more *social* features into your platforms. And that, not surprisingly, is precisely what they have been doing.

Today, Web 2.0 social sites have passed the tipping point. It's estimated that more than 600 million people will be logged onto social networking sites by 2012. No wonder media moguls, scrambling to re-aggregate shrinking customer bases (eyeballs, audiences, readership), are launching or buying Web 2.0 properties to climb back up the value chain. In 2005, Rupert Murdoch's News Corp paid $580 million for MySpace – a bargain price when compared with later valuations. Google meanwhile bought YouTube for $1.65 billion. And Microsoft, for its part, paid $240 million for a tiny 1.6% slice of Facebook – valuing the social networking platform at an eye-popping $15 billion. The stakes were ratched up further when, in early 2008, America Online bought Bebo for $850 million. At the same time, Microsoft made an unsolicited $45 billion offer for Yahoo!

Make no mistake, this is big business. Big payoffs. Even bigger risks. There will be further creative destruction – more winners and losers.

Beyond the high-stakes gamesmanship of corporate takeovers, Web 2.0 e-ruptions threaten to sweep away old business models, management methods and bureaucratic cultures. If so, the consequences for consumer markets, organizational behaviour and democratic participation will be far-reaching. In the chapters that follow, we describe these new dynamics with terms that have been employed elsewhere: Markets 2.0, Enterprise 2.0 and Democracy 2.0.

- **Markets 2.0**. No longer captive to monopoly business models, consumers can disintermediate market gatekeepers and transact directly with suppliers. Consumers can, moreover, compete with suppliers as producers themselves. Budding pop stars don't need EMI or Universal Music to market their music, they can build a fan base directly on YouTube or MySpace. Creative entrepreneurs no longer need to turn to traditional sources to secure financing for their ideas and get their products to market. In a marketplace where power has shifted to consumers, everybody can be a producer – or *prosumer*.[3]
- **Enterprise 2.0**. In the workplace, Web 2.0 tools promise to revitalize organizations by harnessing collective intelligence. Social networks, blogs, wikis, mashups and RSS feeds can facilitate networked conversations, information-sharing and problem-solving. Rigid hierarchies, corporate silos and walled-off R&D departments can be ripped down and replaced by transparent, open-ended "crowdsourcing" strategies that even bring customers into the collaborative dialogue. Power is shifting from executive C-suites to employee cubicles, from companies to customers, from monopolists to markets. The potential upside: improved morale, enhanced collective knowledge, increased productivity, sharpened strategic focus, greater innovation. And on the bottom line, higher profits.
- **Democracy 2.0**. Social networking sites are opening up civil participation to make electoral mobilization and voter feedback more direct and effective. MySpace and Facebook are now indispensible communications tools for democratic dialogue. Both John McCain and Barack Obama were collecting "friends" on their Facebook profiles during the American presidential campaign in 2008. They understood that power is shifting away from political organizations towards people. Thanks to social media, you don't need organizations to get politically organized. For politicians it means that, to win elections, they need "friends" in low places.

Sounds fascinating. It's hard to argue with the "power of us" – mass collaboration, cooperation and participation.[4] But the positive spin on Web 2.0 overlooks a powerful human instinct: the fear factor. In highly structured organizations, social media threaten to destabilize entrenched hierarchies, challenge existing arrangements, shake things up. For many, their first instinct is not how to leverage the dynamics of social media, but how to contain and tame them – if not stop them altogether.

7

Scarcely a week goes by without a media report about yet another embarrassing incident involving institutional resistance to MySpace or Facebook. If you were living in Michigan in early 2007, you might have read in the local papers about a Catholic high school, St Hugo of the Hills, whose strict principal, Sister Margaret Van Velzen, banned pupils from using MySpace under threat of expulsion. The interdiction, predictably, prompted a student rebellion – not in the school corridors, but in cyberspace. Cheeky MySpace pages suddenly began popping up with jeering satires of stern Sister Margaret. Needless to say, the kids were all right. The schoolmarm nun came off as preposterously archaic and, worse, just plain silly.

Oxford University's aquatint facades and gothic spires are a long way from Middle America, but in cyberspace the same e-ruptions are breaking out with similar outcomes. During the spring term of 2007, administrators at the venerable English university decided to crack down on so-called "trashing". At Oxford, trashing is an undergraduate ritual that entails rushing fellow students emerging from their final exams and covering them with a mixture of flour, foam, champagne and broken eggs. It's a messy business, but it's little more than a posh version of the usual campus hi-jinks. No matter, meddling Oxford officials wanted to put a stop to it. So they began systematically spying on student Facebook postings to catch the "trouble-makers" who were posting incriminating photos of their harum-scarum trashing antics. The guilty students, moreover, were given stiff fines ranging from $80 to $1000. When the press got wind of the story, however, Oxford quickly found itself, like Sister Margaret Van Velzen, with egg all over its face – without the flour, foam and champagne.[5]

Many governments, motivated by like-minded conservatism, have banned access to MySpace and Facebook – not only to their employees, but to their entire populations. China's state censors routinely monitor and block access to the Internet – though, curiously, they are decidedly more indulgent towards the pirating of music and movies. Copyright infringement is one thing, but free speech is something else. Syria, too, has banned Facebook in an effort to thwart what the autocratic regime calls "Israeli penetration". Despotic states fear MySpace and Facebook because they promote the emergence of robust civil societies with open access to freely shared and disseminated information.

Not only dictatorships fear the power of online social networking. In the United States, where the CIA is using Facebook as a recruitment tool to scan for future spies, the Pentagon has banned MySpace for army personnel. Congressional legislators in Washington meanwhile have proposed a law that would ban social networking sites in schools and libraries. To the north in liberal-minded Canada, the government has brought the hammer down on Facebook, albeit for bureaucrats only. Canada's biggest city, Toronto, has decreed Facebook off-limits for municipal employees. Ditto in the provincial government of Ontario. And the same ban is in place for national government employees in Ottawa. For Canada's state bureaucrats, Facebook is in the same category as online gambling and hardcore sex sites. It's a no-go zone.

People are getting the message: Facebook may be great for your social life, but it can hurt your career. Look at what's happening in Britain. Figures released under the Freedom of Information Act at the end of 2007 revealed that British government departments had disciplined hundreds of employees for using Facebook and similar sites at work. The Ministry of Justice had dismissed 30 employees, while the Department for Work and Pensions had reprimanded 313 staff members. London's Metropolitan Police, for its part, had disciplined 187 employees. In Hertfordshire, the police department disciplined 140 officers and civilian staff for circulating an online video clip deemed racist (it showed a black man, pursued by police, being decapitated on railings when jumping from a flyover). In total, 132 British government bureaucrats had been sacked over the previous three years, 41 had been forced to resign, 868 had received formal warnings and 686 had been demoted or punished. All for the same crime: logging onto social networking sites at work. When King's Mill Hospital in Nottinghamshire banned Facebook for staff members, more than 100 hospital employees protested by starting an online "Bring Facebook Back" campaign. In Kent, the Medway NHS Trust imposed a similar ban on its health workers on the grounds that they were using Facebook to "throw sheep" at one another while at work, prompting a crackdown on frivolous online "time-wasting".[6]

The fear factor is equally widespread in private-sector corporations. In London's financial district, more than two-thirds of City firms have banned or restricted access to Facebook. The clampdown has been spearheaded by Credit Suisse and Dresdner Kleinwort, which use security systems to block access to social networking sites. British Gas and Lloyds TSB use firewall software.[7] In New York, financial powerhouses Citigroup, Goldman Sachs, JPMorgan, UBS and Lehman Brothers restrict access to Facebook. Barracuda Networks, a leading maker of software security systems, reported at the end of 2007 that more than half the companies using its Web filters were blocking either MySpace or Facebook. Barracuda's chief executive, Dean Draco, declared confidently: "You won't see a lot of financial institutions running to get their employees on Facebook. Maybe someday, but not now."[8]

Why so much fear, distrust and paranoia? The hostility towards Web 2.0 finds justification in many plausible rationales. Social networking is dismissed not only as a wasteful employee distraction, but as a threat to personal privacy, an open invitation for slander and defamation and a danger to the security of competitive information. These concerns are not without legitimacy. But behind every official rationale lurks a deep-seated fear of potential threats to something much more important in most bureaucracies: the status quo.

*

Tension between network dynamics and institutional structures is not new. It has, in fact, been playing out since the beginning of civilization.

Networks are horizontal expressions of dynamic social power; organizations are vertical constructions that represent formal institutional power. Networks and institutions can co-exist, interstitially, without decisively producing winners or losers. But the inherent tension between them produces inevitable ruptures at critical points when new forces emerge and threaten established forms of power.

We argue in this book that the "Facebook phenomenon" represents one of these critical rupture points. We believe, moreover, that to understand the inner dynamics driving this e-ruption, there is much to learn from the past. Sites like MySpace and Facebook are teaching us a very old lesson: power resides in networks. Yet, as history amply demonstrates, networks have not always triumphed. In fact, their resurgence today comes after a long dormancy of several centuries during which centralized institutions have been the pervasive and dominant forms of social organization. To find the last great epoch of network power, we have to travel back in time nearly a millennium to the Middle Ages.

The mythological image of the Middle Ages that has come down to us from legend and gothic literature presents an heroic tableau featuring armoured knights mounted on satin-draped horses and turreted castles ringed by murky moats. This richly embroidered tapestry woven into our collective imagination evokes historical figures like the Knights Templar and the quest for the Holy Grail. Cultural mythology does not always faithfully reflect historical reality.

But the story of the Knights Templar is rich in lessons about the rise and fall of network power.

We know the Knights Templar from chivalrous legends about their heroic exploits during the Crusades. Famous for their white mantles emblazoned with a red cross, they have recently captured the popular imagination through blockbuster movies like *Indiana Jones and the Treasure of the Templars* and the bestselling novel, *The Da Vinci Code*. Even videogames – such as *Broken Sword: The Shadow of the Templars* – have revived the Templar legend.

Popular mythology has focused on their status as a "secret" society carrying forward sacred Christian relics like the Holy Grail. Like all legends, the heroic account of the Knights Templar tells only part of the story. True, the Templars were a Christian military order created during the 12th century Crusades to protect the Holy Land from so-called "Infidels" – the medieval pejorative for Moslems. The first Templars were chivalrous French knights who selflessly took vows of poverty, chastity and obedience to pursue their sacred mission as Defenders of the Faith. Their austere, matrix-style organizational discipline was famous for its Spartan efficiency.

Beyond the legend, however, the Knights Templar were the Pope's de facto standing army. During the Middle Ages, all emperors, kings and princes were the Pontiff of Rome's vassals. Yet for centuries the Pope had no means of *coercion* – except, of course, excommunication. The Crusades gave the Pope a timely pretext to possess serious firepower. The Templars thus became the Vatican's private militia – or "army of Christ". Pope Innocent II sanctified the Templars' official status in 1130, effectively making them accountable only to God. The monastic order was, accordingly, exempted from all earthly laws – including *taxes*.

You don't have to be an investment banker to understand why the Templars immediately attracted a great deal of interest. The monastic order effectively enjoyed, thanks to Papal dispensation, the medieval status of a multinational corporation exempt from all tariffs and taxes in every known jurisdiction. When word got out, thousands of wealthy noblemen throughout Christendom began turning over to the Templars their assets in cash and property. The Templars were the medieval equivalent of a modern-day mega-IPO on the New York Stock Exchange. Think gothic Google.

The feverish take-up was overwhelming. The heirless King Alphonse I of Castile left the military knights a third of his entire kingdom. England's Henry II granted the Templars vast tracts of land, including prime real estate in London; and later the unpopular King John of Magna Carta fame granted the order Lundy Island off the coast near Bristol. By 1300, the Templars were powerful landowners and merchants throughout Europe, controlling a vast network of some 9000 manors and nearly 900 castles. In the Holy Land, they had established their headquarters on Temple Mount in the al-Aqsa Mosque, believed to be the site of King Solomon's Temple where Christ was crucified, buried and resurrected. It was this connection that gave the Templars a lucrative business opportunity which they did not neglect to exploit: trading holy relics associated with Jesus Christ. The market for holy artefacts – most of which, if not all, happened to be counterfeit – found many wealthy buyers, including kings, throughout Christendom.[9]

The main source of Templar revenue, however, was banking. Economic historians credit the Templars with establishing the world's first merchant banking operation using the modern-day equivalent of traveller's cheques. Like the world's biggest banks today, the Templar bank gave the monastic order tremendous power. Few crowned heads of Europe were not in debt, literally and figuratively, to the Templar banking operation. When France's Louis IX was captured and taken hostage by the Infidels during one of the Crusades, it was the Templars who paid his ransom. It was also Templar banking profits that financed the construction of magnificent gothic cathedrals throughout Christendom – including the one in Chartres. The Templar bank was the equivalent of the Federal Reserve, Bank of America, World Bank and International Monetary Fund all rolled into one. The order's Grand Master was, ex officio, regarded much like today's powerful CEOs of global corporations. He could hold his head up in the presence of kings. He was, after all, not accountable to their laws.

This state of affairs did not sit well with France's Philippe IV, commonly known as "Philippe le Bel" due to his famously handsome features. Philippe le Bel would be a media superstar today, followed everywhere by paparazzi and global news cameras. With his square jaw, blue eyes and long blond hair, the French monarch was the John F. Kennedy of his epoch. But looks were deceiving. Even by medieval standards, Philippe le Bel was a cunning and ruthless prince. His calculated propensity for violence inspired the writings of Machiavelli.

A gruesome illustration of Philippe's cold, unflinching brutality was his reaction upon discovering that a pair of royal courtiers had seduced his two daughters-in-law – including the wife of his heir, Prince Louis. Philippe immediately ordered the arrest and imprisonment of the two princesses. A more gruesome fate awaited their unfortunate Lotharios. Found guilty of *lèse majesté*, they were dragged to their place of execution and burnt alive. Their roasted corpses were decapitated, their genitals were hacked off and thrown to a pack of ravenous dogs and the remains of their mutilated cadavers were dragged to the gibbets and hung in public. The two adulterous princesses were escorted to this shocking scene and forced to look on, horrified, as their illicit lovers were burnt at the stake and butchered. Philippe le Bel was definitely not a man to be crossed.

Whatever misgivings historians have about Philippe le Bel's moral character, most agree that he was the first modern nation-builder to emerge out of the chaos of medieval Europe. Centralized power had collapsed in the 5th century with the fall of Rome, and the Church had emerged from its ruins to impose a less structured, horizontal form of networked power throughout Christendom. The so-called Dark Ages were a particularly nasty period. By the early 14th century, Europe had evolved into a rough patchwork of feudal fiefdoms engaged in a continual state of war for territory and legitimacy. As kings struggled to assert their authority over rival barons, power systems were diffuse, multilayered, shifting – located in the volatile alchemy of alliances and networks. Philippe le Bel, surrounded by battalions of legal advisors, was focused on constructing a centrally controlled, territorially defined nation called France. But two powerful forces were in his way: the Pope and the Knights Templar.

The Pope was Boniface VIII, a cunning survivor of many backroom Vatican intrigues. Sixty-two when anointed Holy Father in 1295, the Pontiff must have regarded the 27-year-old Philippe le Bel as a mere pup who could easily be house-trained. He was wrong. Philippe was a fox. The Pope learned this, to his astonishment, after issuing a Papal decree reminding Philippe that he had no taxing powers over Church property. Refusing to roll over, Philippe promptly blocked all gold from leaving his kingdom – thus depriving the Vatican of its income from France. Furious, the Pope excommunicated the French king.

What happened next was an incident that remains one of the most extraordinary events in medieval history. It would not be out of place in one of the more violent episodes of *The Sopranos*. To put it bluntly, Philippe put a contract on the Pope's life.

In September 1303, the French king dispatched an army of 1500 soldiers and 600 cavalry to Rome where they joined a *condottiere* led by Boniface VIII's enemies from his early days of backroom Vatican plots. Fearing for his life, the Pope – now an elderly man of 78 – fled to his home town of Anagni. But Philippe's hit men tracked him down, sacking, pillaging and burning the local cathedral with Carthaginian belligerence. The assailants penetrated the Pope's private quarters, physically seizing the aged Pontiff. Some historians claim the Pope was beaten; other accounts say he was slapped on the face as a gesture of contempt. One fact is not disputed: dragged by his captors back to Rome, Pope Boniface VIII, broken and humiliated, died a few weeks later. Philippe le Bel didn't stop there. After a brief Papal interregnum, the next anointed Pontiff, Clement V, was a French cardinal name Bertrand de Got – hand-picked by none other than Philippe le Bel. This time, Philippe was taking no chances. He had the Papacy moved – lock, stock and barrel – from Rome to Avignon so he could keep the Church on a tight leash.

Philippe was now ready to make his move on the Templars. When Philippe le Bel had inherited the French throne in 1285, his kingdom was deeply in debt. The Templars, meanwhile, had established their banking headquarters right in his backyard in Paris, which had become the financial hub of Christendom. But Philippe could not control the Templars. Nor could he tax them. In fact, he owed them money. But he was not inclined to make payments to a network of Papal warriors.

The showdown came on Friday October 13, 1307 – the original unlucky "Friday the 13th". At dawn on the fateful morning, Philippe's secret police swooped down and arrested hundreds of Templars in a series of well-timed raids. Among those rounded up and imprisoned was the order's Grand Master, Jacques de Molay. He was accused by Philippe's inquisitors of presiding over a secretive organization guilty of many heinous crimes – blasphemy, buggery, even infanticide. In medieval Christendom, these were serious accusations. Philippe meanwhile ordered Pope Clement to issue a Papal bull, *Pastoralis Praeeminentiae*, commanding all Christian monarchs to seize Templar assets. In one stroke of the Papal pen, the Knights Templar were dissolved. After two centuries, the Templars no longer existed. They had been driven out of business by the king of France.

Jacques de Molay finally broke down under torture, confessing to all charges brought against him. He was tried and sentenced to be burnt at the stake. In 1314, he went courageously to his death in front of Notre Dame Cathedral in Paris. According to legend, while Molay was being engulfed by hell fire, he angrily cursed his two persecutors, Philippe le Bel and Pope Clement V, predicting that both would meet a similar end within a year. He was right on both accounts. Pope Clement died from a painful illness seven months later. And Philippe le Bel was killed soon afterwards in a hunting accident, ravaged by a wild boar.

So what is the lesson of this gruesome medieval saga? The Knights Templar, after two centuries of glory as the most influential network in Christendom, were smashed to pieces because they had become too powerful. The inexorable logic of centralized state-building crushed a monastic order with its own codes, rituals, agenda and power. Modernity won over feudalism. Rational calculation defeated religious fervour. Machiavellian *realpolitik* prevailed over the Church's spiritual authority. The commanding logic of vertical power asserted its iron law over the horizontal influence of dynamic social networks. If we put the outcome on a scoreboard, it would read: Centralized Institutions 1, Horizontal Networks 0.

But the war was not over. Philippe le Bel had only won a battle. The Templars would go dormant, morphing gradually into other networks – like the Freemasons – who would re-emerge and play an important role in the overthrow of the French monarchy several centuries later in the French Revolution. Revenge takes time, even centuries – and it's sometimes served hot, not cold.

And, in like manner, the complex dynamics between centralizing institutions and horizontal networks form a perpetual process of conflict and change. It continues today – even in cyberspace.

*

This book is about the Web 2.0 e-ruption, it's not a companion guide to medievalist videogames like *Crusader Kings* or *Knights of Honour*. The feudal saga of Philippe le Bel and the Templars nonetheless contains valuable lessons for the themes examined in this book, and that story will be threaded throughout the pages that follow.

Medieval scholars caution us against seizing on grotesquely gothic stereotypes of the uncivilized "Dark Ages" where daily life, following the collapse of the orderly Roman Empire, was a ceaseless spectacle of raping, pillaging and violent death. These stereotypes can be experienced virtually in popular videogames like *Medieval II: Total War*. The phrase from urban slang to "go medieval" on someone expresses the same stereotype in a way that is instantly understood. Billionaire Edgar Bronfman, owner of Universal Music, reportedly threatened to "go medieval on Napster's ass".

We conceptualize the medieval social order according to a certain number of defining dynamics: the absence of centralized power; the presence of overlapping authority; uncertain political boundaries; multilayered identities; social relations based on fealty, spirituality and horizontally structured loyalties; the privatization of coercion; and widespread use of force and violence. Medieval social dynamics, above all, were essentially *horizontal* and dominated by *networks*. In the Middle Ages, the Christian religion mobilized network power. Today, network power is re-emerging on the Web thanks to social media. This can be contrasted sharply with the *vertical* structure of the modern nation-state system that supplanted feudalism.

Our historical analogy is not novel. A significant body of scholarly literature has drawn parallels between the post-modern world and medieval forms of social interaction and organization. For some, we are witnessing the "end of the nation-state" and the emergence of a "new feudalism". The logic of "territory" has been rendered obsolete as neomedieval forms of networked loyalty and social organization emerge and take hold.

The term *network* is embedded in most accounts of social transformation. Power is shifting from states to networks – namely, to non-governmental organizations, foundations, religions, cults, mafias and so on. Old structures are collapsing as insurgent network forces impose new modes of behaviour and new forms of social organization. This idea was expressed with particular resonance by Spanish sociologist Manuel Castells in his ambitious book, *The Rise of Network Society*. Castells asserts that our social fabric is being transformed by information technologies creating new forms of social interaction that are "replacing vertically integrated hierarchies as the dominant form of social organization."[10] These vertical structures are familiar to us all: schools, corporations, governments, churches. It could well be, indeed, that territorially based, command-and-control power systems – mainly states – will be studied by future historians as a fleeting chapter in the long march of civilization. Others describe a post-modern "horizontal society" inhabited by sovereign individuals liberated from the rigid constraints of government laws and regulations. Most identify the driving forces behind these transformations as communications technologies, market forces and, more generally, the dynamics of *globalization*. Some fret about the negative consequences of a globalized world. Others believe globalization will be good for democracy, justice, economic development and community.[11]

It is no coincidence that neomedieval theories emerged in full force precisely when the Internet was first taking off in the 1990s.[12] Among neomedievalists in this wave was French thinker Alain Minc, whose 1993 book, *The New Middle Ages*, observed that modern society was taking a giant leap backwards to the chaotic social organization associated with feudalism. Wharton business professor Stephen Kobrin, in an essay on Internet financial transactions, wrote five years later: "Cyberspace is not physical, geometric or geographic. The construction of markets as electronic networks renders space once again relational and symbolic, or metaphysical. External reality seen through the World Wide Web may be closer to medieval Christian representation of the world than to a modern atlas."[13]

Christian theology is a recurrent theme in the Web 2.0 e-ruption. Numerous books have been published over the past decade on the spiritual dimension of cyberspace. As early as 1996, *Time* magazine published a cover story featuring a portrait of Christ under the headline: "Jesus Online". Since then, numerous buzzwords have been coined to forge a linkage between spirituality and virtuality: techno-spiritualism, virtual faith and e-religion, to name a few. We even have the reassuring prospect of finding ourselves, one blessed day, before the Pearly Gates of Cyberspace.[14]

Medieval Christianity and cyberspace also share a conception of the human body. The pervasive Christian ideology during the Middle Ages was *contemptus mundi* – contempt for the material world, especially our mortal flesh. Precisely the same ethos prevails in cyberspace, where social interactions are frequently said to be disembodied. A social networking site popular with British teenagers is called ProfileHeaven. Its zippy slogan, emblazoned on its home page, is: "Fun in the Afterlife".

The Christian connection to cyberspace has found its way onto business cards in Silicon Valley, where "Chief Evangelist" is a corporate title. Vint Cerf, for example, is Google's "Chief Internet Evangelist". It's not a gimmick; that's his real job title. It could even be said, with only slight exaggeration, that the global software industry is managed not as a business, but as a religion. It is no secret, for example, that Apple's marketing strategy is based on the principles of Christian evangelism. In May 2006, *Time* magazine asked Gen-X cyber-novelist Douglas Coupland a question that he had probably been asked many times before: "Is Google God?" Coupland, who makes that very comparison in his novel *JPod*, gave the following answer: "Not so much Google itself, but the way you feel after using it really intensely for a long time. Suddenly you know the answer to everything . . . This is what God must be like – knowing everything."[15]

For Web 2.0 evangelists, social media hold great promise for both individuals and organizations. In market transactions, consumers can reap the benefits of so-called "long tail" effects that have made available, often for free, vast amounts of niche content. Think of the limitless number of books, songs and videos available on commercial sites like Amazon.com and iTunes and media-sharing sites like YouTube.

Online social networks have also empowered elderly people, who are no longer condemned to lead sadly isolated lives. Senior citizens can now remain connected to their families, create new friends and participate in social activities. So can people who, because of the dislocations and alienation of post-modern life, feel disconnected from others and who lead lives of quiet desperation. Social networking sites also bring together childhood friends and re-establish lost ties between loved ones. Hospital care, too, has been revolutionized as online diagnosis and treatment no longer requires physical proximity. Volunteer organizations similarly have reorganized and improved the way they operate thanks to the advantages of network effects. Web 2.0 sites also help animal rescue shelters find good homes for abandoned, abused or surrendered dogs and cats and other domestic animals.

Good deeds require goodwill. But what about the fear factor in organizations? The fact remains that, despite growing enthusiasm about social media's potential, Web 2.0 tools have not benefited from widespread "buy in" in most corporations and government bureaucracies. When Web 2.0 software is deployed, it's sometimes little more than an "optics" strategy by senior managers who want to talk a good game about IT-empowered knowledge-sharing and mass-collaboration strategies. In truth, many managers don't want to walk into the sharp end of Web 2.0. For them, Web 2.0 isn't leading edge, it's "bleeding edge". Knowledge-sharing and mass collaboration are nifty management concepts, and doubtless have been endorsed in a million memos. In the real world where human nature meets organizational behaviour, however, people behave according to their basic survival instincts. And most senior managers know that, if you share knowledge, you surrender power. Which is why bold talk about Web 2.0 implementation often hits familiar roadblocks: bureaucratic foot-dragging, vicious compliance and open resistance. Web 2.0 tools are thus deployed in a manner that reasserts the centralizing logic that serves existing institutional biases. The problem isn't the technology, it's the people who manage it.

Is there reason to be more optimistic? Perhaps. One major challenge will be to embed a sufficient degree of *trust* into the dynamics of social media in order to encourage widespread adoption in corporations. In the short term, Web 2.0 will continue to be regarded in the same way that many contemplate heaven: everybody wants to get there, but nobody wants to die first. We agree with Michael Mann who, in his exhaustive book *The Sources of Social Power*, asserted that "social life is always more complex than its dominant institutions". Put more simply, there is always a lag between social realities and organizational behaviour. It's the classic lag between *facts* and *values*. Social facts tend to race ahead of institutionalized values.[16]

For Web 2.0 evangelists, the good news is that some forward-looking CEOs are already tuning out the paranoia and focusing on the business case for social media. Corporate executives are increasingly showing interest in strategies that *leverage* social media, instead of deploying tactics that pay lipservice to Web 2.0 tools while scrambling to *contain* their effects. As investment levels increase, talk about implementing social media in the workplace is shifting from techno-hype to a more bottom-line focus on *performance*. Senior executives will want to know what Web 2.0 can do for "ROI" – return on investment. In truth, corporations have no choice. In a globalized economy, companies are facing growing pressures to innovate in order to remain competitive. Corporations today must constantly reinvent themselves with new business models, more adaptable structures and smarter strategies.

Social media deployment will gain further momentum now that the world's most powerful high-tech brands – Intel, SAP, IBM, Cisco, Google, Jive – have embraced Web 2.0 software. In 2006, Intel led the pack by releasing Web 2.0 applications called SuiteTwo. IBM followed a year later with its Lotus Connections suite – dubbed "MySpace for the Workplace". Lotus Connections was a direct challenge to Microsoft's SharePoint Server software. Then Google brought out its Open-Social software. Today, there are numerous companies selling Web 2.0 software tools to facilitate social networking in organizations: Contact Networks, Leverage Software, SelectMinds, SAP's Enterprise Portal and Oracle's Visible Path. It may be too early to talk about an Enterprise 2.0 tipping point, but social media are starting to reshape the life of corporations. General Motors, for example, uses an internal blog, FastLane, as a corporate "focus group" that attracts some 5000 visits daily, including from consumers.[17] And at a California software company called Serena, "Facebook Fridays" give employees a free hour every Friday to update their Facebook profiles and keep in touch online with colleagues. Other global corporations that have integrated social networking into their organizational strategies include FedEx,

Shell Oil, Motorola, General Electric, Kodak, British Telecom, Kraft Foods, McDonald's and Lockheed Martin.

The technology push behind Web 2.0 is now in overdrive with IBM, Microsoft and Google at the wheel. The real tipping factor, however, will be demographic. It won't be long before Generation V kids (V as in Virtual) – born since the Internet explosion in the early 1990s – begin pushing out of schools into corporations and up the management ranks.[18] Gen V youths rate music, rate movies, rate friends, rate celebrities, rate teachers, rate everything. They're going to rate their bosses too. They will rate and rank whether social networking sites are banned or not. And one day, they just might be your boss – throwing sheep in the boardroom.

*

This book, as noted in the Preface, is divided into three parts: Identity, Status and Power. A good way to remember the book's thematic progression is through the acronym: ISP. **I** for *identity*. **S** for *status*. **P** for *power*.

Our ISP thematic structure reflects the inexorable dynamic of social organization since the dawn of human history. The first phase of all social organization is *identity* construction, both individual and collective. The second phase is unequal distribution of social capital that confers competitive advantages based on *status* attributes. And thirdly, social capital is deployed as *power* in various forms of domination, material and symbolic, as societies are managed by institutional structures which allocate scarce and surplus resources. We have followed this dynamic, sequentially, in the pages that follow through our ISP thematic framework.

The analytical grid superimposed on this thematic structure can be called "3-D": *disaggregation, democratization* and *diffusion*. We argue that Web 2.0 social media are producing three profound social e-ruptions: identities are becoming *disaggregated*, status is becoming *democratized* and power is becoming *diffuse*.

Identity. The first part of the book is animated by a distinction between real-world and virtual identities. While our identities in the real world are *socially* constructed according to institutional values, cyberspace creates a wider horizontal space that facilitates the *personal* fabrication of identities. More to the point, whereas real-world identities are generally *unitary*, in cyberspace identities are frequently *multiple*. We call this identity *disaggregation*, a Latinate word for splintered, unbundled or multifaceted. The social consequences of identity disaggregation, as we shall see, can be profoundly liberating and deeply troubling.

In Chapter 1, we examine the consequences of multiple identity management on social networking sites. In the virtual world, not only can you have your identity *stolen*, it's also possible to discover that someone has *created* your identity without your involvement. You can even discover that your identity has been *deleted* without your permission.

Chapter 2 examines the phenomenon of online "friendship" and the strength of weak ties on social networking sites. Millions of online social networkers routinely collect hundreds of "friends" on their personal pages. Most are distant acquaintances, many complete strangers. It would appear, at first blush, that the accumulation of online "friends" is a vacuous ritual that reveals the shallowness of social interaction in the virtual world. Online social networking can indeed produce dangerously negative effects. Yet at the same time, as we shall see, many social networkers rely on "weak tie" *e-quaintances* to make their way in the online world.

In Chapter 3, we examine the tension between "open" and "closed" social groups – specifically, how both have been replicated in the virtual world and the implications for social adhesion and defection. While online sites frequently attempt to impose real-world social codes and rules, the unique characteristics of disembodied identities in the virtual world can radically transform rules that traditionally govern social groups.

Chapter 4 analyses the most puzzling paradox in the virtual world: *privacy*. Never before have so many people put so much personal information about themselves in the public sphere; and yet, at the same time, never before have we been so preoccupied by the danger of identity theft, fraud and other cybercrimes that are becoming increasingly difficult to police. In the virtual world, your life is an open Facebook. And the consequences can be alarmingly unexpected. More and more people in job interviews are being confronted by the same paralysing remark: "We Googled you . . ."

Chapter 5, the last segment of the Identity section, examines how people are managing online identities in virtual worlds like Second Life and Cyworld. A first lesson, as we shall see, is that the reflex to reassert real-world institutional values and regulations on virtual interaction is powerful – and sometimes has regrettable consequences. Beyond these e-ruptions, virtual reality has far-reaching implications not only for commerce and business, but also for profoundly existential questions of life and death.

Status. The second part of this book examines the motivations – in particular, the attraction of psychic rewards in the form of esteem and prestige – that drive people to socially interact on online networks. In a word, social *status*. High-status people are usually said to possess "social capital". Traditionally, social capital has been conferred by institutionalized norms related to class, education, profession, title, age, gender and so forth. But the virtual world creates spaces where fame, prestige, esteem, influence and even wealth are conferred according to an entirely different system of values. Virtual environments create level playing fields where traditional attributes that confer status are regarded not only as unjust and inefficient, but also irrelevant. We call this phenomenon the *democratization* of status.

In Chapter 6, we conceptualize social capital and examine how status is conferred in virtual reality according to the democratic measures of *efficiency*. We also put social status into historical context and provide a number of case studies to illustrate our theory of status *democratization*.

Chapter 7 examines "fame" on social networking sites like MySpace, Facebook and YouTube. The absence of traditional gatekeepers in cyberspace means that fame can be achieved directly, unfiltered and globally. Andy Warhol once remarked that in the future everybody will be famous for 15 minutes. In cyberspace, it might be said that everybody can be famous for 15 *megabytes*. We also examine the rise and fall of *blockbuster* culture and its implications for the democratization of fame.

In Chapter 8 we examine the attribution of status inside complex organizations. Those at the top of traditional hierarchies, thanks to their ascribed status of rank and position, preserve power by monopolizing "asymmetrical" information. In virtual organizations, on the other hand, it doesn't matter what it says on your business card. You are assessed on the basis of what you bring to the table. Loveable fools are out, competent jerks are in.

Chapter 9 examines the question of reputation, both personal and organizational. Social media expose our reputations to the instant judgement of others. We are all living in a virtual Gong Show from which no reputation can hide, and all opinions can be universally disseminated. But there is one key difference from real-world reputation management: in the virtual world, everybody gets to be judge. Kids rate their friends, pupils grade their teachers, university students rate their professors, customers rate their suppliers, consumers rate their service providers, employees rate their bosses. Also, online merchants like Amazon have business models that give open forums to customer ratings. And, as we shall see, sometimes the virtual culture of rating and ranking can produce surprisingly unintended consequences.

In Chapter 10, we conclude the section on Status by examining the issue of trust. Online crime has made trust paramount for online commercial sites like Amazon, eBay and Dell. Corporations, too, must know how to use Web 2.0 tools – especially blogs – to inspire trust in their brands. As some corporate executives have learned the hard way, blogging can quickly backfire when the message seems insincere, dishonest or fraudulent.

Power. The third part brings us to the key theme of this book. In the final analysis, *power* is how we get things done. Social interaction is not an end in itself. We socially interact to achieve goals. And the achievement of goals implies a power relationship. Traditional forms of power, especially in organizations, are exercised through centralized, top-down, command-and-control systems of domination. In the virtual world, power is shifting to the edges, the margins, the periphery. Virtual power is embedded in networks. We call this phenomenon the *diffusion* of power.

We don't argue that institutions are powerless. We also recognize that the initial reaction to social media in many institutions, corporations and bureaucracies will be to assert "control" over them to protect existing organizational arrangements. Technological e-ruptions invariably meet resistance that, initially, seeks to appropriate their energies to the service of old systems. This part of the book analyses the e-ruptive effects of social media on power.

Chapter 11 conceptualizes power and puts it into historical context. In particular, we discuss how, throughout history, social power has always resided in networks. We look, furthermore, at how social networks are using the Web to assert power in ways that can counter institutional forms of domination, especially by authoritarian states.

In Chapter 12, we examine the Web-driven power shift from "professionals" to "amateurs". By diffusing social power to the margins, Web 2.0 media have triggered a social e-ruption that we can call the revenge of the amateur. A highly visible terrain on which this power shift is taking place is journalism. The Web has put power into the hands of "citizen" journalists who are challenging the monopoly privileges and status rewards of self-styled journalistic professionals.

Chapter 13 examines the power shift in the marketplace towards consumers. To illustrate our Markets 2.0 thesis, we provide a case-study analysis of how Internet downloading and the iPod toppled the

Big Four music cartel and e-rupted the industry's business model. We also examine the emergence of the consumer as producer, as aspiring musical artists can now reach fans directly via the Web without depending on a music label.

In Chapter 14, we examine how power is shifting inside organizations from vertical top-down hierarchies to horizontal networks. The Enterprise 2.0 business model is based on decentralized collaboration and open innovation. We argue that, while Web 2.0 tools pose real threats to organizational arrangements, senior executives will ignore them at their peril. It's time for CEOs to give meaning to the buzzword "business transformation".

Chapter 15 focuses on an issue that concerns us all: civic engagement. Social networking sites like Facebook are revitalizing the democratic process. Politicians, as we shall see, have been quicker to embrace social networking sites than CEOs. The reason is not a mystery: elections cannot afford to ignore social power. Using Web 2.0 tools to transform government bureaucracies, however, runs into the same obstacles found in corporate hierarchies. Even so, there is some momentum in favour of e-government initiatives to make public services more efficient and accountable. The Internet may one day facilitate civil participation that gives true meaning to the word democracy.

Make no mistake, the power of social media, despite organizational resistance, is turning old models on their heads. In the Web 2.0 world, fans become celebrities, students become teachers, customers become producers, employees become bosses, citizens become politicians, Davids become Goliaths.

Social media are here to stay. They are transforming your life, your work and your world. There can be no looking back. Except, of course, back to the Middle Ages.

PART I

Identity

"You've got my resume, but it's impossible to know the real me without reading my blog."

1

The I's have it: multiple selves in virtual worlds

The assassination of Benazir Bhutto in December 2007 shocked the world. The exiled Pakistani leader was widely considered to embody the only hope for democratic renewal in a volatile Moslem country ruled by generals and fraught with Islamic terrorism.

The Bhutto family, like the Kennedys in America, was a cursed political dynasty. Benazir's father Zulfikar Ali Bhutto, also a former Pakistani prime minister, had been put to death by the country's military regime. Now Benazir too was dead, her cortege blown up by a terrorist bomb.

The tragedy of assassination, when it afflicts political dynasties, instantly raises the question of succession. Immediately after Benazir's death, the hot glare of global media attention frantically fixed on the person who was the Bhutto clan's most likely political heir: her 19-year-old son, Bilawal Bhutto Zardari.

Until his mother's murder, not much was known about young Bilawal. He was an undergraduate at Oxford University, where his mother had once been president of the famed Oxford Union. Bilawal, however, was a decidedly more discreet figure at the ancient university. Enrolled at Christ Church college, the unlikely Bhutto heir was living under the name "Bilawal Lawalib" (the last name a backward spelling of his first name) to protect his privacy. When the press began poking around and asking questions, Bilawal was definitely not a Big Man on Campus. Nobody was expecting this obscure teenager to be suddenly thrust into the international spotlight. Including Bilawal himself.

Then the media got lucky. An enterprising journalist discovered that Bilawal, like many undergraduates his age, kept a Facebook profile. Even better, it was filled with surprisingly juicy bits about his personal predilections. Bilawal seemed to be having a roaring good time at Oxford while his mother was bravely returning to Pakistan to face the daunting challenge of destiny. On his Facebook profile, Bilawal listed his only interest as "women". He also confessed to a culinary taste for "junk food" and declared that he was a huge fan of TV shows *Buffy the Vampire Slayer* and *West Wing*. There was more. Bilawal's Facebook page featured a photo of him dressed up in a red devil's costume, his face plastered in make-up with evil horns popping out of his forehead. The photo was accompanied by Bilawal's ghoulish menace: "We're ready to bring hell on earth . . . *waaahahahahahah.*"

This was very intriguing indeed. What the media really wanted to know, however, was whether Bilawal Bhutto Zardari was ready to assume the political mantle of his martyred mother. On that subject, the young Bhutto used his Facebook profile to put out a message that was oddly equivocal: "I am not a born leader. I'm not a politician or a great thinker. I'm merely a student." On his religion, Bilawal's comments were puzzling to say the least, describing Islamic extremism as "strict adherence to a particular interpretation of seventh century Islamic law as practised by the prophet Mohammed, and when I say 'strict adherence', I'm not kidding around. Men are forced to pray, wear their beards a certain length." Another of Bilawal's Facebook declarations was that "well-behaved women rarely make history."

For the heir of a political dynasty in a country armed with nuclear bombs, Bilawal's Facebook page was decidedly out-of-character, if not utterly ill-advised. The press, needless to say, jumped on it. The French news agency, Agence France Presse, rushed out a solemn dispatch that reported: "The 19-year-old, whose mother and grandfather were famed for their rhetorical skills during their terms in power, chose the social networking site Facebook on Monday to make his biggest public statement yet since her killing. In a message on Facebook – where he has attracted more than 1200 'friends' – he admitted that he was 'not a born leader' despite having taken on the leadership of Bhutto's party just three days after her death." Britain's *Daily Telegraph, Guardian* and *Daily Mail* reported the story's Facebook angle. So did Canada's national daily, *Globe and Mail* and Australia's ABC television network. In the United States, the *Los Angeles Times* sourced Facebook in a column about the Bhutto destiny. *Time* magazine also covered the story. So did MTV News and the influential Democratic website, HuffingtonPost.

There was one big problem, however. The Facebook profile was bogus. It was a hoax. The world's major media outlets had been "punked" by an Internet prankster.[1]

When the magnitude of this blunder became apparent, it was a bad day for journalism – a profession already suffering major erosion of audiences and readership and plagued by ethical scandals about fabricated stories. Now this. Suckered by a prankster who'd concocted a phoney Facebook profile. The *Los Angeles Times* took the high road and published an embarrassed correction. At Agence France Presse, management issued an abject *mea culpa* and, internally, banned its journalists from consulting Facebook, Wikipedia and all other "virtual sources".[2]

Facebook, for its part, quickly issued a statement saying the company had "disabled" two Bilawal Bhutto Zardari profiles deemed "not authentic." Facebook spokesperson Clare Gayner added: "Anyone violating Facebook's terms of use is removed from the site."

That's precisely what British politician Steve Webb had already discovered to his immense bewilderment. Like many elected officials, the Member of Parliament had been using Facebook to connect with his local constituency voters. Webb, a Liberal Democrat, counted some 2500 "friends" on his Facebook page. He'd been one of the first British politicians to use online social networking as a campaigning tool. Then one day in December 2007 – only a couple of weeks before the assassination of Benazir Bhutto – Webb tried to log onto his Facebook profile. But it had been disabled. The MP was flummoxed. When he contacted Facebook for an answer, the company informed him that it had received reliable information that Steve Webb did not, in fact, exist. Webb was dumbfounded. He was a ten-year veteran of the House of Commons, an outspoken proponent of online social networking, and what's more was frequently quoted in the press on the issue. Hadn't anybody noticed?

"They had concluded that my profile was a fake, that I wasn't really Steve Webb," the MP told the press. "I was essentially accused of impersonating a Member of Parliament. You realize the power these organizations really have. If they'd been really determined, they could have deactivated me completely and then you kind of don't know where you stand. It's actually hard for a genuine person to prove they exist." The MP's friends quickly came to the rescue of his misplaced identity by setting up a parallel Facebook group called "Steve Webb is real!"[3]

It turns out that Bilawal Bhutto Zardari was real too: the young Bhutto actually had a Facebook profile. But it wasn't the one quoted by media outlets around the world. The authentic profile was part of a group Facebook site called Christ Church Freshers 2007. The real Bilawal, it turned out, was more interested in equestrian sports than in womanizing, gorging himself on Big Macs and flopping out in front of his television set to watch endless reruns of *Buffy the Vampire Slayer*.

Bilawal Bhutto Zardari's clever Facebook impostor, it seems, pulled off his hoax with impunity. The Facebook prankster was never tracked down. But manipulating false identities on the Internet can sometimes have deeply troubling consequences. Consider what happened to a 26-year-old Moroccan computer engineer called Fouad Mourtada. In January 2008, he posted a fake Facebook page claiming to be the profile of 37-year-old Prince Moulay Rachid, brother of Morocco's King Mohammed VI. Shortly after he put up the phoney Facebook page, Mourtada mysteriously disappeared. His family had no idea what had happened to him until they learned he was languishing in prison. On February 5, 2008, he'd been forced into a vehicle by two Moroccan secret servicemen, blindfolded and driven to a police station. In jail, he recounted later, he was beaten to the point of losing consciousness.

When his family finally saw Mourtada again, he was locked up in Casablanca's Oukacha jail awaiting trial for "villainous practices". His crime: identity fraud – punishable in Morocco by five years' incarceration. His real crime, of course, was *lèse majesté*.

Pleading for clemency, Mourtada – a graduate of the prestigious Mohammedia Engineers School in Rabat – told Moroccan police that his Facebook profile had been an innocuous hoax. "I created this account on January 15, 2008," he said in a statement. "It remained online a few days before somebody closed it. There are so many profiles of celebrities on Facebook. I never thought that by creating a profile of His Highness Prince Moulay Rachid I was harming him in any way. As a matter of fact, I did not send any message from that account to anyone. It was just a joke, a gag."

Mourtada's lawyer, Ali Ammar, sought his client's release on bail on the grounds that no fraud had been committed against anyone. "This is a cultural problem, this is the first time that a Moroccan poses as a very important personality on the Internet," he said. "This is already a common practice in Europe and USA." The Moroccan authorities, implacable, were unmoved. The request for bail was denied. In late February 2008, Mourtada received a three-year prison term. Facebook, meanwhile, denied giving the Moroccan authorities information leading them to Mourtada.[4]

As Mourtada began serving hard time in a Moroccan prison, he could console himself with the fact that, paradoxically, his true identity was receiving more international attention than the Moroccan prince he'd imitated on Facebook. Mourtada's predicament had made CNN's newscast and was published in newspapers around the world including *The New York Times*. A sudden *cause célèbre* on many human rights Websites and blogs, Mourtada even earned his own Wikipedia biography. A "Help Fouad" site was created to rally support for his legal appeal. The international pressure worked. After groups like Amnesty International got involved, Mourtada received a royal pardon.[5]

In Britain, meanwhile, a 23-year-old woman called Kerry Harvey discovered to her horror that scam artists had stolen her online details – including her date of birth and mobile phone number – and reconstructed her identity on Facebook as a prostitute soliciting clients online. Kerry, an advertising executive from Glousestershire, was at first baffled when she started getting calls from "punters" looking for sex. Then she learned that she had a parallel life on Facebook, where malicious fraudsters had stolen her photo from another website and, combining it with accurate details like her phone number, transformed her into a Facebook hooker.

Harvey says the Facebook scam severely undermined her self-esteem. "These sites are too open to abuse and should be closed down or made safer," she said. "Since it happened I've become really self conscious. I can't just go up to people and talk to them because my confidence has gone. The person who created [the phoney profile] is sick and should be banned from websites like this."[6]

Let's step back and consider the implications of these Facebook identity conundrums.

Many of us worry about having our identities stolen by Internet hackers seeking to drain our bank accounts. These anxieties are well-founded. Cyber-fraud is now a billion-dollar criminal racket. For fraud to be perpetrated successfully, however, nobody can know about it. A fraudster furtively *borrows* your identity in order to steal your money in a criminal act that initially goes unnoticed. On social networking sites like Facebook, however, your identity can be *created* or *deleted*. What's more, the entire world may quickly know about it. In cyberspace, as Bilawal Bhutto Zardari and Steve Webb discovered, your virtual self can be brought to life, and killed off, like characters in a play. And you have no control over it.

It's even more complicated. We can now play an active role, like a playwright, in the creation and manipulation of our own online identities. Since the explosion of social networking websites circa 2005, millions of people have been constructing *multiple* identities as they socially interact, build networks and collect "friends". Virtual reality has given a new meaning to the term "facelift". Online self-representation is disembodied and exempt from the immediate consequences of direct eye-to-eye contact. Millions of online social networkers thus have become masters of self-fabrication, distortion, misrepresentation and outright imposture.

On sites like MySpace and Facebook, anyone can hide behind a self-constructed virtual identity. Plain girls become hot babes. Shy nerds become sociable extraverts. Fatties become thin, pipsqueaks become towering, weaklings become buff. In the virtual social universe where status is conferred by the accumulation of "friends", self-presentation has been transformed into a ritual of self-fabrication. It's called putting your best cyberface forward.

We call this identity *disaggregation*. The construction, and maintenance, of multiple identities on social networking sites is rapidly becoming the expected norm. In the online world, the *unitary* self has morphed into the *multiple* self. Identities in cyberspace are multifaceted, splintered, concocted, fluid, negotiated, unexpected and sometimes deceptive.

Multiple cyber-identities can have a perverse dark side. Men can play women; and women can play men. The bad play good; and the vicious play virtuous. On sites like MySpace, dangerous paedophiles can pretend to be children in order to prey on innocent victims. For many parents, understandably, this online danger is a source of tremendous anxiety. Cyber identity construction can also destroy marriages. It's difficult to keep a marriage interesting when one partner spends all night on Facebook, especially when the lure of pornography and virtual adultery is only a click away. In 2007, *Time* magazine announced: "Facebook More Popular than Porn". Many adults who navigate virtual sites like Second Life are, in fact, looking for sexual adventure.[7] Facebook is also being used to reconnect with old sweethearts and flings. In marriages, suspicious minds are now cyber-stalking their own spouses by snooping on their online profiles. Checking a list of "friends" sometimes comes across an inadvertent slip that reveals a fatal crack in the marriage. The snooper may also be stalking from outside the marriage. Adulterers beware: the Bunny Boiler is prying into your Facebook profile.

Social networking sites have also been blamed for serving as online catalysts for shocking tragedies. In the quiet Welsh town of Bridgend, residents were horrified in early 2008 to discover a rash of suicides among local teenagers whose morbid pact had apparently been conceived on the Bebo site. When Bridgend's local tragedy hit the national media, the whole of Britain was stunned and perplexed. What was it about socially interacting on a website that pushed these Welsh teenagers to end their lives?[8]

This all-too-common phenomenon is called the "Werther Effect", after Goethe's *Sorrows of Young Werther*. In Goethe's 18th century *sturm und drang* novel, the melancholic hero Werther shoots himself in the head over his unrequited love for a girl called Lotte. When the book first appeared in 1774, it triggered an epidemic of similar acts of despair – the first-known examples of "copycat suicides" in modern history. *Sorrows of Young Werther*, which Napoleon counted among the greatest works of literature, was banned in several countries. Today, the "Werther Effect" is plaguing the MySpace generation as adolescents struggle with identity construction between real and virtual worlds.

Identity formation is a complex process. Some might argue that, fundamentally, we are all unknowable mysteries. The psychoanalytical tradition from Freud to Lacan posits that our identities are essentially illusory. There is little disagreement, however, about one powerful fact: our identities are *socially* constructed. The social construction of identities is based on institutionalized values – family, community, church, profession, nation and so on. For most of us, our identities have been assembled and shaped by dominant values given social expression by institutions.[9]

During the Roman Empire, identity construction was simple: you were either a Roman or a Barbarian. True, within the empire there was a distinction between *citizens* and *slaves*, but the most significant identity distinction was a sharp us-and-them dichotomy between Roman citizens and the uncivilized hordes beyond the limits of empire – Germans, Celts, Britons, Huns, Vandals and Visigoths. When Rome finally collapsed in the 5th century after a Barbarian invasion, Christianity emerged from its imperial ruins. The Catholic Church's administrative system was grafted directly onto old Roman dioceses. The new religion, fittingly, was called Roman Catholicism.

In Christendom, identities were no longer constructed according to notions of *citizenship*. They were fashioned by the spiritual values of a *religious* community. If you asked someone in medieval Europe the question, "who are you?", they would not have replied French, German, British, Spanish or Italian. Those concepts did not even exist. Identities in the Middle Ages were complex and multilayered, integrating sacred and profane. Most people considered themselves, above everything else, to be "Christian". It was in this historical context that monastic orders like the Knights Templar emerged as powerful social networks. The young French noblemen who joined the Templars were, to be sure, attracted to the order by the prospect of influence and power. But more fundamentally, they were sorting out their own identities. It must have been deeply reassuring in 13th century Christendom to be regarded, and revered, as a benighted Defender of the Faith.

After modern nation-states overthrew the medieval order, states based their authority on *legal-rational* forms of domination exercised through strong, centralized bureaucracies. When modern states first emerged in the 17th century, with the Treaty of Westphalia in 1648, what we today call "national identities" did not exist. Identities were based on a fusion of feudal loyalties and religious devotion. Nationalism as we know it today would not finally emerge until the end of the 18th century with the French Revolution. While modern states imposed their authority through centralized institutions and strong armies, they needed something else to forge social cohesiveness among their disparate populations who frequently spoke different languages. Thus was born *national identity*.

In his classic work, *Imagined Communities*, Benedict Anderson observed that modern nations are essentially *mythological* constructs. They are "imagined" because their members do not know most of their fellow citizens; they never come into contact with one another. And yet, thanks to a strange psychosocial alchemy called national identity, nations are forged by a common *image* that joins people in feelings of common loyalty and purpose. The word frequently used to describe this phenomenon is *patriotism*. In the 18th century, Dr Johnson famously remarked that patriotism is the "last refuge of the scoundrel". For modern states, however, patriotism had a function. It ensured social cohesion and legitimized the state's authority.[10]

States proved remarkably successful at identity construction. All manner of rituals and symbols – including flags, anthems and folk heroes – were cobbled together, and sometimes fabricated, in the cause of nation-building. It was an extraordinary achievement, especially since some nations – like Belgium – were in fact artificially invented and held together by national symbols that were either concocted or borrowed. Yet it worked. For the past two or three centuries, most people have maintained a primary self-concept fused with an essentially *national* sense of belonging. The Olympic Games are organized according to these national identity constructions. So is World Cup soccer. When you land at a foreign airport and present yourself at customs, you are asked for a passport – a document attesting to your national identity. Warfare is the most violent, and tragic, expression of national identity. Think of how many millions have laid down their lives for their country. During the 19th and 20th centuries, patriotism had real consequences on many battlefields.

Today, states no longer exercise the same degree of symbolic power capable of structuring identities and commanding loyalties. After three centuries of unchallenged authority, and countless millions killed in wars, nationalism has a blemished reputation. The monopoly of centralized states on identity construction and social mobilization is now being challenged by competing loyalties. New forms of identity construction are being organized not by vertical institutions, but rather by *networks*. And many of these networks operate on the Internet. Identity construction is shifting to the virtual world.

That challenge to state power was laid down, perhaps over-dramatically, in 1996 when self-styled cyberguru John Perry Barlow flew to Davos to make his unilateral Declaration of the Independence of Cyberspace. "Governments of the Industrial World, you weary giants of flesh and steel, I come from Cyberspace, the new home of Mind. On behalf of the future, I ask you of the past to leave us alone," he announced. "You are not welcome among us. You have no sovereignty where we gather . . . Our world is different. Cyberspace consists of transactions, relationships and thought itself, arrayed like a standing wave in the web of our communications. Ours is a world that is both everywhere and nowhere, but it is not where bodies live. We are creating a world that all may enter without privilege or prejudice accorded by race, economic power, military force or station of birth. We are creating a world where anyone, anywhere may express his or her beliefs, no matter how singular, without fear of being coerced into silence or conformity. Your legal concepts of property, expression, identity, movement and context do not apply to us. They are all based on matter, and there is no matter here."

Is this just bombastic, over-the-top, neo-hippie, cyber-Utopian lunacy? Or should we accredit John Perry Barlow's taunting Declaration of Independence as a bona fide draft constitution for hundreds of millions of members of MySpace, Facebook, Bebo, Orkut, Cyworld and other social networking sites?

So long as we are holding passports while travelling in real space and time, it might reasonably be argued, national identities are here to stay. It cannot be doubted, however, that the line between real-world and virtual identities is becoming increasingly blurred and ambiguous.

A useful way to conceptualize this tension is by contrasting *social* and *personal* identity construction. Traditional theories, as noted, posit that identities are fundamentally *social* constructs. Social identities connect us to communities based on feelings of *sameness* with other members. Personal identities, on the other hand, are constructed not to reinforce our similarity to others, but rather to assert our *uniqueness*.[11]

Virtual reality is an ideal sphere for *personal* identities. The quest for uniqueness on online social networks, as we have seen, can sometimes inspire highly imaginative forms of self-presentation, including fabrication and invention. Virtual identities are multifaceted and chameleon-like. For some, it must feel liberating and rebellious in a way that reconnects with the hippie culture of the 1960s when John Perry Barlow was writing lyrics for the Grateful Dead. No longer dependent on socially defined values of established institutions, young people on MySpace and Bebo are free to cultivate, albeit narcissistically, highly personalized notions of self.

There is, however, an unavoidable caveat: the blurred line between "true" and "false" identities can be disturbingly deceptive.[12]

The fate of the Friendster social networking site provides a fascinating case study that illustrates this troubling ambiguity. Launched in 2002, Friendster was one of the first American social networking sites. Like other sites that came later, its main function was connecting people – in fact, it started off as a "dating" site. Friendster's social architecture, however, quickly produced a series of unintended consequences. The site's original design limited any member's circle of "friends" to only those less than *four degrees* away (defined as friends of friends of friends of friends). This was an even more restrictive version of the famous "six degrees of separation" which, apparently, links us all. The owners of Friendster were, in effect, regulating the site in order to create some semblance of social cohesion – or "close ties".

The two-degree difference turned out, unexpectedly, to be a significant factor in the way Friendster members began to behave on the site. Most "Friendsters" – as the site's members were called – had joined the site, in keeping with its name, to validate themselves socially by collecting a maximum number of "friends". They were not bothered by having hundreds of "friends" who were, in truth, vague acquaintances or total strangers. Yet the site's owners had arbitrarily erected a social barrier around the fourth degree. Reacting against this restriction, some Friendsters began padding out their "friend" lists with fake profiles in order to cut through the two-degree filter. These persona fabricators quickly became known as "Fakesters". A great deal of creativity and inventiveness was often invested in the fabrication of these fake profiles. Indeed, Fakesters soon became immensely popular on the site. Collecting Fakester friends became cool. For many, paradoxically, their most fascinating "friends" were people who, in fact, did not actually exist.

The owners of Friendster, failing to understand the appeal of this paradox, reacted by cracking down on the "Fakester" epidemic. They began frantically deleting all phoney profiles. Punishing your own customers is never a good idea. Then the owners of Friendster made another serious management blunder. They began deleting profiles of *suspected* Fakesters who, in fact, turned out to be real members and not fakes at all.[13] Authentic Friendsters – like the British MP Steven Webb – were waking up to discover that their online identities had been deleted. Zap, you don't exist.

This ill-advised meddling produced disastrous consequences for Friendster. The snooping and heavy-handed regulation triggered a mass defection from the site. Fed up with the site's uncool owners, many founding Friendster members checked out. In the United States, Friendster never fully recovered from the exodus. In America, the site was quickly overtaken by MySpace, which shrewdly offered a user-friendly alternative to Friendster. If Friendster's owners had shown more flexibility and openness towards multiple identities popping up on the site, it might today be the most popular social networking site in the world. After the disgruntled exodus of its American membership, however, Friendster was forced to shift its membership focus to Asia.

The lesson? In virtual reality, the coexistence of *real* and *false* identities has been instinctively integrated into online social interaction. People actively want to construct and manipulate *multiple* identities in the virtual world. Any attempt to ban it, or meddle with it, will alienate and trigger mass defections.

There's now a new twist to the online identity conundrum. People are actually stealing virtual identities to make themselves appear more attractive. It's call "cut-and-paste-personality" theft.

One victim is New York-based humorist Hugh Gallagher, who tracked down more than 50 online profiles using bits and pieces of his famous college entrance essay published in *Harper's* magazine. Gallagher's essay, composed as a string of funny one-liners, featured self-descriptions such as: "I am a dynamic figure, often seen scaling walls and crushing ice. . . . I write award-winning operas. . . . I woo women with my sensuous and godlike trombone playing. . . . I cook Thirty-Minute Brownies in twenty minutes. . . . I am an expert in stucco, a veteran in love, and an outlaw in Peru." Gallagher discovered to his stupefaction that other men, clearly less endowed with natural charm, had shamelessly purloined these lines and fraudulently used them for their own online mating rituals. One of these cyber-identity thieves was Jim Carey, a 38-year-old pharmaceutical salesman from Washington State. Carey, cynically believing that ends justify means, confessed to the *Wall Street Journal* that he'd stolen Gallagher's personality because he wanted women to think he was funny but was too lazy to make things up himself. Another cut-and-paste-personality thief confessed to luring 20 women out on dates thanks to pickup lines stolen on the Web, including: "You will soon learn that I'm a raging egomaniac."[14]

Cut-and-paste-personality theft may be distasteful, but it's growing. A MySpace search in early 2008 discovered more than 700 recent comments accusing others of stealing from their online personalities – avatars, favourite songs, witty remarks, background designs, even entire profiles. Among women, a favourite cut-and-pasted line is: "If you love mushroom ravioli, romantic nights by a fire and spring camping trips, please reply!" A popular line for dull men looking to steroid-inject their boring online personas is: "I guarantee I can change the oil in your car in 10 minutes flat." When Engage.com surveyed more than 400 online daters, 9% confessed to copying from someone else's profile. In the high-stakes ritual of online mating, people feel so much competitive pressure to stand out in the crowd that they will go to any length – including identity theft – to sell "themselves" as an attractive prospect. For the unscrupulous, putting your best cyber-face forward entails using someone else's face. It gives new meaning to the term "two-faced".

What is astonishing is how casual opportunistic online behaviour has become. The *Online Dating for Dummies* guide, while not inciting readers to steal from other profiles, nonetheless advises them not to worry too much about copying. The cut-and-paste personality game has even become a business. At TheProfileCoach.com, you can buy a dozen "proven" profiles for just four dollars. Yahoo Personals, for its part, at least has some pretence to ethical probity. It attaches a proviso to its samples: "Don't copy these profiles exactly." Note the last word in that caveat.

A site called FriendFlood will, for a fee, post messages from attractive "friends" on your profile to create the impression that you, like your friends, are attractive and fascinating. Another service popped up with a brand name, FakeYourSpace, that at least has the virtue of being brazenly honest about the service it offers. No false advertising here. With a promise to "turn cyberlosers into social magnets", Fake-YourSpace offered to fill your wall with an eye-popping collection of hot-looking, hard-bodied friends. The site ran into legal problems in early 2007, however, after complaints that it was using photographs of fashion models from iStockPhoto.com without permission. iStock-Photo.com issued a cease and desist order.[15] Meanwhile, cyberlosers who rip off profiles are increasingly being upbraided with angry messages like the following complaint from an aggrieved identity-theft victim: "Dude, u like copied my whole MySpace post." A 34-year-old New Jersey woman posted the following outburst on her Plentyoffish. com profile: "To the girl who copied my profile and denies it . . . You shit!"

In the real world, the false personality phenomenon is not new. In fact, we are all guilty of identity fabricating, albeit innocently, at some point in our lives. On a highly formalized level, the tradition of fancy-dress parties and masquerade balls taps into the same desire to present oneself socially in a disguise. But while masquerade balls are elaborate rituals, Facebook and MySpace profiles are spontaneous and constantly updated forms of social interaction. Online identity fabrication is a daily habit, not a once-a-season social event.

In the real world, social roles are constricted by an abiding awareness of institutionalized norms and values. We are supposed to know our "cues". In the virtual world of MySpace and Facebook, on the other hand, role-playing is less constrained by social codes. Self-regulated by its own "netiquette", online social interaction doesn't defer to conventional norms. On Facebook you might tag a photo, provide an update or share a confidence with hundreds of "friends" who you scarcely know; yet you would never think of making the same gestures to mere acquaintances in the real world.

Another difference involves *control*. In the real world, we have less control over our own identities because, as noted, they are *socially* constructed. Social norms tell us who we are supposed to be. The *personal* fabrication of identities in cyberspace, on the other hand, affords more control on who we wish to be and how we present ourselves. Cyber-sociologists describe the fabrication of self on social networking sites as "writing yourself into being". As the authors of our own personal identities, we have control over the construction of the cyber-personality we fabricate and display in the virtual world. On MySpace or Facebook, people make up who they are, possibly in multiple personas, with a keen eye on what kind of impression they wish to create. In the real world the self is *presented*; in the virtual world it is *invented*.[16]

The fabrication of false identities was first theorized by Erving Goffman in his classic 1959 microsociological study, *The Presentation of Self in Everyday Life*.[17] Goffman examined "symbolic interaction" between people in everyday circumstances. Expanding on "role" theories about human interaction, Goffman concluded that, for most people, the presentation of self is akin to a dramatic stage "performance" whose function vis-à-vis others is a ritualized form of "impression management". In a later essay called "Face Work" – whose title sounds strangely similar to Facebook – Goffman elaborated on his theory by introducing notions of "stigma" and "prestige". As social actors, he observed, we seek to create impressions that reflect well on ourselves. The primary goals of self-presentation are *stigma avoidance* and *prestige enhancement*.

Goffman was writing long before the advent of the Web, of course, but his theories contain many fascinating insights. In cyberspace, as we shall see in subsequent chapters, stigma avoidance and prestige enhancement are prime motivators in online social interaction. In cyberspace, however, rewards for *fame* and punishments for *shame* are sometimes distributed in unexpected ways. Online personal identities are constructed, and presented, as a *social performance*. In cyberspace, the old adage "know thyself" becomes "show thyself".[18]

In sum, online social networking is a virtual catwalk. Impression management involves constantly changing identities, much like fashion models switch outfits. Except that, in the virtual world, the curtain never comes down on the ritual of identity fabrication and self-exhibition. The popularity contest is a moveable feast where all "friends" are invited. And when it's time to vote for your "Top Friend", the Is definitely have it.

2

The kindness of strangers: the ties that bind

Most of us, at some point in our lives, ask ourselves: "How many real *friends* do I have?" It's a question that can't be posed without some trepidation. It requires us to look, unflinchingly, into a long-neglected existential mirror and wonder, honestly, how many souls in this world we can truly call *friends* – people on whom we can count for genuine support and consolation, who will stand by us in good times and bad, whether our fortunes are up or down, whether we are in the loop or out of favour.

It's a troubling question because it induces dreaded anxiety – a sinking feeling that, in truth, the number of our true friends is despairingly smaller than we wish to believe.

No more worries. Online social networks have rescued us from this soul-searching, angst-inducing self-interrogation. It's now possible to have dozens, hundreds, even thousands of "friends" on social sites like MySpace, Facebook, Bebo, Orkut and others. With a simple click, we can "add" new friends, connect to friends of friends and list our "Top Friends".

Collecting friends, indeed, is the main appeal of many social networking sites. No wonder that one of the first sites to gain widespread popularity was called Friendster. In the virtual culture of narcissism, the composition of our "friends" network has become a key identity signature. It's a social barometer that validates self-esteem, confers status and measures social capital. It allows us – if we have loads of "friends" – to project ourselves into the cyberworld with greater self-confidence.

For critics of online friendships, social networking sites have become virtual secondary schools that reproduce the maddeningly, and sometimes dangerous, psycho-politics encountered in the real world. On many sites, the socially ambitious boast their extensive network of "friends", thus signalling their superior social skills. The online ritual of collecting, and displaying, "friends" has become a pervasive – some would say perverse – obsession that is consuming the lives of millions of young people worldwide.

The word *friend* has even become a verb. People spend countless hours *friending* on social sites in a frantic, competitive drive to acquire, maintain and build what they believe is social capital. Competitive *friending* has become an online expression of invidious comparison. Millions of people go online and jealously check the profiles of others to see how many "friends" they've accumulated. In the old days, men with status envy looked for "trophy girlfriends". Today, the prize catch on social networking sites is a "trophy friend". No sex required.[1] Many concoct wholly invented "friends" and add them to their personal page to create the illusion of popularity. That trick is called "Fakebooking". In the online world, if you can't find real friends, you can always make them up.

The online "friends" e-ruption has confounded courts of law, which manifestly are confused by the distinction between virtual and real-world social interaction. In March 2008, a 34-year-old British man was the first person in the UK charged with harassment on a social networking site. Michael Hurst's ex-girlfriend Sophie Sladden accused Hurst of harassing her by contacting her on Facebook. In his own defence, Hurst told Birmingham magistrates that he'd merely "sent her an electronic message requesting her friendship." The judge agreed with Hurst and threw the case out of court, ruling that his contact with his ex-girlfriend was innocuous because Facebook "friends" cannot be defined as "friendship in the traditional sense." But Dillon Osborn wasn't so lucky before another British court. He was sentenced to a week in jail for sending Facebook "friend" requests to his ex-wife in defiance of a court order stipulating that he not contact her.

Many other cases of marital "stalking" of spouses do not result in arrests, criminal charges and court appearances. The reason for this is simple: husbands and wives are cyber-stalking their spouses while still married and living together, usually to confirm suspicions of adultery. Snooping on a spouse's Facebook page to inspect their "friend" list is a growing trend with troubling consequences. As in the real world, when a spouse describes someone as "just a friend", it often means much more. The online Urban Dictionary even features a definition for "Facebook stalker".[2] Sometimes, online marital snooping can trigger violent outcomes that land in the courts. In May 2008, a British man was sentenced to a three-month suspended sentence for physically assaulting and breaking the jaw of his wife's lover, a former boyfriend with whom she'd reconnected on Facebook. When 39-year-old Stephen Henshaw's wife Tammy told him she was leaving the marriage, he discovered on her Facebook page that she was carrying on an affair with her teenage sweetheart, Jake Hamon. She had even travelled to the Channel Islands for romantic trysts. The Facebook-cuckolded husband Henshaw, from Manchester, flew to the Channel Islands to track down Hamon. Henshaw was later found guilty of unlawful and malicious wounding, but was spared hard time in prison. In Yorkshire, meanwhile, a woman's body was found murdered in her garden shed after she'd revealed on Facebook that she was leaving her husband Gary, an electrical engineer. Shortly after Tracey Grinhaff's battered body was found, police discovered Gary's body nearby with self-inflicted head injuries. This shocking murder–suicide had been provoked by one short sentence on Tracey Grinhaff's Facebook page: "Currently splitting up from my husband." Stunned neighbours said the Grinhaffs seemed like a "perfect little family."[3]

Less tragically, online "friendship" can be fraught with the same petty hypocrisies that many encounter in the real world. Consider what happened to Jerome Kerviel, the 31-year-old rogue trader in Paris who burned through $7 billion of a major French bank's money through allegedly fraudulent transactions. The day before Kerviel got nabbed for the biggest bank scandal in history, he counted ten "friends" on his Facebook profile, most of them colleagues at his bank. As soon as news of his arrest hit the media, however, Kerviel had been abandoned by all his Facebook "friends" – except one. The single brave soul who stuck by him must have been a true friend indeed – or perhaps was away on holiday. In an ironic twist, Kerviel (who bears an uncanny resemblance to movie star Tom Cruise) suddenly found himself embraced by thousands of "friends" throughout the world who created "Jerome Kerviel Fan Club" pages on Facebook. Thanks to the rebellious, anti-establishment values of cyberspace, the French rogue trader was transformed into a global Robin Hood. Kerviel may have lost his "Top Friends" on Facebook, but he gained the "friendship" of thousands of people he didn't even know.[4]

The virtual ritual of making, and abandoning, "friends" has raised anguishing matters of online etiquette. How should you respond to a request to be someone's "friend" when you frankly loathe the person? Or how to handle the indelicate matter of *de-friending* someone. Saul Hansell wrote of this painful experience in the *New York Times* in a story titled "He Didn't Want to be That Kind of Friend". After someone called Bob Mason, a chief technology officer at a New England video company, invited Hansell to become an online "friend", Mason had a change of heart. Mason wrote to Hansell: "I hope you don't mind, but I am in the process of moving industry colleagues and partners from Facebook to LinkedIn. From a professional perspective I've decided to keep my Facebook relationships strictly at a personal level. As such I am planning on removing you as a Facebook friend, but would welcome the chance to link up in LinkedIn." Ouch, that hurts.

Mason was effectively telling Hansell that he wasn't really a "friend" – he was merely a *contact*. Hansell was remarkably steady about his social downgrading. "No one likes to be jilted by anyone for anything," he wrote, "but I can't say that I was being cut off by someone I thought was my best buddy."[5]

In Britain, the upper-crust bible, Debrett's, has attempted to resolve these netiquette dilemmas for more rarefied sensibilities. Debrett's, which has been publishing genealogical guides to the British aristocracy since 1769 and is considered to be the last word on matters of etiquette, entered the Internet era in 2008 by releasing a guide to good manners on social networking sites. The Debrett's guide – in the tradition of *Debrett's Guide to Entertaining* and *Debrett's Etiquette and Modern Manners* – provides online rules on "sociable social networking".

Jo Bryant, a Debrett's etiquette adviser, said the purpose of the latest guide was to help online social networkers to know what to do in awkward situations, including getting "poked" and being invited to become someone's "friend". Not surprisingly, Debrett's advice – based on a desire to keep old friends and avoid making unwanted new ones – is cautious, conservative and punctilious about correct form. "It can sometimes feel odd when someone who you don't necessary know asks you to be their friend," said Bryant. "What do you do? You automatically feel like you should say yes but that can seem a bit weird because you don't actually know them. The trend for social networking has made new demands on traditional etiquette. My advice is to play it safe, and always employ your usual good manners when online, treating others with kindness or respect. Social networking is meant to complement and enhance your existing social life, not complicate it."[6]

The Debrett's guidelines might be useful in certain social circles. But the plain fact is that, for millions of teenagers struggling with the turbulent emotions of youth, the finer points of correct form are not likely to be top-of-mind when friending online. For kids with unformed – and hence fragile – identities, emotional reactions to online social interaction are not always so stoical and stiff-upper-lipped. Youths desperately need approval and want to make friends. It's easy to imagine the self-esteem injury suffered by a teenager – or anyone – who upon checking the profile of one of their own "Top Friends", discovers that the honour has not been reciprocated.[7] These injuries can have tragic consequences. Some emotionally vulnerable teenagers have even been driven to suicide by online rejection and bullying.

In a disturbingly perverse case that was widely reported in the media, a pretty 13-year-old American girl from Missouri called Megan Meier killed herself in October 2006 after becoming emotionally attached on MySpace to a cute 16-year-old boy. As the *New Yorker* magazine noted in a journalistic exposé of Megan's troubling suicide, she was no different from millions of fragile teenagers who turn to MySpace, Facebook and other sites in search of themselves. "Like many teenagers, Megan and her peers carried on an online social life that was more mercurial, and perhaps more crucial to their sense of status and acceptance, than the one they inhabited in the flesh," noted the *New Yorker*. "On MySpace, and on other social-networking sites, such as Friendster and Facebook, a person can project a larger, more confident self, a nervy collection of favorite music, books, quotations, pleasures, and complaints. He or she, able to play with different personas, is released from some of the petty humiliations of being a middle-schooler – all it takes to be a Ludacris fan is a couple of keystrokes. But trying on identities is, in the fluid environment of the Internet, a riskier experiment than raiding Mom's makeup bag. Squabbles that would take days to percolate in person can within seconds explode into full-blown wars. Disputes can also become painfully public."[8]

Megan, still not fourteen, was legally too young to have a MySpace account. But her parents made a fatal mistake by allowing her to join MySpace, which did not require identity authentification for new members. The same rules – or lack of rules – applied to the cute teenage boy called Josh. After he contacted Megan on her MySpace page, the two immediately began an online flirtation that quickly became intense. Megan was instantly smitten by Josh's gorgeous photo, showing a teen-idol hunk with blue eyes, chiselled features and brown wavy hair. Josh charmed the impressionable teenager by listing his height as six-foot-three and revealing that his "turn-ons" included tongue-piercing and that he loved being nibbled on the ear. Megan begged her parents to allow her to add Josh as a "friend". When they agreed, that was their second fatal mistake.

As soon as Megan was infatuated with Josh, he turned angrily on her. He began insulting her as "fat" and called her a "slut". He also sent her a note saying: "You're a shitty person and the world would be a better place without you in it." Fifteen minutes later, Megan hung herself with a belt in her bedroom closet.

It was later discovered that Josh did not exist. His photo has been stolen and pasted on his phoney MySpace profile. Everything about him had been made up. There was no Josh. He was a false persona maliciously concocted by 47-year-old Lori Drew, the mother of one of Megan's former classmates. The Drews lived only four doors away from Megan's family on a suburban St Louis street. Drew, who attended Megan's funeral before being found out, confessed to police that she had been harassing the girl as revenge after Megan had dropped her daughter as a friend – not online, but in the real world.

Lori Drew, publicly exposed as an evil busybody, became notorious in a Wikipedia entry about Megan's suicide – but at first no criminal charges were laid against her.[9] Then, in May 2008, nineteen months after Megan's suicide, Drew was indicted on one count of conspiracy and three counts of accessing a protected computer without authorization to access information used to inflict emotional distress. The tragic consequences of online identity manipulation had come to Middle America.

"The Internet is a world unto itself, people must know how far they can go before they must stop," said FBI agent Salvador Hernandez when the indictments against Lori Drew were announced. "They exploited a young girl's weaknesses. Whether the defendant could have foreseen the results, she's responsible for her actions."[10]

After the charges were laid, Megan's mother Tina Meier appeared on the national television show "Good Morning America" to say she wanted Lori Drew to receive the maximum prison sentence for her role in her daughter's death. "I am hopeful she will face the maximum 20 years in prison," said Meier. "Twenty years is unfortunately not enough for her. She played a ridiculous game with my daughter's life."[11]

Sometimes suicide, when it happens online as a dramatically symbolic gesture, can have less wrenching consequences. In a mock gesture called "Facebook suicide", a 27-year-old English woman from

London called Stephanie Painter decided to "kill" herself on February 11, 2008. But it was her *virtual* self that committed suicide. After giving her online friends a final, sad-faced "poke", Painter killed off her Facebook persona. "It was hard to kill the profile I'd spent so long creating," she told the British press, "but I felt it was the only way out." What was the problem? Painter's Facebook identity was damaging her real-world relationship with her boyfriend Danny, especially after ex-boyfriends and random flings from her past got in touch online and asked her to be their "friend". The situation became awkward because Danny, as one of her Facebook "friends", could view her profile page including her other male "friends" and their flirtatious messages. "In the end, Facebook was causing so many arguments between us that I decided the best thing would be to log off," she said. "As soon as my Facebook profile died, our relationship improved."[12]

The "friendship" stakes have become so frenetic, and confusing, it's perhaps worth asking the age-old question: *What are friends for?*

The word "friend" can be ambiguous if the subtleties of cultural context and social nuances are not understood. Silicon Valley geeks are evidently quite relaxed about approaching strangers in person and asking them if they can become their online "friend". At a Palo Alto business gathering, you might overhear someone saying: "I read your blog, can I be your friend?"[13] In other social circumstances, the word "friend" can be wickedly ironic. At a stuffy cocktail party, if someone you know well crosses the room with a stranger in tow and intones, "Let me introduce you to my *friend* Bob Jones", you know instantly what your close friend really thinks of Bobby Boy. When someone curtly begins a sentence with, "Listen, my friend . . .", there can little doubt that the word signifies precisely its opposite.

Just how many friends can one person have anyway? In the virtual world, hyper-friendship inflation doesn't seem to have any reasonable limits. Many young people casually accumulate hundreds of friends and display them, frequently accompanied by tagged photos, on their profile pages. A 17-year-old American girl called Brittnie Sarnes, from Ohio, boasted a total of 5036 "friends" on a social networking site. There have been other reports of people collecting as many as 26000 online friends.[14] If we are all linked to one another by the famous "six degrees of separation", maybe this isn't so astounding. Why not a thousand, ten thousand, a hundred thousand "friends"? Yet for most of us, it doesn't seem manageable. How can someone stay in contact with so many people? Surely there must be a maximum number of friends we can keep up without deforming the very meaning of the word. Indeed, is there a maximum number of friends that any one person can reasonably claim to have?

The answer that to question, it seems, is *yes*. There does seem to be a cognitive limit to any one person's close circle of friends. It's called Dunbar's Law – named after British anthropologist Robin Dunbar. In the early 1990s he calculated, based on a complex analysis of non-human primates and the size of the human neocortex, that the maximum number of people with whom any human being can maintain stable social relationships is about 150. The 150 figure – frequently referred to as "Dunbar's Number" – happened to correspond to the size of Neolithic villages as functional units. It also matched the size of Hutterite colonies before they split off to form a new community. And, interestingly, the ancient Roman army was divided into legions of 5000 soldiers split into units of – you guessed it – 150 men. In fact, the same figure – 150 – endured until modern times as the number of soldiers in an army company. There seems to be something magic, sociologically, about the number 150 as the maximum limit for maintaining functional cohesion in human groupings. Beyond the 150 threshold, something happens to human behaviour. The necessary ritual of social "grooming" becomes too difficult to manage and, consequently, group cohesion breaks down. A group larger than 150 requires rules and regulations to enforce stability. There is even evidence that when social-dominant online games like *Castle Marrach* reach approximately 150 active users, group cohesion collapses, resulting in dissatisfaction and defection. Similarly, Wikipedia involvement tends to plateau at about 150 active administrators.[15]

If Dunbar's Law were strictly applicable to the virtual world, anyone boasting more than 150 "friends" on a social networking site would be exaggerating. In fact, the Friendster site originally limited the number of "friends" for any single member to a specific capped figure: 150. Fascinating. Were the Friendster founders astute students of Dunbar's Law? Perhaps. But as we shall see, social networkers in the virtual world often behave in ways that defy all known laws of social anthropology. It should be noted, incidentally, that Dunbar did not argue that we can maintain *close* personal relationships with as many as 150 people. In fact, he explicitly stated that core circles of friends – or "sympathy groups" – with whom any one person can maintain "intense" relations generally do not exceed 12 people. This figure appears to indicate that the best numerical grouping for a "My Top Friends" list is a dozen. Any number beyond that is a sign that someone is being generously diplomatic.

We frequently use images from knitting to describe the texture of our social relations. Our true friends, those to whom we are linked by close personal ties, form our *close-knit* group. Our wider network of social acquaintances and contacts, on the other hand, belong in a larger group that we often call a *loose-knit* network. But what about people beyond the magic 150 figure – people we know only vaguely, on a "nodding" basis in an office corridor, familiar faces we see at cocktail parties or members of our alumni association? If the differential between 12 and 150 separates close friends from acquaintances, what about those who belong in the amorphous group beyond Dunbar's number? Extending these categories beyond 150, as we shall see, opens up fascinating insights with meaningful consequences – not only for individuals, but also for organizations. We are referring here to the often-discussed distinction between "strong" and "weak" ties. When we examine the inner dynamics of "weak" ties within networks, it quickly becomes apparent that these connections are much more powerful than we might otherwise believe possible.

In a famous, ground-breaking 1973 essay called "The Strength of Weak Ties", American sociologist Mark Granovetter argued that "weak ties" frequently play important social roles in our lives even though, in many instances, we scarcely know these people.[16] Granovetter's definition of "weak ties" is social relationships characterized by infrequent contact, an absence of emotional closeness and no history of reciprocal favours. In professional parlance, you might say people in your "extended network". You know who they are, but you don't really *know* them. More importantly, they are people who owe you nothing, and vice versa. Most of us, if we sat down with pen and paper, could list dozens of people, perhaps hundreds, who belong in this nebulous social category. They are out there somewhere, but we rarely give much thought to their existence. Until, that is, we need them.

Granovetter's fascinating finding is precisely that: we rely on "weak tie" connections much more often than we think. Call it the "kindness of strangers" theory. The classic example of this unexpected dependency is job searching. Ask yourself: if you are looking for a new job, who are you going to turn to? Your family and close friends? In most cases, they won't be much help – unless you are the happy beneficiary of nepotism or cronyism. Most intelligent jobseekers turn to their "network". Indeed, people who are job hunting or switching careers often say that they are "reactivating their network" – in other words, letting everybody know they're on the job market. This means, by implication, that "weak tie" networks are usually dormant. For

Granovetter, "weak ties" are located in the world of loose "egocentric networks" where everyone, fundamentally, is a rational actor. We are willing to help out vague social contacts, usually with useful information, because one day we may rely on the kindness of these same strangers. Also, it always feels good to do someone a good turn.

Granovetter's empirical evidence, published in his 1974 book *Getting a Job*, confirmed that most people find jobs not through close friends, but via weak-tie acquaintances. In fact, the vast majority of those surveyed reported that they found jobs through an acquaintance they'd seen only occasionally or rarely.[17] Granovetter was turning many long-established sociological assumptions on their head. Social research until that time – the late 1960s – had focused largely on the importance of "close" ties for social mobility. These notions still stubbornly linger in our thinking. We tend to believe, perhaps cynically, that others get jobs through family connections, close friends and cronies. We regard "networks" as closed, invitation-only groups restricted to like-minded people bonded by a common past. Yet, in fact, most business networks are based on relatively "weak tie" associations. Even "old boy" networks, alumni allegiances, Freemasons, Rotarians and other alleged cliques are essentially loose-knit. Think about it: how well do their members actually *know* one another? The answer is: for most of them, not very well at all. So what is their bond? Their bond is the strength of weak ties.

When the Internet first exploded, many jobseekers used email to plug into "weak tie" networks. Today, social networking sites like LinkedIn and Facebook serve the same function. Any site will work, so long as you are connected to a network of "friends". Collecting online "friends" – or *e-quaintances* – is not merely a hollow ritual for the vain, insecure and narcissistic. Online friendships have a function. They give social substance to an online community harnessing the strength of weak ties.

Let's return briefly to where this book began: the Knights Templar. The Templars are a classic example of an egocentric network that operated according to "weak tie" dynamics. The Templars, it will be recalled, were created by a group of French noblemen following the recapture of Jerusalem in 1099 and the expulsion of the so-called Infidels. But who were these French noblemen? They were Hugues de Payens and Godefroy de Saint-Omer. Left to their own devices, these two men never could have transformed the Templars into a powerful crusading force throughout Christendom. They needed Papal blessing to sanctify their operations. Fortuitously, Payens and Omer had a strategically important Church contact from their home region of Champagne. His name was Bernard de Clairvaux. In the 12th century, Clairvaux was perhaps the most well-connected man in Christendom. Widely considered the "conscience" of the Church, today Clairvaux would be known as a power-broker, a go-to guy, a rainmaker, an *éminence grise*. His views were not only listened to, but also widely solicited. Clairvaux was a major player in the most important ecclesiastical discussions of his epoch. Pope Innocent II, before his elevation to the Papacy, had been one of Bernard de Clairvaux's disciples.

Clairvaux was, above all, stridently neoconservative – to employ a modern term – about driving the Infidels from the Holy Land. When Hugues de Payens and Godefroy de Saint-Omer were assembling their military order to protect Christian pilgrims from the heathens, they knew who to turn to. Clairvaux not only spread the word about the Templars, he wrote a flattering tract called *De laude novae militae* praising the formation of this "new militia". Most importantly, in 1129 Clairvaux personally intervened with Pope Innocent II to secure Papal blessing for the Templar organization. The idea for the Templars had come from a small group of French knights, but it was Bernard de Clairvaux who made things happen. The Knights Templar were launched, thanks to the interventions of Clairvaux, on the strength of weak ties. Clairvaux, incidentally, was posthumously canonized as Saint Bernard.

Not much has changed since the 12th century. It could be argued, in fact, that the entire capitalist system was founded on the strength of weak ties. Economic historians tell us that the rise of capitalism – a complex process that occurred over several centuries – overthrew the feudal economic system. The feudal order was founded on traditional reflexes of personal *fealty* – or loyalty of vassals to their lords. The medieval system of economic exchange reflected this social order. It was based on an agrarian peasantry, local fiefdoms, relations of servitude, organized craftsmen and personalized bartering. The notion of "trust" in economic exchanges was embedded in these personal relations. With the emergence of capitalism, however, money exchanges and mercantile activity gradually imposed a more rational economic system based not on personal loyalties, but on *impersonal* transactions. By definition, capitalist expansion was founded on the belief that people can conduct economic exchanges without close personal ties. In other words, on the strength of weak ties.

True, capitalists are "kept honest" by the constant threat of coercion in the form of legal actions and, in the international economy, retaliatory trade measures. Business executives today operate according to a "trust-but-verify" ethos, hence the necessity of due diligence. Still, the extraordinary success of capitalism pays tribute to the uncanny willingness of people to transact on the basis of implicit *trust*, guided by rational calculation instead of vile instincts, in order to pursue mutual benefits. Adam Smith, the intellectual father of capitalism and author of *The Wealth of Nations*, was acutely aware of the interdependence of mutual self-interest and transactional probity. It helped, of course, that the "spirit" of capitalism – to cite Max Weber – was driven by a burgeoning Protestant culture actively overthrowing what it saw as corrupt Catholic institutions. Whatever one may say about the unvarnished aspect and habits of the Puritans and Quakers – who were dismissed as "Fanaticks" in 17th century England and expelled to America – they carried forward fundamental values of hard work and honesty in their commercial dealings. Capitalism worked because people brought together by "weak ties" agreed to deal with one another honestly and without recourse to violent behaviour. As anyone who has watched an episode of *The Sopranos* knows, Mafia economies are governed by "close tie" relationships – often bloodlines – but there's a good chance that, sooner or later, "family" members will end up in a dumpster with a bullet in their head. Capitalism, true enough, has produced crooks and fraudsters, but they rarely win in the long term. As James Surowiecki puts it in his insightful book, *The Wisdom of Crowds*: "It may be, in the end, that a good society is defined more by how people treat strangers than by how they treat those they know."[18]

Not surprisingly, social networking sites have leveraged the strength of weak tie e-quaintances around specific consumer needs. The travel and hotel industries, for example, were early adopters of Web 2.0 software to aggregate their customers as e-quaintance networks. This makes perfect sense. Frequent travellers, especially business people, often bump into the same faces at airports and in hotel lobbies without getting to know them beyond a nod or casual chat. Similarly, well-to-do people often have fetish resorts and hotels which they visit the same week every year with the predictability of migratory birds. In these exclusive precincts they invariably come across the same faithful clientele who have identical holiday habits. Why not create e-quaintance networks around these customers to socially cement brand loyalty? A social networking site called Dopplr.com is already doing just that. It connects high-end – and often solitary – business travellers to facilitate serendipitous meetings. When members log onto the site and type their travel itinerary, Dopplr alerts them (online or on mobile devices) if someone they know will also be in the same location. The Starwood hotel chain, meanwhile, has launched a social site, TheLobby.com, designed for its "Starwood Preferred Guests". Starwood, which owns Sheraton hotels, also redesigned its Sheraton.com site, which now invites customers to share photos and videos from their trips, make comments, blog and offer tips. Starwood is trying to attract online connectors who are happy to spend time online to share information and experiences. It's not so much social networking as social marketing.

The strength of weak ties can have an even more powerful impact inside organizations. If the miracle of capitalism is that people, given a rational incentive to seek mutual benefits, will conduct honest dealings with strangers, the potential of Web 2.0 tools for organizations resides in a similar insight. Thanks to Web 2.0 tools like wikis, corporations can leverage the power of collaborative networks which are replacing traditional institutional resources for problem-solving. If given the right environment and tools, employees will cooperate and collaborate with unknown colleagues, even with customers, to achieve organizational goals – including profitability.

Organizational behaviour research has shown that collaborative Web 2.0 tools are particularly effective where *technical* knowledge is valued. In complex organizations like multinational corporations, finding someone who possesses highly specific expertise is often difficult. One reason is that expertise remains "hidden" – and consequently unexploited – within organizational structures. In vertical corporate hierarchies characterized by institutional silos and hierarchical organizational roles, there is no incentive for employees to look beyond their familiar workplace setting of nearby colleagues as informational resources. Most managers and employees consult colleagues with whom they have "close" professional ties. It is a basic fact of human nature that, in organizational settings, people tend to provide information to, and share knowledge with, those they know and like – especially if they have helped them with favours in the past. When seeking solutions to problems, most people do not diversify their human options. They go with people they know. While this instinct is understandable, countless studies have demonstrated that it's also counterproductive. When employees work in an "echo chamber" where colleagues invited to meetings mouth the same attitudes and viewpoints, the only winner is the status quo. Everybody loses – except, of course, entrenched management. The really big losers are shareholders.[19]

Web 2.0 software knocks down corporate silos, moats and walls by encouraging open communication and information sharing. Expertise and solutions to problems no longer remain "hidden", they are actively sought out and exploited. Since Web 2.0 tools foster transparent communication visible to all, the collaborative input of any employee, even far down the formal hierarchy, will be known, recognized and perhaps rewarded. Status and prestige incentives are thus built into the collaborative process. When collaboration is a win-win for everybody, buy-in is universal.

Web 2.0 tools can offer competitive advantages to firms in sectors where *innovation* produces winners and losers. Senior executives in large-scale corporations are increasingly aware that innovation is not restricted to R&D departments, but is a dynamic *social* process. To reinforce this point, here is Steve Jobs's description of how innovation works at Apple: "Innovation comes from people meeting up in the hallways or calling each other at 10:30 at night with a new idea, or because they realized something that shoots holes in how we've been thinking about a problem. It's ad hoc meetings of six people called by someone who thinks he has figured out the coolest new thing ever and who wants to know what other people think of his idea."

Innovation at Apple, clearly, relies on *social* interaction.[20] When you look at Apple's revenue and profit figures – not to mention its revolutionary impact on personal technology and social wellbeing – it makes a convincing case for "Facebook Fridays" at the office.

The list of major corporations using Web 2.0 software tools to promote productivity and foster innovation is growing: FedEx, Shell Oil, Motorola, General Electric, Kodak, British Telecom, Kraft Foods, McDonald's, and Lockheed Martin. Multinational corporations like Procter & Gamble are outsourcing R&D on websites to invite customer input, thus blurring the line between *producer* and *consumer*. If customers are already helping P&G to produce new brands of toothpaste and shampoo, they may soon be designing cars for General Motors, Ford and Renault.

These are seismic changes. Power is shifting from vertical corporate hierarchies to horizontal collaborative networks. The wiki workplace is unleashing the "power of us". CEOs must rethink the way they manage their companies to achieve the necessary business transformation that will, in the final analysis, produce greater employee satisfaction and shareholder value.[21]

If mass collaboration and bottom-up innovation promote the greater good, they nonetheless pose serious threats. As Harvard business professor Andrew McAfee warns, the forces of resistance inside organizations are powerful, especially among middle managers. McAfee quotes Max Weber to underscore this point: "Every bureaucracy seeks to increase the superiority of the professionally informed by keeping their knowledge and intentions secret." Old org charts die hard. People in organizations protect their power bases.

McAfee nonetheless remains optimistic about the strength of weak ties: "The implication for social networking sites is obvious: Facebook and its peers should be highly valuable for businesses because they're tools for increasing the density of weak ties within a company, as well as outside it. My Facebook friends are a large group of people from diverse backgrounds who have very little in common with each other. Furthermore, their profiles give me a decent way to evaluate their expertise. These online friends, in other words, are a large group of bridges to other networks."[22] In sum, if individuals can benefit from the kindness of strangers, so can organizations.

Maybe so, but this basic truism has not been enthusiastically embraced in many countries, especially in Asia where "close" ties are vitally important for business transactions. Chinese business operates according to the principle of *guanxi*, which translates roughly as "personal relationship". *Guanxi* affirms the old saying: "It's not *what* you now, it's *who* you know." As many Western business leaders have learned to their immense frustration, the Chinese do business only with those with whom they have a *personal* relationship. This Asian tradition provides business transactions with structured relationships that replicate extended family or clan networks. It is the Chinese way of embedding *trust* in their business dealings. For Western business people, who are generally willing to do business with anybody who can read a contract, *guanxi* is a time-consuming distraction that frequently requires them – if they wish to gain access to the huge Chinese market – to spend countless hours in Beijing and Shanghai restaurants grinning suspiciously at alarmingly exotic culinary dishes and slamming back high-octane liqueurs to an interminable number of toasts. It's through these elaborate, and sometimes intoxicating, social rituals that Westerners can establish some semblance of a "close tie" – or *tong* – as an indispensable cultural preamble to getting a business deal signed.

Interestingly, online social networks of e-quaintances seem uniquely compatible with the Chinese *guanxi* imperative because they ritualize the semblance of friendship without actually establishing close personal bonds. As Allison Luong of the Internet consultancy Pearl Research told *The Economist*, online social networking is a natural cultural extension of *guanxi* relationships in Chinese society.[23] Sites like MySpace and Facebook have been called *guanxi* enablers because they impose obligations to be "friends" on their members. There are other fascinating parallels between Asian social customs and online social interactions. One is the ritual of gift-giving. In China, gift-giving and personal favours (including bribes in business relations) constitute an important dimension of *guanxi*, which is based on reciprocal obligation and indebtedness.[24] Studies of interactions on social networking sites reveal that gift-giving has similarly been integrated into personal interaction as a way of establishing and maintaining bonds. A study of online "gift" exchange on the LiveJournal site, for example, found that users were offering material and virtual "gifts" to others in order to maintain social bonds. On sites like Facebook, too, members exchange digital gifts – like teddy bear icons – with "friends" to maintain network e-quaintances.[25]

We can conclude that, despite the outlandishly expansive notion of "friends" on many social networking sites like Facebook and MySpace, users do seem to make efforts to create some semblance of a personal connection with complete strangers. As we have seen, "weak" ties can be indispensably important to get many things done in the real world. In the online world, e-quaintances can serve a similar function. We would agree with cyber-blogger Jeff Jarvis that grasping the consequences of this social e-ruption requires an acceptance of demographic dynamics. Younger generations don't consider weak-tie "friend" networks of e-quaintances as inauthentic or shallow.

"For today's young people, keeping in touch won't be so difficult," notes Jarvis. "They are all Google-able and will have threads permanently connecting them in Facebook or whatever follows . . . I think this means that they will maintain friendships longer in life. Which, in turn, could lead to richer friendships. No longer can you escape relationships when you move on; you will be tied to your past – and to the consequences of your actions. I hope this could make us better friends." [26]

You probably don't need Facebook if you're Bill Gates. The Microsoft founder once maintained a profile on Facebook but stopped using it because too many people wanted to be his "friend". In early 2008, Gates opted instead to join the professional LinkedIn social networking site, though it's doubtful he needs to network to look for a new job. On his LinkedIn profile, Gates describes himself as a "technologist" and "philanthropist" and lists his interests as reading, tennis and bridge. The coincidental timing of his membership to LinkedIn did not escape industry followers. Microsoft was just about to launch an advertising campaign on the site.

For most of us, meanwhile, e-quaintances can prove unexpectedly strong, compelling and necessary. Collaborative innovation in the workplace is a positive example of how "weak tie" e-quaintances can be leveraged in organizations. Beyond organizations in our personal lives, the tragic story of Megan Meier is a sad, shocking demonstration of the dark side of online networking. Multiple online identities can create confusion between strong and weak bonds. Sometimes, depending on the kindness of strangers can have tragic consequences.

Social rejection is less perilous when you belong to an online social network in which loyalty and defection are negotiable. It's a small world, even in cyberspace. Which is why, as we shall see in the next chapter, we need to have genuine incentives to remain loyal and wide-open exit doors if we choose to leave.

3

It's a small world: exit, voice and loyalty

The phenomenal success of social networking sites, it cannot be doubted, is down to a novel idea that is generally discouraged in most social groupings: an open-door, come-one-come-all invitation policy. It's dead easy to join virtually any social site – MySpace, Facebook, Bebo, Orkut, you name it. Just sign up and you're a fully entitled member. Let the "friendship" stakes begin!

No wonder these highly trafficked sites, in only a few years, have attracted a worldwide membership that measures, in total, in the hundreds of millions. Everybody is invited to the party, regardless of region, race, religion, gender, class or sexual orientation. And you can come and go when you wish. The revolving door is always open. No pressure, no hard sells, no nasty surprises.

Sounds fabulous. In truth, however, it's not rigorously true. Many social networking sites, in fact, have imported familiar social distinctions from real-world experience – especially the impulse to erect social barriers to entry. Even cyberspace can be a small world. Just when you thought the Web was a wide-open world, its doors are beginning to bang shut. The open/closed conundrum on social networking sites provides fascinating anthropological insights into human nature and social organization. It also reveals how the Internet, despite real-world social reflexes, is transforming the way we join, participate in and defect from social groups.

Facebook offers a textbook case study of the open/closed paradox. With more than 125 million members, it's difficult to think of

Facebook as a *closed* social network. Facebook has, in fact, been struggling to manage the paradox of its closed architecture since the site was launched in 2004. When Harvard geek Mark Zuckerberg created Facebook, it was originally intended for fellow campus undergrads. Right from the start, Facebook was exclusive: Harvard students only. It was designed as a virtual walled garden, restricted and closed.

Facebook later opened up to other Ivy League colleges in New England, such as Yale and MIT, and then to anyone with an appropriate "edu" or other email address from a university or high school. By definition, this entrance qualification made Facebook a closed online social sphere. If you didn't have an educational affiliation, you couldn't join. Then, in late 2006, Zuckerberg adopted a so-called "open signup" model that took the site off campus and reached out to the entire world. Facebook was finally living up to the potential of online social networking: open, ubiquitous, nondiscriminatory.

Not so fast. Facebook still remained relatively closed despite open signup. Members did not have access to the profiles of all other users. In other words, Facebook was still not fully leveraging so-called network effects by linking all members. Zuckerberg did open up Facebook to outside software developers who could integrate "widget" applications – like sheep-throwing and super-poking – onto the site's functionality. This gave Zuckerberg bragging rights that Facebook was the Web's "social operating system". That expression, presumably, was an indirect swipe at Microsoft and Google, which had neglected the *social* potential of the Web. Facebook's socially driven software, said Zuckerberg, was bringing "elegant organization" to online communities.

Maybe so, but Facebook stubbornly remained a walled garden. Some criticized Facebook as "the new America Online". The comparison to a closed, branded community was not meant to be flattering. As cyber-blogger Jeff Jarvis, a Facebook admirer, put it: "As impressed as I am with the platform, I still wish it were more open. I want to combine my presence on Facebook with my presences on my blog, del.icio.us, Twitter, YouTube, Flickr, iTunes, Daylife, Amazon, eBay, and lots of other places . . . I also want them to interact with each other and with my friends' presences in those places to see what surprises result. Maybe I start to see that my friends are buying the same books. Or I put together a Twitter group for an event. Or I find that my blog readers who are in my same group are going to the same event."[1]

Jarvis's complaint was this: once you entered Facebook, you were condemned to socially interact inside its cyberwalls. Facebook had opened its entry door, but once inside there were no social windows.

You couldn't look outside. Facebook had an even more troubling problem. Facebook members who decided to drop out and move on discovered, to their consternation, that it was devilishly difficult to escape without leaving footprints. There were not only no windows, there were no exit doors. Those who managed to find an exit door discovered that it was bolted shut. If you insisted on getting out, you were forced to strip down and leave all your belongings behind.

Facebook, for its part, insisted that its policy allowed members to "deactivate" their accounts. Facebook's official terms-of-use wording did say: "You may remove your user content from the site at any time." True enough, but *deleting* your profile entirely was another matter. As the Facebook fine-print caveat stated: "You acknowledge that the company may retain archived copies of your user content."

Leaving aside the basic issue of personal privacy, this raised concerns that Facebook was commercially exploiting profile information and other user-related data for commercial advertising purposes. One disgruntled Facebook member described his frustrating predicament by citing the lyrics of a well-known Eagles song: "It's like the Hotel California – you can check out any time you like, but you can never leave."[2]

This tension between open and closed social networks is nothing new. In fact, it stretches back to the darkest recesses of human history. We have always sought the reassurances procured through membership in closed social groupings with their own codes, values and protections. The trade-off, however, has been that, once accepted inside a closed community – as in Facebook – making an exit is easier said than done. Most cohesive forms of social organization actively discourage, and frequently punish, any form of disloyalty or defection.

To illustrate this time-honoured conundrum, let's return to our Knights Templar saga. Only noble-born knights could become members of the Templars, and defection from the monastic order was punishable by death. The Templars, though structured as a matrix organization that emphasized efficiency over hierarchy, was a military order. Defection could not be tolerated. Throughout history, indeed, military deserters have usually been summarily executed. In the modern era, religious sects like the Church of Scientology are frequently criticized for putting intense pressure on members who express a desire to exit. The internal discipline of criminal organizations, too, is characterized by aggressive, indeed physically violent, behaviour towards defectors. In the Mafia, once a member is "made" there is no getting out. The Mafia is family.

Most modern nations treat their citizens in the same manner, albeit with less violence. Most of us are born with a national identity certified by the passports we carry. Defecting from our national community is a complex process. Even if we become a citizen of another country, we usually retain our original nationality. Some states deny their citizens the right to join another national community. Those who defect to enemy nations – frequently called spies – are stripped of their citizenship as traitors and, if caught, punished either by execution or exceedingly long periods of incarceration. Expulsion is another possible punishment, especially when dealing with citizens from other countries. The Catholic Church can invoke its power of excommunication, which is a form of expulsion. Religious sects like Hutterites expel members by shunning them through the silent treatment. But unilateral defection is another matter. In strict observance to an enduring rule of social organization – in families, communities, clubs, churches, corporations and nations – extraordinary efforts are normally deployed to dissuade any gesture of unilateral defection.

This tension was theorized by economist Albert O. Hirschman in his classic book, *Exit, Voice and Loyalty*.[3] First published in 1970, Hirschman's book began as a series of reflections on the underlying reasons behind the decline of firms, but expanded into a series of powerful insights into the nature of belonging, protest and defection from markets, organizations and nations. In a nutshell, Hirschman argued that people, when faced with declining service quality as consumers, employees and voters, generally have two options to manifest their dissatisfaction: *exit* or *voice*.

When consumers are dissatisfied with a product or service quality, they can *exit* from the relationship by refusing to buy the product or cancelling service (except, of course, in monopolistic situations). Similarly, when employees are frustrated with their jobs, they can manifest their disenchantment by quitting and seeking employment elsewhere. Finally, when citizens are unhappy with conditions in their country, they can exit by emigrating to another country. These *exit* reactions are implicit messages of discontent – to suppliers, to employers and to political leaders.

A more explicit reaction is *voice*. Consumers dissatisfied with a product or service can complain by calling the supplier's customer service department. Contacting consumer organizations or the media is another *voice* option. Disgruntled employees stuck in unpleasant jobs can file a grievance or complain to management in the hope of effecting change in the workplace. And citizens who are unhappy with living conditions can protest, revolt and sometimes even over-throw a regime through violent revolution.

Exit and *voice* are symptoms of decline in firms, organizations and regimes. The former is generally an early warning sign of decline; the latter a more dramatic, and potentially disruptive, symptom.

Loyalty is a highly valued asset because it tempers any temptation to exit or voice dissatisfaction. A successful product seeks to achieve *brand loyalty*, corporations strive to instil *employee loyalty* and states are generally comforted by strong feelings of *patriotism* that foster loyalty among their citizenry. Loyalty is a positive virtue because, in downturns, it can affect an individual's cost–benefit calculation when assessing the advantages of *exit* and *voice*. If you are loyal to a product brand, you are not likely to stop buying it and defect to a competing product merely because it's temporarily out of stock. If you are loyal to your company, you're not likely to quit merely because its stock value is falling. And if loyal to your country, you are not likely to move to another country merely because you are angry with a government policy.

Hirschman wrote *Exit, Voice and Loyalty* long before the advent of the Web, yet his rich insights are remarkably relevant for social networking sites facing the open/closed paradox. Facebook is not alone in struggling with the *exit* option of its members. In fact, this same dilemma was being encountered during the earliest days of the Internet.

Take the example of Prodigy, one of the first online communities, launched in 1984 by CBS, IBM and Sears Roebuck. After quickly ramping up to more than a million subscribers, Prodigy was accused of spying on its own members and censoring user forums. On Prodigy forums, for example, potentially offensive words – such as "beaver" – were banned. This created absurd situations where members couldn't post comments on the 1950s television show "Leave it to Beaver". Prodigy members got around this ludicrous interdiction by using the Latin name for the beaver species: *castor*. But it stopped being funny pretty fast. Compounding the negative reaction to its fussy meddling, Prodigy committed a fatal management blunder when it abandoned its "unlimited chat" service and switched to an hourly fee structure. The reaction was immediate: mass exodus. Prodigy members opted for *exit*.

The same happened at GeoCities, a site founded in 1994 and later purchased by Yahoo for an eye-popping $3.6 billion. Under Yahoo management, the site's fortunes began to flounder. Why? Because

Yahoo was first to make a mistake that Facebook would copy a decade later: it imposed terms-of-service rules on members stipulating that it, not members, owned all content on the site. This policy, even though Yahoo quickly reversed its decision, triggered a mass exodus. GeoCities members didn't like the restriction, so they ran for the *exit* doors.

The most spectacular example of an *exit* disaster, however, is Friendster. In Chapter 1, we briefly recounted how Friendster members defected en masse from the site after the company began deleting so-called "Fakester" profiles. That was only one setback in a much larger Friendster catastrophe. Friendster, which had been among the first social networking sites after its launch in 2002, was on its way to becoming a billion-dollar online powerhouse. Then oversized egos, incessant infighting and bad management decisions destroyed the site's soaring fortunes in America.

Founded by former Netscape programmer Jonathan Abrams, Friendster was originally designed as a "dating" site to compete with Match.com. In its start-up phase, Friendster was a huge success. Abrams became a media celebrity and was lionized by Silicon Valley's big-money players. In 2003, when Google offered him $30 million for the site, Abrams snubbed the overture. He had bigger plans. His rebuff took counsel from two Stanford computer grads called Larry Page and Sergey Brin, who had decided to launch a search engine called Google only after Yahoo had refused to buy their technology for a paltry $1.6 million. Abrams believed Friendster would become a social Google. At one point, Friendster execs were kicking the tyres of a small start-up at Harvard called Facebook. But they'd decided to take a pass.

Friendster members meanwhile had morphed into a curious mixture of "freaks, geeks and queers". The site had become a dating platform for gay men while so-called "Burners" (a geek community formed around the Burning Man festival in the Nevada Desert) also had coalesced around Friendster. Besides these core constituencies, there were assorted hangers-on of various affiliations, including so-called Fraudsters using the site to deal drugs, run prostitution rings and exploit the site as an advertising platform to attract new clients.[4]

Friendster's real problem was its basic architecture. The site was designed as a *closed* system whose members had to be linked to one another by at least "four degrees" of separation. As the *New York Times* described it: "The holy grail at Friendster – and the cause of most of its technical problems – was its closed system: users at Friendster could view only the profiles of those on a relatively short chain of acquaintances."[5] Aliases and multiple identities were also banned. Worse, Friendster administrators began sending "nasty-grams" to members in violation of site rules. The Friendster founders had failed to grasp the social dynamics of the site's success. They were behaving like a rigid, vertical bureaucracy harassing their own members with rules and regulations, instead of harnessing the social potential of the platform that was making them rich.

Exasperated by excessive meddling, Friendster members reacted by opting for *exit*. The site suffered mass defections. As Internet sociologist Danah Boyd, who has studied the history of Friendster, described it: "There is a tipping point to get on and a tipping point to get off. Once mass departure began with a few pissed-off folks, it spiralled quickly. While the early adopters left storm-like, cancelling their accounts, most users simply stopped logging in frequently because it was no longer the place where their friends were."[6] In the end, Friendster's high-flying days as the new media darling of the American social networking landscape had lasted a little more than a year. Friendster's only option was to focus on its popularity outside the United States – mainly in Singapore, Malaysia and the Philippines.

The founders of an upstart site called MySpace, meanwhile, were carefully analysing Friendster's missteps. When Tom Anderson and Chris DeWolfe launched MySpace, they deliberately took a different approach. MySpace marketed itself as a cool, hip, music-oriented site that, above all, was *open* to anybody. No busybody social restrictions. MySpace encouraged members to check out anybody's profile and do just about whatever they pleased on the site. Result: while Friendster's numbers were falling in America, MySpace's membership soared. In 2005, Friendster was running out of cash and had fired Abrams before going into exile in Asia. The same year, Rupert Murdoch paid $580 million for MySpace.

Friendster made two fatal mistakes: it failed to understand the *identity* dynamics of online social networking; and it underestimated the consequences of *exit* reactions. MySpace's success, built on the lessons of Friendster's blunders, proved that first-mover advantages don't always pay off.

Other social networking sites have resorted to overregulation in order to create an aura of exclusivity. Consider the example of aSmallWorld, a jet-set networking site that has been called "Facebook for the few" and "MySpace for millionaires". aSmallWorld appeals to the super-rich and famous confronted with everyday quandaries like leasing a private island in Fiji, finding a string of Argentine polo horses for the Palm Beach season or hiring a fleet of Aston Martins in a jiffy for an A-list soirée in Switzerland. Problems that your average Facebook "friend" won't likely help you solve.

aSmallWorld, created in 2004 as an online country club for the global elite, advertises itself as a virtual space where celebrities and the super-rich can connect with no worries about fan harassment, paparazzi, hangers-on and everybody else on the planet. Quintessentially medieval in its social architecture, aSmallWorld cuts off its global aristocracy from the masses by erecting an online fortress circled by an intimidating virtual moat. The site's exalted membership reportedly includes fashion model Naomi Campbell, socialites Paris Hilton and Ivanka Trump, pop star James Blunt, golf pro Tiger Woods, Microsoft billionaire Paul Allen, Hollywood movie director Quentin Tarantino, as well as scions of America's Old Money capitalist dynasties with names like Firestone, Rockefeller and Forbes.[7]

aSmallWorld is the brainchild of New York-based investment banker Erik Wachtmeister, the son of a Swedish diplomat whose upbringing appears to have given him an expansive, horizontal vision of the global elite. "I came to the realization that there is an existing community out there of people that are connected to each other, directly or indirectly," said Wachtmeister, whose handsome blond looks give the impression that he would be perfectly at ease among the Beautiful People attracted to his site. "These are people that you constantly see at the same places at the same time of year, over and over again, and they keep running into each other and saying to each other, 'Oh, what a small world. What are you doing here?' That was the first 'aha' moment that I had. The second thing is, what they have in common is not only that they know a lot of the same people, but they also have similar needs, tastes, desires, and they constantly want to know who's where and who's doing what."[8]

aSmallWorld has seen its rarefied ranks soar from a small clique of 500 invitation-only members to roughly 300 000 glitterati worldwide. Apart from the psychic rewards of being a member, aSmallWorld keeps its members abreast of more practical matters, such as the scheduling of real-world VIP events in global hot spots like Palm Beach, Cannes, Dubai, Paris, New York City and the Hamptons. To gain admission into this gated community in cyberspace, you need to be put up by no fewer than *five* members. What's more, all members must be linked by no more than *three* degrees of separation – half the *six* degrees that, according to the famous "small world" theory, separate most mere mortals.[9] The aSmallWorld site, moreover, has a "no-jumping-the-velvet-rope" rule that gives invitation privileges only to a fraction of its top-drawer members. This rule evidently keeps out cyber-social climbers and assorted other vulgarians and riff-raff from the lower fringes of the moneyed classes.

There was nothing spontaneous about aSmallWorld's creation. It was founded as a business from the outset.[10] Wachtmeister, faithful to his Wall Street training, crunched the numbers and studied the sociology of networking sites. aSmallWorld's main function is *information sharing* and its value system is based on *trust*. The site's super-rich members must feel they can trust other members. Paris Hilton isn't going to ask just anyone where to go for a pedicure in Monte Carlo. On aSmallWorld, however, she can get trusted information.

The intriguing thing about aSmallWorld's business model is that it appears to contradict the driving logic of *network effects*. The standard definition of network effects is this: a network is more socially *useful* as the number of its members *increases*. This axiom is sometimes called Metcalfe's Law – named after Ethernet inventor Robert Metcalfe – which posits that the value of a network is proportional to the square of the number of people it connects. Metcalfe's Law was modified by David Reed, who argued that Metcalfe underestimated the *utility* value of network growth. According to Reed, the utility of a network – including social networks – grows *exponentially* with its size.[11] What Metcalfe and Reed were both observing was this: large networks are infinitely more useful, and hence valuable, than small networks. Metcalfe noted that, from an economic point of view, after a certain critical mass of network connectivity is reached – the tipping point – the network's benefits grow more than its costs.

The classic illustration of network effects is the telephone system. During the telephone's early years at the end of the 19th century, when very few people were connected, the telephone network offered little utility value. During the 1870s, most people were quite happy sending written messages via telegraph. Alexander Graham Bell put phones in urban hotel rooms which at first shocked many Victorian ladies when they discovered people were actually speaking to complete strangers while in a state of undress. Yet the network was still limited. After telephone penetration reached a critical mass, however, its network value soared – not only for new adopters, but also for early adopters who now had more people to ring up.

The law of network effects has applied to many other technologies: fax machines, mobile phones, Internet, Skype and so on. The more people who use these technologies, the more useful they are to users. Which leads logically to the question: if the value of a network increases exponentially with the number of its users, what is the value of a social network like aSmallWorld, whose raison d'être is to *minimize* the number of its members?

The obvious answer, from a strictly sociological point of view, is that people value small, like-minded, exclusive networks. It's an enduring fact of human nature that people seek to manifest superior social standing through points of *distinction* – wealth, class, accent, values, education, manners, taste, dress. Aristotle, in his *Rhetoric*, observed that people "love those who are like themselves". This time-honoured reflex of *homophily* drives many to seek out the company of "people like us".

In the virtual world, this social instinct can be translated into a single concept: the *social graph*.[12] Contrary to the strictly *quantitative* measure of network effects based on size, the social graph is based on a *qualitative* assessment of the type of social connections in a network. In short, the social graph concept focuses on the *sociological content* of a network, whereas network effects describe only its structural dynamics.

Wachtmeister made this point explicitly in late 2006: "Companies like MySpace, Friendster, Facebook and Google's Orkut have received most of the attention, as they are mostly oriented to teenagers and young adults where members can maximise quantity but not necessarily the quality of interaction . . . aSmallWorld has an entirely different approach. We try to follow a code of civilised behaviour within our online community that emulates the real world, capture real-life relationships between people, not random contacts. Unlike other online communities, we are unique because we don't allow aliases or false names, rude or aggressive behaviour towards other members, and allow only genuine and quality content."

Note that Wachtmeister unapologetically uses the term "real-life" and "real world" when describing aSmallWorld. This doubtless explains, or at least justifies, the site's ban on multiple identities. Even more interesting, aSmallWorld has a "free from commercial bias" policy. No advertising clutter on aSmallWorld. However laudable, the combination of real-world values and a commercial-free business model reveals an intriguing contradiction at the core of aSmallWorld's business model. How do you monetize a social networking site based on *minimizing* not only your membership numbers but also your commercial advertising revenue? The quick answer is: you can't.

Wachtmeister finally – and predictably – bit the bullet and opted for an advertising model based on targeting luxury brands like Moët & Chandon, Cartier, Jaguar and Burberry. But Wachtmeister overlooked one important factor. By deciding to sell advertising, he had put aSmallWorld's business model squarely behind the Old Media logic of aggregating audiences. When your business model – in television or newspapers – is based on selling audiences to advertisers, your main incentive, even with high-end demographics, is to *increase* audience size. It may be a small world, but advertisers like big numbers.

This paradox may explain why, after aSmallWorld's membership had soared to nearly 300 000, Wachtmeister was boldly predicting that he expected the number to rocket to a million. He was now employing the language of *network effects*. As aSmallWorld's numbers grew, however, so did tensions between the embedded *trust* in the social graph and the *commercial bias* in favour of network effects. There were even reports that aSmallWorld memberships were being sold on the open market. As the site's top-drawer members began discreetly slipping out the exit doors, aSmallWorld's velvet rope was starting to droop lazily towards the floor.

aSmallWorld insisted that it was policing the site to keep out cyber-social climbers. New rules were imposed: any member making a direct online approach to a stranger, or selling products too aggressively, would face expulsion. aSmallWorld even created a sister site, called aBigWorld, which served as a cyber-limbo to which the B-list crowds of sycophants, publicists, party-promoters and gate-crashers were politely banished. Still, elitist members were sniffing about a riff-raff invasion. Among complaints on the site's bulletin board was this one: "I've been to a few aSmallWorld-only events that one would have thought were for Facebook (or even MySpace) people." Another member remarked: "Is it just me, but lately I see people on ASW who really shouldn't be there. Who invites these people?"[13] aSmallWorld was learning the lesson of *voice* and *exit*.

Wachtmeister, interestingly, had originally been inspired to launch aSmallWorld after studying the Friendster model. It seems, in retrospect, that he took the emulation to the point of replicating Friendster's mistakes. The parallels went further. Just as MySpace learned from Friendster's mistakes and then stole its members by offering a more *open*, unstructured social networking experience, aSmallWorld's competitors were quick to pounce on its membership dissatisfaction by offering a more *closed*, exclusive community.

A rival snob site called DiamondLounge launched in October 2007 with a business model designed to avoid aSmallWorld's pitfalls. DiamondLounge charges subscription fees of $60 per month, claiming that its paid-subscription approach avoids the advertising trap and keeps out the tiresome publicists and PR people who had penetrated aSmallWorld. Also, DiamondLounge members are allowed to maintain two "identities". One identity is your *social* profile in "the Lounge"; the other your *business* profile in "the Boardroom." This personality bifurcation is managed in the following way: in the Lounge, members restrict who can view them based on social criteria like age, gender and physical appearance; in the Boardroom, profile information like industry, job title and income are provided. Members exchange gifts much like Facebook friends, but in the DiamondLounge icons of teddy bears are replaced by real Gucci bags.[14]

Arya Marafie, DiamondLounge's managing director, points out that sites like aSmallWorld claim to be for rich Beautiful People but then fling open the doors to everybody. "We'd rather have 100 members than 5000 of the wrong kinds of people," Marafie told the *New York Times* in 2007. "Once you have the wrong people on these social networks, the whole thing is over."[15] No jumping the velvet rope at DiamondLounge. The obvious question is: how will DiamondLounge, competing with a well-branded gated site like aSmallWorld, make money by being even *more closed*?

DiamondLounge is not the only walled site whose marketing strategy – officially, at least – is based on attracting as *few* members as possible. Another site called Beautiful People advertises itself as the "most exclusive little black book in the world". Shamelessly skin-deep, Beautiful People requires prospective members to submit a recent photograph – girls preferably in bikinis, boys buffed and showing six-packs. Photos are posted on the Beautiful People site for three days while members cast their votes, like on a TV reality show, based on a "four-point attractiveness" scale.[16] A similar site, ModelsHotel, has an even more selective door policy: top fashion models only. Founded by 24-year-old male model Jesper Lannung, the site is restricted to models from "top 50" agencies. Lannung says he created ModelsHotel because he was fed up with all the "poseurs and wannabes" on MySpace. ModelsHotel, adds Lannung, promises members that it "weeds out the creepy people". Lannung told the *Wall Street Journal* in late 2007 that his site had rejected more than half of the 2000 applications it had received. No off-putting membership fees for the happy few, ModelsHotel's revenue projections are based on advertising from luxury fitness clubs and fashion brands like Diesel jeans.[17]

Russian playboy billionaire Mikhail Prokhorov, meanwhile, has created a social networking site called Snob aimed exclusively at super-rich Russians like him. A similar site called OutOrIn is restricted to high net-worth members described as "sophisticated cosmopolitans, aristocracy and business leaders" who have attended a "a renowned university or boarding school". And in New York, an invitation-only site called CarbonNYC attracts the Big Apple's jet-set plutocracy with average annual incomes of $1 million.[18]

Other *closed* sites have been organized around social exclusion based on professional status: Pingsta for computer industry network-ers, MyDealBook for commercial real estate professionals, Sermo for doctors, INmobile for wireless industry executives, AdGabber for adverting people and Reuters Space for hedge-fund managers, traders and analysts. These sites are not seeking to leverage network effects. They all have a sign on their cyber-door that reads: Members Only. To join, you have to show up with real-life credentials on paper. Busi-ness models in this category vary. Reuters, for example, is charging subscriber fees. Sermo, however, monetizes its members, charging from $100 000 to $150 000 a year to nonmedical businesses for the privilege of monitoring online discussions among doctors. Institu-tional investors and pharmaceutical executives, it would appear, are willing to pay steep fees for fly-on-the-wall access to doctor informa-tion about the growth potential of new drugs.[19]

So where does this leave the open/closed debate? Sceptics, it can be expected, will persist with the view that the logic of *closed*, propri-etary and commercial systems will always prevail. Other critics note that social networking sites adopt open strategies in order to leverage network effects, but once critical mass is achieved they quickly capture value by pulling up the drawbridge and monetizing the community locked inside. Some sites, like aSmallWorld, seem to want the best of both worlds: the aura of exclusiveness along with the advantages of network effects. It's a contradiction difficult to reconcile.

There is indisputable evidence to support these criticisms. Still, the advocates of *open* systems are gaining momentum. Google's Open-Social, even if a salvo at Facebook, was a move in that direction. Even Microsoft, after decades cast in the unenviable role of nonproprietary software's fiercest enemy, appears to have finally embraced the open-source model. In February 2008, Microsoft stunned the world by announcing the company was going open-source. Some in the open-source movement called the Microsoft announcement "smoke and mirrors", but most applauded the software giant for making a bold move. We could well be witnessing the early days of an open-network e-ruption.

In the final analysis, the *open* vs. *closed* debate will be resolved according to the measure of greater social good. True, it's a fact of human nature that people organize themselves in social hierarchies and seek status attributes that encourage values of distinction, exclusion and closure. Homophily has long been an entrenched principle of social organization and, in the real world, there is little prospect of that changing any time soon. Yet the laws of genetics warn us against the dangers of inbreeding, just as the dictates of decency counsel us against the inconsideration of snobbery. It is difficult to make a convincing argument in favour of a society whose citizens are cloistered inside social echo chambers in which they are constantly comforted and reassured by the opinions and values of other people just like them. Philosophically, that conception of social organization flouts the basic precepts of liberal values: individualism, pluralism and freedom of expression.

Which brings us back to the third theme in Albert Hirschman's book: *loyalty*. Our analysis of social networking sites – notably Friendster and Facebook – confirms Hirschman's insight. He observed that, when *exit* is impossible (for consumers, employees, citizens), they invariably resort to *voice*. But if voice is given a hearing, and heeded, *loyalty* is possible.

Let's look at how Facebook – unlike Friendster – managed to win customer loyalty. Mark Zuckerberg had obviously been following the sorry plight of Friendster after its blunders. At first, however, Zuckerberg imposed even tighter controls on Facebook. By taking a "Hotel California" approach, Zuckerberg was effectively pre-empting any risk of membership *exit*. You can check out any time you like, but you can never leave – because Facebook gets to keep your identity. This put another interesting twist on the virtual identity conundrum. On Facebook, your identity can be stolen, created, copied, fractured and plasticized into a thousand different forms. But like material wealth after death, you can't take it with you. Your Facebook identity isn't portable. It's a lifetime contract. You can leave, but your identity stays.

Zuckerberg may have believed he'd solved the *exit* problem by bolting the doors shut, but he would soon find himself confronted with a more direct challenge: *voice*.

Some Facebook members, frustrated with the site's no-exit policy, began vociferously protesting – even using their Facebook profiles to voice their complaints. A Facebook group called "How to Permanently Delete Your Facebook Account" counted more than 4000 members. A Quebec-based blogger called Steven Mansour proved an even more effective *voice* protestor. Mansour posted on his home page a sarcastic link called "2504 Steps to Closing Your Facebook Account", which ended up on Digg.com and by early 2008 had been viewed

90 000 times. Mansour jubilantly announced on his blog: "Yes, it's true! I finally managed to close my Facebook account. It was a long, arduous road – the hardest part was slaying the Gorgon on level 16 – and I'm glad it's finally over."[20]

When these protests started sounding off, Facebook was still emerging from a painful damage-control exercise following its disastrous "Beacon" advertising program in late 2007. Beacon was a scarcely veiled strategy to monetize Facebook members by feeding their online commercial activities through a stream of "stories" made visible to other members. Beacon was an attempt to create so-called "social ads" that give the impression members are endorsing products to their online "friends". If a Facebook member purchased a song on iTunes, for example, his entire list of "friends" would know about it. Beacon, in a word, was a viral advertising strategy based on leveraging network effects. Facebook's slogan to potential advertisers was: *"Promote your business in an organic, social way"*.

Facebook members didn't like the idea of being monetized to generate ad revenues – especially without their knowledge or consent. Their hostile reaction was immediate and loud. An American political advocacy group called MoveOn.org gathered almost 70 000 signatures in protest, claiming that Beacon lacked an adequate opt-out function. Worse for Facebook, the Beacon initiative rekindled long-simmering resentment towards the site's no-exit policy. Now it seemed abundantly clear why Facebook was so difficult to escape. The site's business model, it seemed, was based on monetizing membership data to drive commercial revenue.

The timing could not have been worse for Zuckerberg. Google had just gazumped Facebook with its loudly trumpeted "OpenSocial" project allowing software developers to write applications for all social networks with no closed-wall restrictions. Some speculated that OpenSocial was Google's revenge after Facebook snubbed its buyout overture. Turning Google down, Zuckerberg had opted instead to take a small minority investment from Microsoft, which bought a 1.6% stake in Facebook for $240 million. Spiteful or not, Google was now announcing to the world: Facebook is a *closed* world, Google is socially *open*. At the same time, ratings were showing that Facebook's membership growth was starting to stall. To make things even worse, there were dark conspiracy-theory rumours about Facebook's financial backers, who reportedly were wealthy American "neo-cons" with CIA connections exploiting the site to push a dark ideological agenda.[21]

Under attack from all quarters, Zuckerberg decided to come clean. In early December 2007, he posted a blog entry admitting his mistake and reversing Facebook's policy. "About a month ago, we released a new feature called Beacon to try to help people share information with their friends about things they do on the web," said Zuckerberg. "We've made a lot of mistakes building this feature, but we've made even more with how we've handled them. We simply did a bad job with this release, and I apologise for it. While I am disappointed with our mistakes, we appreciate all the feedback we have received from our users." Henceforth, said Zuckerberg, the Beacon program would be opt-in, not opt-out. Two months later, Zuckerberg took further steps to make it easier for Facebook members to delete their profiles.[22]

It had taken Facebook four weeks to deal with the Beacon disaster, and four months to bring closure to the no-exit controversy. But to his credit, Zuckerberg – unlike the Friendster founders – listened to Facebook members and remedied the problem. By dealing honestly with Facebook's voice protests, Zuckerberg was rewarded with customer *loyalty*, not punished by mass *exit*.

The *loyalty* theory contains powerful lessons for all corporations and organizations. Many corporate executives instinctively distrust open networks, which threaten vested interests and existing arrangements in established hierarchies. This entrenched distrust is based on more than the psycho-politics of bureaucratic survival. There is another puzzling paradox at play here. While open networks are more valuable thanks to the law of *network effects*, corporations undervalue them because they are difficult to own and control. Open networks are, moreover, difficult to *value* as intangible assets. We know that Web 2.0 tools, like IT software, create economic value. But many corporations have stubbornly conservative attitudes towards these intangible assets for the purposes of corporate *valuation*. Many companies regard Web 2.0 software not as an intangible asset that creates value, but as a cost centre that needs to be managed.[23] Executives are reluctant to put a value on anything they can't control, often citing "operational risk management".

The real problem, in truth, is the fear factor. And yet corporate managers keep learning the same lessons. Companies whose leaders enforce rigidly defined roles inside suffocating bureaucratic silos and soundproof boardrooms are more frequently punished by *exit* and *voice*. Whereas companies whose leaders encourage individual creativity and open collaboration, and who genuinely listen to their employees and customers, are more frequently rewarded by *loyalty*.

Closed systems benefit established interests in centralized, vertical hierarchies. Open networks foster creativity, innovation and economic value. When the two collide, an unpleasant e-ruption is inevitable. But the best outcome should be obvious.

We are under no illusions. Velvet ropes, VIP parties and snobby country clubs have undeniable appeal in real-world social hierarchies. But in the open networks of cyberspace, smart people bet on the strength of weak ties, the social utility of e-quaintances and the wisdom of diverse crowds. The virtue of open networks won't get much applause among the Beautiful People. But open networks are the way the world works.

4

We Googled you: the privacy paradox

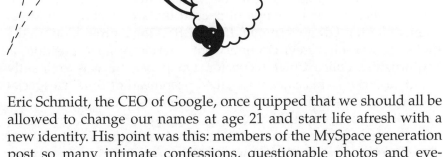

Eric Schmidt, the CEO of Google, once quipped that we should all be allowed to change our names at age 21 and start life afresh with a new identity. His point was this: members of the MySpace generation post so many intimate confessions, questionable photos and eye-popping details about their personal lives on social networking sites that, years later when they enter the real world with its social codes and institutional pressures, many are haunted by a sinking feeling of dread as they realize that embarrassing traces of many past foibles – silly comments, dumb pranks, sick jokes, harum-scarum antics – have been left indelibly on a social networking site in full view of the entire planet.

It's no joke. Just ask the American university student who, after graduating from the University of Illinois, was poised to land a job as an intern at a Chicago consulting company. It was a foot in the door to a promising career, he told the *New York Times* in 2006. After the company's CEO checked the young applicant's Facebook profile, however, his values seemed disturbingly incompatible with hard work. On the profile, he described his main interests in life as smoking dope, screwing girls, and shooting people – each one of these activities expressed in graphic youth slang. The coveted job offer never came. He was toast.[1]

This kind of boomerang blunder is not restricted to the young. Every day it comes back and hits thousands of card-carrying adults who discover, to their everlasting regret, that a door has just been politely closed in their face due to some questionable detail found online. It could be a stupid photo showing a younger, embarrassing version of themselves – mooning before a camera or guzzling down a bottle of Jack Daniels. Or something more serious, like a shameful event – an arrest for drink-driving or drug possession – that keeps popping up on Google.

Haunted by their virtual selves, more and more people know how it feels to wish they could start anew, *tabula rasa*, erasing dark facts and colourful fictions from their past. They are learning the hard way that keeping a blog, or maintaining an online profile, can be a "wealth hazard". Like it or not, our lives are becoming an open Facebook. Everybody's kimono is open.

Consider what happened to Inspector Chris Dreyfus, a senior British police officer in charge of special units protecting the Royal Family and top UK government figures. Seeking a promotion up the ranks, 30-year-old Dreyfus underwent interviews for a position as Bedfordshire Police Chief Inspector. On paper, he was eminently qualified. Prior to his current job, he'd been head of Britain's special Counter-Terrorism Proactive Unit where he was in charge of 30 officers. With those credentials, it was no surprise when he was offered the Chief Inspector's position. But then, suddenly, the offer was withdrawn. After a series of background checks on the Web, it was discovered that Dreyfus was homosexual. That wasn't the problem. The issue was his online behaviour. Dreyfus had been flamboyantly advertising his gay lifestyle on his Facebook profile, including provocative photo postings and suggestive references to using "Vaseline".

Faced with the grim prospect of a career setback, Inspector Dreyfus argued that there was nothing wrong with posting details of his *private* life online. "As long as I do not do anything to disgrace the force then what I do privately is acceptable," he claimed. Maybe so. But Dreyfus' superiors in the Royal Family protection unit had already warned him in writing about his flamboyant Facebook existence.

The British tabloid press, needless to say, had loads of fun with the Dreyfus affair, quipping that the gay copper had received a "spanking" for his homosexual Facebook antics. For Dreyfus, the consequences were less amusing. He didn't get the promotion.[2]

If Dreyfus's career-limiting move seems like a gay version of No-Sex-Please-We're-British, this kind of professional setback can be seriously traumatizing. Every week there's yet another media report about an employee who has been fired due to some posting on a social networking site. Sometimes these collisions lead to painful and costly legal battles. For everyone involved, they end badly. Reputations are destroyed. Careers are ruined. Financial situations collapse. Rebounding often seems impossible. Families can be torn apart. People sink into dark depressions. Employers, for their part, attract unwanted negative publicity. Employee morale is undermined. Everybody is on edge. Big Brother is watching. Nobody wins.

At the end of 2007, Britain's Information Commissioner estimated that nearly 5 million young people in the UK had online profiles featuring content that could, if consulted by universities or potential employers, damage their higher education and career prospects. By ratio-based extrapolation, that would mean that some 25 million American youths are in the same boat, and countless millions more worldwide. In Britain, 60% of youths polled had no idea that their profile postings were permanent and could come back to haunt them. Even more intriguing, 70% of youngsters polled said they were unconcerned that their online profiles could be viewed by strangers.[3] They didn't give a damn.

Given this high level of apathy, the UK Information Commissioner issued a number of tips to encourage young Britons to "wise up" about the potential consequences of posting intimate details about their lives. One key warning was: *a blog is for life*. Another message was: *reputation is everything*.

The normative underpinnings of *privacy* and *reputation* have been challenged, indeed transformed, by the e-ruptions we have been examining in this book – namely, a clash between real-world and virtual-world norms, between personal and social identities, between horizontal networks and vertical institutions. In this chapter, we call this virtual e-ruption the Privacy Paradox. The paradox is this: never before have so many people exhibited their deeply personal and intimate selves so publicly, for the whole world to see, and yet never before has the danger of privacy invasion, identity theft and reputational damage been so preoccupying.

Some believe that the Privacy Paradox is an outdated issue. As Sheldon Teitelbaum put it in *Wired* magazine: "Privacy is history – get over it."[4]

Maybe so, but privacy has a history. We have long been obsessed with privacy and the reputational consequences of its violation.

In many cultures, the naked human body, like the sexual act, has been considered a deeply private zone. In English, a person's genitalia are referred to as "*private* parts" – frequently covered by a fig leaf on statues and in paintings. Beyond intimate spaces, privacy frequently has meant secrecy. Social networks like the Knights Templar, to return to our historical saga, were famous for their secret codes and rituals understood only by initiated members. Today, Freemasons, the descendants of the Templars, are like their forbearers known for their strict codes of secrecy. The same goes for religious sects and cults. Modern states, too, are obsessively secretive about their covert activities – and invasive about those of others. In modern corporations, an iron rule is secrecy. The quickest way for an executive to destroy his career is through a reckless indiscretion.

The modern notion of privacy finds its origins in the Enlightenment philosophy and the emergence of capitalism, whose values were based on *private* property as a fundamental principle of individual liberty. Privacy is a fundamental freedom protected in the Universal Declaration of Human Rights. Robert Ellis Smith, editor of *Privacy Journal*, defines this freedom in the following terms: "The desire by each of us for physical space where we can be free of interruption, intrusion, embarrassment, or accountability and the attempt to control the time and manner of disclosures of personal information about ourselves."[5]

Before the invention of the printing press in the 15th century, privacy was violated by gossip, rumour and innuendo. The advent of books and pamphleteering gave free reign to opinion-making and, despite the constant threat of censorship, gave birth to a mass-produced form of slander and defamation. In the late 19th century, newspapers gave press barons the power to shape opinion and destroy reputations. The explosion of electronic mass media and the emergence of professional journalism institutionalized this power in the hands of the media.

Today, the Web is the latest technological e-ruption that – much more powerfully than its predecessors – is challenging traditional notions of privacy. On the Internet, there is no professional class of gatekeepers – journalists – who determine what is "fit to print". There are no filters, no self-censorship, no ethical reflexes of prior restraint. Anybody can express an opinion on the Web. The explosion of blogs, wikis and social media means that, at any instant, our personal privacy and reputational integrity can be exposed to unwelcome scrutiny. There is no place to hide.

The advent of social networking sites has created virtual norms that no longer make a meaningful distinction between *private* and *public*. In the online world – where people create multiple identities while collecting "friends" – the line between *personal* and *social* identity has become blurred. Which might explain why so many young people are so indifferent to the reputational consequences of the posts they display on their personal pages. They are just being themselves, having fun, doing what kids do – why should their youthful antics be held against them for their entire lives?

The day will come, probably sooner rather than later, when none of these questions will matter. For the moment, however, the problem is that real-world values have not caught up with online values. And the lag between the two can produce serious consequences – especially in the form of a tainted *reputation*. You can be a superstar on Facebook, but you can also be a pariah when you show up at the office.

When a reputation is damaged, the injury is frequently inflicted by embarrassing truths, but it can also be caused by cruel distortions and defamatory lies. Outside a court of law, it doesn't matter how "true" a privacy violation is, the reputational damage is often permanent. This explains why courts take reputational damage so seriously, and indeed frequently award significant amounts of money to injured parties. Courts recognize that reputation is the cornerstone of *identity*. As American law professor Daniel Solove stated in his book, *The Future of Reputation*: "Our reputation can be a key dimension of our self, something that affects the very core of our identity. Beyond its internal influence on our self-conception, our reputation affects our ability to engage in basic activities in society. We depend on others to engage in transactions with us, to employ us, to befriend us, and to listen to us. Without the cooperation of others in society, we often are unable to do what we want to do. Without the respect of others, our actions and accomplishments can lose their purpose and meaning."[6]

A reputation is usually destroyed in one of two ways: people bring disrepute upon themselves through their behaviour or actions; or others inflict reputational injury through malicious gossip, innuendo or disturbing revelations. In the virtual world, the first type of reputational damage is frequently the consequence of narcissistic *self-exhibition* – in other words, online revelations that come back to haunt someone in the real world. In the second category, reputations are destroyed online by deliberate acts of privacy violation. These wilfully destructive gestures are known as *shaming*.

Let's first examine reputational risk through *self-exhibition*. As we saw in Chapter 1, social interaction in the virtual world is an elaborate ritual of self-presentation and impression management – or putting one's best cyberface forward. Since disembodied interaction is exempt from the normal constraints of *space*, self-presentation is not immediately subject to face-to-face verification. You can be anybody you wish online. Imposture is not only indulged, it's expected. Virtual reality has also transformed the traditional social parameters of *time*. In the real world, we manage our social interactions according to a normatively accepted rhythm. Romantic and marital relations are continuous and intense. We interact with loved ones and close friends regularly. We keep up with social friends less frequently. And we remain in touch with acquaintances only occasionally. In the virtual world, on the other hand, the presentation of self vis-à-vis "friends" is a sociological ritual whose rhythm is daily, hourly, even minute-by-minute. Online social interaction can be like a webcam that is never turned off – round-the-clock, always-on, full disclosure. Virtual time, paradoxically, is real time.

The real-time immediacy of self-exhibition is facilitated by social media like Twitter (text) and Flickr (photos). Twitter, a micro-blogging networking site, advertises itself as a service that lets you get constantly updated answers from friends to the question: "What are you doing?" Launched in 2006, Twitter facilitates "many-to-many" mobile messaging via brief text posts – or "tweets" – limited to 140 characters. Messages on Twitter – and similar services like Pownce, Dodgeball and Frazr – can be mind-numbingly banal, trivial and pointless. Twitter is akin to the hit 1990s television series *Seinfeld*, which was famously "about nothing". Typical Twitter patter features comments like, "doing lunch and picking up father-in-law from senior centre" or "falling asleep at my desk. 2 more hours till cocktails!" While such mundane actions and thoughts are essentially devoid of meaning, relating them to others somehow gives them existential significance. Twitter makes us feel connected.

But Twitter is also considered dangerous – especially in corporations. Twitter encourages people to type quick comments to networked friends, who sometimes number in the dozens or hundreds. Many companies fear that Twitter poses a threat to privacy, reputation and corporate secrecy. What happens, for example, when a senior manager attending a confidential boardroom meeting sends an unguarded remark ("my bonehead CEO is stumbling through a lame presentation about why we should pay a 40% premium to buy our main competitor – this will be his Waterloo") to a network of Twitter friends? After a tweet like that starts making the rounds, it's easy to predict who is going to get fired first. Here's a clue: not the CEO.[7]

The most widespread form of self-exhibition is blogging. Virtually everybody can create their own blog. In the language of economics, there are no barriers to entry to the blogosphere, except the cost of a computer and an Internet connection. The blogosphere is a libertarian paradise where every voice can find expression. All you have to do is log onto Google's Blogger.com or another blogging website, and away you go. In early 2008 there were more than 110 million blogs worldwide. By the time you are holding this book in your hands, millions more have been created. Blogging has transformed the ritual of self-exhibition into a *narrative* form of identity construction. Internet sociologist Jenny Sundén made the linkage between virtual narration and identity construction when she argued that people use Web-based self-narration to *write* themselves into existence.[8] Every day, millions of people use their blog, Twitter and Flickr to send the world a constantly updated account of their thoughts, emotions and daily activities.

Virtual autobiography can be a liberating form of self-expression that, in some cases, achieves the status of literature. In many respects, blogging represents a return to forms of literary expression popular in the 17th century, when Samuel Pepys kept his famous diary in Restoration England. On the Internet, however, the public nature of this form of self-exhibition can have serious consequences not only for personal privacy, but for the reputation of others.

Staying with our literary analogy, a fascinating new form of online literature has emerged that seems inspired by epistolary novels from the 18th century like Samuel Richardson's *Clarissa: the History of a Young Lady*. Like their literary antecedents, online confessions betray an obsession with a familiar archetypal heroine: the attractive, ambitious young woman making her way into society, rising and falling with the vagaries of fortune, sometimes rewarded for her virtues, more frequently punished for her vices. Unlike their literary ancestors, however, in the virtual literary sphere sensational blogs are *autobiographies* written by the young women themselves. Many have grown up as teenagers exchanging gossip online with their girlfriends and, later in life, continue using the Web to give narrative form to their impressions. Sometimes, it is true, online literary diaries read like English romance novels in the tradition of *Pamela, or Virtue Rewarded*. But more frequently, they resemble the classic 18th century French epistolary novel, *Les Liaisons Dangeureuses*. More to the point, given the public nature of this form of online self-exhibition – which is, effectively, a virtual *roman à clef* narrative – the consequences for privacy and reputation can be unexpected and often controversial.[9]

Consider the Internet morality tale of 26-year-old Asian-American beauty Jessica Cutler, whose spectacular rise – and fall – in the Washington DC power elite is a tale worthy of *Moll Flanders*. Cutler was an ambitious young Congressional aide working for US Senator Michael DeWine, a Republican from Ohio. Cutler's sexual conquests on Capitol Hill were so prodigious that she was juggling six powerful men at the same time. Then she had a brainwave. Like millions of other young American women, she was a fan of the hit television show, *Sex and the City*, in which actress Sarah Jessica Parker plays a newspaper columnist who writes about her big-city sexual adventures. So Cutler, inspired by the TV show, started keeping an anonymous blog about her exploits in the corridors (and bedrooms) of Washington power politics.

The blog, called The Washingtonienne, immediately scandalized the American capital with its steamy details about wild sex between a sultry young Congressional aide and powerful players who pay her for sex. The blog, started in 2004, described the "spanking" fetish of one of Cutler's lovers. Another, she wrote, liked to "talk dirty". Everybody in Washington was talking dirty, too – about the blog and who was behind it. Then another blog, called Wonkette, revealed that the Washingtonienne seductress was an exotically attractive assistant to a United States senator. The scandal rocked the US capital. Senator DeWine promptly fired Cutler. But once Cutler's online mask had been lifted, her erstwhile leg-over partners felt exposed. One of Cutler's colleagues in Senator DeWine's office – the man who she'd described as liking "spanking" – sued her for $20 million.

Cutler meanwhile accepted a large sum of money to pose nude for *Playboy* and published a kiss-and-tell novel whose title, *The Washingtonienne*, was borrowed from her blog. In the end, however, Cutler's online indiscretions tainted not only the reputation of others, but damaged her own. Run out of Washington and unable to find work, she filed for bankruptcy to avoid liabilities in the lawsuit against her. Today, she keeps her own website at JessicaCutler.com. On the site, she describes herself this way: "I am a published author who jumps out of cakes for money". A donation button on her home page reads: "Please, I need money for slutty clothes and drugs!"[10]

The online phenomenon of *shaming* is, for obvious reasons, more controversial than self-exhibition. Shaming must be distinguished from another online act of aggression known as *flaming*. When you *flame* someone online, you make an emotional and frontal attack on their reputation. Online *shaming*, less direct, is the violation of someone's privacy with the express purpose of humiliating the targeted person through discredit. Shaming is an online pillory and stockade. Or to continue our literary analogy, online shaming is a virtual scarlet letter.

There are many forms of online shaming – some comical, some scandalous, others tragic. The most common type of online shaming, of course, is gossip. Countless blogs and websites traffic in malicious innuendo that spreads virally. Gossip can be cruel, vicious and shockingly defamatory. Many reputations have, sadly, been broken by its poison. When analysed as a sociological phenomenon, though, it can be argued that gossip – however destructive – serves a function. Gossip heightens the rational social instinct to preserve a good *reputation*. Social psychologists observe, indeed, that most use of language in social interactions is a form of *reputation management*.[11]

As Robin Dunbar notes in his book *Grooming, Gossip and the Evolution of Language*: "You can pass on information about yourself in order to influence your listeners' perceptions of you. You can tell them about your likes and dislikes, how you would behave (or how you think you *ought* to behave) in different circumstances, what you believe in and how strongly you believe it, what you disapprove of, and so on. You can be deliberately rude or obsequiously nice; you can insult them or flatter them. It can allow you to sort the sheep from the goats very quickly by driving away those whom you know you would never get on with or encouraging those who might be of interest to stay and further their acquaintance with you. Or, of course, you can engage in black propaganda, sowing the seeds of doubt about enemies in people's minds or praising a slightly dubious friend to the hilt so that he or she gets the job." The good news is that criticism and negative gossip accounts for only 5% of verbal exchanges. Most social conversation is devoted to recounting personal experience and gossiping about who-is-doing-what-with-whom.[12] The important point here is that gossip has a *function*. By sending signals about *reputational consequences*, gossip constitutes a form of social control because it encourages conformity to established social norms.

One long-established social norm dictates that we pay our taxes. Most of us make our fiscal contributions honestly and in a timely manner, if only because we wish to avoid the opprobrium of being known as tax cheats. The negative reputational consequences of being exposed as a *free rider* are unpleasant, especially in the eyes of others who pay their taxes. In the United States, a country where proud Americans like to be regarded as paying their "fair share" of taxes, state governments use online shaming to expose tax scofflaws, whose names are posted on sites with names like CyberShame, DelinqNet, Caught in the Web and Website of Shame. The tactic, which inflicts public ignominy on fiscal free riders, is remarkably effective. Most people, as noted, are terrified of public stigma, and will promptly pay their taxes if they know that failure to do so will expose them to contempt in the eyes of their community. Louisiana, Georgia, South

Carolina and 15 other US states now send notices to tax deadbeats warning them that, if they don't pay up within 30 days, their names will posted online for all to see.

"We're trying to shame people," said Danny Brazell of the South Carolina Department of Revenue, adding that his state's shaming website, Debtor's Corner, was shaking down tax slackers for millions every year. "To have your neighbours able to see your debt, that would be embarrassing of course, and that's the whole idea."[13]

Online shaming also targets annoying, dangerous or anti-social behaviour, which is captured on camera and posted on websites to humiliate the perpetrators. In South Korea, a teenage girl was shamed before the entire country when, on a train with her tiny dog, her pet pooped and the mishap was filmed by another passenger using a cell phone camera. In a country where shame is a culturally devastating stigma, the so-called Dog Poop Girl was so haunted by the online video campaign against her that she dropped out of university. Other targets of online shaming are bad driving, illegal parking, littering, abusive nannies, loud cell phone yapping and lewd whistling at women. All these delinquent acts are now routinely caught on camera and posted on websites, with close-up photos, in order to shame the culprits. Remarkably, shaming victims – even when dead guilty – frequently react angrily by threatening lawsuits on the grounds of privacy invasion.[14]

Online shaming can also, sadly, be scandalous and painful. If hell hath no fury like a woman scorned, it's even worse on YouTube. When 49-year-old British playwright Tricia Walsh-Smith divorced from her rich husband, she was furious with the financial terms of the marital rupture. Walsh-Smith claimed that her 74-year-old husband, New York impresario Phillip Smith and biggest theatre owner on Broadway, was worth about $60 million but was giving her only $400 a week. In a rash act of vengeance, Walsh-Smith posted an astonishing video on YouTube. The video showed an emotional Walsh-Smith showing up at her husband's office and making embarrassing comments about her husband's sexual performance to a secretary. One news report described Walsh-Smith's emotional online outburst as an attempt to "spill the secrets of a marriage in an apparent effort to gain leverage and humiliate the other side."

"This is absolutely a new step, and I think it's scary," high-profile divorce lawyer Bonnie Rabin told the Associated Press. "People used to worry about getting on Page Six (the gossip page of the *New York Post*). But this? It brings the concept of humiliation to a whole new level."[15]

The sad case of Pulitzer-prize-winning American novelist Robert Olen Butler undoubtedly took humiliation to an even lower level. During the summer of 2007, Butler's wife Elizabeth Dewberry left him for another man. Ironically, Dewberry was also a published novelist, and her most recent book was titled, *His Lovely Wife*. Butler, a bald and bookish-looking 62-year-old, was understandably devastated to learn that his younger, attractive 44-year-old wife was leaving him for a fabulously rich and famous rival.

"Put down your cup of coffee or you might spill it," Butler wrote in an email to a group of his Florida State University students. "Elizabeth is leaving me for Ted Turner."

There was more. Butler's long, agonising email claimed that his wife had been "molested by her grandfather" and this trauma caused her later in life to enter into a "decade-long abusive marriage" with her first husband. Olen also claimed Dewberry was jealous of his Pulitzer Prize. Then he speculated on his estranged wife's new relationship: "She will not be Ted's only girlfriend. Ted is permanently and avowedly non-monogamous."

This irrational outburst set the blogosphere ablaze. Celebrity blogs had a field day with this juicy story about a flamboyant billionaire stealing a hot-babe literary Southern Belle from a gnomish, balding, jilted novelist with a high-pitched voice. A blog called American Digest: News from the New America, posted a trenchant account of the saga under the title: "This American Wife: Elizabeth Dewberry and Her Reborn Molester Ted Turner as Told by the Cuckolded Husband". Butler, amazingly, reacted angrily to the Internet publicity that his own pathetic outburst had triggered. While attempting to shame his wife and her billionaire lover, Butler failed to foresee the reputational consequences of his desperate gesture for his own privacy and dignity.

The good news for Butler is that, as a Pulitzer-prize winning novelist in his sixties, he won't likely find himself in the future enduring the anxiety of a job interview. For thousands of others, however, the search for a job is now accompanied by a dreaded feeling that some dark fact, or shameful episode, in their past will resurface and frustrate their ability to find gainful employment. At many job interviews these days, job applicants shudder when they suddenly hear the probing words, "We Googled you . . ."

Call it MySpace versus WorkPlace. It happens a lot more frequently than you think. In 2007, the privacy think tank, Ponemon Institute, found that 35% of managers were using Google to do online background checks, 23% looked up candidates on social networking sites and roughly 33% of Web-based searches led to rejections. "Companies don't want to go on record about Googling candidates but everybody is doing it," says Michael Fertik, CEO of ReputationDefender, whose firm specializes in finding and removing negative online content that violates privacy and threatens to damage reputations. "Your CV is no longer what you send to your employer – it's the first ten things that show up on Google." Firms like ReputationDefender – so-called "reputation-cleansing" services – deal with everything from unsubstantiated criminal accusations to a bogus obituary about a targeted person's child. Fees can be steep. Tiger Two, a reputation cleanser that counts a lot of celebrity clients, charges as much as $10 000 a month.[16]

Should companies hire people who they know have Web-tarnished reputations? In June 2007, the *Harvard Business Review* published a fascinating case study titled "We Googled You", describing this wrenching recruitment dilemma without offering a definite solution.[17] The dilemma is this: Fred Westen is CEO of a Philadelphia-based luxury apparel retailer, Hathaway Jones, whose strategic goal is to crack the lucrative Chinese market with its clothing line for Chinese yuppies (or "chuppies"). Looking for the right candidate to lead the company's drive into China, Westen believes he has found her: a bright, attractive Chinese-American called Mimi Brewster. Mimi has the perfect background and CV for the job. After growing up in China, speaking both Mandarin and local dialects, she moved to the United States where she studied modern Chinese history at Berkeley before choosing Stanford over Yale for her MBA. Mimi has another advantage that puts her ahead of the pack: her father, John Brewster, an American journalist in China, was John Westen's roommate at Andover. Following her easy-going, in-the-bag interview with Westen, Mimi winks at him and says, "Thanks, boss".

But there is one nagging problem. The company's HR director, a stuffy woman called Virginia Flanders who has never liked Westen's management style, has done a background check on Mimi. On a Google search, something troubling came up. On the website of a radical journal called *Alternative Review*, Mimi was identified in a ten-year-old story as a leader of an anti-globalization protest movement at Berkeley. What's more, a newspaper site shows an old photo of the younger Mimi Brewster marching outside China's consulate in San Francisco to protest the communist regime's treatment of dissidents. Was Mimi really the right person to lead the company's commercial strategy into the Chinese market?

When Virginia Flanders presents Westen with the Google results, his initial reaction is defensive. "For heaven's sake," he snaps, "Google anyone hard enough and you'll find some dirt." Then, after some reflection, he adds: "Let's get Mimi back in here to tell her side of the story." Virginia Flanders takes a more formal HR stance. She believes the company's lawyers should be consulted.

Westen is troubled by his dilemma. "The problem is that I have a responsibility to Hathaway Jones to hire the best people I can find," he thinks. "And how am I going to do that if I can only consider the ones who have always played it safe?"

He goes home that night anxious to seek his wife Martha's valued advice. What should he do?

Good question. But the *Harvard Business Review* doesn't offer an answer. We are meant to ponder the dilemma, consult the published advice of an expert panel and come up with an answer ourselves.

Sometimes the "We Googled You" syndrome is manifestly unfair. Take the example of a 34-year-old man from Boston whose predicament was chronicled by the *Boston Globe* in 2003. At that time, he was working at a Boston medical school – and hiding desperately from his past. More than fifteen years earlier, when he was only 17, he had been a drug addict who landed in jail for burglary. When out of prison and turning his life around a few years later, he decided to write about his earlier setbacks in a few specialized publications. What he couldn't predict, however, was the explosion of the Web. Some of those publications which had published his confessions had since posted their content online. His offline confessions about drug addiction, petty larceny and incarceration were now on the Web for the whole world to see.

It almost destroyed his life. Girls who took an interest in him dropped him cold without an explanation. When he was looking for a flat to share, he met with more than thirty potential housemates – but none called back. Then his online shame started to affect his ability to make a living. Actively courted for one job, he went through three rounds of intensive interviews before making the short list. Then, to his puzzlement, the employer stopped calling – and didn't return his phone calls. Baffled, he came to the only conceivable conclusion: they'd Googled him. Worse, they hadn't given him an opportunity to explain himself.[18]

One option would have been to turn to services like Reputation-Defender. Clients for online reputation management services can pay as much as $10 000 to have their virtual identities cleaned up. But there are no guarantees. Andy Beal, an online reputation consultant who blogs at MarketingPilgrim, believes that the best approach is a pro-active attitude to online personas. Beal's philosophy is simple:

since Google is essentially a "reputation engine", the best way to ensure that you don't become its victim is by taking control and becoming the author of your own virtual identity – before somebody else does it for you.[19]

Beal, author of *Radically Transparent: Monitoring & Managing Reputations Online*, markets reputation management solutions including a software called Trakur. It's an online reputation monitoring tool that automatically searches the Web for keywords. While the software tracks news, blogs and all social media, it also tracks your name, your company brands, industry trends and competitor news. Beal also proposes a ten-point programme to help people manage their online reputations pro-actively: (1) Get your own web site, called yourpersonalname.com; (2) Start a blog, via Blogger.com or Wordpress.com; (3) Add a sub-domain to your site; (4) Create a social networking profile on MySpace, Facebook or another site; (5) Create your own social network, via Ning.com; (6) Create a business profile on LinkedIn; (7) share your photos on Flickr; (8) Claim your identity, via Naymz.com; (9) Create your own wiki, via Wetpaint.com; (10) Get a free page from Google, via Googlepages.com.

"Build up credibility in the eyes of Google," says Beal. "You're being searched all the time, whether you know it or not."

Sometimes, reputational damage from online privacy invasions is neither self-inflicted by the indiscretions of self-exhibition nor maliciously perpetrated by others. Imagine discovering, for example, that your entire medical record is accessible on an online database? You could suffer severe reputational damage if, for example, you have a history of mental illness, alcoholism or have contracted a sexually transmitted disease like AIDS.

Sounds like a Big Brother scenario that could never happen? Think again. Both Google and Microsoft already store medical records for a number of US clinics. Privacy watchdogs are concerned that, once medical records are transferred to external services operated by Google or Microsoft, their confidentiality could be violated for a variety of purposes, including commercial exploitation for marketing campaigns by pharmaceutical companies. Given recent scandals in Britain, where in late 2007 government cock-ups led to disclosures of millions of computerized records containing personal information on British citizens, sometimes the most dreaded privacy mishaps can become shockingly real. If you think it can't happen, think again.[20]

Meanwhile, millions of online social networkers are increasingly suspicious about the monitoring – and monetizing – of their virtual profiles by the very sites (MySpace, Facebook, Bebo, Orkut) on which they construct their identities, collect "friends", chat about their habits and open up their hearts. There is widespread concern that sites like Facebook are snooping on their own members. These anxieties are not alleviated by Facebook and other social sites informing their members that they, not members, effectively "own" all data posted on profiles. Nor does it help when members discover that – as we saw in Chapter 3 – it's devilishly difficult to delete their personal profiles when they decide to exit a site. The issue of identity portability is a question that remains open – and unresolved.

Who else is watching us? The CIA? MI5? Religious cults? Criminal organizations? There is evidence that none of these possibilities can be excluded. In fact, the CIA admits openly that it monitors YouTube and other sites to collect intelligence.[21]

Should we even care? So what if somebody shames us? If a potential employer digs up a goofy Facebook posting from a decade earlier, if they don't like what they see, maybe you wouldn't want to work for them anyway. Perhaps employers should understand what is plainly obvious: life is a long and complex movie, with many plot twists, not a single snapshot. As media critic Jeff Jarvis put it on his BuzzMachine blog: "Young people have a different view of privacy and publicness because they realize you can't make connections with people unless you reveal something of yourself: you won't find fellow skiers unless you tell the world that you, too, ski. Privacy advocates would be appalled that I have revealed my most private information on my blog: my health data. But by writing about the heart condition I share with Tony Blair, fibrillation, I have found advice and support from others. Publicness has its benefits." [22]

If Jarvis is right, more power to Mimi Brewster – and down with China's communist regime. So what if some stuffy HR bureaucrat like Virginia Flanders wants to make a stink about a decade-old article that popped up on Google? It won't be long before everybody – the entire Gen V – has a Facebook trail in their past. When that day comes, a new generation of CEOs and HR managers, unburdened by outdated norms, will have a refreshingly different attitude towards recruitment. Today, it seems, we're navigating through the e-ruptive fallout after a collision between the conflicting values of virtual networks and vertical bureaucracies. The turbulence won't last. Remember what Sheldon Teitelbaum asserted in *Wired*: "Privacy is history – get over it."

"The answer isn't more fog but more light: transparency," added Teitelbaum. "If any citizen can read the billionaire's tax return or the politician's bank statement, if no thug – or policeman – can ever be sure his actions are unobserved, if no government agency or corporate boardroom is safe from whistle-blowers, we'll have something precious to help make up for lost privacy: freedom."[23]

In the final analysis, does it really come down to a trade-off – less privacy for more freedom? It sounds tempting, so long as we have freedom from harassment, humiliation, job dismissal and financial ruin. The leap of faith between lost privacy and gained freedom is still one that many would be reluctant to make.

So did Fred Westen decide to hire Mimi Brewster in the end? We will never know. The only clue we are given is the considered advice of his trusted wife Martha, who reminded her husband:

"Internet postings are like tattoos. They never go away."

5

Virtual reality: Second Life and death

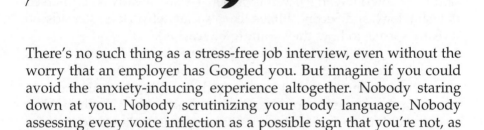

There's no such thing as a stress-free job interview, even without the worry that an employer has Googled you. But imagine if you could avoid the anxiety-inducing experience altogether. Nobody staring down at you. Nobody scrutinizing your body language. Nobody assessing every voice inflection as a possible sign that you're not, as they say, a good fit.

Imagine that nobody ever has to show up for a job interview. We just send a perfect digital version of ourselves to do all the talking.

No, it's not some sci-fi fantasy set in the distant future. The virtual-reality job interview is already happening. In fact, virtual job interviews are becoming increasingly common in large corporations. More and more, Fortune 500 companies and head-hunters are using online 3-D worlds like Second Life to interview candidates who don't necessarily show up dressed in suitable business attire, but are morphed into outlandish virtual avatars – trolls, angels, witches, dragons, monsters, you name it.

Virtual job interviewing has several advantages for both employers and applicants. Traditional barriers are removed in a more relaxed setting unburdened by the stress and awkwardness imposed by bureaucratic values. Also, top executives who would not normally have time, or are travelling abroad on a business trip, can drop into a virtual setting in avatar form and discreetly take part. Professional recruiters say that a simulated meeting between employer and job-seeker often opens up the dialogue and brings out the candidate's potential more quickly. Virtual interviews also lower the cost of recruitment, as companies no longer have to fly dozens of candidates into the city where the head office is located. Virtual interviews are a cost-free way of whittling down to a short list.

In 2007, the global recruitment firm TMP Worldwide held a job fair on Second Life that connected some 800 applicants with a blue-chip roster of employers including Microsoft, eBay, Hewlett Packard and Verizon. True, these are the kind of companies that are looking for tech-savvy people whose Second Life navigational skills provide a reliable indicator of their suitability to work creatively in the high-tech sector. It's expected, however, that, as the younger generation moves into the work force – Gen Y today, Gen V tomorrow – virtual interviews will be standard HR practice.

"We saw it as a very cool and interactive way of allowing job-seekers to interact with recruiters," TMP Worldwide's Louis Vong said in an interview in early 2008. "Gen Y's are already so immersed in technology, and Second Life is like a social network on steroids, so it really speaks to how they want to be reached."[1]

There are even netiquette rules about what kinds of virtual avatars are advisable for job interviews. Even though visually transformed into a cyber-being, you will be assessed according to your *choice* of avatar. In short, you *are* your avatar. So if you're applying for a job at a company known for its conservative corporate culture, don't show up as a mermaid.

Finding the right avatar is, in economic terms, a form of *identity purchase*. Sartorial taste, as in the real world, is a strong indicator about your virtual identity. For the fashion-challenged, there are now sites like StarDoll – a virtual-avatar fashion emporium that boasts more than 14 million members – supplying off-the-rack avatar attire. The upscale Second Life crowd apparently eschews *prêt-à-porter* avatar fashion, preferring *haut de gamme* self-exhibition. Once you've selected your outfit, you should have a good technical mastery of your avatar, because moving around Second Life can be challenging. Second Life defies basic laws of gravity. While most avatars get about by running and jumping (not usual modes of ambulation in most modern cities), many fly from place to place at altitudes ranging upwards to roughly 200 metres. Familiar vehicles – from go-karts and helicopters to sub-marines and hot-air balloons – are also available for transportation. None of these are absolutely necessary, however, because avatars can *teleport* directly to any location. In an embarrassing job interview that has become infamous, the applicant kept banging his head against the virtual walls of the boardroom. Not a smart way to make a good first impression.[2]

Second Life, the best-known 3-D virtual environment, was launched in 2003 and counts roughly 600 000 monthly visitors among a total membership of some 13 million members, called "residents". But Second Life – whose original financial backers included Amazon CEO Jeff Bezos and Lotus founder Mitch Kapor – was not the first virtual world. There.com, a virtual social world aimed at the twentysomething generation, was founded in 1998 and has been used by MTV to launch virtual locations. Cyworld, a Korean virtual space with more than 20 million monthly visitors, was launched four years before Second Life. Also, so-called massively multiplayer online role-playing games (MMORPGs) are hugely popular worldwide: *World of Warcraft, EverQuest, RuneScape, Final Fantasy, CounterStrike* and *Lineage II. World of Warcraft*, by far the most popular online virtual game, was launched in 1994 and today counts nearly ten million gamers. Also, millions of kids and teenagers visit online virtual worlds such as Habbo Hotel, Barbie Girls, Zookazoo, Neopets, Club Penguin, WeeWorld, Webkinz and Zwinktopia. In mid-2008, Habbo Hotel was clocking more than ten million visitors and counted some 100 million virtual avatars on the site.

Second Life, a latecomer to virtual reality, didn't become a global brand until 2006 when major corporations like IBM began using, and promoting, the site as a place for company meetings. Buy-in by Fortune 500 companies gave Second Life major brand momentum, and major media coverage – including a *Business Week* cover story – soon followed.[3] Second Life provides further proof that first mover advantages don't necessarily produce brand dominance and market leaders. Latecomers can often learn from the mistakes of early entrants. But as we'll see with Second Life, they can also make their own mistakes that lead to equally challenging problems.

Many still believe Second Life is a videogame – a sort of cross between *SimCity* and *Grand Theft Auto*. In truth, Second Life's inspiration was literary. Founder Philip Rosedale created Second Life after reading Neal Stephenson's cyberpunk novel, *Snow Crash*, in which he coined the term "metaverse" to describe a user-defined virtual world. While the conduct of Second Life's residents has sometimes been controversial, the site has definitely succeeded as a commercial and artistic showcase. A Shakespearean theatre troupe has performed *Hamlet* on the site. The Royal Liverpool Philharmonic gave a live performance of works by Ravel and Rachmaninov before an audience of roughly 80 avatars in a virtual replica of the symphony's real-life Art Deco concert hall.[4] Second Life also features virtual art gallery openings, stand-up comedy acts and pop concerts by singers like Suzanne Vega. The late novelist, Kurt Vonnegut Jr, gave his very last interview on Second Life. The news agency Reuters has posted a reporter on Second Life, and Sky News opened a virtual studio on the site. Also, as part of a movement in favour of virtual diplomacy, governments of small nations like Sweden, Estonia and the Maldives have established virtual embassies on the site's Diplomacy Island. While these virtual embassies appear to be mainly online tourist bureaus that promote travel to real-world locations, diplomatic activity on Second Life is also a way for small nations to gain profile on an international chessboard dominated by global powers.[5]

Some have criticized virtual worlds as a gimmicky fad that corporations – from IBM and Coca-Cola to Adidas and Ben & Jerry's – are exploiting, mainly for marketing and PR purposes, to create the optics of being hip, leading-edge companies. Still, there is a burgeoning virtual economy whose value can be measured in hard currency. Forecasts for online virtual worlds are generally robust. According to the Gartner consultancy, 80% of active Internet users will have a virtual identity by 2011. And while 3-D environments present significant risks to businesses – including security, confidentiality and brand reputation – Gartner predicts that 20% of major retailers will have a marketing presence in virtual worlds and online games by 2010.[6]

Marketing hard goods on virtual sites is one thing, selling virtual products is something else. Leave selling *atoms* to traditional retailers, virtual sites are now selling binary *bits* – lots of them. Virtual currency isn't funny money from a Monopoly board game. Thanks to real-money trading instruments – called RMT – digital funds can be turned into hard cash. Some estimates put the burgeoning virtual economy's annual transactional value at $12 billion. Take HotOrNot.com, an online dating site that charges subscriber fees. The site makes roughly 40% of revenues selling virtual goods (such as virtual flowers with a romantic digital card attached). Habbo Hotel, the world-building site popular with youths, counts more than 75 million avatars and 90% of its $60 million in annual revenue is generated by sales of virtual goods like furniture.[7]

Virtual sales can be for a good cause. A Facebook application called "Causes", launched in early 2007, allows users to send virtual charity gifts to "friends" – anything from digital blankets to a laptop computer. Proceeds from virtual gifts, purchased with real money at $1 apiece, go to charities such as the Red Cross or Breast Cancer Awareness. Donations are made in the *recipient's* name and posted on his/her Facebook profile. Some have noted, uncharitably, that Facebook launched the application in early February to exploit the frenzied, status-driven ritual of Valentine's Day gift-giving. Still, in the year after Facebook introduced the micro-payment application (with 9 million installs), an estimated $15 million was raised for charity. While free, advertising sponsored gifts have been the most popular, holiday-themed gifts (Santa hat, eggnog, Happy New Year message) and romantic gifts ("Be Mine" cookies, box of chocolates) top the paid category. Less message-specific digital gifts, and thus less popular, include espresso beans, beach balls, lemons and gingerbread cookies.[8] Petlover sites Dogster and Catster, which boast nearly 600 000 registered users, also monetize virtual gifts, ranging from doggy bones and mice icons to wool balls and party balloons.

In the human world, critics claim that digital-gift markets amount to pouring money down the virtual drain. According to a strictly economic analysis, however, the theory of *marginal utility* can explain why people bother buying and sending digital gifts. To use a simple illustration, one dollar spent on sending someone a digital birthday greeting has more marginal utility than running out and buying a $1 birthday card and sending it in the post. Why? First, sending a digital card requires less effort; second, the digital card will arrive on time, never be thrown into the trash bin, and what's more all the recipient's online friends will see that you've sent the card.[9]

The rationale for buying virtual gifts provides fascinating insights into the *social* dimension of virtual worlds. Virtual reality is not only a vast shopping centre, it's a place where people interact in all the complexity of human social life, for better or worse. And vices, like virtues, are part of the social dynamic.

As we saw in Chapter 2, gift-giving constitutes an important component of the social ritual that the Chinese call *guanxi*, which cements social ties based on reciprocal obligation and indebtedness. Studies of online gift exchange reveal that people offer virtual gifts in order to create and maintain social ties with "friends" and e-quaintances.[10] Virtual gifts therefore have a social *function*. Digital gift-giving adds a virtual twist to another all-too-familiar human compulsion known as *conspicuous consumption*. The twist is this: it's not so much the *value* of the gift that matters, but rather the fact that others see, on the recipient's home page, that they have given or received a gift. Virtual gift-giving is therefore *private* and *public* simultaneously. When you give a virtual gift, it's not just the "thought" that counts; what really matters is that the whole world knows about it.

Let's look at the implications for virtual worlds of the themes we've been exploring in this part of the book: identity construction, social ties, open-versus-closed networks and privacy.

First, *identities*. The market for virtual commodities, as we saw above with the selection and purchase of avatars, is intimately linked to identity construction. Virtual avatars take online identity to a whole new level – from *fabrication* to *transmogrification*. In worlds like Second Life and Cyworld, the merger of personal identity and virtual avatar selection has created a market for virtual goods. You literally *buy* who you wish to *be*. Studies of virtual avatars reveal that people tend to create *idealized* versions – younger, stronger, cooler, better-looking – of their real-world social identities. Dowdy women become hot babes; nerdy guys morph into buff hunks.

Second, *social ties*. Social interaction in virtual worlds is, with a few exceptions, conducted mostly on a "weak tie" e-quaintance basis. You don't normally visit Second Life to hang out with your best friends from the real world – or "meatspace". When you are making your way through *World of Warcraft*'s mythical realm of Azeroth slaying monsters, thousands of other avatar warrior orcs and night-elf wizards are playing along too.

Third, *open-versus-closed networks*. Virtual reality is essentially an *open* social environment. There are no Small World or Beautiful People entry barriers. How, after all, do you discriminate against someone dressed in a Batman costume when you look like a Roman gladiator? Virtual reality is an exciting and stimulating social space precisely because it facilitates open-minded exploration.

Fourth, *privacy*. Virtual worlds are, by definition, indifferent to personal privacy because so-called "in-world" social interaction takes place between fantastical avatar creations that conceal social identities. If your true identity is known to your interlocutors (say, in a virtual job interview) you are willingly surrendering information about yourself. But, like on sites like MySpace and Facebook, virtual privacy is problematic, and sometimes controversial, given the attraction of sites like Second Life for perverse sexual activity.

We can say, therefore, that virtual worlds should, in theory, be socially open spaces where transmogrified identities conduct weak-tie interactions with others relatively unconcerned about personal privacy. If this is so, a puzzling question is unavoidable. Why has Second Life failed to construct a social architecture that leverages these inherent virtual-world dynamics?

Second Life, it seems, has opted for a counter-intuitive strategy that, instead of harnessing the social power of online network dynamics, has constructed a virtual reality inspired by the all-too-familiar institutional values of meatspace. Second Life, paradoxically, is real life in cyberspace. The site, for example, has instituted an "identity verification system" and bans residents from "impersonating" any other person. Also, Second Life is restricted to adults only. You have to be 18 years old to join (minors are directed to Teen Second Life, where adults are banned entry). Overall, Second Life has a strict privacy policy, though it arrogates to itself the right to "collect and aggregate" all sorts of information and behavioural data about its residents.

A closer look at Second Life's ethos provides a possible explanation for this paradox. Second Life's founding ethos was inspired by the values of *private property*. There is nothing wrong with this, of course, as private property rights are fundamental to Enlightenment philosophy that ushered in modern capitalism and liberal democracy. But Second Life adopted a basic architecture that was, in essence, a virtual extension, and faithful replication, of a real-world modern capitalist economy – including its most alarming dysfunctions. The site's property-based logic quickly transformed the site into a virtual sphere that placed greater emphasis on *commercial* transactions than on *social* interactions. This dynamic was complicated by Second Life's relatively liberal attitude towards the real-world vices, commonly called the Seven Deadly Sins. Given that Second Life's GDP has been estimated at roughly $220 million, it's perhaps not surprising that greed was given special pride-of-place at the site's table of honour.[11] In the real world, reckless greed is generally indulged more willingly than sexual perversion. Which might explain why, when greed was joined by lust, the honour quickly degenerated into dishonour. No wonder that Second Life – after a brief flurry of media hype in 2006 – has been besieged by scandal and controversy.

A Reuters reporter who covers Second Life (as a journalistic avatar called Adam Reuters) has exposed alleged fraud and other defalcations in its virtual economy. In 2007, Second Life was forced to call in the FBI before banning virtual casinos and all forms of gambling on the site. In Britain, the real-world Institute of Chartered Accountants' fraud advisory panel warned that criminal gangs and terrorist networks may be using Second Life in illegal money-laundering rackets.

"There's nothing virtual about online crime, it is all too real," said Steven Phillipsohn, chairman of the panel's cybercrime working group. "It is time government took this seriously. The legitimate benefits of virtual communities will prove enormous, but people need to be aware that this cutting-edge technology has a darker side."[12]

Second Life's most serious reputational crisis hit when an elaborate Ponzi scheme was exposed. Economists had been expressing doubts for some time about Second Life's "phony economics" and questionable monetary policy. Specifically, they questioned Second Life's economic policy of running up deficits and issuing more of its currency, "Linden dollars", redeemable against real American currency (originally pegged at L$270 = US$1). Economists criticized Second Life for compensating for deficits by increasing money supply not backed up by 100% reserves.

"As opportunists and capitalists, we're not particularly bothered by indications that Second Life generates most of its economic 'wealth' through a rampant virtual real estate bubble which makes San Francisco, Marina District condo look like a bargain," noted economist Randolph Harrison in a blistering critique of Second Life's economic system. "Nor are we particularly bothered that the virtual playground provides a safe harbour for what is effectively the phone-sex industry reinvented. And Internet gambling, despite the US Federal Government's recent protestations to the contrary, is inevitable. So why not profit off of it? And how better, than in a utopian Ayn Rand open market capitalistic metaverse?" What was bothering Harrison was this: markets in Second Life were "rigged" and there was no "trust" in its economy. "Second Life is a giant magnet for the desperate, uninformed, easily victimized," he concluded. Matthew Beller, a former Federal Reserve employee, followed with an equally critical paper published by the US-based libertarian think tank, Ludwig von Mises Institute. Describing Second Life's financial institutions as "wildcat banking", Beller observed: "Banks with no underlying loans and no ability to redeem all deposits . . . are essentially Ponzi schemes, and therefore fraudulent."[13]

These criticisms proved right on the money. In early 2008, Second Life's unregulated financial system collapsed following a run on its virtual banks. One bank in particular, Ginko Financial, was offering 44% returns on the $220 000 of its real-money deposits made by some 10 000 account holders. In August 2007, after a run on deposits, Ginko declared insolvency and skipped town on Second Life.[14] This embarrassing scandal shook confidence in Second Life's virtual economy. At a time when the real-world global banking system was reeling from a devastating sub-prime mortgage crisis, Second Life's virtual banks had been offering eye-popping annual interests rates – some as high as 60%. Clearly, some investors – guilty of either credulity or avarice – believed that normal laws of economics didn't apply to virtual reality. True, the estimated $750 000 lost by Second Life's bank depositors was minuscule compared with the $100 billion in banking write-offs in the real world, but it was real money nonetheless.

The crisis for Second Life was more serious. Not only were the foundations of its virtual banking system shaken, but the scandal shattered faith in the indispensible *trust* factor in virtual transactions. Second Life's founders at Linden Lab, despite their avowed commitment to an Invisible Hand towards virtual commerce, scrambled frantically in damage control mode. When they finally acted, many doubtless were surprised by their decidedly real-world approach to the crisis: heavy-handed intervention. So much for the Invisible Hand. Announcing its new monetary policy, Second Life pulled the plug on all unregulated banks. Henceforth, only banks with "proof of an applicable government registration statement or financial institution charter" were allowed to operate in its virtual economy.

Behnam Dayanim, an e-commerce lawyer with Washington firm Paul, Hastings, Janofsky & Walker, offered the following analysis of Second Life's financial crisis: "When virtual environments first started, they were viewed as libertarian dreams with no interference. As companies that sponsor these environments become more accountable to investors or regulators, they are starting to encounter real-world limitations."[15]

Perhaps in reaction to these market failures, Second Life is now inhabited by an organized group of zealous anti-capitalists and assorted other forms of radicalized thuggery. Virtual vandals – called "griefers" – maraud around the site to harass, attack and disrupt anything they find objectionable. Griefers attacked the Toyota space with missiles. Another group of virtual pranksters harassed a wealthy Second Life real estate developer, Anshe Chung, by bombarding her with "flying penises". Chung, whose avatar was featured as a sexy Asian hottie on *Business Week*'s cover in May 2006, was apparently a Second Life escort girl before going into real estate. Her transition from social interaction to commercial transaction evidently proved tremendously lucrative.[16]

In early 2007, a Second Life location called Porcupine was the scene of violent clashes between right-wing extremists and leftist protestors after French politician Jean-Marie Le Pen's far-right Front National party opened political headquarters. In running battles that normally would have ended in bloodshed, leftist activists threw "exploding pigs" at their right-wing adversaries. But the menace to the Front National was real. A group calling itself the Second Life Left Unity purchased land next to the Front National headquarters and issued a press release threatening continued disruptions aimed at running "fascists" off the island. The following day, the Front National closed down its Porcupine HQ and moved to another Second Life location called Axel.[17]

Second Life's dirty secret – and doubtless the reason that minors are banned from the site – is that many residents, when they aren't hustling real estate deals, are looking for virtual sex. The two most popular spots on Second Life are called, fittingly, Money Island and Sexy Beach. And, while Second Life doesn't shout it from the rooftops, there's an active BDSM – bondage, discipline and sado-masochism – community on the site. It is estimated that 18% of all real estate in Second Life is devoted to sexual activity. In fact, the site's first bona fide copyright suit was a dispute over the invention of a digital "SexGen" bed – a software application that facilitates virtual leg-over activity. More troubling, Second Life faced serious reputational issues when residents were caught conducting virtual recreations of pornographic scenes with avatars of children.[18]

In the murky wake of these scandals, Second Life's media honeymoon is definitely over. In *Forbes* magazine, Allison Fass sniffed: "There is nothing to do in Second Life except, pardon my bluntness, try to get laid."[19] *Time* included Second Life in its "5 Worst Websites", along with eHarmony, Evite, Meez and MySpace (sites that the magazine included in its "25 Sites We Can't Live Without" included Amazon, Wikipedia, Del.icio.us, Digg, eBay, Facebook, Flickr, Google and YouTube). Others have noted that, while Second Life boasts nearly 13 million residents, only about 15 000 are logged on at any one time. What's more, "meetings" cannot accommodate any more than 75 to 100 avatars. There is also doubt about Second Life's business model, which charges users a monthly $9.95 fee and higher amounts to premium users who want to buy – and sell – virtual land. *Wired* magazine, an early Second Life cheerleader, later revised its assessment in an article titled, "How Madison Avenue Is Wasting Millions on a Deserted Second Life". The magazine's editor Chris Anderson, author of *The Long Tail*, joined this negative chorus in a blog post, "Why I Gave Up on Second Life."[20]

Others call Second Life a "virtual nanny state" which has imposed "community behaviour" standards governing intolerance, harassment, assault, indecency and disturbing the peace. The Invisible Hand, it seems, has given way to Big Brother. One Second Life critic is Nathalie Rothschild, who came to the following conclusion: "To me, the most striking thing about Second Life is just how un-striking it is – and how much it replicates the real world's regrettable levels of policing of interpersonal relations and monitoring of our behaviour. Even in this virtual world, where we're supposed to be able to let our imaginations run riot, we are actually being watched over and reined in by censorious moderators and touchy individuals."[21] Still other Second Life observers note that the site has been a disappointment for those who had high expectations for new business models and alternative modes of social interaction. As Axel Bruns observed in his book *Blogs, Wikipedia, Second Life and Beyond*, the site is regarded as a "consumerist paradise and an extrapolation from first-life capitalism."[22]

Besieged by setbacks and criticism, Second Life founder Philip Rosedale stepped down as CEO in March 2008. To be fair, however, Second Life is not the only virtual world that, tainted by scandal, has desperately reached out to the real world for rescue. Virtual worlds, it would appear, are still going through an early phase of their evolution marked by e-ruptive collisions with the institutionalized values of the real world. And there doubtless are more e-ruptions to come.

On the youth virtual site, Habbo Hotel, a 17-year-old Dutch teenager was arrested for stealing about $6000 worth of virtual furniture with five 15-year-old accomplices. Habbo, which counts six million members in 30 countries, said in a statement: "In Habbo, as in many other virtual worlds, scamming for other people's personal information such as user names has been problematic for quite a while. We have had much of this scamming going on in many countries but this is the first case where the police have taken legal action."[23] In 2005, a 41-year-old Chinese man, Qiu Chengwei, was sentenced to death for murdering a fellow online gamer for stealing, and reselling, his virtual "dragon sword" used to kill on *Legend of Mir 3*, a so-called massively multiplayer online role-playing game. Qiu had lent the hard-earned, highly-coveted virtual sword to 26-year-old Zhu Caoyuan. Then Zhu greedily made a fatal error of judgement. Aware of the virtual sword's high scarcity value, due to the enormous in-game effort required to possess one, he sold it to someone else for currency convertible to roughly $1000. When Qiu reported the theft to Chinese police, he was told they had no authority over online disputes. So Qiu resolved the matter by himself, using not a virtual sword but a real knife. He broke into Zhu's house and, finding him in bed, stabbed him repeatedly in the chest. This shocking incident alerted authorities to the obsessive nature of virtual worlds. *Legend of Mir 3*, an isometric 3-D game that features warriors wielding enormous swords, was certified by the *Guinness Book of World Records* for having 750000 gamers playing online simultaneously. The horrific nature of this game-related crime also led to calls for

Chinese courts (who commuted Qiu's sentence to life in prison) to rethink the way they treat virtual theft, given that items like dragon swords are considered personal property, bought and sold with real money.[24]

China was at the centre of another virtual-world controversy when it was discovered that the country was home to organized gaming sweatshops where online players of *World of Warcraft* and other games hack and slaughter their way up the ladders of these violent medieval fantasylands to grab a piece of the estimated $2 billion global trade in virtual items like dragon swords. *World of Warcraft*, with its eight million subscribers worldwide, uses virtual gold coins as in-world currency – hence the term "gold farms" for these Chinese gaming workshops. The online auction giant eBay was drawn into the Chinese "gold farm" controversy due to its role as a clearing house for real-money trading of virtual property. It was estimated in 2007 that the online games section of eBay was clocking roughly $10 million in business annually.[25]

As the commercial success of Second Life's real-estate millionaire Anshe Chung illustrates, the lure of virtual economies cannot be underestimated. In 2001, when economist Edward Castronova conducted a study of virtual economic activity in Sony's virtual game, *EverQuest*, he calculated that the in-game land of Norrath's GNP made it, when compared with real-world nations, the 77th richest country on the planet, roughly equivalent to Bulgaria. Castronova discovered, moreover, that 20% of so-called Norrathians actually considered themselves residents of the in-game nation, 22% desired to spend all their time there and 40% said they'd quit their real-world jobs if they could make a living in Norrath.[26] Sony, which owns *EverQuest*, was only too aware of the lucrative economics of Norrath's virtual economy. Taking a strict "you're in our world now" position towards gamers, Sony asserted its ownership over all virtual assets and characters in *EverQuest*. The company also pressured eBay to ban the sale of virtual goods from *EverQuest*. Interestingly, Sony's proprietary move to shut down all virtual asset sales provoked a loud protest by *EverQuest* gamers – another example of virtual *voice* to express discontent, with the implied threat of *exit* defection.[27] In 2007, eBay – worried about getting entangled in complex and costly lawsuits – decided to ban the sale of all virtual assets on the grounds that their ownership is less clear than property rights of *tangible* goods. Yet eBay, interestingly, exempted Second Life property, claiming that Second Life is not a *game*. eBay's decision was, in effect, assigning to Second Life's virtual reality the attributes of a tangible territory.

Virtual worlds, despite inevitable dysfunctions, are not the exclusive domain of perverts, freaks, vandals, hucksters, swindlers and sword-wielding murderers. As we saw with digital gifts, virtual worlds can be online platforms for altruism, education and social wellbeing. Thanks to virtual reality, charities now sponsor virtual "walks" to raise money for breast cancer. There are virtual animal shelters that help find loving homes for abandoned animals. Some of the world's top MBA schools, such as INSEAD, are using virtual environments to teach team-building and innovation skills while other universities offer virtual courses through e-learning programmes. In health care, virtual interaction has not only changed the nature of doctor–patient consultations but is transforming the way professionals conceive, and manage, private and state-funded health systems. In early 2008, a new publicly-financed hospital in San Diego, California – Palomar West Medical Center – had its virtual opening on Second Life three years before its official opening in the real world. In Britain, real hospitals are using e-health technology to offer virtual health care using Cisco's HealthPresence system.[28]

Meanwhile, some are predicting a shakeup in the virtual reality space. With unclear visibility about future moves by major players, consultancies like Forrester are cautioning business clients against betting heavily on any single site like Second Life. According to Forrester, new players with big pockets, facing virtual-world start-up costs of only $75 million and potential monthly revenues of $90 million for successful sites, can be expected to move into the space.[29] Sony, which owns the online game *EverQuest*, is well-positioned to construct a new virtual world. In July 2008, Google launched its own virtual world, Lively, as a powerful competitor to Second Life. Some argue that Second Life, though it has enjoyed a great deal of media attention in Western countries, is hardly the best virtual-world model. A better place to look is South Korea, a country with 100% broadband penetration, a massively popular mobile device culture and, most importantly, a leading-edge virtual reality site: Cyworld.

Launched in 1999 by a subsidiary of SK Telecom, Cyworld is Second Life, MySpace, YouTube, Flickr, Habbo Hotel, Amazon, eBay and iTunes all rolled into one. Now consider this: nearly 45% of South Korea's entire population of roughly 50 million people are Cyworld users. No wonder some 30000 corporations have a business presence on the site. As the authors of *Digital Korea* put it: "Cyworld is by far the most advanced virtual ecosystem and the most complete virtual economy, as well as the most complete social networking service yet created anywhere."[30] The translation of the Korean *cultural* model, however, might be incompatible with Western values and behavioural reflexes in online worlds. A study of Cyworld discovered, for example, that the online "friends" (called *Cy-Ilchons*) are virtual extensions of the Korean concept *yons*, or strong kinship ties – also called "Cy-ties". In contrast to sites like MySpace and Facebook, where "friends" include not only weak-tie e-quaintances but often celebrities and complete strangers, Cyworld appears to function essentially as a forum for *pre-existing* friendships.[31] Yet some online behavioural traits, it would seem, are universal – like vanity, narcissism and the desire to put your best cyberface forward. Many South Koreans, it is said, spend more on clothing and accessories for their virtual avatars than they lay out for their real wardrobes. Cyworld's virtual-goods market, which uses convertible "acorns" as currency, is estimated at nearly $500 000 per day – or about $180 million annually.

With all this economic activity in virtual worlds, it won't be long till the taxman shows up. Guess what, he's already at the door. The idea of taxing "virtual assets" was first raised in 2001 by American economist Edward Castronova, who predicted that virtual economies would be producing revenues of $1.5 billion within three years.[32] A few years later, an American online gamer, Julian Dibbell, auctioned on eBay some of his virtual assets collected on the *Ultima* game and reported his capital gains to the US Internal Revenue Service. Dibbell later published a book titled *Play Money: Or How I Quit My Day Job and Struck it Rich in Virtual Loot Farming*. A title like that was, presumably, sufficiently taunting to attract the attention of American legislators.

In late 2006, the US Congress Joint Economic Committee launched a probe into virtual taxes. It was estimated, at that time, that daily user-to-user transactions on Second Life were generating about $500 000. A year later, good news came for virtual free marketers. The Congressional committee had decided against taxing virtual transactions. "In my opinion the less government regulation you have on virtual worlds, the more they'll thrive and develop," said Dan Miller, a senior economist for the Congressional committee, adding however that the Internal Revenue Service might take a different view.[33]

Benjamin Franklin famously remarked that "in this world nothing can be said to be certain, except death and taxes". If virtual taxes are on hold, what about the other inevitability – death? Is cyberspace a virtual metaphor for eternity?

Cyberspace's quasi-religious dimension was seized on by Web evangelists from the earliest days of the Internet in the 1990s. The spiritual linkage between religion and cyberspace was being explored, for example, by Catholic theologian Tom Beaudoin in his GenX quest titled *Virtual Faith*, in which he sought to reconcile the values of American pop culture and existential questions related to his belief in God. At roughly the same time, Margaret Wertheim published a fascinating book called *The Pearly Gates of Cyberspace*, a Dante-esque journey which makes a spiritual connection between the two spheres, real and virtual, through a comparison of cyberspace and medieval Christendom. Wertheim argued that the Christian visions of the Holy City and New Jerusalem have found new expression in the virtual eternity of cyberspace.

"Where early Christians conceived of Heaven as a realm where their 'souls' would be freed from the failings and frailties of the flesh," she observed, "so today's champions of cyberspace hail their realm as a place where we will be freed from the limitations and embarrassments of physical embodiment."

The Book of Revelation, it seems, may be a dazzling spectacle that will explode into the virtual heavens of cyber-eternity. If eternity is indeed a virtual space, perhaps death is like uploading our psyches and shooting through the virtual heavens towards everlasting life. For those of us living in the here-and-now, meanwhile, we can already procure burial plots in virtual cemeteries. There are virtual cemeteries and memorial sites where the dearly departed live in perpetuity in our hearts: Legacy, Tributes, SweetMemoriesSite, SweetMemoriesAndMore. And, in anticipation of our own eternal journey, we can also write our own obituaries on sites like YouDied.org. There are even virtual pet cemeteries that keep alive the memories of beloved animal companions.

The quest for the Holy Grail is often portrayed as a journey of spiritual self-discovery – a quest for *identity*. There is no more fundamental question than, "who am I?" Virtual reality has opened up the infinite possibilities posed by that question. For now, however, it remains tantalizingly unanswered.

PART II

Status

"I can't explain it—it's just a funny feeling that I'm being Googled."

6

Social capital: monkeysphere to cyberspace

On the first day of 2008, the announcement was trumpeted with great fanfare: members of Facebook's global community had just elected its first president.

The victor in cyberspace's first democratic vote was a sharply dressed 28-year-old Frenchman named Arash Derambarsh. Facebook's new president, who resembled a stock-market golden boy in his expensive pin-striped suit and hip designer glasses, was the first elected politician of the Web 2.0 era.

"I have a power that is unique," he declared in a press release after the vote. "No one on the Internet can reach as many people as me."

Derambarsh's electoral triumph was uniquely fascinating. Social networking sites, it seemed, were not just loose, horizontal platforms for collecting "friends". They were being transformed into cohesive global communities represented by democratically elected leaders. Following the free and open election on Facebook, Derambarsh had appropriated the attributes of a sovereign head of state. It was no small victory. Facebook's vast global population, after all, surpasses that of France and Britain.

The media immediately took interest in Derambarsh's electoral watershed. France's conservative daily newspaper, *Le Figaro*, described him as a "quasi world president". Derambarsh had made contact with French President Nicolas Sarkozy, said another report, and was also forming a partnership with UNESCO. Clearly enjoying his status as a world political leader, Derambarsh declared that, during his first mandate, he hoped to promote goodwill, tolerance and literacy throughout the world.

Yet there was something about Derambarsh that seemed just a little too slick. After a few background checks, it turned out that Derambarsh was no "world president", quasi or otherwise. There was no such thing as an elected Facebook "president". The established media had been "punked" again. The young Frenchman, a skilled grandstander, was a bona fide cyberspace scam artist.

Derambarsh's preposterous claim had been concocted on the strength of a vote using Canadian-made software called ClutterMe, which had virally sent out an application called "ePresident". Those who downloaded the application were urged to "vote" for a Facebook president. In the running for this exalted office were no fewer than 41 440 candidates – an open field by any standard. Some 142 849 votes were cast – in other words, more than 25% of the voters were actual candidates. At best, this "election" was little more than a light-hearted charade deploying the latest Facebook widget – like throwing sheep, super-poking and vampire biting.[1]

But Derambarsh, seeing his main chance, campaigned hard. When the votes were tallied, he unilaterally declared his electoral victory as Facebook "president" on the strength of just 9156 votes. Do the maths: roughly 143 000 people voted out of 65 million Facebook members at the time. That surely must constitute a new world record for low voter turnout. And Derambarsh's paltry 9000 votes, as a percentage of the entire Facebook population, must be the slenderest claim to electoral legitimacy since the birth of democracy in ancient Athens.

Derambarsh's motives, interestingly, turned out to be more complicated than those of your average Web prankster. When embarrassed journalists scratched harder to discover the true identity of the dapper young Frenchman who had scammed them, they learned that Derambarsh was no geek. He was, in fact, a savvy political operator standing for election as a local councillor in a suburban Paris constituency. Derambarsh's loudly proclaimed "election" as Facebook president had been a clever publicity stunt aimed at attracting media attention to bolster his electoral fortunes in the hardnosed world of local French politics.

Derambarsh was a nobody who, by cleverly mobilizing social resources on the Web, was trying to become a somebody. He was, in a word, a *status*-seeker.

Judged by real world standards, Derambarsh's dubious grandstanding displayed an intriguing combination of outrageous cheek and shrewd opportunism. Judged by the values of virtual reality, however, his gambit was not particularly outrageous. Social networking sites like Facebook are, after all, online platforms for personal identity fabrication, impression management and status building. The mercurial and rebellious culture of online social networks is highly indulgent towards dare-to-be-great flourishes, however self-serving. In many respects, Derambarsh was merely playing the game by familiar rules widely accepted in the virtual culture of narcissism.

Status attainment is a powerful motivator on social networking sites. The difference between real-world and virtual-world status, as we have seen in previous chapters, resides in the link between social status and *identity*. While status rewards in the real world are generally conferred on those whose identities are constructed *socially* according to institutionalized values of conformity, in virtual reality status can be achieved through the assertion of *personal* identities that emphasize unique and exceptional qualities.

In the online world, social status is highly personalized. The constant reference point is the self – who we are, how we're feeling, where we are, what we're doing, who we're seeing. Every day, countless millions of people "update" their social status on networking sites and on mobile platforms like Twitter. Social-status updating has become a micro-sociological obsession. Many social networkers update their social status every hour, some every fifteen minutes. In most instances, it's a mundane gesture that merely lets networked "friends" know what they're up to ("Cathy is going to the gym, back home at 6."). On a deeper level, it's a form of status anxiety motivated by a compulsive need to feel constantly connected to our social environment. Status-updating may seem like a self-reflexively narcissistic ritual, but in truth it merely acknowledges that social status is, by definition, conferred by others.

Status anxieties in the real world are all too familiar. Life in the material world is, in fact, a ceaseless ritual of *status updating* performed in full view of our social networks. A new wardrobe replete with designer labels, a new-model BMW or Mercedes, a grander house in a tonier neighbourhood – these status updates send definite, and deliberate, signals to others around us. The familiar term "keeping up with the Joneses" expresses the competitive dimension of status anxiety. Most people, whatever their social class, feel driven to improve their lot not only through material gain, but also – and perhaps more importantly – by attaining greater *status* recognition conferred by social advancement.

So-called *status symbols* – like luxury cars – favourably distinguish us from others, especially those lower down in the social order. It is curiously ironic that Henry Ford, the American inventor of the automobile, failed to understand the importance of cars as an attribute of social status. Perhaps the most famous quote attributed to Ford was his statement that "any customer can have a car painted any colour he wants – so long as it is black." Whether Ford actually said it is not the point. It is a fact that early Ford Model-T cars were all black, without exception. Alfred P. Sloan, the chairman of General Motors, understood the status significance of cars. GM sold cars in many colours, thus allowing consumers to select individual models on points of *distinction* that conferred social status. GM quickly surpassed Ford in sales to become America's largest car manufacturer. Henry Ford was a great inventor, but a poor salesman – and an even worse social anthropologist.

The obvious question flowing from these illustrations concerns, as noted, differences between status in the real and virtual worlds. We saw in the first part of this book how *identity construction* is radically different in the online world. Can we say the same of *status*? The answer, as we shall see in the next four chapters, resides less in basic impulses that motivate status attainment than in the manner in which status is conferred.

The social architecture of status has been reconfigured radically in the virtual world. In the real world, status is conferred by institutionalized *position*. In the online world, status is conferred on the basis of *performance*. In cyberspace, status is not *assigned*, it is *earned*. Status in the online world, moreover, is based not on *values*, but on *facts* – the measurable facts that attest to expertise, efficiency and effectiveness. In sum, real-world oligarchies have been deposed by online democracies. We call this the *democratization* of status.

The history of social status is a fascinating saga – indeed, the inexorable quest for status attainment underlies the vanity of all human endeavour. Traditionally, social status was conferred by institutionalized values based on *ascriptive* criteria such as rank, position, title, wealth, race and so on. From the beginning of human history, status was socially organized as a *vertical* system of values – in most cases, in pyramidal form. The small group at the top enjoyed higher social status than the vast majority at the bottom. Status therefore was an attribute that confirmed *domination* – and therefore was instrumentally linked to power.

In the Middle Ages, aristocracies assimilated the values of "honour" and prestige into warfare, thus assigning status to their coercive domination of lower social orders. The aristocracy even monopolized the use of weapons, banning commoners from owning or bearing arms.

In fact, the reason the Templars admitted only knights into their ranks was because, as beneficiaries of the aristocratic monopoly on arms, they were ideal candidates for a new monastic militia. The Templars were not only powerful, but as knights they also enjoyed the benefits of status and prestige throughout Christendom. As one 19th century account put it: "Honour and respect awaited the Templars wherever they appeared, and persons of all ranks were eager to do what might be grateful to them".[2] In Philippe le Bel's eyes, that was precisely the problem: the Templars were not only armed, they were stealing his thunder.

Anthropologists tell us that our instinct to form status hierarchies was inherited from our primate ancestors. Behavioural studies of the monkeysphere have shown that the ritual of social grooming – think of apes affectionately picking through one another's body hair – is an interactive way of maintaining cohesiveness and sorting out hierarchical roles. Robin Dunbar – father of "Dunbar's Number" establishing 150 as the maximum size of a cohesive social group – argues that humans have carried forward this complex ritual of social grooming – except for one major difference. In human societies, we have replaced physical grooming with *language* – in particular, with *gossip*.[3] That people are given to constant chattering (like monkeys, as it were) about others behind their backs is a social ritual that hardly needs to be demonstrated. Water-cooler chit-chat may seem trivial and petty, but it actually has a social function. Gossip is a primordial social grooming ritual that forges bonds, establishes norms and sorts out status relationships. As anybody who has worked in a complex organization knows, if you really want to know who's in and who's out, or who's up and who's down (not to mention who's sleeping with whom), the best way to find out is by gossiping for ten minutes with low-ranking employees chattering through their cigarette break, these days outdoors near the car park. In many corporations, lowly secretaries frequently possess more reliable information about what's really going on than senior vice-presidents. Office cafeterias are, functionally speaking, bureaucratic settings for human monkey troops. It is for this reason, as we saw in Chapter 4 on the privacy paradox, that the social barometer of *reputation* plays such a crucial role in the assignment of *status*. When people gossip about friends or colleagues, they are establishing status updates on allies and adversaries.

A key concept for understanding social status is *distinction*. We owe much of our conceptual understanding of social distinction to 19th century American economist Thorstein Veblen, who is remembered – and championed by progressive liberals – for his enduringly controversial insights into the underlying motivations of economic behaviour. Veblen, like Robin Dunbar, took an anthropological approach in his famous analysis of the inexorable human drive towards status distinction in modern capitalistic societies. In his 1899 classic book, *Theory of the Leisure Class*, Veblen argued that "conspicuous consumption" – a term he invented – is not merely a by-product of capitalism, but its end goal. Wealth, like rank, is an ascriptive form of social status. But it's the *status* that matters to the wealthy, not the money. Veblen observed that economic elites accumulate wealth not for the comforts it affords, but rather – as in medieval aristocracies – for the "honour" it confers. As Veblen put it: "So soon as the possession of property becomes the basis of popular esteem, therefore, it becomes also a requisite to the complacency which we call self-respect."[4]

Veblen's theory of "pecuniary emulation" was especially irritating to members of America's status-seeking capitalist oligarchy at the end of the Robber Baron era. Victorian capitalists found little comfort in Veblen's comparisons of leisure class manners with those of high-status members of primitive tribes.[5] According to Veblen, the wealthy accumulate material possessions not only to satisfy their own sense of self worth, but also to inspire in others feelings of "invidious comparison" – another one of his famous semantic coinages. "In order to gain and to hold the esteem of men it is not sufficient merely to possess wealth or power," noted Veblen. "The wealth or power must be put in evidence, for esteem is awarded only on evidence." This explains why the so-called *nouveaux riches*, who generally possess wealth without status, frequently make an ostentatious display of their newly acquired material possessions. The possession of a Louis Vuitton handbag or Cartier watch, buying a grand house in a smart address, taking out a membership at a posh social club, sending the kids to prestigious private schools – all these publicly displayed manifestations of wealth are forms of invidious comparison whose underlying purpose is to assert social status.

Inheritors of established fortunes, by contrast, tend to mark their superior status through more subtle distinctions such as speech, manners, poise and culture. The French sociologist Pierre Bourdieu argued, in his epic work *La Distinction*, that finer points of social distinction are, in fact, a form of domination that asserts power through subtle status codes.[6] Traditionally, in class-based societies like Britain, simply listening to the way people spoke was an instantaneous way of sorting out their social status – or "station" – and, consequently, establishing their "place" in the social order.

Britain's Prince Charles, in fact, was once accused of stating that people should know their station in life. "What is wrong with people nowadays?" wrote the Prince of Wales to senior members of his household staff in a 2004 memo that was leaked to the press. "Why do they all seem to think they are qualified to do things far above their capabilities? This is all to do with the learning culture in schools. It is a consequence of a child-centred education system which tells people they can become pop stars, high court judges or brilliant TV presenters or infinitely more competent heads of state without ever putting in the necessary work or having the natural ability. It is a result of social utopianism which believes humanity can be genetically engineered to contradict the lessons of history."[7] The Prince's remarks were understandably controversial, especially from a personage of his exalted rank who his entire life has enjoyed the rewards of ascriptive status. Yet his comments, as we shall see, were rich in ironic insights into the *democratization* of status in the online world.

Since the Victorian era when Thorstein Veblen wrote about the manners of the leisure classes, notions of status and power have benefited from further conceptual refinements. One is the notion of *social capital*. Most of us know someone who is said to be in abundant possession of social capital. These people are generally regarded, and invariably admired, as well-connected, highly esteemed and above all *influential*. They are commonly referred to as "players". Social capital is generally possessed by those who benefit from *ascribed* status conferred by institutionally validated positions. CEOs, ambassadors, government ministers, university presidents, archbishops and newspaper editors – all possess social capital produced by ascriptive social status thanks to their rank or positions. Arash Derambarsh, the phony Facebook "president", was clearly attempting to appropriate social capital associated with ascriptive title and rank. Some possess social capital not thanks to their formal position in society, but due to their strategic *positioning* that allows them to act as brokers between influential power networks. These people, fittingly, are called "power brokers".

Social capital, by definition, is no different from economic capital invested to produce a financial return. We can say, indeed, that social capital is an *investment in social relations with expected returns*. This may sound coldly rational, but it is nonetheless an accurate formal definition. As sociologist Nin Lan puts it in his book *Social Capital*: "Individuals engage in interactions and networking in order to produce profits."[8]

How can these "profits" be recognized and measured? According to neocapital theory, they take the form of *information, influence, social credentials* and *recognition*. In other words, social capital procures *competitive advantages* conferred by privileged access to *resources* located in social networks. It's for this reason, indeed, that *social* resources are generally valued as more useful than *personal* resources. To illustrate this, compare an immensely wealthy person living reclusively with a moderately wealthy person who is actively involved in a multitude of social networks. There can be no doubt that, despite the ascriptive status conferred by enormous wealth, the less wealthy – but *well-connected* – person possesses more social capital. Money can buy influence, to be sure, but social capital is much more influential.

This theory of social capital posits, as noted, that we don't engage in social interaction for purely altruistic reasons. When someone joins the Rotary Club or Parent Teacher Association, the social investment (in terms of time and effort) is expected to produce a "profit" in the form of a competitive advantage – *privileged information, influence, recognition, prestige* and so forth. To express this profit motive in simple terms, we can say that, just as *economic* capital's production of surplus value is shared by those who control its ownership, *social* capital is a collective asset that produces competitive advantages for members of defined groups or networks who control it. People join prestigious social clubs not for the inherent pleasure it procures, but for the outward status it confers.

The same logic applied to the Knights Templar in the Middle Ages. The French aristocrats who joined the Templars were not, contrary to popular mythology, motivated purely by Christian faith and a desire to rid the Holy Land of heathens. Most Templars – many of whom paid a considerable entry fee in either land or money – were expecting to reap benefits (in both profits and honour) from their association with the Papal militia. Controlling land in Palestine, once they'd booted out the Infidels, was not absent from their calculations. The Templars' formidable power for two centuries was based on a powerful combination of profits generated by investments in economic and social capital. Several centuries later, the Templars' organizational reincarnation, the Freemasons, were similarly motivated by social capital advantages conferred by their adhesion to an influential network.

The concept of *network* brings us back to our distinction between closed cliques and open networks discussed in the earlier chapter on the "Small World" phenomenon. It's frequently observed that social capital is most efficiently deployed inside *closed* and *tightly knit* groups characterized by dense interactions that enforce mutual recognition and trust. Groups like the Freemasons, exclusive social clubs and alumni associations distribute social capital to their members – for example, competitive advantages in the form of information about potential employment or contracts. Here is the important point: the exclusive nature of this social capital depends on *closure*.[9] Members inside these networks mutually recognize and trust one another because they know their group is *closed* to outsiders.

The closure theory – emphasizing the existence of closed, hierarchical, institutionally based groups with strong enforcement codes for the exclusive distribution of social capital – describes an observable truth throughout human history. Most forms of social organization have been closed. Still, closure theory presents a number of weaknesses that open up insights into how social capital functions in the online world. While closed cliques enjoy higher levels of implicit trust, they generally are adverse to innovation and creativity due to the "echo chamber" effect. In a nut shell, they are hostile to change. Members of closed structures, which distribute social capital advantages within a tight circle, tend to have conservative reflexes that reinforce their own values and predispositions. Close-knit groups are efficient at monopolizing social capital amongst their exclusive members, but highly inefficient when it comes to vitally important instincts, like flexibility, adaptability and open communication.

History is cluttered with examples of the catastrophic consequences of the echo-chamber loopback.[10] The French monarchy circa 1789 comes to mind. Its oligarchic leaders, including the king, stubbornly barricaded themselves behind the ramparts of their own archaic values – and ended up on a tumbrel on the way to the scaffold. In modern France, it is similarly observed that the poor performance of major French corporations is due to the institutionalized cronyism that results from a time-honoured educational tradition. In France, a small number of *grandes écoles* produce the country's bureaucratic and corporate elites noted for their homogenous, inward-looking value system based on ascriptive professional status.[11] Sometimes the existence of closed, opaque elites can produced unintended consequences. Jerome Kerviel, it will be remembered, was the French rogue trader who destabilized the French banking establishment when he lost $7 billion through allegedly fraudulent transactions. It was later discovered that Kerviel had not actually been motivated by greed, for he hadn't pocketed any money himself. His real motivation was *status* attainment. Unlike the top traders at the Société Générale bank, Kerviel was not educated at France's elite schools and consequently possessed no ascriptively conferred social capital giving him access into the top-drawer ranks of his profession. His trading frenzy, which at first had been spectacularly successful, was Kerviel's way of compensating through *performance* for his lack of ascribed social status.

Here is how *Business Week* described the status chip on Kerviel's shoulder that led to the biggest banking meltdown in history: "Determined to break into trading, Kerviel grabbed the first job that came his way, an opening on SocGen's so-called Delta One trading desk, which handles generally low-risk futures hedging on European stock market indexes. Yet even at Delta One, Kerviel was dogged by his lack of credentials – a reflection of France's rigidly hierarchical education system, in which top students who gain admission to a handful of *grandes écoles* easily find prestigious jobs in government and business, while those who attend more ordinary schools find it far more difficult to advance. That frustration, and a desire to prove that he could play in the big leagues, led Kerviel to begin making unauthorized trades almost immediately upon joining Delta One. It was a decision that ultimately led to a $7.1 billion loss that could topple one of Europe's biggest banks."

Kerviel himself confessed to French prosecutors that his lack of status had driven him to go for broke on the bank's Delta One trading desk. "I was aware, starting from my first meeting in 2005, that I was less well-considered than the others, as regarding my university degree and my professional and personal background," he said. "I had not come directly to the front office, but had passed through the middle office, and I was the only [trader] to have done that."[12]

Kerviel almost pulled it off. His gains, at one point, reached $2 billion. But then he got overtaken by events. And when the bubble burst, Kerviel was the fall guy. In the eyes of the French banking establishment, he was a climber who didn't know his place. The one place where Kerviel found bona fide social status was the last place he expected – Facebook. The online world heralded him as an anti-establishment cult hero. Kerviel had received no respect in the vertical hierarchy of a major French bank, but in the wide open, horizontal world of online social networks he was a star.

Let's be clear, we don't mean to suggest that social capital, without exception, is a coveted asset jealously monopolized by oligarchic elites inhabiting closed, inward-looking cliques on a fast-track to corporate self-destruction. In fact, social capital can be a positive virtue associated with excellent public health, low crime rates and indeed efficient financial markets.[13] Social capital is also credited with producing high levels of *civic engagement*. If people are primarily motivated to join PTAs, church groups, unions, Freemasons, political parties and community organizations in order to extract "profits" in the form of competitive advantages, self-interested motivation nonetheless produces positive benefits for society as a whole. Just as *financial capital* investment produces increased economic growth and higher levels of prosperity, *social capital* investment produces increased civic engagement that strengthens democratic values and institutions. Alexis de Tocqueville marvelled at the linkage between civic engagement and democracy during his tour of the young American republic in the 1830s. Americans of all ages and stations in life, Tocqueville noted in *Democracy in America*, were constantly forming and joining associations. He observed: "There are not only commercial and industrial associations in which all take part, but others of a thousand different types – religious, moral, serious, futile, very general and very limited, immensely large and very minute . . . Nothing, in my view, deserves more attention than the intellectual and moral associations in America."[14]

About 150 years after Tocqueville's visit to America, Robert Putnam lamented the decline of social capital in America in a widely discussed book, *Bowling Alone*. First published in essay form in 1995, Putnam's book argued that the robust democracy Tocqueville had described started to vanish after the 1960s. Putnam was looking back nostalgically not to America in the early 19th century, but to the white-picket-fence America evoked in Norman Rockwell paintings – a golden age where the American Way of Life meant family values, community involvement and civic engagement. Since the 1970s, Putnam argued, America has been suffering from a severe social capital deficit whose pervasive symptoms are low voter turnout, disengagement from local community activities, declining membership in unions, apathy towards politics and so forth. To illustrate his argument, Putnam used the social metaphor of bowling. Bowling leagues had once been a popular form of social interaction in America. Bowling was an activity that produced social capital. Today, as Americans retreat from civic engagement, people are forced to "bowl alone" as isolated, disconnected, atomized and socially alienated individuals.[15]

Putnam cited a number of social dislocations that supported his theory. One of them, which he called the *technological transformation of leisure*, blamed television and other media for what he called the "virtual reality helmet". Putnam observed: "There is reason to believe that deep-seated technological trends are radically 'privatizing' or 'individualizing' our use of leisure time and thus disrupting many opportunities for social-capital formation. The most obvious and probably the most powerful instrument of this revolution is television. Time-budget studies in the 1960s showed that the growth in time spent watching television dwarfed all other changes in the way Americans passed their days and nights. Television has made our communities (or, rather, what we experience as our communities) wider and shallower. In the language of economics, electronic technology enables individual tastes to be satisfied more fully, but at the cost of the positive social externalities associated with more primitive forms of entertainment. The same logic applies to the replacement of Vaudeville by the movies and now of movies by the VCR. The new 'virtual reality' helmets that we will soon don to be entertained in total isolation are merely the latest extension of this trend."

Putnam's "bowling alone" theory has been criticized on a number of points, notably for its failure to take into consideration the changing nature of social ties.[16] Its main weakness, though, is its dismissal of electronic communication as a platform for social interaction. Putnam's theory was constructed with a built-in bias that regarded social capital exclusively as the product of face-to-face interaction. This conceptual bias blinded his analysis to a powerful fact that was e-rupting all around him: social capital was shifting from real-world interactions to virtual interactions on the Web.[17] If social capital was indeed declining in America, as Putnam argued, it was re-emerging on the Internet – everywhere from MySpace and Facebook to e-Masonry to e-government. As sociologist Nan Lin observed: "There is little doubt that the hypothesis that social capital is declining can be refuted if one goes beyond the traditional interpersonal networks and analyses the cybernetworks that emerged in the 1990s. We are witnessing the beginnings of a new era in which social capital is far outpacing personal capital in significance and effect."[18]

That observation succinctly expresses the theme underpinning this part of the book: the creation, possession and accumulation of social capital are shifting towards the online world. The starting point of our analysis of status begins with that assertion. More importantly, we examine how social capital is created and acquired; and, above all, how *status* rewards and benefits are assigned. As we shall see, sites like MySpace and Facebook can produce social capital in unique ways. Online social capital is attributed according to the values of *personal identity* liberated from the constraints of institutionalized social identity construction.[19] This winning combination – personal identity and social capital – represents a profound e-ruption for status rewards. As noted above, whereas status traditionally has been based on institutional values emphasizing ascriptive notions of rank and position, in cyberspace status is conferred according to *facts* related to performance: *expertise, efficiency* and *effectiveness*. Or, as previously noted, the *democratization of status*. As the distribution of social capital moves from the real to the virtual world, its status rewards are shifting from oligarchic to democratic values.

One important caveat must accompany this assertion however. As we saw in the Small World and Second Life chapters, the initial reaction to social e-ruptions is frequently a reflex favouring the *replication* of traditional forms of social organization in the virtual world. Some social networking sites have, as we have seen, based their business models on the enforcement of *closure* rules to create dense social interactions. There is some evidence that, in India, members of the Orkut social networking site are organizing themselves according to that country's traditional castes. In the United States, there is evidence that MySpace and Facebook mark class differences among America's youth. While Facebook tends to attract middle-class kids, MySpace seems to be more popular among teenagers from ethnic, working-class and other marginalized social groups. Internet sociologist Danah Boyd even suggests that the US military's banning of MySpace is a symptom of this class bias: enlisted soldiers use MySpace, whereas officers are drawn to Facebook. Others have observed that, while Facebook is associated with "geek" culture status, MySpace members are more "glam".[20] Whatever the precise cleavages, there can be little doubt that – in an initial phase – some networking sites tend to replicate real-world social hierarchies.

The online phenomenon of "hazing" gives further support to this observation. On university campuses, the annual ritual of hazing – leaving aside criticisms about the cruelty of these practices – serves the function of enforcing status hierarchies through mild forms of violence and, most of all, severe feelings of humiliation. Hazing transmits norms, however perversely, from dominant members of a social group (upper classmen) to younger members (freshmen). In British public schools, the so-called "fagging" system is a year-round ritual of social subordination of younger boys whose function is to enforce status hierarchies and transmit norms. In American-style university fraternity and sorority houses, freshers are forced to make "pledges" of loyalty to the group. In the online world, virtual groups are now subjecting new members to similar initiation rituals. One group is called X-Filesaholics, fans of the television show X-Files. In a study of X-Filesaholic hazing published in 2005, it was observed that new members were given virtual toothbrushes and forced to clean and scrub virtual apartments of senior members.[21] True, online hazing doesn't inflict physical duress; but the status values of domination and subordination are just as effectively transmitted.

The ritual of virtual gift-giving is another form of traditional status assertion that has migrated to the online world. As we saw in Chapter 5, while the function of digital gifts is to reinforce social ties with online "friends" and e-quaintances, digital gift-giving can also be an expression of *invidious comparison* driven by a desire to offer, and display, more expensive gifts than others. This impulse, as Thorstein Veblen so eloquently analysed, is straight out of a longstanding tradition of socio-anthropology. On the surface, nothing much seems to have changed with virtual gift-giving. As marketing executive Dave Coffey, who bought his wife a virtual pair of shoes on Facebook, observed: "For the person who gets the gift, it is like a badge of honour." Coffey also bought a virtual can of Whoop-Ass juice for a friend who'd just landed a new job, and a virtual can of beer for his boss to pay off a lost bet. The first virtual gift affirmed his friend's new status; the second affirmed his own status as a good loser. Kel Kelly, a marketing executive in Boston, says she has spent about $100 on virtual gifts on Facebook, usually on high-status items like champagne bottle icons that her clients can post on their pages. "Anyone can send an email that says 'Congratulations on your recent partnership' or whatever," said Kelly, adding that her high-end virtual gifts, for which she pays between $5 and $10, are "just a really cool way to stand out."[22] Standing out, in other circumstances, is called either *invidious comparison* or *conspicuous consumption*. Kelly is a status-seeker.

Let's apply more rigorous analysis to the gesture of digital gifts. The value, or *status*, of a virtual gift is linked to the economic notion of *scarcity*. The value of a gift, indeed of anything, is determined by how rare it is. The scarcer something is, the more we value it – even if it's utterly useless. Adam Smith, in *Wealth of Nations*, famously illustrated this principle through the so-called *paradox of value* theorem, sometimes called the Diamond–Water Paradox. Smith was intrigued by the relative values of water and diamonds: while water is much more vital to human survival, the value assigned to diamonds is much higher, even though the stone has virtually no social utility. This led Smith to the conclusion, frequently called the Labour Theory of Value, that "the real price of everything, what everything really costs to the man who wants to acquire it, is the toil and trouble of acquiring it." In a word, diamonds are *scarce*, whereas water is plentiful. Diamonds are a girl's best friend not because of their aesthetic properties, but rather because of the tremendous effort and cost required to find, extract, shape and polish them. And the bigger the rock on the dainty wedding finger, the higher the social status for the lucky lady – and, of course, for the groom who offered it. Romantic devotion, conspicuous consumption and invidious comparison are definitely the three motivating impulses here – though not necessarily in that order.

The scarcity principle goes only so far in the online world. And the reason is simple: virtual gifts are not, in fact, scarce.[23] Think about it: anything that can be digitally reproduced into a million, even a zillion, copies at no marginal cost is hardly scarce. That explains why most virtual gifts are exchanged in micropayment markets at prices of only $1 and $10. As the global music industry discovered, the technical ability to copy digital products reduces their value because, instead of being monetized in *closed* retail markets, they are disseminated virally in *open* networks. Indeed, as we have seen with the *World of Warcraft* example, the most profitable business model for virtual goods leverages *network effects* based on high volume, not high margins on low volumes. Needless to say, this produces the effect of lowering the *status* value of virtual goods, because in truth they are never scarce. If sending a virtual bottle of champagne that costs $5 may be more impressive than offering a $1 bouquet of virtual flowers, there are precious little invidious comparison advantages in the differential. Digital gifts may be ideal for transactions in charity markets, where value is not associated with cost. But in the *status* stakes, their lack of scarcity value only comforts the theme that animates this part of the book. Status in the online world is *democratic* – and based on *facts*, not values.

Reflexes that seek to impose and enforce real-world status hierarchies in virtual social spheres are expressions of conservative instincts that fail to understand the dynamics and potential of online networks. In cyberspace, fame, prestige, esteem, influence and wealth are conferred directly in a ceaseless democratic ritual of plebiscite and disavowal.

The four chapters that follow each examine a different aspect of the status e-ruption – fame, corporate roles, ratings and rankings and brand reputation.

To win fame online, you don't need a music label, movie studio, television producer or publisher – you can appeal directly to the global democracy of YouTube. In the online world, taste gatekeepers can't dictate which cultural products get to be blockbusters, and which talents get to become stars. Everybody gets a fair shot at recognition – and the winners are announced when the votes are counted. In virtual reality, as we shall see, fame is *decentralized* and *democratic*.

Social media are also challenging traditional bureaucracies in which valuable competence and expertise too frequently remain "hidden", and thus unproductive, merely to minimize potential threats to existing status hierarchies. In these organizations, loveable fools are more popular, and enjoy higher status, than competent jerks. The result is status sclerosis: entrenched management cliques win, frustrated shareholders lose. Thanks to Web 2.0 tools, you don't need to flatter and cajole your way up the ladder – mainly because there is no ladder. You can directly prove your abilities through virtual collaboration. Social media facilitate the emergence of networked organizational structures, where collaboration is transparent and horizontal. A lofty title and a corner office are no longer sufficient to assert status. Rewards are attributed on the basis of performance, not position.

The online world's democratic culture, in which status rewards are attributed according to achievement and merit, has a natural bias in favour of quantitative measurement. Hence the online obsession with ratings and rankings as statistical methods of sorting out status and distributing its rewards. Even fame can be measured scientifically, thus bypassing the judgement filters of taste gatekeepers who like to give us status guidance about what to eat, buy and wear. True, intermediaries who control fame markets are digging in to protect their prerogatives; but, as we shall see, their conservatism can sometimes produce scandalous consequences. If tyranny of the majority is a constant danger in democratic systems, it can make a greater claim on efficiency and legitimacy than tyranny of the few.

When everybody has a vote, and anyone can have a voice on a blog, reputational risk for organizations becomes a growing preoccupation – for some, the source of corporate paranoia. An organization's brand status, as we shall see, can be damaged instantly, and irreparably, by the viral reactivity of social media. Unlike in the past when corporations and governments could effectively manage protest – whether from consumers, shareholders or voters – the power of online opinion can be a virtual nightmare for organizations that put a foot wrong. Blogs have become such powerful social media tools, indeed, that some CEOs are now blogging themselves to manage their status, reputation and brand.

There is a lesson in the power of social media to redefine status. Organizations that remain rigidly locked in their vertical status hierarchies are paying the price for their conservatism. Those who are changing the way they do business, and turning closed echo chambers into dynamically open networks, are those who have grasped the radically e-rupted dynamics of status.

7

Me, MySpace and I: the fame game

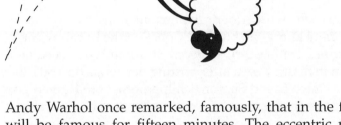

Andy Warhol once remarked, famously, that in the future everyone will be famous for fifteen minutes. The eccentric pop artist, who himself enjoyed fame for much longer than 15 minutes, died in 1987, several years before the explosion of the Web. If Warhol had lived longer, he may well have reformulated his celebrated quote by asserting: "In the future everybody will be famous for fifteen *megabytes*".

Fame on the Internet is a real-time, direct global democracy in action. Never before has it been so easy to become so famous so fast. You don't need an agent, a publisher, a music label, a movie studio or a television network. If you have talent – even if you don't – you can upload your work directly on MySpace, YouTube, your own blog or onto countless other social sites. Your shot at fame will be judged on a global Gong Show on which the curtain never comes down.

Rarely a week goes by without news of another "YouTube sensation" rocketing to worldwide fame. The YouTube fame launch pad even has its own name: YouToo. As in, yes, *you too* can become famous.

It worked for a wholesome American girl named Lisa Donovan, who shot to fame with online comic skits on YouTube using her *nom de web*, LisaNova. When her YouTube clips started attracting upwards of 11 million viewers, LisaNova's online fame led to a contract to shoot four episodes on the Fox television show, *MadTV*. YouTube also worked for comedy team Luke Barats and Joe Bereta, a.k.a "BaratsAndBereta", who began uploading their comedy sketches when both were undergrads at a Jesuit college in Spokane, Washington. Their YouTube routines were soon attracting more than 16 million viewers. The comedy team was soon signed to develop a series for the major American television network, NBC.[1]

The *faming* impulse was actually the original inspiration for the first social networking sites launched. Both Friendster and MySpace started off as fame platforms. Among early-adopters on Friendster were "indie" rock bands from Los Angeles who uploaded their music in the hope of gaining recognition. When Friendster's owners booted the bands off the site, the aspiring musicians quickly defected to MySpace, whose early growth was based on its "bands-and-fans" ethos.[2] Friendster's owners over-regulated the fame game; MySpace empowered it.

Faming isn't an exclusively American phenomenon. The mad Internet rush for notoriety knows no borders. Consider the uncanny celebrity of a 19-year-old British girl, Rebecca Strachan, who became a singing sensation in South Korea after posting her songs on YouTube. Strachan and her Dutch friend Sharon Schilperoord, both Korean pop fans, met on an Internet forum for "K-Pop" enthusiasts and were soon making their own videos of Korean pop songs. Calling themselves "DGDY", the pair posted a song called "Promise You" on YouTube. Almost instantly, the video became a hit on Korean social networking sites like Gypsii. Strachan, from the English town of Basingstoke, became so famous in Korea that the owners of the Gypsii site paid her travelling expenses to perform in Korea. She was also reportedly in discussions with a Korean music label, J-Tune, about a record deal.[3]

There is now a website, called Taltopia which is devoted to discovering and launching new talent. Created in March 2007, Taltopia bills itself as a free-of-charge, worldwide stage for anyone seeking Web celebrity. Fame-seekers upload their videos and, like ancient Roman gladiators subject to life-or-death "thumbs up" and "thumbs down" signals from a roaring Coliseum throng, watch their fortunes rise and fall via so-called "fame" and "shame" votes.

Perhaps the most remarkable example of Web fame thus far is Tila Nguyen, a Vietnamese beauty who moved to the United States from Singapore when she was a small child. In 2002, at age 20, Nguyen was featured as Playboy's "Cyber Girl of the Month". She changed her name to "Tila Tequila" and, in 2003, launched a MySpace page as a platform to sell her personal brand – her look, sex appeal and songs. And it worked. Tequila became fabulously famous online. Indeed, she was the most popular person on MySpace by far, with nearly two million "friends". Tequila, an online fame pioneer, is still credited with starting the "friends" syndrome on social networking sites. It wasn't long before Tequila had her own clothing line, a cellphone endorsement contract and was appearing scantily-clad on the covers of lad magazines like *Stuff* and *Maxim*, which ranked her in their "100 Sexiest Women" lists. By 2007, she was a star on MTV, hosting a bisexual dating show called *A Shot at Love with Tila Tequila*. Her songs, true enough, have been described as "skank pop". But Tequila is undaunted. In 2007, she released her first single, "I Love U" on iTunes and posted the video version on her MySpace page. As *Time* magazine put it in a profile of this one-woman, Vietnamese-American, fame-driven media brand: "Nguyen clearly grasps the logic of Web 2.0 in a way that would make most CEOs weep". *Slate* published a profile of her entitled "Tila Tequila for President".[4]

In the spring of 2008, the virtual inhabitants of an eccentric Pantheon of Internet celebrities attended a conference on the prestigious MIT campus. Organized by David Weinberger – a fellow at Harvard Law School and an early Web 2.0 evangelist – the conference was dubbed ROFL for "Rolling On the Floor Laughing". Web stars like Tila Tequila shunned this event. With her MTV career, she doubtless was regarded as too "old media" for ROFL. The event was dedicated to the pop cultural phenomenon of inadvertent celebrities, or Internet *memes*, sporting geekish monikers like Ben Huh, Tron Guy, Leeroy Jenkins, JibJab Guy and One Red Paper Clip Guy.

Sounds ridiculous, but some of these Web-celebrated oddballs are household names in America. JibJab Guy's political parodies have appeared on Jay Leno's *Tonight Show*. And Tron Guy has been a guest several times on *Jimmy Kimmel Live*. Leeroy Jenkins, as the initiated would know, is a character in the world's most popular online game, *World of Warcraft*. This Ubuesque cast of characters appears to belong in Andy Warhol's hall of fame, but the very fact that they are out there, enjoying online notoriety, tells us something about the changing nature of fame. Weinberger, co-author of the *Cluetrain Manifesto*, says he organized the event to celebrate the "democratization of fame". Web celebrities, he notes, are "our famous" – unlike mass-media-produced celebrities whose fame is "based on alienation".

"What's famous on the Web looks like it was done by a human hand," says Weinberger, "They still feel like ours. It's not just the homespun quality of what's famous on the Web. It's how fame works – it's becoming much more DIY. Fame is now living in a long tail, or a long continuum of ways to be famous."[5]

The compulsion to become famous has motivated the quest for human grandeur since the beginning of civilization. In the ancient world, fame was associated with "glory", hence the Latin adage *sic transit gloria*, reminding triumphant Roman generals that glory is fleeting so savour the moment. The ancient world also gave us classic works – Suetonius's *Twelve Caesars* and Plutarch's *Lives of the Illustrious Greeks and Romans* – about the glory of great men, especially emperors. In medieval Christendom, the pervasive *contemptus mundi* ethos rejected classical culture's ideology of human triumph as "vainglorious". Medieval Christians preferred the mythology of chivalric "honour", though the rise of Italian city states controlled by dynasties like the Medicis soon brought back humanist values of worldly achievement. With the advent of the printing press and the emergence of nation states, fame underwent yet another cultural transformation as the Renaissance returned to a cultural validation of worldly classical virtues. The 18th century Scottish philosopher David Hume, in his *Enquiry Concerning Human Understanding*, observed that the "love of fame" among men was the "grand object of all their designs and undertakings".

Traditionally, fame has been limited by the constraints of time and space. Mozart and Liszt were famous in their day mainly because they travelled throughout Europe to give piano concerts. If spatial distance could be overcome through travel, extending fame in time was more challenging. Great artists who achieved extraordinary fame in their lifetimes were sometimes forgotten by future generations. Some today might recognize the names Edmund Keane, Maria Malibran, Sarah Bernhardt and Enrico Caruso, but they would not likely poll highly on name-recognition surveys. And yet they were all massively famous figures of the theatre and opera in the 19th century. Marie Lloyd was the most famous English music hall singer of her generation in Edwardian England. When she died in 1922, more than 100000 adoring fans attended her funeral in London. Less than a century later, few would even recognize her name, even in England – though her legend has recently been revived by a BBC drama. Sometimes famous figures vanish into obscurity but then, generations after their deaths, rise phoenix-like after rediscovery of their work. Consider these names: Mozart, Vivaldi, Oscar Wilde, Kafka, F. Scott Fitzgerald. All are famous names today, yet all died in relative obscurity. If you are never a prophet in your own land, many are refused the honour in their own time.

The poet Lord Byron was one of the first literary figures to achieve adulatory fame in the modern sense. Byron even wrote, "I woke up one day and found myself famous". The ennobled poet was, in many respects, a prototype of the modern pop star, including the scandalous suggestion of shocking sexual proclivities. That Byron was a great poet cannot be doubted. But his fame was owed to the economics of industrial production: his books could be mass-produced and distributed widely to adoring fans. Byron's fame must be put into quantitative perspective however. Look at the numbers: the first edition of Byron's most celebrated poem, *Childe Harold*, made him famous after an initial print run of 500 copies was sold out in three days. His fame soared when *The Corsair* sold 10 000 copies on the first day, and 25 000 copies in the first month. In Regency England, those were big numbers. Today, they wouldn't get a book even close to the bottom ranks of a major bestseller list.

In the 20th century, the economics of industrial production transformed fame into a mass-audience phenomenon with the advent of motion pictures and recorded music. In particular, the economics of *marginal costs* – which dramatically reduce the added expense of reproducing a single unit of intellectual property – produced huge profits in these industries. All you needed to do was cover the costs of several dozen copies of a motion picture to be projected in major cities and millions of tickets could be sold, with no additional cost for each additional ticket purchased. Likewise for records: the marginal cost of each vinyl disc stamped out was next to zero. The economies of scale in these industries made them among the most profitable in the history of capitalism.

This economic model, needless to say, produced massively famous stars. In the period following the First World War, no one had ever achieved global fame on the scale of movie stars like Charlie Chaplin, Douglas Fairbanks, Mary Pickford and Rudolf Valentino. In recorded music, singers like Frank Sinatra were extraordinarily famous worldwide more than a decade before rock n' roll hit radio airwaves in the 1950s. In the 1960s, the convergence of counter-culture music, mass-audience television and control of the global music industry by a small number of major music labels propelled groups like The Beatles and The Rolling Stones to a level of fame never before known for musicians. These pop stars, understandably, became acutely conscious of their own fame. The Beatles were so adulated throughout the world in the 1960s that John Lennon declared, controversially, that the group was "more famous than Jesus Christ". John Lennon, of course, became a martyred victim of his own global fame when he was tragically murdered by a deranged fan. His killer, Mark David Chapman, later confessed that he'd shot the ex-Beatle dead in order to "steal" his fame.[6]

Andy Warhol understood that industrial mass-production was transforming not only artistic fame, but the nature of art itself. His Campbell's Soup can was an ironic statement about the industrial production of art. And his mass-produced portraits of superstars like Marilyn Monroe were trenchant commentaries on the connection between industrial production and celebrity. Warhol himself was, paradoxically, both a critic of the aesthetics of mass production and one of its most famous proponents. That his critique was lost on millions who worshipped movie stars and pop idols like him did not seem to trouble Warhol. His fame, however ambiguous, brought him tremendous status and its many rewards, especially money.

The German-born social theorist Theodor Adorno had grasped the dynamics of the "cultural industries" – a term he coined in the 1940s – before the pop art movement more than a decade later. Adorno, a leading figure of the Marxist-inspired Frankfurt School, argued in his 1941 work, *On Popular Music*, that industrially manufactured popular music resulted in *standardization* and *pseudo-individualization* which, when consumed by mass audiences, produces an alienating effect that leads to physical and social isolation. Adorno also applied the Marxist notion of *cultural fetishism* to popular music. He argued that the cultural industries distract audiences from the underlying power relationships of capitalist production. In other words, that pop stars are, when you strip away the fame factor, merely products of capitalist marketing machines.[7]

Adorno was describing the *blockbuster* economic model that has driven the media and entertainment industries for the past half century. The blockbuster model, to express it formally, is a capitalist means of extracting maximized rents from a limited number of products through cost-efficient risk-reduction strategies. In simpler language, the blockbuster model is a strategy based on earning high margins produced by a small number of superstars, frequently to the exclusion of many other lesser-known artists. Hollywood studios and major music labels invest heavily in selected "bankable" stars whose products benefit from blitzkrieg marketing strategies based on "buying" market share. In a word, market *saturation*. The economic principle of *cross-subsidy* also comes into play in blockbuster economics. Because producers feel compelled to spread their risks, the huge profits generated by a small number of "hits" are deployed to cover the production costs of movies, songs and other products that fail to generate profits. Hollywood studios generally make most of their profits in a given year on a small fraction of the movies they produce – like *Titanic* or *Jurassic Park* or *Harry Potter*. This ratio is often called the "80/20 Rule". In other words, 20% of new releases account for 80% of revenues (and, in many cases, for 100% of profits). In pop music, only one CD out of every ten turns a profit. In music, therefore, it's the "90/10 Rule".[8]

The blockbuster model is driven by a winner-takes-all ethos. The lucky few who get picked by Hollywood studios, major music labels and giant publishing houses become the beneficiaries of massive publicity machines that, if all goes well, bring global fame and staggering financial rewards.[9] World-famous superstars – Mick Jagger, Angelina Jolie, Brad Pitt, George Clooney, Nicole Kidman, Mariah Carey – also become the focus of intense gossip in celebrity magazines, especially rumours about their sexual partnerships. Gossip, as we have seen, performs an anthropological function of sorting out *status*. There is no more powerful sign of status ranking than which physically attractive superstars are sleeping together.

The blockbuster model, it cannot be doubted, has produced enormously talented stars who richly deserve their millions of adoring fans. Most would agree that The Beatles, The Rolling Stones, Led Zeppelin, Bob Dylan, David Bowie, Elton John, Pink Floyd, The Who, Michael Jackson, Madonna and other superstars are legendary pop artists who have produced "classic" songs. Similarly, in cinema many movie stars – James Dean, Marlon Brando, Marilyn Monroe – possessed powerful charisma and talent that still attracts tremendous fascination. Some bestselling books are actually worthy of the megasales they generate. Still, the blockbuster model has a flaw that critics never tire of pointing out: it produces *poor quality*. If risk-reduction strategies based on "hits" produced The Beatles, Elton John and David Bowie, they also gave us memorable pop acts like The Monkees, Bay City Rollers and Vanilla Ice. And let's face it, most of the Hollywood movies that top the box-office hit parade can hardly be described as classics. The same goes for fiction on the bestseller lists.

If this is true, why do blockbuster economics produce cultural goods that *qualitatively* don't appear to merit their enormous popularity?

The question, it turns out, intrigued American economist Tyler Cowen enough for him to devote an entire book to formulating a hypothesis. In *What Price Fame?*, Cowen made a conceptual distinction between *fame* and *merit* – in other words, that some people become famous even though, by any reasonable standard, they don't deserve their notoriety.

"The separation of fame and merit is a central dilemma for any evaluation of a modern market economy," asserted Cowen in his book, published in 2000. "A system based on voluntary exchange does not reward merit with a concomitant degree of recognition."[10]

Cowen correctly identified factors that make "fame markets" fail, such as hype-driven snowball effects, fan clubs and payola bribes. But he identified *blockbuster economics* as the principal reason for the failure of fame markets. While it might be argued that fame markets are driven by *supply*-side factors, Cowen's analysis kept *demand* in the equation. "The oversimplications of modern fame are part of the price we voluntarily pay for the mobilisation of large audiences at low cost," he observed. "Commercial promotions do not give fans the stars they want the most in absolute terms, but they do give fans the stars they are willing to pay for." In other words, the disconnect between fame and merit is acceptable because it is dictated by market forces. Cowen, as an economist, appears to approve of that outcome.

That still doesn't resolve the issue of blockbuster economics and the fame/merit disconnect. Cowen's essentially optimistic view of fame markets takes statistical comfort in the declining importance of blockbuster economics. Tracking the Billboard charts, Hollywood box-office figures and TV ratings over the past half century, Cowen observed that there were more blockbuster hits in the period from the 1950s to 1980s than there have been since. In other words, there's a growing trend towards "decentralization of rewards", mainly due to increased *supply* via cable, satellite TV and other media platforms. The phenomenon of *fame decentralization* has, according to Cowen's analysis, narrowed the gap between fame and merit. How? Increased supply lowers the cost of fame by shifting power to the demand side – i.e. consumers. When more people have a shot at fame, due to increased supply, its rewards are more evenly, and justly, distributed according to merit – not according to arbitrary choices made by taste-gatekeeper corporations who pick winners.

There can be no doubt that blockbusters, as Cowen suggests, have been declining. The 500-channel universe means that TV eyeballs are now spread over so many channels, and musical tastes over so many different outlets, that stars today are not nearly as famous as celebrities were a half century ago. In the 1950s, the *I Love Lucy* show was watched by 75% of American households and throughout the world. Today, a hit show on American television would be happy with a 15% share. In the 1950s, Lucille Ball was much more famous than the female star of a hit television show today, like Marg Helgenberger from *CSI: Crime Scene Investigation*.

Rolling Stone magazine's "Greatest Albums of All Time" reveals the same bias towards the past, but with a strong fame-merit connection.

Not a single album in the Top 10 of *Rolling Stone's* list was produced after the 1970s: *Sgt. Pepper's Lonely Hearts Club Band*, The Beatles (1967); *Pet Sounds*, The Beach Boys (1966); *Revolver*, The Beatles (1966); *Highway 61 Revisited*, Bob Dylan (1965); *Rubber Soul*, The Beatles (1965); *What's Going On*, Marvin Gaye (1971); *Exile on Main St.*, Rolling Stones (1972); *London Calling*, The Clash (1979); *Blonde on Blonde*, Bob Dylan (1966); *The White Album*, The Beatles (1968). *Rolling Stone*, which published the list in 2003, made a qualitative judgement that no album recorded since 1979 merited a place in the Top 10.[11] Even the best-selling records of all time – a strictly *quantitative* measure – show the same trend: Eagles' *Greatest Hits*, Michael Jackson's *Thriller*, Pink Floyd's *The Wall*, Led Zeppelin *IV*, AC/DC's *Back in Black*, Billy Joel's *Greatest Hits*, Fleetwood Mac's *Rumours*, The Beatles' *White Album*, Shania Twain's *Come on Over* and Boston's self-titled album *Boston*.[12] Only one of these albums, Shania Twain's *Come on Over*, was released in the last 25 years. We can say, therefore, that blockbusters do indeed appear to be declining. If we give credence to *Rolling Stone's* merit ranking, and compare it with the bestseller list to find commonalities, there's a merit connection in only one instance: The Beatles' *White Album*.

If Tyler Cowen is right, more people are less famous today due to the decline of the blockbuster, and therefore fame is increasingly the reward of genuine merit. In other words, fame markets are less distorted. We believe, however, that a more powerful answer to Cowen's dilemma about the inefficiency of fame markets can be found elsewhere: the Internet.

The Web has produced dramatic e-ruptions that are transforming not only the underlying economics of media and entertainment markets, but more importantly how they distribute rewards like fame and celebrity. As traditional bricks-and-mortar distribution systems have been displaced by online retailers like Amazon, iTunes, Netflix and others, the blockbuster model has not just declined, it has become virtually irrelevant. This undoubtedly explains why Web-based retail selling of movies, songs, books and other cultural products was originally resisted by established players (Hollywood studios, Big Four music labels, major book chains) whose commercial strategies were based on managing, despite imperfections, the blockbuster model of extracting high margins from "hits" and "superstars". It is a testimony to their market power that these powerful gatekeepers succeeded in resisting the Web for so long. But when consumers realized the benefits of online retail transactions – product diversity, low price points, efficient delivery – demand reached a tipping point.

Gatekeeper resistance was no longer possible. The democratic floodgates had been flung open.

The economics of Web-based retailing turned the blockbuster model on its head thanks to one powerful factor: *lower inventory costs*. iTunes can store millions of songs on its online "shelves" to create a digital jukebox that costs virtually zero to manage. When inventory costs are next to zero, or relatively low, and capacity is unlimited, suppliers can offer a much wider variety of products to consumers instead of manipulating supply in favour of blockbuster "hits" produced by selected superstars. This market model has famously been called the "long tail" after Chris Anderson's 2006 book, *The Long Tail: How Endless Choice is Creating Unlimited Demand*.[13] The book, which in effect was a well-argued obituary for the blockbuster model, starts with a key insight about the economic bias of fame markets: "A hit-driven economy is a hit-driven culture". In other words, we consume blockbuster products because that's what the market supplies. The good news, for consumers, is that "long tail" economics liberate them from the blockbuster syndrome. The 80/20 Rule has been replaced by the "98% Rule". Instead of the blockbuster model's reliance on 20% of product releases to generate 80% of revenues, on the Internet consumers purchase 98% of products made available to them. The "long tail" business model connects supply and demand more democratically, argues Anderson, because production, distribution and product "search" costs are virtually non-existent. Anybody can record a song and post it on YouTube, and anybody with a computer can find that song.

Illustrated graphically as supply-and-demand metrics, "long tail" economics replace the traditional bell-bulge graph with a dropped hockey-stick shape that falls off abruptly and trails off towards the right. The "long tail" running along the bottom of the graph represents the cornucopia of niche products, a million flowers blooming that consumers are willing to buy at the right price – hard-to-find songs, cult movies, rare books, early jazz recordings, B-sides, remixes, obscure artists, foreign films and CDs, you name it. This model transcends the constraints of time and space: on the Web, you can find niche products made in the distant past (a rare Bessie Smith blues number from the 1920s) and far away in distance (a hard-to-find early recording by French pop legend Serge Gainsbourg). If you live somewhere in Middle America, try walking into any music retailer and asking for either. Chances are, you won't find them on the shelf. But they're almost certainly both available on the Web. So are songs and movies from virtually every era and every culture throughout the world – in French, German, Italian, Portuguese, Spanish, Farsi, Hindi, Arab, Chinese, Japanese, Korean and others.

The logic of "long tail" economics has obvious consequences for fame. When supply is virtually unlimited and meets demand at the right price, fame is more *democratically* conferred and the term "popular" comes closer to its true meaning. Elitists and monopolists, it is true, don't like democracy, because it either offends their tastes or threatens their oligarchic power. But why, rationally, should fame markets be controlled by a small clutch of executives at Hollywood studios, Big Four music labels, major TV networks and big publishing houses entrusted with "picking winners" in the marketplace? That's Blockbuster Think.

The "long tail" model has attracted criticism, to be sure, mainly from those who believe it doesn't deliver on its promise. Wharton business professor Kartik Hosanagar observes that online retailers like Amazon actually tend to *reinforce* the blockbuster logic of media markets, especially through "recommender" systems. Amazon and iTunes rarely recommend obscure, hard-to-find songs, movies and books, but tend to suggest blockbuster products that have already benefited from significant snowball effects. Hosanagar notes, in particular, recommender systems that propose products based on *sales* and consumer *ratings* create "rich-get-richer effects for popular products and vice versa for unpopular ones". Others argue that Google and Yahoo! would be more efficient, and impartial, platforms for product searches because, unlike Amazon, Google is relatively indifferent to which products consumers buy. For Amazon, on the other hand, its recommender system is revenue-driven. Still, online recommenders are more efficient than old-style bestseller lists. Moreover, it can hardly be claimed that recommender systems undermine "long tail" effects. In the final analysis, whatever Amazon or iTunes may be recommending, consumers can still find almost any product, however obscure, somewhere on their virtual shelves. The critique, in sum, is directed at the supply-side "push" dynamic of online retailing. But consumer "pull", whatever the online retailer's marketing strategy, remains sovereign.[14]

A more troubling critique of the "long tail" model relates to the nature of democracy: while the Web undoubtedly *democratizes* fame markets, it also *trivializes* them. The Web confers dubious notoriety on fame-seekers for reasons that, on the surface, seem wholly disconnected to merit. The explosion of "reality" television shows has produced an intriguing roster of so-called celebrities who are "famous for being famous". This phenomenon even has a name: the Paris

Hilton Rule. She originally became famous, it will be recalled, for her private version of reality television: performing intimate sex acts on videotapes that were sent out on the Web. Another personality in this category is Nicole Richie, who starred with Paris Hilton in the reality show, *The Simple Life*. An online illustration of the Paris Hilton Rule is the sad fate of Ghyslain Raza. He's the chubby Canadian teen who, in 2003, became world famous as the "Star Wars Kid" after his home-made video of himself awkwardly brandishing a light sabre, imitating Darth Maul, was posted on the Web. Raza's global fame was trivialized because the millions who played the video laughed at his physical clumsiness. Raza became so famous online that major old media outlets – *New York Times*, CBS News in America and BBC News in Britain – reported on his notoriety. But his fame proved to be a poisoned chalice. Harassed in school by classmates, Raza was soon in therapy to deal with the stress. His parents ended up launching a "cyber-bullying" civil suit, claiming $351 000 against the families of their son's classmates who had posted the video online.[15] If the Star Wars Kid had attended the Internet fame conference at MIT in the spring of 2008, he undoubtedly would have been enthusiastically applauded along with Ben Huh, Tron Guy Leeroy Jenkins, JibJab Guy and One Red Paper Clip Guy.

Sometimes infamy is marketed as a substitute for fame, especially if there's money to be made. Ashley Dupré, the 22-year-old New Jersey prostitute who shot to fame after New York Governor Eliot Spitzer was caught paying premium rates for her sexual services, turned her sudden infamy into a lucrative career opportunity. Before getting drawn into the vortex of New York's netherworld of high-class prostitution where she was earning $4500 an hour, Dupré had been struggling to make a living like thousands of other girls in the Big Apple. When her furtive rendezvous with the New York governor in Washington's Mayflower Hotel was exposed, Spitzer's downfall was immediate. Dupré, for her part, discovered that she was suddenly famous.[16]

Within a day after the sex scandal hit American newspapers, more than five million people had converged on Dupré's MySpace page where she shared her dreams of becoming a pop singer. She already had, in fact, recorded a couple of songs – one called "What We Want" and another "Move Ya Body" – that sounded like Britney Spears imitations. The tunes were promptly posted on the music-sharing site Aime Street, which pays artists 70% cut download fees. Then New York radio station, Z100, started playing "What We Want" as a gimmick. But surprisingly, the tunes caught on. "After the first play, a lot of the reaction was negative," the station's programme director Sharon Dastur told the *New York Times*. "But after the second play, it became, 'Play that song again', and 'Hey, that song's not bad'."[17] The songs generated so many downloads, in fact, that Dupré quickly had earned more than $200 000. In the meantime, she was receiving $1-million offers to pose nude in porn magazines. Dupré learned that, thanks to her MySpace page, the line between scarlet and starlet can be astoundingly blurry.

Flash-in-the-pan fame is nothing new. But the Web has the merit of providing a reliable measure of fame – whether ephemeral or enduring – that can be quantified with precision never before possible. Bestseller lists, despite their claims of statistical accuracy, are not always based on science – indeed, their methodologies are often contested as sloppy or, worse, rigged. And while *Billboard* charts and box-office receipts give a measure of sales, they don't necessarily provide any insights into *fame* markets. Indeed, if there's a gap between *fame* and *merit*, there can also be a disconnection between *fame* and *success*. The reason for this is that, while success can be *quantified* (in sales figures), fame is largely a *qualitative* measure. Many hugely famous artists, to be sure, are also immensely successful. Pop divas Madonna and Mariah Carey are massively famous worldwide, and also sell millions of records. Some of the best-selling records of all time, however, were made by recording artists who, if they walked down Oxford Street in London, would not be recognized by anyone. Consider the following pop acts who have produced some of the highest-selling records of all time: Backstreet Boys (40 million units of *Millennium*), Ace of Base (23 million units of *Happy Nation*), Dido (21 million units of *No Angel*), Boston (18 million units of *Boston*) and Evanescence (15 million units of *Fallen*). Some of us may remember the names of these rock groups, but few would recognize the names of their members. They are not famous. Paul McCartney and David Bowie are famous, and yet their success, when statistically measured, is not particularly impressive. Neither has made a best-selling record in years. Fame can outlive success; and success can be achieved without enduring fame.

The Web, as noted, has revolutionized the metrics of fame. It has also allowed us, thanks to search engines, to get a precise sociological reading of how famous a celebrity really is. Interestingly, it took an astronomer, not an economist, to come up with a Web-based system of measuring the socio-metrics of fame. Eric Schulman began quantifying fame in the 1990s by using Web search engines like Alta Vista, Google, Excite and Lycos. In 1999, Schulman calculated that five billion people (most of the planet's six billion people at that time) recognized the name Jesus Christ. Only half that number, or roughly 2.2 billion, recognized the name Bill Clinton (who in 1999 was President of the United States). Some 1.8 billion recognized the name Bill Gates, the world's richest person in 1999. And more than 650 million people recognized the name Monica Lewinsky, the White House intern who was at the centre of a scandal when her adulterous sexual liaison with Bill Clinton came to light. Schulman, moreover, found empirical confirmation of the so-called "Lennon Theorem", based on John Lennon's assertion in 1966 that "the Beatles are more famous than Jesus". Schulman discovered on Google that the term "The Beatles" received 1 550 000 hits while "Jesus Christ" scored only 1 440 000 hits. Jesus was more famous than both Bill Gates and Bill Clinton, who were neck-and-neck at about 750 000 hits each, but less famous than the Beatles.[18]

Schulman produced even more fascinating findings in 2006, this time offering a less academic, more easy-to-use method for measuring "celebrities" as a function of fame. Rejecting superficial notions of "celebrity" found in magazines like *People, Time* and *National Enquirer*, Schulman argued that mass-media standards are highly subjective, biased, arbitrary and what's more lack methods to classify people with low levels of fame. In a word, mass-media measurements are mostly interested in *blockbuster* fame. *People* doesn't put mildly famous people on its cover. The magazine is interested in superstars and categories like the "Sexiest Man Alive".

Schulman took a different approach. Applying the Weber–Fechner Law of human perception to fame measurement, he scientifically categorized celebrities using a logarithmic standard unit of fame, according to familiar "A-List" and "B-List" distinctions, but going all the way down to an "H-List" for lesser celebrities in a wide variety of fields from business and politics to music, movies, religion, science and sports. Exploiting data from Google hits in October 2005, Schulman's A-List included, in ranked order: Bill Gates, Bill Clinton, Jesus Christ, The Beatles, Albert Einstein, Jennifer Lopez, Paul McCartney, Tiger Woods and John Lennon (this time, interestingly, Jesus was more famous than The Beatles, thus repudiating the Lennon Theorem). Schulman suggested that his fame index, especially in lower category notoriety, has practical applications for charities seeking to solicit celebrities for fundraising purposes.[19]

Schulman's work has been studied and modified by others who have proposed a distinction between *fame* and *celebrity*. According to one revised definition, "Fame is being known. Celebrity is being known by your first name". According to the GFNR (Google First Name Rank) measure that produces a Celebrity Index, Bill Gates ranks higher than Bill Clinton. This can apparently be explained by the triumph of the computer. According to a Microsoft research paper: "A comparison of Bill Gates and Bill Clinton suggests that, in this era of blogging, celebrity depends more on the computer screen than on the TV screen."[20] There is, moreover, a stronger connection between *fame* and *merit* than between *celebrity* and *merit*. People who become hugely famous tend to deserve the distinction, and moreover their fame usually endures through time. Celebrity, on the other hand, is not only ephemeral, but it is frequently undeserved. Paul McCartney is famous; Paris Hilton is a celebrity.

The good news is that, thanks to the economics of social media and online commerce, access to fame is no longer controlled by institutionalized taste oligarchies exercising a tight stranglehold on supply. Taste oligarchies perpetuate disconnections between fame and merit because they decide, arbitrarily, who gets to become famous. Sometimes they are right; frequently they are not. True, democratic fame can be trivialized by vulgarians and publicity seekers. But the blockbuster model, as we have seen, fails to resolve the *quality* problem of fame markets. Social media at least give consumers the power to participate fully, unmediated by marketing intermediaries and taste gatekeepers. On the Web, everybody has a shot at fame; and everybody has a vote in who gets to be famous. The fame game today is *decentralized* and *democratic*.

Fame may last fifteen minutes, or fifteen decades. The difference today is that, from now on, it's you who chooses. And what's more, YouToo can become famous on YouTube.

8

Status hierarchies: loveable fools and competent jerks

When someone says "CEO of the year," you don't normally think of a corporate boss whose most impressive job credential is his hard-won status as an online gladiator, honing valuable leadership skills through mercilessly slaying mortal enemies on *World of Warcraft*. But the day may not be far off when top CEOs will be boasting executive skills, especially those necessary for hacking their way to the top, learned on virtual games.

Some major corporations, in fact, are already preparing for a new generation of dragon-slaying CEOs. Today, the average age of gamers in virtual worlds like *World of Warcraft* is not fifteen, but twice that age. Seasoned gamers are now in their thirties. Serious research shows, moreover, that the cognitive skills acquired by virtual gamers can be transformed, no joke, into effective leadership abilities in corporate environments. As IBM studies published in 2007 demonstrate, as Gen Y and Gen V move into the workforce, management challenges will increasingly resemble complex videogames.[1] The demographic shift from Gen Y to Gen V is already under way in many organizations. And make no mistake, its most powerful e-ruption will be a radical redefinition of *status* in corporate hierarchies.

"For Generation V, the virtual environment provides many aspects of a level playing field, where age, gender, class and income of individuals are less important and less rewarded than competence, motivation and effort," says Adam Sarner, principal analyst at Gartner. Sarner predicts that, by 2015, companies will be spending more on marketing to multiple and anonymous online personas than on today's conventional offline marketing campaigns.

Note the words *competence, motivation* and *effort* in the Gartner forecast. This analysis confirms what we have been arguing in this book: GenVers are much more *performance*-oriented than previous generations whose values in organizational structures have been based on ascriptive notions of position and rank. As Sarner puts it: "An 11-year old individual can be the leading 'go to' person for advice on how to upgrade or hack a digital video recorder for more recording space. An unpopular office worker can be a highly revered, accomplished 40th-level half-elf in *World of Warcraft*. The opportunity for reputation, prestige, influence and personal growth provides a powerful social draw for the masses to spend more time in a virtual world."[2]

The implications of this status e-ruption will be revolutionary. The Web 2.0 organization is a genuine democracy where everybody gets a fair shot at slaying a monster, or solving a management problem, and becoming a corporate hero if they succeed. Social media tools solicit and empower the best expertise. In corporate environments where knowledge-sharing and peer collaboration are transparent and horizontal, the power of collective intelligence will produce the optimal decision.

Management guru Gary Hamel, in his book *The Future of Management*, calls this e-ruption in organizations a Democracy of Ideas – or *thoughtocracy*.[3] If this vision of a radically democratic corporate bureaucracy won't inspire CEOs to get an Xbox installed in their offices, it's an e-ruption that they will ignore at their peril.

But, as noted at the outset of this book, there's one major obstacle: the *fear factor*. Most companies don't have IBM's corporate culture. In many organizations, senior executives behave like oligarchic political leaders: they are not generally inclined to usher in sweeping democratic reforms that promise to threaten their prerogatives, privileges and power. Many senior managers are highly talented at corporate gamesmanship without ever having played *World of Warcraft* – and they intend to keep it that way. Democracy is a noble ideal, but in most corporate hierarchies it has never been in vogue.

America's Declaration of Independence famously declared that we are all created equal. Yet another immutable law of human nature, it seems, is that when people find themselves in bureaucratic settings, they waste little time organizing themselves in vertical hierarchies that rigorously enforce status distinctions. Perhaps the French revolutionaries got it right when they declared in 1789 – thirteen years after the US Declaration of Independence – that while "men are born and remain free and equal in rights," social distinctions are justified when they promote the *"general good."*[4] This fine point of principle invites us to reflect on what kinds of social inequality are susceptible to contribute to the common good. If some people are going to enjoy higher status than others, what are the best criteria for conferring status unequally?

Anthropologists tell us that primate societies accorded higher social status to those whose activities were believed to be vital for the *survival* of the whole group. Accordingly, medicine men and skilled hunters enjoyed higher status in recognition of their specific, and vitally utilitarian, *expertise*. In sum, status was conferred on top performers. In aristocratic and oligarchic forms of social organization, by contrast, social status was conferred by *ascription* – in other words, according to a vertically structured value system based on rank, title, property, wealth, education and other signs of *social standing*. Status was conferred not on the basis of *performance*, but rather according to distinctions of *position*.

Status tension between these two value systems – rank versus expertise – has produced many notable disruptions throughout history, not to mention the occasional war. The late Middle Ages – when the logic of states and capitalism was gradually deposing the moral orders of religion and aristocracy as organizing principles – was particularly instructive in this regard. Returning to our leitmotif saga of Philippe le Bel and the Knights Templar, it will be recalled that the French king's biggest headache was the Pope. In medieval Europe, the Pontiff of Rome was, theoretically, the most powerful figure in Christendom. All princes, kings and emperors were the Pope's vassals. Henry IV, the Holy Roman Emperor at the end of the 11th century, was one of the first secular rulers to grow intensely frustrated with this state of affairs. When Pope Gregory VII decreed so-called "investiture" reforms asserting papal authority over the appointment of bishops and other high-ranking church officials, the Pontiff was effectively usurping the Holy Roman Emperor's traditional power over the church throughout his Germanic realm. Gregory VII pushed the envelope further by challenging the emperor's "divine right" powers, thereby rallying the support of German aristocrats who resented Henry IV's feudal power over them. For Henry IV, this was a bridge too far. He promptly renounced the Pope, refusing to submit to Rome. The Pontiff, in turn, excommunicated the recalcitrant Holy Roman Emperor. Then Pope Gregory drove in the nail with an ultimatum: after a one-year deadline, Henry's excommunication would be irrevocable. The Holy Roman Emperor's soul would be beyond salvation.

This historical showdown, undoubtedly one of the most bizarre incidents in medieval history, was essentially a *status* standoff. At stake was who held higher rank, the Pope or the Holy Roman Emperor. In a world whose organizing principle was the Christian religion, it didn't take long for the winner to be declared. A humbled Henry IV, desperate to have his excommunication lifted before the deadline and facing an imminent revolt by his nobles, was forced to perform public penance before the Pontiff to save his soul. In the cold winter of 1077, Henry trekked across the Alps to an Italian castle at Canossa where the Pope was in residence. According to historical accounts, Henry was barefoot and dressed in penitent hair-shirt as an outward sign of his humiliation, which lasted three howling nights before the Canossa castle gates. Finally brought before the Pope, Henry knelt before the Pontiff and begged for absolution. Fortunately for the Holy Roman Emperor, in the 11th century there were no round-the-clock CNN and BBC news cameras to broadcast his ignominy to the entire planet. Still, Henry IV's humiliation left no doubt throughout Christendom who was boss. It also had the effect of delaying Germany's emergence as a centralized nation until the late 19th century. The Canossa episode put power in the hands of a loose network of local German aristocrats for nine centuries. It was for this reason that Voltaire famously remarked that the Holy Roman Empire was "neither holy, nor Roman, nor an empire". One of those local German dynasties, the dukes of Saxe-Cobourg-Gotha, produced the direct ancestors of Britain's current monarch, Queen Elizabeth II.

France's Philippe le Bel, as we have seen, handled this same status showdown in precisely the opposite manner. In 1302, Boniface VIII issued a papal decree, *Unam Sanctum,* asserting that all spiritual and temporal powers in Christendom were under the Pope's jurisdiction. After Philippe renounced the Pope, he was – like Henry IV more than two centuries earlier – promptly excommunicated. But Philippe refused to back down. Showing the Pope who was in charge, the French king sent an assassination squad to Italy and had the Pope murdered. Then he dealt with the Pontiff's unofficial army, the Knights Templar, by having their leaders charged with blasphemy and executed. His victory over the Pope marked the birth of the modern state, unyoked by religious power. France thus centralized state power relatively early and emerged as a strong nation at a time when Germany remained a loose patchwork of minor aristocratic kingdoms, duchies and principalities. Philippe le Bel's victory over the Papal-blessed Knights Templar was a triumph of vertical power over horizontal networks.

Modern capitalist societies, driven by a need for functional efficiency, attempted to reconcile this status tension. Modern states constructed – as Max Weber famously described – "legal-rational" bureaucracies to assert authority over defined territories and their populations. These bureaucracies were, by definition, *vertically* structured and based on strict deference to *rank*. But modern states borrowed a normative principle from one of Philippe le Bel's unique innovations. The French king, instead of surrounding himself with grand aristocrats of exalted rank, ruled over France with advice from battalions of jurists. Philippe thus placed superior value on *expertise, performance* and *efficiency*. It could be argued, indeed, that Philippe le Bel's rule marked the birth of France's longstanding preference for government by *technocrats*.

Philippe le Bel's legacy – merging hierarchical status and functional expertise – was uniquely forward-looking. And yet it was not followed in other countries like Britain, where aristocratic elites rejected both capitalism and rational administration. Government in Britain was a monopoly controlled by high-born nobles, not experts. Britain's landed aristocracy generally disdained capitalism as "trade" and appropriated for itself the most powerful roles of state, army and Church.[5] In France, a centralized state took control of capitalistic enterprises through *dirigiste* intervention and trained technocrats to run its institutions, Britain, by contrast, maintained a time-honoured tradition of government by elitist "amateurs" educated at Oxford and Cambridge. This cultural difference possibly explains Britain's long resistance, until very recently, to MBA business schools and elite public administration schools, which in France stretch back to the 19th century. It might even be argued, interestingly, that it also explains the stark difference between French and English gardens: the former being formally designed according to strict rules of rigid geometry, the latter's wild and unruly indifference to regularity betraying the unmistakable hand of the amateur.

The legacy of this status tension still lingers in our values, attitudes and organizational biases. The evolution of two familiar professions – acting and athletics – provide interesting illustrations of how these tensions have evolved. Until the mid-19th century, acting was regarded in respectable social circles as a disreputable occupation and actors were not admitted into polite society. The theatre was considered sinful and people with stage careers were considered unfrequentable. On occasion, actresses became the mistresses of princes and kings; but this only reinforced the theatre's reputation as sinful.

After the advent of cinema and the Hollywood commercial machinery, the acting profession benefited from a status reversal. Today, actors rank among the most famous and admired personalities in the world. The actors who achieve the greatest fame are generally those whose films are commercial successes. Thus, the assignment of status is directly related to measures of economic *performance*. Many sports, in like manner, have evolved from "amateur" activities (still in force in the Olympics) to professional status with enormous financial rewards. In sport, as in acting, emoluments tend to be linked to quantifiable *performance* measures. Thus, star players are usually those who score the most goals, hit the most home-runs, win the most tournaments and so on. The world's top-seeded tennis player – a ranking based on tournament wins – usually makes more money and enjoys higher status than a player who is ranked 150th. Today, the world's best actors and athletes are judged according to the professional standards of performance.

It's a logical assumption that modern capitalism – like acting and athletics – has a strong bias in favour of performance. It would be churlish to suggest that capitalist enterprises are not motivated by efficiency maximization. And yet the realities of organizational behaviour compel us to confront a puzzling paradox, namely the persistence of entrenched reflexes in favour of ascriptive status, social position and other qualitative criteria incompatible with rational goals of expertise and efficiency. Many CEOs, to be sure, are highly remunerated for delivering excellent financial results; and many small, medium-sized and Fortune 500 companies are notably well-managed and achieve high levels of productivity and profitability. But as the ongoing debate about executive compensation amply demonstrates, if the emoluments of senior executives in salary, bonus, stock options and other perquisites were based on their firm's share price and/or profit performance, many would be abruptly shown the exit door.

How can we explain this paradox? The most obvious answer is that modern capitalists have inadequately studied the example of Philippe le Bel. Many corporations today still fail to make the status connection between values of ascriptive *position* and facts of measurable *performance*. To put it more bluntly, too many executives with impressive business cards, lucrative compensation packages and impeccable social connections are not producing optimal results in the organizations they lead. Corporations seem to be socially designed with inefficiency built into their status hierarchies.

There are, of course, *cultural* differences that influence attitudes towards ascriptive rank in organizations. In cultures that are relatively homogenous and characterized by values of conformity, bureaucratic settings tend to be rigidly hierarchical with clearly defined and understood roles. These so-called "tight" cultures – notably in Asia – impose strict behavioural norms that limit individual autonomy. In "loose" cultures – particularly Anglo-American countries – hierarchies are less rigid, individual autonomy less constricted and social mobility more likely.[6] While "tight" cultures, with their greater emphasis on conformity, may be more efficient in manufacturing sectors where individual autonomy is not functionally valued, "loose" cultures tend to foster greater potential efficiency optimization through informal collaboration. There are, at the same time, cultural differences within Western cultures regarding *social-capital* effects on performance. American executives, for example, are more accustomed than French managers to working in porous bureaucratic environments that allow for networked exchanges outside the company. French bureaucracies, due to France's inductive intellectual tradition that inhibits pragmatism, are generally more regulated, hierarchical environments with absolute notions of authority. Anglo-American managers, by contrast, are open to taking much more pragmatic approaches to problem-solving. This explains why American executives tend to work in "loose" networks, while French managers – as rogue trader Jerome Kerviel learned – are accustomed to "dense" networks based on common values learned in elitist schools, state planning agencies and state-owned firms.[7] We're back to our horticultural analogy: loosely informal versus rigidly geometric gardens.

Allowing for these cultural factors, it can still be said that *ascriptive* forms of social capital sometimes undermine rational organizational goals of performance and efficiency. Management studies consistently demonstrate that people in organizations who are regarded as benefitting from impressively diverse and dense social connections are invariably more popular and respected than those who are viewed as possessing less social capital. In a word, *well-connected* people get more respect than people without impressive connections – even in the absence of objective measures of actual *competence*. In fact, there is a definite tendency to confuse the two in ways that show a bias in favour of ascriptive status. Studies show that people who are regarded as having prominent friends generally benefit from enhanced *performance reputations* and are considered to be *influential*. This finding makes an interesting connection between status and performance: people within organizations who benefit from ascriptive status are not only highly esteemed, they are also regarded, *ipso facto*, as top performers.[8]

This value-based status/performance linkage – the impression that high-status, well-connected people are highly competent – confirms another organizational behaviour syndrome summed up by the following phrase: "It's not what you *do*, but who you *are*." To express this reflex in familiar terms, people tend to believe that because someone has "Executive Vice President" on his/her business card and is known to be well-connected inside and outside an organization, they must be competent, respected and influential. Such people therefore enjoy high-status reputations, even in the absence of measurable evidence. To express it inversely, the higher a manager's social status, the less likely he/she will encounter negative opinions. Studies have indeed found that, when questionable conduct or deviant behaviour is attributed to both well-connected senior executives and lower-ranking marginal employees, the former can count on more indulgent reactions whereas the latter are invariably judged more severely.[9]

Let's express this status tension in Web 2.0 language. If a junior employee keeps a blog on which he slags off the company's strategy, nobody will be surprised when he's disciplined or dismissed. But if the CEO of the same company causes offense to numerous employees in a corporate blog, or in comments to the media, few are surprised when the affront goes unsanctioned. In sum, managers have an incentive to accumulate social capital, and benefit from its status rewards, in order to enhance their performance reputations and strengthen their positions within an organization. It shouldn't be surprising, therefore, to learn that this is precisely what many senior managers do, instinctively, if not by calculation.

Few will be alarmed by the above observations, for they confirm what is generally known and widely accepted. Another phenomenon of organizational behaviour, however, will be regarded as somewhat more troubling. It's the answer to the following question: "Who's really sharing?"

Most agree that information-sharing in organizations optimizes decision-making rationality because it maximizes the number of inputs into problem-solving exercises. Decision theory experts call this "perfect information". It may be impossible to achieve, as a practical matter, but most intelligent managers seek to maximize information inputs before taking a decision. This fact, on the surface, seems to make a rational case for information-sharing in organizations. In reality, however, information *withholding* is a fact of everyday life in most complex organizations.

We know, furthermore, that some people are more likely to share, or withhold, information than others. The findings here are paradoxical, and yet not surprising given the basic facts of human nature. Studies show that those in possession of genuine expertise in organizations are more likely to promote information-sharing than nonexperts. Put simply, people who know what they're talking about don't mind sharing what they know. They indeed may actively desire to share their knowledge in order to gain status, build goodwill or simply allow others to benefit from their expertise. This confirms Malcolm Gladwell's observation in *The Tipping Point* about how experts – or "mavens" – actively share their specialized knowledge.

Now here's the problem. In organizations where senior managers owe their positions to ascriptive advantages of *rank*, instead of *expertise*, it is more likely that they will create structures that frustrate information-sharing. In other words, nonexpert managers who are more preoccupied with values of vertical *status* are more likely to knowingly withhold important facts, and thus frustrate "perfect information", in order to protect their own positions. The classic example of this syndrome is familiar to anybody who has worked in management: the senior executive who briefs colleagues on a particular issue without giving them the "whole picture". The knock-on effect for the organization is nonoptimal decision-making due to "discussion biases" that frame issues without the benefit of all information inputs.[10]

Why is such nonoptimal behaviour so pervasive in so many organizations? An easy answer might point to the human proclivity to protect one's own interests and promote one's own status – commonly called "protecting one's ass". Most managers in complex organizations don't like open, transparent and horizontal networks because, frankly, they are threatening. Openly sharing information for the benefit of the organization as a whole is not a widespread human reflex. Most people like to work and share information exclusively with people they know, like and trust – especially if they have a history of reciprocal favours. Given a choice between working with someone they *like* or someone who is *competent*, most people choose the former – even if the person they like has no particular expertise.

This fascinating hypothesis was demonstrated in a *Harvard Business Review* paper called "Competent Jerks, Lovable Fools, and the Formation of Social Networks." The authors started with an assertion that seemed unimpeachably rational: when colleagues are tasked with solving a complex problem, they naturally have an interest in calling on others whose *expertise* makes them most qualified to collaborate. This seems logical ten times out of ten. But here's the surprise: the answer is no. People invariably choose *likeability* over *ability*. In most organizations, employees prefer to work with others who share their own values, attitudes and ways of thinking – even if they don't possess any demonstrated competence. Even, indeed, if they are more or less incompetent. Conversely, employees tend to avoid, and marginalize, those who are considered unpleasant – even if they possess excellent technical expertise that could be indispensible to solve a problem. In sum, *loveable fools* are more popular in organizations than *competent jerks*. This explains why so many unlikely people get invited to meetings. Take a closer look: there's a good chance they're loveable fools. Competent jerks, by contrast, are rigorously kept out of the loop. True, most prefer to work with a *loveable star*, and nobody wants to work with an *incompetent jerk*. But given the choice between a *loveable fool* and a *competent jerk*, the former invariably gets selected.[11]

This finding, clearly, can have serious implications for organizational performance and efficiency. First of all, the tendency towards *homophily* – working with "people like us" – creates an echo-chamber syndrome where managers hear only the familiar reverberation of their own biases. Echo chambers, we know, frustrate innovation and creativity because they discourage openness to change – sometimes referred to as "out-of-the-box" thinking. Echo chambers are heavily biased in favour of the status quo. The exclusion of competent jerks means that valuable expertise goes untapped. Also, when knowledge and expertise are unrecognized and unrewarded, the result is often low employee morale due to the general perception that the organization is run by a closed clique of incompetent managers. The winners, in the short term, are the entrenched managers who like the sound of their own voices – and keep their jobs. The losers, in the long term, almost assuredly are investors. Loveable fools may be fun to hang around with, but they are rarely good for shareholder value.

The "Competent Jerks, Lovable Fools" authors offer a remedy based largely on "human relations" strategies aimed at boosting the status of employees. The answer: *leverage the likeable* and *work on the jerk*. Sounds pithy. It assumes, however, that competent jerks actually require reforming. It may be just possible, though, that the real problem is elsewhere. It may reside, for example, in the selfish institutional interests of a tight management clique who jealously arrogate for themselves the power to confer positive and negative status. More fundamentally, the problem may find its origins in the basic value structure of an organization that assigns higher status to *ascribed position* than to *expert performance*. Maybe the jerk doesn't need to be worked on – but promoted.

There is a vast body of management literature that takes this same HR approach, treating people in organizations as a "problem" while ignoring more fundamental issues related to status values. The proliferation of How-To management books frequently fall into this category. Many of these tomes spoon-feed easy-to-digest advice, sprinkled with trendy buzzwords, on how to tackle the "problem people" challenge. While some recognize that bureaucratic values are the source of people problems, few offer prescriptions that challenge core assumptions inside status hierarchies. They instead focus on individuals, often taking a quasi-psychiatric approach to organizational behaviour. Solutions consequently emphasize the need to *energize* and *motivate* difficult employees categorized into intriguing archetypes like "Queen Bees", "Wanabees" and "Afraid to Bees". Sometimes the diagnosis is more brutal. Marsha Petrie Sue's book, *Toxic People: Decontaminating Difficult People at Work Without Using Weapons or Duct Tape*, classifies "toxic" employees into six recognizable pigeon holes: Backstabbers, Steamrollers, Know-it-Alls, Zipper Lips, Needy Weenies and Whine and Cheesers.[12] We've all met these people at some point in our careers.

The *problem people* approach is undoubtedly intriguing, even entertaining, and sometimes contains valuable insights into behaviour in workplace bureaucracies. This kind of analysis, however, remains trapped in existing *hierarchical* structures. While employees may feel better about being motivated or energized, they still remain prisoners of the same organizational environment. A more fruitful approach would be looking into the dynamics of organizational structure to locate status tensions that so frequently frustrate communication, undermine optimal decision-making and thwart the achievement of corporate goals. Let's put it in a very colloquial manner. It's not people – it's the *structure*, stupid.

Let's briefly examine four structural models that provide comparative insights into the point we are making: *traditional hierarchies, flat structures, virtual corporations* and *network organizations*.

First, the traditional bureaucratic hierarchy, which emerged in the United States in the late 19th century to manage complex corporate organizations, is the familiar top-down pyramid structure. Managerial control is centralized and the workplace environment is heavily regulated. Status in traditional hierarchies is ascriptively assigned according to *rank*. These structures are generally *low-trust* environments. Employees are considered to be motivated chiefly by *extrinsic* factors, mainly *homo œconomicus* incentives in the form of salaries.[13]

Second, flat structures push decision-making either up or down by eliminating middle-management layers. The two main advantages of the flat organizational model are increased information-flow efficiency and reduced costs. Cost reduction by eliminating middle management layers requires no explanation. Information flow in flat organizations is more efficient for two reasons: first, it's not slowed down by multiple layers of bureaucracy; and second, it doesn't get distorted, sidetracked or simply buried by managers with their own agendas. Flat organizations are generally *high-trust* environments due to their decentralized structures. Napoleon, for example, organized his *Grande Armée* into a flat command structure: its 150 000 soldiers were divided into six autonomous corps commanded by roughly 20 officers each. It was Napoleon's shrewd choice of a flexible decision-making system that led to France's great military victories in the campaigns of 1806–1807.

Third, the virtual corporation is a variation of the flat structure. But whereas flat organizations push authority up or down, virtual corporations move decision-making to the margins and beyond their boundaries. The motivation for doing so is related to *transaction costs*. Because transactional costs outside a firm's boundaries are dramatically reduced by information technology, many corporations no longer need to maintain expensive bureaucratic units for these transactional functions. They therefore contract out commodity-like functions and products. Virtual corporations are characterized by high levels of trust between company and contractor.[14]

Finally, the network organization takes the logic of the virtual organization one step further by eliminating hierarchy altogether. The social architecture of the network organization is essentially medieval: absence of central regulating authority, multilayered zones of sovereignty, horizontally structured power relations. Or as Francis Fukuyama and Abram Shulsky put it in their book on the *Virtual Corporation*, a networked corporate structure has "no sovereign source of authority; all of the members of the organisation cooperate with one another on a more or less equal basis."[15] Network organizations are generally characterized by *informal trust networks*. Instead of *homo œconomicus* employees responding to extrinsic pecuniary incentives, they are *intrinsically* motivated based on personal satisfaction. The advantage of network organizations is their adaptiveness and capacity to innovate when faced with change and uncertainty. The network organization, in that respect, is like the Internet – lacking a controlling centre but functioning as a platform for collaboration, innovation and creativity.

The contrast between traditional hierarchies and network organizations can have powerful ramifications for organizational behaviour. Traditional hierarchies are low-trust environments in which status is assigned according to values of vertical *rank*. Network organizations, on the other hand, operate horizontally according to values of informal trust and assign status *democratically* according to *performance*.

Now ask yourself: which kind of organization would you choose to work in?

Network organizations, needless to say, are the natural habitat of Web 2.0 social media. The literature and case-study work on knowledge-based collaboration – from Harvard professor Andrew McAfee's published and blogged analysis to Don Tapscott's book *Wikinomics* – is rich in insights.[16] As we shall see in Chapter 14 on Enterprise 2.0, social media – blogs, wikis, social networks, mashups, social bookmarking, RSS feeds – can effectively supersede existing knowledge management systems. Enterprise 2.0 social tools are different from existing enterprise software in one crucial way: whereas traditional software tools impose structure prior to use, social media tools empower users as a priority and let the structure emerge from functional requirements. The e-ruptive impact on existing structures is obvious. Deployed in organizations, Web 2.0 software constructs open-ended platforms on which, in theory, everybody is equal. Collaboration is a horizontal democracy, not a vertical hierarchy – and status rewards are distributed accordingly. The person who has the winning brainwave might be a low-level employee working in the bowels of the company (possibly playing *World of Warcraft*); or may be a customer located outside of the corporate walls.

Logically, Web 2.0 should be a no-brainer. In a perfectly rational world, shareholders should be clamouring for the deployment of Web 2.0 tools in the corporations they own. Corporate directors, too, should be pushing executive management to get with the programme and implement social media solutions without further delay – or face the consequences of failing to do so. The problem, however, is that we don't live in a perfectly rational world. In fact, organizations have been on this corporate merry-go-round before.

The end of vertical bureaucracy was trumpeted several decades ago by Alvin Toffler, who in his groundbreaking book, *Future Shock*, predicted that archaic corporate bureaucracies would be replaced by dynamic horizontal *adhocracies*. At the end of the counter-culture

1960s when Toffler's book was an international bestseller, this was exciting stuff. Toffler's concept of *adhocracy* captured the spirit of the times. Adhocracy was proclaimed as a new form of organization that would kick down bureaucratic walls and bring people together to capture opportunities and find innovative solutions.[17]

In the wake of Toffler's exhilarating forecasts, techno-hype about how information technology would soon revolutionize knowledge management in organizations continued throughout the 1970s and 1980s. In 1988, management consultant Robert Schrank made this prediction: "In the workplace, knowledge is power. Knowledge that used to be proprietary information is now available to anyone who knows how to call it up."

Jim Maxmin, CEO of British conglomerate Thorn EMI, agreed. "The old-style corporation, with a fixed hierarchy of authority and information flow, is becoming a dinosaur," said Maxmin, whose EMI music unit had included The Beatles, The Rolling Stones, Pink Floyd and Queen. Looking towards the 1990s, Maxmin made the following prediction: "In the last decade, excellence in business meant doing one thing well. In the decade to come, though, you'll have to do everything well, and do it everywhere. The image of the corporation as a pyramid is dead. The new corporation will be more like a holo-gram, with shared information making each person, each part, contain the whole."[18]

This vision found eloquent expression in a 1988 book, *In the Age of the Smart Machine*, by Harvard business professor Shoshana Zuboff, who described how information technology was leading to new net-worked forms of corporate organization. Zuboff, who also happened to be Jim Maxmin's wife, was a leading evangelist in the 1980s for the new-age vision of computer-based technology toppling old forms of corporate hierarchies and encouraging horizontal information flows and power-sharing among employees.[19]

After the Internet exploded in the 1990s, the visionary techno-optimism began spreading to areas like workplace ecology. Trumpet-ing this vision, author Malcolm Gladwell published a fascinating *New Yorker* article, "Designs for Working", in which he explained to readers "why your bosses want to turn your new office into Greenwich Village". The office as hip, spontaneous, urban streetscape had defi-nite appeal. Gladwell asked: "Who, after all, has a direct interest in creating vital spaces that foster creativity and serendipity?" His answer: "Employers do".[20]

Oh no they don't. Gladwell may be proved right one day. But since his article appeared in 2000, corporate managers have not exactly been stampeding to embrace a "social" vision of the workplace. Neither have they embraced Zuboff's vision of a networked workplace. In fact, a decade after her book first appeared Zuboff acknowledged: "The paradise of shared knowledge and a more egalitarian working environment just isn't happening. Knowledge isn't really shared because management doesn't want to share authority and power."[21] In 2003, Zuboff and husband Jim Maxmin published a new book, *The Support Economy: Why Corporations Are Failing Individuals and the Next Episode of Capitalism*, which argued that the potential of information technology failed because of resistance by the corrupted culture of "managerial capitalism".[22]

"Managers are at the centre, preoccupied with their own interests," said Zuboff. "But their path has become corrupted, they are insulated and have become a source of governance catastrophes." Despite institutionalized resistance to technology e-ruptions, Zuboff remains confident that a new form of networked capitalism is on the horizon now that power is shifting from producers to consumers. "People have opinions, they want choices – they are not like their parents and grandparents who had certain roles to play," she says.[23]

Don Tapscott, an articulate Web 2.0 evangelist and mass collaboration advocate, nonetheless remains realistic about the threats it represents. "Mass collaboration can empower a growing cohort of connected individuals and organizations to create extraordinary wealth and reach unprecedented heights in learning and scientific discovery," Tapscott and co-author Anthony Williams noted in *Wikinomics*. They added, however, that "the new participation will also cause great upheaval, dislocation and danger for societies, corporations and individuals that fail to keep up with the relentless change."[24] This declaration, scary stuff for any corporate executive, almost precisely echoes Alvin Toffler's bold predictions nearly forty years earlier. So is the e-ruption for real this time?

For Web 2.0 sceptics, the *fear factor* should never be underestimated. Deployment of social media like blogs and wikis may be great for employee satisfaction and shareholder value, but they threaten entrenched status hierarchies. Web 2.0 tools blow up corporate silos, knock down bureaucratic walls, drain organizational moats and swamps. Many corporate executives, far from seeing the tremendous potential of Web 2.0 for productivity, innovation, communication and recruitment, still regard social media as a time-wasting distraction for employees spending most of the day on YouTube, Facebook and LinkedIn.[25]

For Web 2.0 optimists, there's reason to be more optimistic today than in the post-*Future Shock* generation twenty or thirty years ago. After early reticence in many companies, Web 2.0 tools are enjoying increased buy-in at Fortune 500 corporations. As the Economist Intelligent Unit put it in a 2007 report called *Serious Business: Web 2.0 Goes Corporate*: "Why are large corporations interested in what many see as no more than the latest dot-com fad? The answer is growth and profitability." Some 80% of executives surveyed by *The Economist* said they regarded Web 2.0 information sharing and peer collaboration as an opportunity to increase revenue and margins. As a top executive at Citigroup put it: "Internally we have started using wikis for knowledge management in large projects where there is lots of terminology or processes to be followed. Anything that helps collaboration helps us."[26] If these statements are genuine, and based on concrete plans to aggressively roll out Web 2.0 tools, maybe the revolution is for real. If so, here come the competent jerks.

Let's say Web 2.0 tools do take off. Why would employees feel motivated to participate in an open-communication system and spend time collaborating with people they don't know?

Good question. One answer is organizational citizenship. Just as people deal honestly in commercial transactions if they believe in the overall integrity of the capitalist system, in corporations employees will collaborate openly with others if they feel *intrinsically* motivated by positive attitudes towards the organization.[27] In a word, if employees share organizational *values*. In healthy organizations, *loyalty* is a precondition to working toward corporate objectives; without loyalty, a second option is *exit*.

Another answer is that people will collaborate if there are *incentives* for them to do so. People respond to status rewards, especially if they know the system is fair; in sum, if *status* and *prestige* incentives are built into the collaborative process and rewards are distributed according to *performance*. Or as *Cluetrain Manifesto*'s 50th thesis puts it, when respect is accorded to *hands-on knowledge*, not abstract authority.

When rigid status hierarchies finally come crashing down, it won't be long before a 40th-level half-elf in *World of Warcraft* will be a top-performing CEO in a network organization – and enjoying status benefits that are richly deserved.

9

Everyone's a critic: ratings and rankings

If Generation V can be defined by any single behaviour trait, it's their cultural obsession with ratings and rankings. The same Gen V kids who, a decade ago, were rating Pokémon players are now logged onto social networking sites feverishly rating and ranking their favourite songs, movies, TV shows, photos, comic books, celebrities, you name it. Life in Gen V is instantaneous mass democracy, constantly self-updating, rendering verdicts on just about everything.

It's no coincidence that this obsession has emerged at a time when "Google is God". The popular Web search engine's success is owed to its powerfully efficient page-*ranking* system based on a proprietary Google algorithm. Google itself describes its PageRank system as relying on "the uniquely *democratic* nature of the Web by using its vast link structure as an indicator of an individual page's value."[1]

Gen V's rating and ranking culture also takes inspiration from video games. In *World of Warcraft*, players are ranked according to a strict "honour" system that awards points according to levels of achievement, usually related to killing other players. The attribution of honour is thus related to *performance*. The inspiration from medieval chivalry is obvious, not only in *World of Warcraft* but in many role-playing games where skills are deployed in a frenetic quest to achieve higher rankings. Video games like *Knights of Honour* and *Crusader Kings* are virtual versions of medieval social mythology.

During the Middle Ages, the highly formalized ritual of knightly jousts – a medieval forerunner to modern mass-audience stadium sports – was an elaborate spectacle whose outcome served the function of sorting out ranking and status. These mêlée tournaments, which began in France in the 12th century, were judged by standards of skill and performance that *World of Warcraft* replicated eight centuries later. Medieval jousts also produced the biggest superstars of medieval Christendom. By far the most famous was William Marshal, whose jousting skills were so awesome that barons, counts and dukes jockeyed to claim his friendship. So famous was Marshal that, in 1189, Richard the Lionheart ennobled him as an earl and married him off, at age 43, to England's second richest heiress, 17-year-old Isabel de Clare. As the Earl of Pembroke, Marshal was King John's point man during the Magna Carta negotiations with rebellious barons. When Marshal died in 1219, his wishes to be buried as a Knight Templar were respected. His effigy can still be seen today in London's Temple Church.[2] Interestingly, the highest rank in *World of Warcraft* is "Grand Marshal".

Rating and ranking, to be sure, is hardly a mania exclusive to online virtual worlds. We live in a world where everything is rated and ranked. *Billboard* ranks best-selling songs. *Variety* lists rankings for Hollywood movies according to box-office receipts. Every self-respecting newspaper publishes a bestseller list for books. Neilson rates television shows in ranked order according to millions of viewers. *Fortune* and *Forbes* publish lists of the world's top corporations and richest people. *Business Week* and *Financial Times* rank MBA schools. Every year, *People* announces with great fanfare the identity of the "Sexiest Man Alive". Best-dressed and worst-dressed, who's hot and who's not, thumbs up and thumbs down – our cultural obsession with ratings and ranking is pervasive.

But online ratings and rankings are different. Traditional media select a small number of "experts" who, as intermediary taste gatekeepers, rate and rank products and services. Think of newspapers: they hire battalions of pundits and critics who rate music, movies, books, food, holiday spots and other consumer products. We, as consumers, are asked to defer to their expertise, even when they possess none. On social networking sites, by contrast, judges are not preselected cliques of taste gatekeepers; they are millions of people worldwide stating their opinion directly. Social media, in short, harness the power of collective smarts, mass intelligence and the wisdom of crowds.

The superstardom of pop diva Leona Lewis demonstrates the wisdom of crowds – namely that, as the book of that title asserts, *the many are smarter than the few*.[3] Lewis was an unknown receptionist with a great singing voice from London's working class Hackney district when, in December 2006, she won Britain's massively popular televised talent contest, "The X-Factor". After her victory, Lewis's song "A Moment Like This", was downloaded 50 000 times in thirty minutes. A little more than a year later, in early 2008, Lewis's debut album, *Spirit*, rocketed to number one on the US *Billboard* charts. Today Lewis – who is frequently compared with Mariah Carey – is an international superstar. She owes her phenomenal success and celebrity not to a music label executive who discovered her talent (as was the case for Mariah Carey), but rather to millions of British kids who voted for her on their mobile phones. True, shows like "X-Factor" – and "American Idol" in the US and "Nouvelle Star" in France – feature professional juries who give their views. But in the final analysis, it's the masses who vote for budding stars like Leona Lewis.

To understand the e-ruptive consequences of this technology-empowered form of democratic plebiscite, let's examine how traditional rating and ranking systems work – or rather, why they don't work. When discussing ratings and rankings, we should note, it's actually shorthand that neglects another R: *reviewing*. The three general types of selection systems are: *reviews, ratings* and *rankings*.

First, *reviews* provide subjective evaluations that facilitate choices between multiple options. These options can range from products and services to politicians. The former compete for our disposable income, the latter for our votes. A review is an *opinion* based on either personal experience (movie, book, CD, restaurant, holiday location) or considered judgement (politician).

Second, *ratings* generally assign a "grade" – often using a five-star system – to a product or service. The *Michelin Guide* is a traditional, and prestigious, form of ratings for restaurants and hotels. A three-star Michelin rating for a restaurant can catapult its name to world-wide fame; and a demotion in the guide's star ratings can destroy its fortunes. A five-star hotel creates certain expectations about luxury and quality of service – and price, too. Sometimes movie, music and restaurant reviews are accompanied by a rating.

Third, *rankings* introduce a comparative element into ratings. A democratic election is, in essence, a form of ranking. The politician who wins is ranked first, beating other competitors. Singer Leona Lewis was ranked number 1 in the audience-based election on "X-Factor". Product reviews can be ranked according to price, value and other criteria.

Old "push" media – newspapers, magazines, radio, television networks – hire critics to review, rate and rank everything from books and movies to restaurants and personal hygiene products. In many cases, as noted, these hand-picked pundits cannot make any legitimate claim to particular expertise. They nonetheless write up reviews with a pretence to authority, recommending which movies to go and see, which restaurants to frequent, which books are must-reads, which fashion accessories are must-haves, and so forth. The marketing and advertising industry not only finances this institutionalized system of taste gatekeeping, it also validates its legitimacy by citing reviews and ratings (like a movie critic's "rave") in their publicity campaigns.

Now let's ask a provocative question: why do advertisers, who generate the bulk of revenues for media outlets, continue to bankroll a ratings and ranking system that has such little claim on genuine expertise? If advertisers had faith in the wisdom of crowds, they would be shifting their budgets towards niche websites, blogs and other social media where much more accurate and reliable product ratings are available to everybody. It might be asked, indeed, why newspapers and magazines even hire movie, TV, book and restaurant critics in the first place. It would make economic sense to move those costs off their books and open up their websites to reviews written by their readers. If the wisdom of crowds theorem is correct, and the many are indeed always smarter than the few, not only would newspapers and magazines be reducing costs, they would also be providing a better service to their customers.

Sounds like a no-brainer, right? No doubt about it – except for one factor. Advertisers are suspicious of *democracy*.

The global advertising industry is a multi-billion-dollar marketing machine that invests massively in PR blitzkriegs directed at journalists, frequently in the form of inducements known familiarly as "freebies". In a business where there's no such thing as a free lunch, freebies are proffered in the expectation of a returned favour. Freebies make ratings and rankings more predictable. Sometimes they are not even necessary. Marketing and PR professionals belong to the same socio-professional class as journalists. They are all, by definition, gatekeepers whose function is to intermediate consumer choices about product purchases. In short, journalists, marketing professionals and advertising executives belong to the same socio-professional *oligarchy*. And oligarchies, as a rule, are not energetic advocates of democracy – especially when their own livelihoods are at stake. Direct democracy, on the other hand, is devilishly difficult to manage. It's much easier for the advertising-media oligarchy to operate in a closed world that produces predictable results, managing internal conflict as it arises.

The problem, however, is that sometimes democratic groundswells – as history amply demonstrates – are impossible to hold back. This occurs when the masses are not only disenchanted, but empowered with the weapons of *voice*. The Internet, as everyone knows, has empowered consumers with information they need to make rational choices. They don't have to buy newspapers and magazines, watch television or listen to the radio for information about products. They now have options. In fact, they can be journalists and critics themselves. They can even be producers. Consumers indeed are increasingly turning to *user-generated* ratings instead of relying on taste gatekeepers from the established media oligarchy. When this democratic e-ruption starts to gain momentum, advertisers will start to follow, even if it means breaking up stable socio-professional relations in old cliques. The democratic e-ruption will have been too powerful to contain.

Forrester Research published a study in early 2008 that bears out this trend. Based on a survey of 5000 respondents, Forrester asked consumers what they wanted most from commercial websites in four selected industries (consumer electronics, travel, banking and media). A large majority of 64% ranked *user ratings and reviews* at the top. Consumer-generated ratings were ranked higher than special offers (61%) and price-comparison tools (59%). Nearly half of those surveyed (49%) said they wanted more customer testimonials.[4] These findings confirmed the results of a Deloitte & Touche survey, which polled more than 3300 American consumers aged 17 and over on similar questions. Over 60% said they read online user reviews, and among that group more than 80% said they had been "directly influenced" by online ratings when making purchasing decisions. Also, some 69% said they had shared online reviews with friends, family members or colleagues.

This trend will produce e-ruptive consequences for established oligarchies. As Pat Conroy, head of Deloitte's US consumer products group, put it: "This increasing market transparency can adversely impact the margins, market share and brand equity of consumer product companies. In the past, clever marketers and advertisers shaped brands, but now consumers are increasingly empowered, everyone has a voice, and information and opinions are instantly dispersed."[5]

In the online world, our three Rs will be turned on their head. We won't need taste gatekeepers to review, rate and rank for us.

It's already happening. Sites like Epinions, ReviewCentre, Ciao and Dooyoo already feature reviews about virtually every kind of product and service. There are also niche sites – like SputnikMusic for teenage music buffs – featuring thousands of user-generated reviews. And online retailers like Amazon embed customer reviews into consumer selections as they search for products. In the hotel industry, sites like TripAdvisor encourage customers to review and rate their travel and holiday experiences. TripAdvisor's slogan is: "Get the truth. Then go". For ratings, sites like YahooShopping provide "Merchant Reviews" that include a five-star system in categories such as *price, shipping options, delivery, ease of purchase* and *customer service*. Also, online merchants like Amazon and eBay invite customers to rate their service performance and that of third-party commercial partners. For *rankings*, sites like Shopping.com, YahooShopping, Froogle and Shopzilla rank a wide variety of products according to established criteria. And if you select a product on Amazon, you can immediately see its popularity ranking according to sales. The difference in the online world is that information comes from millions of consumers.

Amazon is undoubtedly the online retailer best known for its customer reviews, ratings and rankings. It uses sophisticated "collaborative filtering" software to provide customers with useful information. Collaborative filtering, in its retail commercial applications, is a complex term for something quite simple: an item-based *recommendation* system that connects like-minded consumers with similar tastes. If you log onto Amazon and click to purchase Leona Lewis's record, *Spirit*, you'll see pop up on your screen a "Recommendation List" composed of other products purchased, or viewed, by customers who also bought the same Leona Lewis record. Amazon's recommendations algorithms can mine much more sophisticated data – such as demographic profiles – but the basic function is to connect clusters of customers based on similar tastes and purchasing habits. It's also a highly effective revenue driver, generating impressive "click through" and "conversion" rates that stimulate purchases.[6]

In the real world, as we have seen, the *commercial* function of recommending is performed by "critics" who work largely for traditional media outlets like newspapers. The *social* function of recommending is performed by so-called "Connectors", as Malcolm Gladwell calls them in *The Tipping Point*.[7] Connectors work on a word-of-mouth basis, using their influence to get the word out. Collaborative filtering makes the traditional role of the critic redundant. It if doesn't quite put Connectors out of work, collaborate filtering makes them largely unnecessary. In fact, it could be argued that collaborative filtering performs the function of all three of Gladwell's social types: Mavens, Connectors and Salesmen. Thanks to collaborative filtering, the review/rating/ranking process is opened up and made more *democratic*. Everybody gets to participate. And the results are displayed directly on your computer screen. Amazon, flush with success, is pushing its sales strategy more deeply into "social shopping" through new software applications that leverage *network effects* on social networking sites. On Facebook, for example, members who add the "Amazon Giver" application to their profile can view the Amazon "wish lists" of their online friends. eBay also offers software applications to Facebook and MySpace members so they can track bidding and make purchases.[8]

Ratings and rankings systems have not been exempt from criticism and controversy. The key to all social interaction, needless to say, is *trust*. The same rule applies to socially based commercial transactions. In the real world, if you are going to act on the advice of a Maven, Connector or Salesman, you must first trust their opinion. If there is no trust, the social function fails. In the online world, it's equally imperative that users *trust* sophisticated software systems that guide their choices. Direct democracy works only when the process is transparent. Any sign of opacity, bias or incomplete information suggests corruption. When this happens, the entire system is discredited and *loyalty* suffers. People opt for *voice* or *exit* to protest their dissatisfaction.

Some argue that online recommendation systems, notably Amazon's, are dysfunctional because, as we noted in Chapter 7, they have a built-in bias towards promoting "blockbuster" products. This would appear to contradict the "long tail" commercial logic of online retailers offering vast inventories of niche products appealing to a wide diversity of tastes. Yet, as a Wharton Business School study discovered, Amazon and other online retailers tend to reinforce the blockbuster logic of media markets because their recommendations are based on consumer *sales* and *ratings*. This system is perfectly democratic. But as the Wharton authors noted, blockbuster products, not niche offerings, generally benefit from the highest sales and ratings. "Thus these recommenders create a rich-get-richer effect for popular products and vice versa for unpopular ones," noted the study.[9]

This finding about blockbuster tendencies echoes Tocqueville's main misgiving about democratic political systems – namely *tyranny of the majority*. Tocqueville observed, after his voyage to the young American republic in the 1830s, that "the moral authority of the majority is partly based on the notion that there is more intelligence and wisdom in a number of men united than a single individual, and that the number of legislators is more important than their quality."

Tocqueville's observation was, as a practical matter, pure "wisdom of crowds" in democratic action. Yet the French aristocrat was concerned that, in democratic societies, differences of opinion are not readily tolerated. Interestingly, Tocqueville took comfort in the fact that America's absence of an aristocracy was compensated by the rise of powerful professional classes – notably lawyers. He believed that lawyers would act as a buffer against democratic tyranny.

"In a community in which lawyers are allowed to occupy without opposition that high station which naturally belongs to them, their general spirit will be eminently conservative and anti-democratic," noted Tocqueville, adding that lawyers "are the most powerful existing security against the excesses of democracy."

Most American lawyers today would not likely confess to feeling emboldened by Tocqueville's endorsement. Yet he was making a valid point about the social role of intermediaries and gatekeepers. Tocqueville was describing a republican democracy in the early 19th century. Today, lawyers and MPs are joined by journalists, television producers, publishers, advertisers and marketing executives that make up the oligarchy of taste gatekeepers who intermediate between supply and demand in the marketplace. Their self-arrogation of oligarchic power serves as a buffer against the will of the majority. Tocqueville undoubtedly would have been satisfied to observe today that, no matter how powerful the forces of direct democracy, elites invariably find a way to assert their intermediary power as selectors, filterers and packagers of how we behave, what we buy and for whom we vote.

This tension between oligarchy and democracy e-rupted recently in Britain, where the anti-democratic professionals were not lawyers, but television producers. The entire UK television industry is still going through a painful soul-searching ordeal following a series of vote-rigging scandals that afflicted popular contest shows, including *The X Factor* which launched the career of pop diva Leona Lewis.

In early 2007, after media reports about vote-rigging and other irregularities on British contest shows, the major UK networks were under tremendous pressure to clean up their acts. The private ITV network asked Deloitte to conduct an investigation into allegations about institutionalized irregularities on some of its most popular shows. Deloitte's findings were shocking. It discovered that *The X Factor* and other shows were guilty of a chronic pattern of deliberate deceptions and technical blunders during phone-in talent contests and televised competitions. *The X Factor*, for example, had received thousands of phone-in votes that were never counted. Even worse,

ITV had been systematically overcharging premium rates for SMS and red-button viewer voting in order to drive up its own revenues. For the contest won by Leona Lewis, viewers had been overcharged by about $400 000. ITV executives also admitted that, in total, they'd extorted roughly $16 million in premium phone-in rates for worthless votes that were never counted.

The Deloitte findings were so serious that they triggered a government inquiry by the Serious Fraud Office. ITV, meanwhile, was facing as much as $140 million in fines for fraudulently charging viewers premium phone-in rates for faked contests.[10] ITV's chairman, Michael Grade, abjectly apologized for the phone-in scandals and promised to reimburse viewers who took part in rigged votes. "This is not an attempt to hide anything or excuse anything," he said. "This is a full confession". Grade blamed the irregularities on a "serious cultural failure within ITV".[11]

ITV wasn't the only British television network to flout the rules of direct democracy. The scandals were even worse at the venerable BBC. During one of the public network's children's shows, BBC producers had hastily enlisted a child visiting the network's studios to pose as a phone-in competition winner, even though some 40 000 children had called the show's premium-rate phone line in the hope of winning a toy. The government watchdog, Ofcom, fined the BBC $100 000 for this incident. Even more ridiculous, the BBC was found guilty of breach of trust for disregarding the votes cast by thousands of children to name the cat on the set of popular kids' show, *Blue Peter*. Viewers had overwhelmingly voted to call the fluffy white cat "Cookie", but the show's producers discarded the vote's results and decided that the cat would instead be called "Socks".

These BBC fakery scandals led to some 25 staffers being dismissed or disciplined, including the resignation of two senior executives. The *Blue Peter* producer behind the "Socks" cock-up was sacked.[12] The BBC's director-general, Mark Thompson, was forced to make a humiliating confession in a corporate blog posting. "Letting down the children who watch 'Blue Peter' and who trust it implicitly is a truly terrible idea – even if all that is at stake is the difference between calling a cat 'Cookie' or 'Socks'", wrote Thompson. His blog post, entitled "Trust and Values", featured a photo of the adorable blue-eyed kitten at the centre of the controversy.[13]

These scandals were only the tip of the iceberg. It quickly became apparent that fakery scams, fraud, extortion and arrogant attitudes towards viewers were endemic throughout the entire British television industry. Channel 4, long considered a quality network, was fined $4 million for gouging viewers on premium call-in shows. Channel 5, for its part, was fined $600 000 for faking winners on its *Brainteaser* quiz show. Using in-house staff members, and sometimes their families, to pose as winning contestants was a widespread practice throughout the UK television industry. Even the BBC charity fundraising show, *Comic Relief*, had used a member of its production team to pose on air as a winning caller.[14]

In May 2008, British regulators slapped an $11 million fine on ITV – much lower than had been expected, but nonetheless a severe reputational setback for Britain's biggest private television network. Britain's Ofcom regular said it had "uncovered institutionalized failure" and "misconduct" within ITV that had driven the network to show "total disregard" for professional ethics and behave in a fraudulent manner vis-à-vis its own viewers. One of ITV's worst embarrassments had been its broadcast of the 2005 British Comedy Awards. Comic actress Catherine Tate had won the "People's Choice Award" voted by viewers, but the organizers of the event wanted pop star Robbie Williams, formerly of the hit group Take That, to present an award. Williams had indicated that he'd be happy to present an award offered to the comedy duo called Ant and Dec. To accommodate the pop star, Catherine Tate was deprived of her democratic victory and the "People's Choice" prize was given, after an arbitrary backroom decision, to Ant and Dec. British television had never stooped so low, or showed so much contempt for viewers.[15]

What on earth had possessed so many seasoned professionals in the British television industry to act with such arrogant disregard for basic ethical principles?

The answer is simple. In the UK television industry, with its time-honoured tradition of Oxbridge paternalism, producers failed to understand – or refused to accept – that direct public participation meant less editorial control for them. In a nutshell, UK television producers were still acting like oligarchic taste gatekeepers. And, fittingly, their cultural arrogance ended up resembling a sketch from Monty Python. When a majority of British children watching *Blue Peter* wanted the cat to be called "Cookie", the show's producers reacted by saying damn the kids, to hell with phone-in direct democracy – the kitty will be called "Socks".

Predictably, the immediate democratic reaction to these TV scandals was a viewer *loyalty* crisis that, inevitably, led to mass *exit*. Ratings dropped as viewers lost trust in these fraudulent shows. ITV's shareholders, moreover, ran for the exit doors and the company's stock went south. The network's revenues also plunged by 9.6% in the first half of 2007 immediately following the scandals.[16] Worst of all, the entire British television industry was thrown into reputational disarray. Regaining the *loyalty* of viewers would be a long hard climb after their shameful conduct.

The persistence of oligarchic taste gatekeepers should never be underestimated however. New oligarchies are even emerging, and asserting control, on online retail sites whose reputation is based on the democratic values of mass participation. That's what novelist Garth Risk Hallberg discovered when his debut novel, *A Field Guide to the North American Family*, was reviewed on the Amazon site in October 2007. The review, written by someone named Grady Harp from Los Angeles, was a rave. "Hallberg is a sensitive observer of human foibles," noted the reviewer. Harp added that Hallberg "also just happens to be a superb writer!"

Hallberg, as a 29-year-old first novelist, was understandably flattered by such high praise from an "enlightened consumer" who'd purchased his book and took the trouble to write such a well-considered assessment of his debut literary effort. But then something caught Hallberg's attention: on the Amazon website, Grady Harp was accorded the status of "Top 10 Reviewer". Harp, it turned out, wasn't an enlightened consumer at all. He was a regular, paid reviewer for Amazon – no different from a freelance book reviewer in the book sections of the *New York Times* or *Daily Telegraph*. Hallberg discovered even more troubling information after contacting his publisher to enquire about the rave review on Amazon.com. His own publicist had solicited the review from Grady Harp. In an instant, Hallberg's faith in the democratic goodwill of enlightened consumers deflated like a punctured tyre. "I suppose I shouldn't have been surprised, but I had imagined Amazon's customer reviews as a refuge from the machinations of the publishing industry," he noted in a published account of his Amazon disenchantment.[17]

Hallberg felt betrayed because he'd been genuinely optimistic about customer reviews. James Marcus, a former Amazon executive, had written in his memoir, *Amazonia: Five Years at the Epicenter of the Dot.Com Juggernaut*, that reviews on the website were "an intelligent and articulate conversation . . . conducted by a group of disinterested, disembodied spirits." In 2001, *Time* had published an article declaring that, thanks to the Web, today everyone's a critic: "The spread of cybercriticism is easy to understand. Everybody has an opinion. But until the Internet came along, not many people could get theirs out to the world at large. Critical approbation was supervised by gatekeeper institutions – newspapers, magazines, TV stations – that chose professional commentators. The Internet blew away the gates, and it did so at the very time that cynicism was growing about whether many professionals were just mouthpieces for the creators of cultural product or out of touch with popular interests. Thus, the unstated premise behind all of these sites is that 'my opinion is as good as anybody's.' That populist philosophy has always made democracy a tough cultural climate for professional critics – the people paid to have views that are supposed to be, well, better."[18] No wonder Hallberg, naively, believed in Amazon's vision of democratic disintermediation of self-appointed elites.

"Amazon had been hailed as a harbinger of 'Web 2.0' – an ideal realm where user-generated consensus trumps the bankrupt pieties of experts," he wrote. "As I explored the murky understory of Amazon's reviewer rankings, however, I came to see the real Web 2.0 as a tangle of hidden agendas – one in which the disinterested amateur may be an endangered species."

What Hallberg discovered was that, in truth, Amazon had been infested with the same politics of cronyism, egomania, vendetta and venality that pervade the cosy elites who control the offline book publishing business. Disillusioned, he conducted an investigation into Amazon's "Top 10 Reviewers" and discovered that strict regard for unimpeachable ethics was not the hallmark of this influential group of paid Amazon critics.[19] Hallberg learned that Amazon reviewers routinely swapped "help votes" in a conspiracy of mutual back-scratching. Their rankings as "Top 10 Reviewers", it turned out, depended on the number of consumer clicks on "this review was helpful". Amazon reviewers, it seemed, were rigging votes to protect their own status as taste gatekeepers. Hallberg came to the dismayed conclusion that Amazon reviewers, like book reviewers at major newspapers and magazines, are well-established members of publishing social circles. And thanks to this status, they are hardly impervious to the usual commercial pressures to review and praise books.

"Web 2.0 stakes its credibility on the transparency of users' motives and their freedom from top-down interference," noted Hallberg. "Amazon, for example, describes its Top Reviewers as 'clear-eyed critics [who] provide their fellow shoppers with helpful, honest, tell-it-like-it-is product information'. But beneath the just-us-folks rhetoric lurks an unresolved tension between transparency and opacity."

The irony of Hallberg's disillusionment was that it came precisely when critics of Web 2.0 were claiming that social media were spawning a so-called "cult of the amateur". Hallberg, for his part, was bemoaning the early death of the amateur. He could have pointed to other websites, like Epinions.com, to justify his pessimism. Epinions was launched in 1999 as a "consumer journalism" site where ordinary people can read, and write, reviews about all manner of products and services. But Epinions' business model is based on *paying* reviewers for their work.[20] And, like Amazon, Epinions ranks its regular reviewers in status categories: Adviser, Top Reviewer and Category Lead. Originally owned by Shopping.com, Epinions is now controlled by eBay following its $620 million purchase of Shopping.com in 2005.

This tension between oligarchy and democracy, it might be argued, will be sorted out in the marketplace through laws of *exit, voice* and *loyalty*. If the system is corrupted, people will walk. Let the marketplace of ideas decide who should be trusted. The idea undoubtedly has merit. But what happens when the *voice* impulse speaks out against institutional power not normally subject to market forces – for example, in corporate hierarchies, government bureaucracies and educational institutions? These precincts, let's face it, are not normally renowned for their democratic values. Employees don't "vote" for their CEO. Bureaucrats don't "vote" for senior managers. And students don't "vote" for their professors. Most large-scale bureaucracies are characterized by rigid status hierarchies based on corporate rank, union protection, academic tenure and other entrenched privileges that are, by definition, hostile to free democratic expression. It may be possible to fire a BBC producer in the wake of a viewer vote-rigging scandal, but it's impossible to dismiss, say, a tenured academic no matter how loud the clamour about longstanding incompetence.

There's a fascinating case study, fortuitously, that provides intriguing insights into precisely that conundrum: RateMyProfessors.com. Launched in 1999, the site today is the most heavily trafficked college website – boasting some seven million users who have generated opinions of roughly one million professors teaching at roughly 6000 collegiate institutions in Anglo-American countries (another site, RateMyTeachers.com, is devoted to primary and secondary schools). Professors are rated on a five-point scale according to straightforward criteria: *easiness, helpfulness, clarity* and the student's *interest* in the class before taking it. Also, "smiley" icons are assigned as general ratings – grinning brightly for high-satisfaction evaluations, frowning glumly for low scores.

John Swapceinski, a Silicon Valley software engineer who founded RateMyProfessors.com, says the site was inspired by the laws of the marketplace. "Students are demanding more information because they see themselves as customers who want the most value for their dollar," he says.[21]

Hard to argue with that. Unless, of course, you are a professor. If professors like to give grades, most deeply resent being evaluated – especially when comments are posted anonymously. Academic careers are based on formal ranks – assistant, associate, full professor – that confer status. Being assessed by non-ranking students is considered an affront to the institutionalized values of professional status.

RateMyProfessors, not surprisingly, has been threatened with a number of legal actions and is constantly the object of complaints and attacks from academic guilds and lobbies. Most of the criticism sidesteps the actual purpose of the site – to rate professors on a graded scale – and focuses on the negative impact on teachers' feelings, reputations and even psychological stability. Some academic unions argue that RateMyProfessors is a form of "cyberbullying". In Britain, one teacher claimed to feel dehumanized when a student described her as a "disinfected cat". Other teachers in Britain claim their students are bullying them on sites like Facebook and Bebo.[22]

"Cyber-bullying takes an age-old issue to new levels," said Mary Bousted, head of Britain's Association of Teachers and Lecturers. "It's an insidious and growing problem in our schools and colleges that goes beyond the school gate. For all its benefits, information technology is allowing pupils and parents to bully teachers and lecturers from afar by phone, email and the Internet, exposing them to public humiliation, damaging their good reputation and taking away their professional pride and confidence."

Michael Hussey, who helped design RateMyProfessors before creating RateMyTeachers, argues that, on the contrary, the site is merely an online platform for what students are saying about their professors anyway. "All we're doing is taking chatter that may be in the lunchroom or the dorm room and organizing it so it can be used by students," says Hussey.[23]

Critics argue that sites like RateMyProfessors are trivialized by student obsession with the physical appearance of their instructors. Students assign "chili pepper" icons to professors they find "hot". The "hotness" ranking indeed appears to be RateMyProfessors' most popular attraction. It has become so popular that RateMyProfessors now features a Top 50 for the "hottest" profs. With these kinds of ratings, we're getting close to seeing *People* magazine announcing, on the cover of a special RateMyProfessors tie-in issue, the "Sexiest Professor Alive". One empirical study of the site found that students tend to like courses taught by professors that they find "hot".[24] Other studies of RateMyProfessors – despite obvious questions about margin-of-error implications when only 50 or 60 students assess a teacher – give top marks to the site's utilitarian function. A study published in the *Journal of Computer-Mediated Communication* concluded that "while issues such as personality and appearance did enter into the postings, these were secondary motivators compared to more salient issues such as competence, knowledge, clarity and helpfulness."[25]

RateMyProfessors has now gone showbiz. In early 2007, MTV bought the site and merged it with its 24-hour college channel, MtvU, which is broadcast on 750 college campuses throughout the United States. Since the MTV takeover, RateMyProfessors has been enhanced with a Facebook application and jazzy features like "Professors Strike Back". Professors have been given their own voice on the site. Their responses to student reviews are even videotaped. You can watch Natalie Jeremijenko, a "hot" blonde art history professor from the University of California in San Diego, respond tartly to a male student who left the following posting: "I have a hard time focusing because I find her magnetic and attractive – she's beautiful. I want to be her personal slave, please. I will be your soldier-boy." Some professors, meanwhile, have started their own site, RateYourStudents.blogspot. com, which feature opinions about students like this one: "I'd just like him to write his own paper once. Or at least crack the spine of that $40 textbook. I'd like to smack his smug face."[26]

Professors in France don't have to rally against their students; they have the courts to protect their interests. When two Parisian entrepreneurs, Stéphane Cola and Anne-Françoise de Lastic, launched a French teacher-rating site called Note2be.com, it was immediately denounced by France's powerful teacher unions as an "incitement to public disorder". The site, which featured some 50000 evaluations of high-school teachers, was attracting about 150000 visits a day. One teacher in Paris complained: "I got the impression that I was being exposed to public gaze. It was an attack on me as a person."[27] Site founder Stéphane Cola, for his part, pointed out that similar sites – like Rate-MyProfessors in the Anglo-American world – were highly successful platforms for information and exchange. But in France, a country where rigid unions are willing to paralyse the country under any pretext if their interests are at stake, the government's dread of a teachers' strike outweighed its indulgence towards online free expression.

Xavier Ducros, France's education minister, took a tough stance against the site that left no doubt which lobbies had the most clout vis-à-vis his ministry. "The evaluation of teachers is the exclusive domain of the Ministry of Education and the civil servants who are appointed to carry it out," asserted Ducros. With implicit direction from the government, French courts effectively shut down the site by prohibiting any teacher's name to be posted. After the court ruling, Note2be went out of business. Philippe le Bel doubtless would have given high marks to this commanding show of state power.

Corporate hierarchies are, as a rule, even less democratic than school bureaucracies. So far, no free-wheeling RateMyBoss or Rate-MyCEO website has been launched. There is one site, called ImprovdeNow.com, that gives employees an opportunity to rate their bosses, anonymously, according to a number of questions, such as "are angry words between you and your boss quickly forgotten?" But Improve-Now is no RateMyProfessors. It's a highly controlled "HR" environment where bosses initiate the ratings by asking employees to log on and conduct evaluations. ImproveNow is primarily a service for managers – with a business model based on revenues from executive training – not a bottom-up democratic platform for employees.[28]

More promising is a site launched in June 2008 called Glassdoor, which stands a chance of becoming the RateMyProfessors of the corporate world. Glassdoor members get access not only to reviews and rankings of CEOs and top executives, but also to insider knowledge about salary and bonus levels, and pros-and-cons of working for specific companies. The site operates on a "give to get" policy. The service is free of charge, but you have to provide information about your own workplace to gain access to information about other employers. Glassdoor thus can lay off on its own members the cost of building its database. Information about corporations is crowdsourced by their own employees – or, in many cases, ex-employees. Another corporate rating-and-ranking site is Criticat, which serves as a collaborative platform for transparent information about companies. Criticat features a box, for example, called Shout, which asks employees to answer the question: "What is one thing you would want to change if you were made the CEO of the company?" If sites like Glassdoor and Criticat take off, it could become a nightmare for HR executives because it would turn the tables on employers by empowering job candidates with strategic information. And maybe that's a long-overdue e-ruption.[29]

Forrester analyst Jeremiah Owyang argues that the crowdsourced corporation has shifted power from top executives to employees – a theme we will examine in greater detail in Part III on *power*. "The conversations that used to take place at the physical watercooler, have now shifted online, organized, and manifest as something greater," notes Owyang. He cautions, however, that corporations will react to this power e-ruption. Job candidates, he says, will have more bargaining clout during the hiring process because they will be armed with detailed salary-and-bonus information, plus more qualitative assessments, thanks to sites like Glassdoor and Salary.com. This will put HR executives and recruiters on the spot, and they will doubtless refute the data gleaned on these sites. "Corporations will flinch," adds Owyang, "and many will set up policies to prevent employees from posting private information outside of the firewall, although many of these internal memos will appear within hours on the very sites they seek to stop."[30]

While CEOs and HR executives fret about their crowdsourced grades on sites like Glassdoor, direct democracy in corporations is emerging thanks to another Web 2.0 tool: *blogging*. While Web 2.0 evangelists counsel CEOs and senior managers to relax and allow employees to express themselves freely, even critically, on corporate blogs, this has proved easier said than done. In vertical bureaucratic structures, allowing open-ended employee opinionizing makes many executives nervous. Most managers fear potential damage to the company's brand and reputation – not to mention their own reputations – if employees are allowed to let loose on blogs. That dreaded *fear factor* again. The challenge is to loosen control without losing control. But most corporations still aren't willing to take that chance.

Sometimes, though, CEOs themselves decide to become blogging bosses. And, as we shall see in the next chapter, that presents an entirely different set of opportunities and challenges.

10

Blogs, bosses and brands: reputation management

eBay must have suspected it was facing a reputational nightmare when it received notice that Harry Potter's creator, J.K. Rowling, was suing the online auction giant.

Rowling had long been accusing eBay of breach of copyright, claiming the multi-billion-dollar auction behemoth was allowing unscrupulous sellers to flog unauthorized electronic versions and fake "signed" copies of her massively popular Harry Potter books. In early 2007, the world-famous author finally won a legal victory when a court in India ordered eBay to cease and desist from listing all illegal copies of Rowling's works.

The court decision was a major blow for eBay. Previously, it had claimed that its site was a free marketplace that's difficult to police. eBay insisted that it had taken steps with its so-called "VeRO" programme (Verified Rights Owner), whereby it removes suspected fake items when notified by the copyright owners. Many nonetheless were growing increasingly frustrated with eBay, claiming that the online auction site was, in fact, overindulgent towards fraud.

Artist Anne Conti was so fed up seeing fake copies of her paintings on the block for a mere $50 that she posted her cautionary tale on the Web under the title, "eBay Art Fraud". Even worse, professional fraudsters were using eBay to pawn off works claiming paternity by Picasso, Chagall, Dali and Miro. In the United States, criminal charges had been laid against a ring of professional art fraudsters caught selling fake works on eBay.[1]

The ire of Harry Potter's creator was an especially big headache for eBay. Its unenviable predicament became even more delicate when Rowling made a direct appeal to her millions of young fans to sign an online petition against eBay. The petition read: "Every year, thousands of forged, fraudulent and illegal Harry Potter items are listed on eBay. J.K. Rowling has repeatedly requested that eBay police these items more carefully. eBay has refused to do so, stating that they can only react to the desires of their customers. In this case, however, the customers in question are often children. By signing this petition we are declaring our support for J.K. Rowling. We feel there is a significant problem with fraud in the area of Harry Potter collectibles on eBay."[2]

These controversies were particularly embarrassing, for eBay. It had built one of the world's most famous, and trusted, online brands thanks to its famous public "reputation system" to ensure a transparent auction market. The J.K. Rowling court victory put eBay in a real spot of bother. Defusing the public indignation of Harry Potter fans is a challenge that not even the most seasoned corporate practitioners of damage control would wish to confront. Dealing deftly with the Harry Potter kerfuffle was a textbook case study in reputational risk and brand management. It required steady nerves, a safe pair of hands and, above all, a willingness to deal honestly with the problem.

And yet eBay, instead of coming clean, decided to go on the attack against J.K. Rowling. The company filed papers in a Delhi high court claiming that the Harry Potter author had caused the company "immense humiliation." eBay, moreover, argued that Rowling and her attorneys were "spreading misinformation" that had damaged the company's "goodwill and reputation."[3]

Harry Potter's creator, it turned out, was not eBay's only powerful adversary. Some of the world's most prestigious luxury brands – Tiffany, Louis Vuitton, Christian Dior, L'Oréal – had also been complaining, and eventually sued eBay over the sale of counterfeit goods sold on its site. Louis Vuitton claimed that some 235 000 counterfeit items had been auctioned off on eBay as authentic Vuitton products. The French luxury goods company estimated that 90% of products bearing its brand on eBay were, in fact, fakes. Its Paris-based parent company, LVMH – which also owns Christian Dior – was seeking roughly $75 million in damages. L'Oréal, for its part, launched a lawsuit against eBay in 2007 following unsuccessful attempts to apply pressure on the auction site to police the sale of fake fragrances and cosmetics bearing its brand.[4] In June 2008, LVMH won its case against eBay when a Paris court awarded the luxury goods giant $63 million damages. After the court ruling, a spokesman for LVMH – whose other brands include Givenchy, Fendi, Emilio Pucci and Marc Jacobs – welcomed the fine against eBay as "an answer to a particularly serious question, on whether the Internet is a free-for-all for the most hateful, parasitic practices."[5]

If these legal battles were not enough, eBay was also facing criticism about robbers buying their tools of the trade and murderers purchasing their weapons on eBay. After the Virginia Tech school massacre in the United States in 2007, it was discovered that the killer, Cho Seung Hui, had bought ammunition clips on eBay before his killing spree. In Britain, a well-organized gang of thieves who pulled off the biggest heist in UK history disguised as policemen had bought their uniforms on eBay. There were also reports of a fraudulent eBay trade in phoney sports memorabilia, including "signed" photographs and jerseys "worn" by English soccer stars like David Beckham. And in Romania, incredibly, fraudsters were scamming astoundingly misinformed buyers on eBay by offering MiG jetfighters at prices as low as $2000.

More generally, eBay critics were complaining that eBay auctions were "fixed" by unscrupulous sellers who were artificially bidding up prices. The auction site was, moreover, accused of distorting charity markets. In late 2007, eBay became a scalper's paradise for tickets to Led Zeppelin's reunion concert in London, the proceeds of which were going to Ahmet Ertegun Education Fund. The rock supergroup's promoter, Harvey Goldsmith, grew so frustrated with the inflationary eBay market controlled by Led Zeppelin ticket touts that he declared publicly: "I wish eBay would drop dead and die."[6]

What had gone so terribly wrong? eBay, after all, had worked hard to build an online "community of trust".[7] Stock analysts consistently ranked eBay, along with Amazon, as an online leader in customer trust and were bullish on the company's outlook. eBay was described as an "invincible" Web-based powerhouse with a fantastic business model: online sales that leveraged network effects with no inventory costs. Meg Whitman, eBay's founder and CEO – and one of the richest women in the world – was media-friendly, likeable and personified the positive face of the dot-com boom. eBay was widely considered to be one of the Internet's best-loved brands.[8]

Nobody, it seemed, saw the *trust* crack in the eBay system. There had been warning signs, however. In 2003, when Al Golin published his book, *Trust or Consequences: Build Trust Today or Lose Your Market Tomorrow*, he could have been talking about eBay when he warned that "the by-products of distrust – suspicion, anger, cynicism and disappointment – drive down stock prices, harm employee recruitment and retention efforts, and cause customer defections to competitors."[9] Complaints about fake items and rigged auctions had been slowly boiling up for years, before they hit the courts. Most of the suspicion, anger and cynicism was being vented in the blogosphere. By the time the Harry Potter controversy hit, in fact, eBay was already under attack from well-informed bloggers who had long been following, and criticizing, market dysfunctions on the site.

The anti-eBay blog hammering was relentless. In October 2007, Kim Peterson, who writes MSN's MoneyBlog, observed that embattled eBay was scrambling to re-aggregate its "community" through a new social networking site called Neighbourhoods, but dismissed the new site as "cringe-worthy". The *New York Times*'s technology blog, meanwhile, drew up a devastating list of eBay's problems: its customer service was broken; its PayPal payment system was inefficient (Amazon's system was judged much better); its auctions were awash in counterfeit goods; it had failed to focus on unique merchandise; its business model was greedy; its management had made poor strategic decisions, notably eBay's $2.6 billion purchase of Internet-based telephone system, Skype (on which it later took a $1.4 billion writedown). There was more. Gary Sattler, who writes the online BloggingStocks column, observed: "eBay's brand image is tarnished, its reputation is trashed, its competition is mounting." Henry Blodget, the former Wall Street dot-com evangelist who now writes the Silicon Alley blog, disclosed that he had a long-term position in eBay before declaring that, in his opinion, it was time for CEO Meg Whitman to go. Virtually every other blogger following eBay's tribulations agreed: Whitman was toast.[10]

eBay was facing a classic *exit/voice/loyalty* dilemma. The company was besieged – from J.K. Rowling's lawsuit to its blog battering – by *voice* protests delivering an unequivocal message about trust issues. There was also evidence of *exit* – not only by eBay customers, but also investors. eBay's stock peaked in early 2005 at close to $60, but three years later in early 2008 it had been cut in half, floating around $30. Sales listings were declining overall and its active "power seller" listings were down roughly 25% in 2007 from a year earlier. The site was also facing an increasingly angry seller base. Then, in early 2008, eBay got hit by a seller boycott. One angry seller made the following threat: "What will change eBay is if everyone leaves. eBay will crumble and other sites with more compassionate managers will benefit. And the sooner the better."[11]

Meg Whitman apparently decided that, for eBay to manage its *loyalty* crisis, she needed to make an *exit* before things got worse. And that's what she did. In late January 2008, Whitman announced that, after a decade in the job, she would step down at the end of March. "It's time for eBay to have new leadership, a new perspective and a new vision," she said before her departure, amidst a chorus of praise and speculation that she would get involved in Republican Party politics. The markets reacted less sanguinely to her exit. As one eBay analyst put it: "The buyside is sick of Meg."[12]

In its post-Whitman era, eBay is coming to terms with a serious lesson about customer loyalty that it should have learned long before. The status of a brand is based on its reputation. A good reputation creates trust, and trust earns loyalty. Without brand *loyalty*, when things go wrong there is a strong risk of *voice* or *exit* – sometimes both, sequentially.

Reputation status generally takes cues from an underlying *value* system. In Anglo-American cultures, as we saw with the scandal that brought down New York governor Eliot Spitzer, a deeply embedded culture of Puritanism is unforgiving, sometimes cruelly, towards the sexual indiscretions of public officials. Private impropriety is interpreted as a breach of public trust. Many UK politicians have learned the same lesson when caught in media scandals about their extramarital distractions. Those who make a claim on public virtue are rarely forgiven private vices. Voters in Anglo-American countries think: if his wife can't *trust* him, why should we? In Latin countries like Italy and France, attitudes towards sexual indiscretions committed by elected officials are comparatively indulgent. Reputations don't suffer for the same sins that would destroy careers and ruin lives in Britain or the United States. Other cultures – China, Japan, India and Moslem countries – have their unique value systems that condition attitudes towards virtues and vice, both public and private.

To briefly return to our Knights Templar saga, Philippe le Bel shrewdly understood the importance of *reputation* and its consequences for trust and loyalty. His dark plot to destroy the monastic order, it will be remembered, was based on tarnishing the Templars' reputation. More to the point, Philippe shrewdly appealed to the underlying values of medieval Christendom to ensure that his hardball tactic produced the desired effects. Using gossip and rumour, he spread throughout his kingdom, and all of Christendom, that the Templars were blasphemous devil-worshippers whose secret rituals involved renouncing Jesus Christ and spitting on the cross. At the outset of the 14th century, it was impossible to imagine more heinous crimes. By destroying the Templars' reputation, Philippe felt more confident, after rounding up Templar leaders and having them executed, that he would not face a public outcry in their defence. Fortunately for the French king, there were no bloggers circa 1300 to react instantly to his deadly machinations.

In business, the operating value system in transactional exchange is *trust*. eBay's reputation suffered, as we have seen, because it lost the trust of its customers. When your entire business model is based on a reputational system designed to win customers' trust, and it fails, you have a serious problem. Especially when your failings are under attack throughout the blogosphere.

Corporations today, as eBay discovered, don't have the luxury of indifference towards the blogosphere's viral influence. Bloggers react much more quickly than traditional media like newspapers and television – their postings are not only instantaneous, they're ubiquitous. Bloggers, moreover, don't feel constrained by customary pressures – deadlines, space limitations, self-censorship – that shape old media content. Perhaps most importantly, the sociology of the blogosphere is, at least in this early phase, radically independent. Most bloggers sound off without fear or favour. That's a big change from the pre-Web 2.0 days, when major corporations could rely on sophisticated PR and "spin" machines to cultivate influential media figures and react pre-emptively to potentially negative stories. Reputational risk was manageable in the closed "media elite" governed by tacit codes of mutual trust and practices of reciprocal favours. The blogosphere, by contrast, is more difficult to co-opt because entry into its ranks is *democratic*. The blogosphere is an open network, not a closed clique.

But how much can bloggers themselves be trusted? The established media often claim, plausibly, that bloggers have no credibility – their main commerce is gossip, rumour and innuendo. The blogosphere, argue critics, is not an organized democracy, but an ungovernable anarchy where it's impossible to distinguish fact and fiction. Perhaps these claims are the self-interested rationalizations of complacent oligarchies afraid of any threat to their comfortable monopoly as taste gatekeepers. Perhaps, too, these claims are not entirely without foundation.

The question therefore can be asked: are bloggers credible? The answer, it seems, is an ambiguous yes and no.

Those who claim that bloggers don't enjoy high-trust reputations can validate this assertion with empirical research. Surveys indicate that people overwhelmingly put more faith in their close *friends* and *family* than in bloggers and MySpace "friends". According to findings published by Forrester Research, when consumers are looking for credible information about a product or service, 83% would trust a "friend or acquaintance", 63% would trust the opinion of a "known expert", while only 30% would put faith in the views of a blogger. Those results confirm Edelman's "Trust Barometer" whose study covered the 2003–2008 period. Edelman found that 58% of respondents said they would trust a "person like me", while only 14% would trust a blogger. The Canadian polling firm Pollara arrived at similar conclusions. Pollara found that 80% of people using social networking sites were "very or somewhat more likely" to consider buying a product recommended by real-world friends and family members, while only 23% said they would trust the opinions of bloggers.[13]

These empirical findings are considered a major blow to Malcolm Gladwell's so-called "Law of the Few" in *The Tipping Point*. Gladwell argued that a small number of influencers – such as "Connectors" – exert disproportionate power in shaping opinion. Gladwell's theory – reanimating "two-step" influence theories stretching back to the 1950s in classic works like *Personal Influence* – was initially embraced by marketing professionals as a powerful insight with tremendous practical value. Gladwell's book spawned works by marketing executives – notably *The Influentials* by Ed Keller and Jon Berry – pursuing the same theme. Keller and Berry argued that 20% of Americans effectively tell the other 80% "how to vote, where to eat, and what to buy".[14] In a word, the real world doesn't actually operate like a democracy. It's an oligarchy.

The polls by Forrester, Edelman and Pollara appeared to debunk these fashionable notions about oligarchic opinion shaping. One well-known social scientist, Duncan Watts, openly challenged the *Tipping Point* theories. He says Gladwell simply got it wrong. "It sort of sounds cool", said Watts in early 2008, "but it's wonderfully persuasive only for as long as you don't think about it." Watts, who heads the Human Social Dynamics group at Yahoo! Research, conducted his own experiments which discovered that, contrary to Gladwell's claims, trends are not dictated by a minority.

"It just doesn't work," said Watts about Gladwell's theory. "A rare bunch of cool people just don't have that power. And when you test the way marketers say the world works, it falls apart. There's no *there* there."[15] Opinion-shaping is not controlled by an oligarchy – it really is a democracy.

What about bloggers? Are they members of Gladwell's oligarchic few? Or are they lost in the crowd of Watts's democratic mass? It's tempting to conclude that bloggers are oligarchic "Connectors" shaping opinion from their virtual Web 2.0 perches. But given the open-ended, horizontal network dynamics of blogging, that elitist conceptualization of the blogosphere doesn't hold up. Most bloggers, after all, solicit comment and feedback, and their blogs read like a long thread of ongoing dialogue and debate. The above-cited Forrester/Edelman/Pollara research, moreover, is actually more nuanced than its big-bullet points appear to indicate. Forrester analyst Josh Bernoff directs our attention to this finding: while people trust friends and family most, they nonetheless manifest high trust levels for consumer reviews by people whom they've never met.

"Why do people trust strangers?" asks Bernoff. "They don't, not as individuals. But they do in groups. Strangers are assumed not to have an axe to grind. If 100 people on eBags say a laptop bag is great, then it *is* great. If they say it's inferior, then it is inferior. Regardless of what a so-called 'expert' might say." Another Forrester study found that the trust factor for bloggers is rising, mainly because consumers trust other individuals more than they trust mass advertising.[16]

We're back, it would seem, to the wisdom of crowds. So long as the blogosphere remains an open-ended mass democracy, the information that emerges from its network effects will be relatively accurate and trustworthy. But openness and diversity are key. Bloggers don't, as a rule, self-censor or withhold information; they actively connect us to just about every other possible point of view imaginable on any given subject, and provide open forums for feedback and discussion. In the blogosphere, we really do depend on the kindness of strangers. Sure, some blogs are PR platforms for special interests. But as we shall see below, the self-correcting mechanism of the blogosphere is quick to *flame* and *shame*. Fierce independence is the governing ethos of the blogosphere. Which is why, for major corporations, it's so difficult to manage reputational risk when the bloggers unleash their wrath against their brands.

The most famous example of the blogosphere's power is the so-called "Dell Hell" saga triggered by Jeff Jarvis on his BuzzMachine blog. In 2005, Jarvis bought a Dell computer which, he quickly realized, was a lemon. He subsequently became even more frustrated when dealing with Dell's poor customer service department. To register his *voice* protest, Jarvis resorted to online shaming. He banged off a blog post entitled: "Dell Lies, Dell Sucks". His anti-Dell rant included the following remarks: "I just got a new Dell laptop and paid a fortune for the four-year, in-home service. The machine is a lemon and the service is a lie. DELL SUCKS. DELL LIES. Put that in your Google and smoke it, Dell." Jarvis followed up with a blog post in the form of an open letter to Dell's CEO, Michael Dell. The letter began with this reminder: "Your customer satisfaction is plummeting, your market share is shrinking, and your stock price is deflating. Let me give you some indication of why."[17]

Jarvis's blog posts unleashed a "Dell Sucks" shaming blaze that spread virally throughout the blogosphere. As Jarvis later recalled: "There was a method to my mad rant: I learned some time ago that you can search Google for any brand, followed by the word 'sucks', to find out just how much ill will is attached . . . All I wanted to do was warn off other unsuspecting customers by joining in Google's wisdom of the crowds, adding just one more critical consumer opinion. But my post snowballed into a saga, a weblog miniseries. Scores of readers left comments with their stories of Dell hell and scores more bloggers linked to my post with their wails of woe."[18]

Dell at first ignored Jarvis's online rants. The democratic ground-swell of outrage became so overwhelming, however, that the company soon found itself sinking, in Dante-esque fashion, into a Dell Hell public relations nightmare. Dell finally had no choice but to squirm frantically out of the quicksand by shifting into damage-control mode. Michael Dell even gave Jeff Jarvis a personal interview that was published in *Business Week* under the title, "Dell Learns to Listen".[19] Jarvis, taking care to ensure that his readers didn't form the view that he'd been spun by Dell executives, continued blogging about his experiences with the company and its products. He kept the discussion going in the blogosphere while he was dialoguing with Michael Dell. Jarvis, to his credit, scored two major victories against Dell. First, the company ended up hiring its own "chief blogger", Lionel Menchaca, to engage the blogosphere about the company and its products. Second, Dell announced that it had decided to give its customers a social platform, called IdeaStorm.[20] The Dell Hell saga, when it was finally over, was a major triumph of open-ended network dynamics over the impenetrable vertical logic of corporate hierarchies.

The Dell Hell protest was a groundswell that started rumbling outside Dell. It began with an *external* shock. But what about blogging *inside* corporations? What happens when the negative reaction is *internal*? If blogs, as Dell learned the hard way, are an excellent way of opening up a dialogue with customers, why not give a voice to *employees* too?

It seems like a great idea in theory. Corporate blogs can help position a company as a "thought leaders", put a human face on the corporation, build a dialogue with customers, capture information for sharing, facilitate collaboration, promote knowledge management, test new ideas, manage media relations and attract new employees.[21] Some leading-edge companies, indeed, have been using social media as corporate platforms for employees and customers to interact and express views in "naked conversations".[22] In a nutshell, to leverage the power of *collective intelligence*. Companies like IBM, Microsoft and Sun Microsystems encourage employees to maintain blogs. Serena Software has even adopted Facebook as a corporate intranet for its 800 employees who go online for "Facebook Fridays".[23] Some studies indicate that employee blogs, even when providing a forum for negative comments, can improve a company's reputation and boost morale because open dialogue enhances credibility and draws people to positive postings. At many companies, however, the instinctive reaction to employee blogging has been to treat it as a potential threat. The hard rule in most corporate environments continues to be: Loose Lips Sink Ships.[24]

Consider what happened to Ellen Simonetti, an attractive 29-year-old flight attendant from North Carolina working for Delta Airlines. In 2003, Simonetti began keeping a blog called Queen of Sky: Diary of a Dysfunctional Flight Attendant. But after she posted sexy photos of herself dressed in a Delta stewardess uniform, she was suspended without pay, then fired. In 2005, Simonetti filed a discrimination complaint with the US Equal Employment Opportunity Commission. She also appeared on American television shows to publicize her plight, and her predicament was reported in prestigious newspapers like the *New York Times*.[25] Delta Airlines, for its part, remained tight-lipped, refusing to discuss "internal company employee matters". Simonetti, meanwhile, published a book based on her blog, which she fittingly renamed *Diary of a* Fired *Flight Attendant*.[26]

British secretary Catherine Sanderson met a similar fate when she was working in Paris at a British accountancy firm called Dixon Wilson. Hiding behind the pseudonym "Petite Anglaise", she started keeping a blog in which she recounted her personal life, referring to her French boyfriend as "Frog" and their new baby as "Tadpole". It all seemed innocent enough, until Sanderson began sharing her office impressions on the blog. In one posting, she described a Dixon Wilson senior partner this way: "He wears braces and sock suspenders, stays in gentlemen's clubs when in London, and calls secretaries 'typists'." Her satirical accounts of the firm's snobby Old School culture got up the noses of the clubby men in the firm's top ranks. Sanderson, an unpretentious Yorkshire lass, was abruptly summoned by her employers and fired for breach of trust.

But her dismissal quickly triggered an unexpected reversal of fortune for Sanderson – and aggravated Dixon Wilson's reputational problems. When the British media got wind of her dismissal, UK newspapers offered her large sums of money for interviews. Dubbed an "Online Bridget Jones", her blog hits soared from 3000 per day to 10 000.[27] Sanderson, meanwhile, hired a lawyer and launched a wrongful dismissal suit against Dixon Wilson. She probably didn't need the money. Penguin had come knocking and offered her more than $900 000 for a two-book deal including *Petite Anglaise* and a follow-up novel. Sanderson, briefly unemployed, was now a richly remunerated literary sensation.[28]

A new word has been coined for career setbacks suffered by employee bloggers: *dooced*. This neologism's origins can be traced to the sacking of a Mormon woman from Tennessee called Heather Hamilton. An attractive blonde in her twenties who graduated from Brigham Young University, Hamilton was working in Los Angeles as a graphic artist when she started a semi-fictional blog called Dooce. While her postings dealt mainly with her personal ordeals – including depression and skin cancer – Hamilton also made acid remarks about work colleagues. In one post, she tartly observed about one vice-president that "lately, he's been an authority on patently grotesque facial hair patterns."

Hamilton eventually got found out and, in 2002, was dismissed for her Dooce postings. Her sacking instantly became a cause célèbre for privacy advocates and, for a while, Hamilton was one of the most famous bloggers in America. "I was naïve," she later reflected with some regret. "I was writing these caricatures of my colleagues . . . I didn't think anyone would be reading it." Now married with a small daughter and living under the name Heather Armstrong, she still keeps up the Dooce site, though its popularity has dropped off sharply as younger, more socially indiscreet, female bloggers have moved into the spotlight. Dooce's legacy will endure, however, in the word its author added to the online English lexicon.

Ironically, while paranoia about employee blogging persists in many corporations, senior executives are starting to blog. In late 2007, a group of major American corporations created a Blog Council, which describes itself as a "professional community of top global brands dedicated to promoting best practices in corporate blogging". Its founding members include Cisco Systems, Coca-Cola, Dell, Gemstar-

TV Guide, General Motors, Microsoft, Nokia, SAP and Wells Fargo. The blogosphere itself, with some exceptions, was decidedly critical of this Big Business blog structure. Jeff Jarvis castigated the Blog Council for its corporate-sounding name, but also added: "It's not about them writing blog posts. It is as much about them reading everybody else's blog posts . . . If they truly realise that we, the customers, are in charge, then that changes the way you comport yourself in this conversation. Again, you listen more than you speak." Business blogger Dave Taylor was less diplomatic on his Intuitive Systems blog when he described the Blog Council this way: "My translation: 'We're all clueless, but don't want anyone to realize just how unplugged our organizations have become from the world of 'marketing 2.0', so we created a club so our ignorance can be shielded from public eyes."[29]

While Fortune 500 companies are doing due diligence on the value of corporate blogs, some trailblazing CEOs have jumped right in as blogging evangelists. There is even a school of management that believes CEO blogging is indispensible. Or as Jonathan Schwartz, president of Sun Microsystems, puts it: "If you want to lead, blog".[30]

Bill Gates doesn't blog, neither does Steve Jobs. Still, there's an impressive, and growing, list of powerful CEOs who are using blogs as management tools. The CEO blogroll includes, besides Schwartz, Mark Zuckerberg (Facebook), Craig Newmark (Craig's List), Mark Cuban (Dallas Mavericks), Kevin Lynch (Adobe), John Dragoon (Novell), Joe Wikert (John Wiley & Sons), Matt Blumberg (Return Path), Richard Charkin (Macmillan Publishers) and billionaire investor Carl Icahn.[31] CEOs who don't blog risk seeing phoney satirical blogs that claim to be written by them. A fake blog called Secret Life of Steve Jobs is kept by *Forbes* columnist Daniel Lyons. There are also fake blogs for Oracle's Larry Ellison (called The Fake Larry Ellison Blog) and ex-eBay CEO Meg Whitman (called The Secret Diary of Meg Whitman).

Sometimes fake blogs – or "flogs" – are created by marketing and PR flaks to promote products under the guise of authentic consumers who appear to be enthusiastically plugging a product. The emergence of flogs, needless to say, has been highly controversial. Major PR firms like Edelman have been taken on in the blogosphere for flogging on behalf of corporate clients. In 2006, Edelman managed a flog for retail giant Wal-Mart, called Wal-Marting Across America. The blog created the impression that it was written by an average American couple, "Jim" and "Laura", who were chronicling their travels across America in a recreation vehicle and making stops in Wal-Mart parking lots. It turned out, however, that the blog was being written by "fake people" – Laura was a freelance writer and Jim was a *Washington Post* staff photographer – paid by a pro-Wal-Mart public relations front, Working Families for Wal-Mart, which had already been at the centre of another phony-blog controversy.[32] Working Families for Wal-Mart had been set up, it turned out, by none other than Richard Edelman, Wal-Mart's well-paid PR consultant.

When media reports, including an exposé in *Business Week*, uncovered the Wal-Mart flog, both Wal-Mart and Edelman hastily beat an embarrassed retreat. But it was too late. The blogosphere had already piled on, blasting Edelman for appropriating the blog form and blurring the line between authentic opinion and PR.[33] The Wal-Mart flogging mess raised serious ethical issues about the general question of corporate-sponsored "PayPerPost" blogs. Richard Edelman, in damage-control mode, was forced to come clean and, in a blog posting on his own corporate site, clarify his firm's policy regarding corporate clients. As blogger Richard Scoble noted: "The nice thing is that when the corrosive effect of money comes into the blogosphere and isn't disclosed, it'll earn a direct blowback."[34] Wal-Mart, meanwhile, decided to seek redemption by launching an authentic blog written by employees called Checkout. The company describes the blog this way: "This is a blog, simply, about a team of experts at Wal-Mart who have really cool jobs working with gadgets, wine, sustainability, fashion and more."[35]

Another controversial flog was Sony's marketing campaign using MySpace profiles and YouTube videos to hype its PSP games console. Sony's flogging was quickly exposed by alert bloggers, such as the *Consumerist*, who swung into a *flaming* and *shaming* operation by posting the phony MySpace profiles and denouncing the "marketing douchebags who appear on the PSP flog pretending that they are kids who want their parents to buy them a PSP for Christmas." Sony immediately yanked the embarrassing flog – proof, once again, that the libertarian democracy of social media has a built-in self-correcting mechanism.[36]

Some CEOs have committed astonishing blunders on their blogs, including attempts to hide behind false identities to promote their brands – and, even more controversially, knock their competition. Whole Foods president John Mackey got busted doing this after he blogged using an identity called "Rahodeb" (a scramble of his wife Deborah's name).

Mackey's flogging was hardly motivated by his enthusiasm for initiating online conservations. His flog posts betrayed a clear conflict of interest. While flogging away, Mackey was trashing another food retailer, Wild Oats, on Yahoo! stock forums. Slagging off competitors is one thing, but it turned out that Whole Foods was making a take-over attempt on Wild Oats while Mackey was flogging about how overvalued the competing retailer was. One of Mackey's flog posts was unequivocally self-interested: "Would Whole Foods buy Wild Oats? Almost surely not at current prices." Then Mackey added that Wild Oats had "no value and no future."[37]

When Mackey's flogging was uncovered, the US Securities Exchange Commission launched an investigation to determine whether he had violated any laws about disclosure of insider infor-mation. The *Wall Street Journal* published an editorial under the headline: "Mr Mackey's Offense". The newspaper noted: "That'll teach Mr. Mackey to flog the virtues of his company on the Web. He made the mistake – in today's hyper-regulated world – of giving the impression in his blogging that he was just another Internet-surfing schmoe with an opinion."[38]

Steven Grover, a vice-president for Burger King, is another top corporate executive who got "punked" by the blogosphere for ques-tionable flogging. He had been using his teenage daughter's email identity to smear a labour group, Coalition of Immokalee Workers, which was petitioning on behalf of Florida tomato-pickers against the company's alleged low wages. One of Grover's flog posts said: "The CIW is an attack organisation lining the leaders' pockets by attacking restaurant companies. They make up issues and collect money from dupes that believe their story. . . ." Unfortunately for Grover, both his daughter and wife were more honest and forthcom-ing than him. They admitted to the press that he'd used his daugh-ter's email to attack the labour organization. The bad optics for Burger King were aggravated by the fact that its competitors, McDonald's and Taco Bell, had agreed to the tomato-pickers' wage demands. Grover's predicament became even more embarrassing when his flog postings showed up on YouTube and on blogs like The Consumerist, whose slogan is "Shoppers Bite Back". The Consumerist remarked: "The next time Burger King VP Stephen Grover goes online to spread FUD (fear, uncertainty and doubt) about labour advocates, he should probably leave his daughter out of it."[39]

These brand-damaging pitfalls only strengthen the arguments of those who believe CEOs should avoid blogging like the plague. Mar-keting strategist Seth Godin warns that CEOs should seriously think twice about blogging. "Here's the problem," says Godin. "Blogs work when they are based on: candour, urgency, timeliness, pithiness and controversy (maybe utility if you want six). Does this sound like a CEO to you?"[40] Blogger Dave Taylor agrees: "For companies of any size, CEOs have more important tasks than writing articles for the company weblog. I'm not saying that the entire executive team at a company should stay far, far away from the company blog. Quite the opposite! I applaud companies like Boeing and General Motors for becoming more accessible and gaining visibility in their marketplace by having executives contribute to their blogs. But neither firm has their CEO blogging, let alone a CEO blog. Frankly, their CEOs are just too darn busy with the challenges of running large companies."[41]

So why do some powerful CEOs, if they're too busy and have more important things to do, not only bother with the hassle of blogging but also claim it's an indispensable management tool?

Sun Microsystems' CEO Jonathan Schwartz says blogging is a matter of corporate survival. "Many senior executives at Sun, including me, have blogs that can be read by anyone, anywhere in the world," he says. "We discuss everything from business strategy to product development to company values . . . In ten years, most of us will communicate directly with customers, employees and the broader business community through blogs. For executives, having a blog is not going to be a matter of choice, any more than using email is today. If you're not part of the conversation, others will speak on your behalf – and I'm not talking about your employees. Blogging lets you participate in communities you want to cultivate – whether it's your employees, potential employees, customers or anyone else – and leverage your corporate culture competitively."[42]

Bob Lutz, vice-chairman of General Motors, is another convert to executive blogging. He contributes to the company's FastLane blog and is known as a pro-corporate blogging evangelist. "The key is to leave the corporate-speak behind and keep the tone conversational, open and honest," says Lutz. "Anyone who has read our blog sees the real deal, as produced by us and not polished by several layers of trained communications pros. Another aspect that helps keep things real is the wealth of comments posted by readers and other bloggers. We don't filter out negative comments, complaints or hate mail. All we do is screen for spam and posts from crackpots using language that most people would find offensive. It's important that we run the bad with the good. We'd take a credibility hit if we posted only rosy compliments, and credibility is the most important attribute a corporate blog can have. Once it's gone, your blog is meaningless."[43]

Honesty does indeed seem to be the key to successful corporate blogging. Dishonesty, as the examples of Wal-Mart and Burger King demonstrated, exposes corporations to serious reputational risk. Honesty builds trust, which is the most valuable form of social capital for brand and reputation management.

We are back to the same fundamental lesson. Trust creates employee and customer *loyalty*. Distrust leads to *voice* and *exit*.

The challenge for many companies, going forward, will entail bringing their employees and customers into the conversation in an open and honest way. In a word, making their organizations more genuinely democratic.

PART III

Power

"I hope you realize you're interrupting my mid-morning podcast."

© Mike Shapiro

11

The anatomy of power:
getting things done

Manchester is famous worldwide for the popular British television drama, *Coronation Street*, a long-running soap that recounts the daily struggles that bond local residents in one of the city's familiar terraced rows. The reality of inner-city life in Manchester, however, is not always so quaintly reassuring. The city is plagued with one of the UK's highest rates of violent crime. That's why Manchester's police are using Facebook to fight crime. Call it Facecrook.

Manchester law enforcement has discovered that Facebook is a more effective – and faster – crime-fighting tool than traditional crime alerts. Facebook members who download the crime-busting application – dubbed "GMP Updates" – can connect directly to Greater Manchester Police's website and its YouTube channel to report crimes. Anyone with a mobile device can report – and even film – crimes in real time. The application also features a "Submit Intelligence" button that allows Facebook members to send in crime tips anonymously.

Manchester police decided to take a social networking approach to crime-fighting after the tragic murder of an 18-year-old local girl who'd been a national inspiration as an aspiring singer on a televised talent show. Kesha Wizzart had shot to fame when, at age 15, she appeared on *Young Stars in Their Eyes* singing a Toni Braxton song, "Unbreak My Heart". In July 2007, she'd just finished her exams and was hoping to study law at university. She also kept a Facebook page. But Kesha's young life was cut short that summer when her bludgeoned body was found along with the corpses of her murdered

13-year-old brother and their mother, a 35-year-old single black woman working as a nurse at Manchester Royal Infirmary. An estranged ex-boyfriend of Kesha's mother was later convicted of all three murders and sentenced to 38 years in prison.

After Kesha's tragic death, thousands of grief-stricken tributes flooded Facebook with messages of condolence. Manchester Police realized that, while too late to save Kesha, the power of social networking sites could be leveraged to fight crime.

"Facebook has 59 million users, seven million of which live in the UK," said assistant chief constable Rob Taylor in April 2008 when the GMP software application was launched. "So we realized that this was an excellent way of spreading our messages to people on a more personal basis. This application allows Greater Manchester Police to further raise awareness of incidents taking place within our local communities in a bid to gain more intelligence and bring offenders to justice."[1]

Social media are also being deployed worldwide to bring mass responsiveness to critical situations. In China, local residents in Shanghai and Nanjing use sites like GoogleMaps and Sougou to draw up "thief maps" that give precise locations of areas where street crimes are committed. One Chinese online network called "Anti-Pickpocket Alliance" uses online forums and SMS messaging to combat criminality. China's online crime-fighting networks – apparently inspired by a popular Chinese movie called *A World Without Thieves* – have been described as "smart mob" crowdsourcing.

On a more macro scale, the power of social media is being harnessed for disaster relief efforts. Social networking tools – instant messaging, blogs, photos, map sites – have proven highly effective in providing early warning when disasters like tsunamis and earthquakes are about to strike. In May 2008, *New Scientist* reported that Facebook, Twitter and GoogleMaps had been more efficient than traditional emergency services – which often rely on mass media – in responding to devastating Californian wildfires and the tragic Virginia Tech shooting rampages the previous year.[2] During the California fires, television reports had focused on the "celebrity" angle as the flames threatened the luxurious homes of Hollywood stars, thus distorting the true picture of the disaster's impact. The American Red Cross is now using Twitter to update information on local disasters. The US Geological Society meanwhile operates a site called "Did You Feel It?" to collect information on earthquakes. When a devastating earthquake struck China in the spring of 2008, the first reports came not from media reports, but from from Twitter "tweets".

Thanks to Twitter, well-known blogger Robert Scoble reported the Chinese disaster an hour before major media like CNN. Scoble had been reading Twitter tweets from people in China while the earthquake was actually shaking the ground under their feet.[3]

"Members of the public play an absolutely critical role in disaster response," said computer scientist Laysia Palen, author of the study published in *New Scientist*. "Now we're seeing what happens when you superimpose a technological layer on top of that. Instead of rumour-mongering, we see socially produced accuracy."[4]

These examples demonstrate that Web 2.0 tools are increasingly valued not only as platforms for social interaction, but as effective instruments of *social power*. Most of the time, Twitter and Facebook updates form a micro-sociological gossip network that, like the television show *Seinfeld*, is mostly about "nothing" (status update: "Jennifer is stripped to the waist, eating a tub of Cool Whip with a big wooden spoon, by the light of the open refrigerator"). But Twitter, Facebook, GoogleMaps and other social networking platforms can spontaneously mobilize social action with measurable utilitarian value. They possess the power to *get things done*.

Spontaneous social action underscores a fundamental difference between *institutional* and *network* power. As we have seen in previous chapters, the distinguishing social architecture of institutions is rigidly vertical status hierarchies. Institutional structures – especially state and corporate bureaucracies – are centralized command-and-control systems in which power is ascriptively assigned and exercised top-down. Social networks, by contrast, are horizontal and animated by informal exchanges, not formal commands. The power dynamic of social networks is not centralized and top-down, but distributed and diffused.

Hence the third "D" in our 3-D analytical framework: online social networks are characterized by horizontal *diffusion* of power.

Another important insight must be underlined here. The e-ruptive impact of social networking power surpasses, in its consequences, the two other ruptures analysed in the previous parts of this book. The *disaggregation* of online identities, as we saw in the first part, is a phenomenon that has produced many fascinating, unintended and sometimes troubling consequences for social interaction and organizational behaviour. The *democratization* of online status, in like manner, has powerful ramifications for social organization, market behaviour and corporate management. These e-ruptions require us to think differently about the nature of personal identity, social status and the distribution of rewards in complex organizations and wider society. The most revolutionary e-ruptions, however, are being produced by the *power* dynamic of social media. The reason for this is not difficult to discover: in the final analysis, power relations determine the dominant form of social organization, its underlying values and its system of rewards and punishment. We argue in this part of the book that power is shifting away from centralized institutions and is being increasingly distributed through diffuse networks. And this e-ruption, we believe, will have far-reaching consequences for social organization in all its complexity.

As noted at the outset of this book, some have compared the e-ruptive power of Web 2.0 with the profound social, political and economic transformations triggered by the invention of the printing press in the 15th century. Gutenberg's moveable type press, which revolutionized book-making by replacing handwritten manuscripts with mass-copying techniques, facilitated the spread of learning and vernacular languages throughout Western civilization. Most significantly, Gutenberg's invention challenged established hierarchies – notably the Catholic Church – whose monopoly on knowledge and power had largely been based on widespread illiteracy and use of Latin as the official language, notably the Vulgate Bible. The printing press unleashed social power throughout the Renaissance – triggering the Protestant Reformation with vernacular translations of the Bible, and later ushered in the scientific and industrial revolutions that produced capitalism and modern states. A single technical innovation, remarkably, was at the origin of all these cataclysmic transformations. The diffusion of information and knowledge empowered people to challenge, and eventually overthrow, established institutional authority. As testimony to Gutenberg's status in the annals of human endeavour, he is frequently ranked number 1 in Top 10 listings of the most important figures in history – ahead of towering figures such as Christopher Columbus, Martin Luther, Galileo, Shakespeare, Isaac Newton, Charles Darwin, Leonardo da Vinci and Beethoven.[5]

The social Web is different from the printing press – and perhaps even more powerful – in one important aspect. The printing press was a machine whose ownership was largely restricted to new elites, including Martin Luther whose *95 Theses*, nailed to the door of the Wittenberg Castle Church in 1517, was translated from Latin and spread throughout Europe. If many people could read in local languages like German, French and English in the 16th century, very few owned a printing press. Two centuries later when newspapers were attracting mass audiences, printing presses were controlled by a tiny minority of capitalist owners. This oligopoly of press owners yielded enormous power. Some were called "press barons" as testimony to their influence – and indeed, some actually were ennobled as barons in Britain's House of Lords. While media messages were diffuse, media power was concentrated.

The invention of motion pictures and recorded music had similar cultural consequences for social power. Just as the printing press had facilitated the "vulgarization" of the Bible and challenged cultural reverence for Greek and Roman classics with new works by vernacular authors bearing names like Shakespeare and Molière, cinema and sound recordings overthrew cultural elitism by harnessing the spontaneous creativity of so-called "low culture". Until the 20th century, dominant cultural tastes in most Western societies were "bourgeois". The masses, true enough, had their popular "folk" culture, but it was assigned lower status. New industrial techniques turned this status hierarchy on its head. The industrialization of cultural production overthrew elite tastes and enthroned mass-audience popular culture – from Charlie Chaplin and Mickey Mouse to rock and roll and rap. But while this rupture effectively marginalized "elite" culture, it also created – as with the printing press – a new oligopoly that tightly controlled cultural supply. In movies and music, the barons were called moguls. Not everybody could make a movie, produce a television show or record a pop song. These were capital-intensive activities driven by an industrial logic. Power remained centralized. Audiences were empowered only as *consumers*.

Web 2.0 social media have radically e-rupted this cultural production model by disintermediating established suppliers. In the Web 2.0 era, there are no barriers to entry. The costs of production are almost zero. Consumers can also be cultural *producers*. Everybody has access to the value chain. Power is no longer centralized in the hands of monopolists and oligopolies; it is widely distributed towards the margins. In a word, power is *diffused*.

Before taking our analysis further, let's first examine the concept of *power* in its different forms. We have informally defined power as *getting things done*. According to a more formal definition, power always entails some form of *coercion*, either direct or indirect. The bottom-line fact about power is that its assertion is required to achieve goals by constraining others to do things they normally would not do. Unavoidably, power involves issuing commands, explicitly or implicitly, and expecting obedience. It can be exercised through threats, inducements or cooptation. Hence, the definition of power according to three categories: *condign*, *compensatory* or *conditioned*. Condign power is exercised through raw coercion; compensatory power is based on pecuniary rewards; and conditioned power wins submission through persuasion. Condign power can range from physical aggression to military invasion. Anyone who is gainfully employed is familiar with the dynamics of compensatory power. Employers assert power over employees through compensation in the form of wages or a salary. And conditioned power can take various forms, from the habits of tradition to "soft power" in international relations through the appeal of culture and values.

Michael Mann, in his exhaustive work *The Sources of Social Power*, identifies, qualitatively, four broad types of power dynamics: *ideological, economic, military* and *political*. None of these concepts requires further elaboration here, except to say that Mann's definition of *ideology* includes religion. Mann argues that power, which he conceives as a form of *collective action*, possesses two main characteristics: first, it's a *dynamic* process exercised in *networks*; and second, it requires *social organization*. Networks therefore have a functional purpose: they *institutionalize* social relations. Personality and property, to be sure, can form the basis of power. Charismatic leaders – from Napoleon and Hitler to Martin Luther King – have exercised power through persuasion. And plutocrats often exercise power through economic forms of coercion. Hence the familiar expression "money buys power". But the principal source of power, according to Mann, is *social organization*.

Of particular relevance to our analysis here are two distinctions Mann makes in describing power dynamics. First, he distinguishes between *intensive* and *extensive* power; and second, between *authoritative* and *diffused* power.

Intensive power is asserted vertically inside tight command-and-control systems like armies and bureaucracies. *Extensive* power, by contrast, is exercised over a vast spatial territory – for example, throughout an empire or inside a multinational corporation. *Authoritative* power is generally associated with vertical command structures that expect obedience. *Diffused* power, by contrast, is more horizontal and exercised less coercively. Mann provides a detailed definition of *diffused* power that is relevant to our analysis in the following chapters. He notes that diffused power "spreads in a more spontaneous, unconscious, decentred way throughout a population, resulting in similar social practices that embody power relations but are not explicitly commanded."[6] These distinctions provide insights that help us understand the network dynamics of Web 2.0 social media in contrast to traditional forms of institutional power. While institutional power is generally *authoritative, intensive* and exercised through *coercion*, network power is *diffused, extensive* and exercised through *cooperation*.

The classic example of institutional power is the modern nation-state, formally defined as exercising a *monopoly of legitimate violence over a defined territory*. States are coercive instruments, directed inwardly towards their own populations. When state violence is turned outside its borders, it's called warfare. We find the same entrenched notion of aggression in widely accepted characteristics of modern capitalist corporations. It's often said that corporations are driven by a relentless desire to *crush* or *wipe out* the competition. Economists employ similarly bellicose terminology when they describe corporations as market *belligerents*. The values of warfare are thus deeply embedded in the spirit, if not in the actual conduct, of modern capitalism. In the marketplace, launching a legal action against a competitor is commercial warfare by other means.

The Middle Ages, needless to say, was a highly belligerent epoch. The clash between Philippe le Bel and the Knights Templar provides us with a perfect illustration of the tension between authoritative/intensive and diffused/extensive power. Templar power was essentially ideological – or, to be precise, *religious* – and was exercised in an *extensive* and *diffused* manner throughout Christendom. Philippe le Bel, as we have seen, feared that Templar power was becoming *authoritative* and *intensive* and consequently threatened to rival his own legitimacy. His paranoia was not entirely unfounded. Few historians would dispute that the Knights Templar were becoming a significant temporal power base throughout Christendom, capable of asserting military, economic, political and ideological coercion. The Teutonic Knights, another Papal order, did precisely that. As Philippe le Bel knew only too well, the Teutonic Knights had invaded the Baltic region and established a monastic state in Prussia. Philippe, determined to neutralize a similar threat in Western Europe, ordered the arrest and execution of the Templar leaders. In economic terms, Philippe was crushing a potential competitor and asserting the French state's monopoly of legitimate violence over his kingdom. The French king was a shrewd monopolist. So were the modern states that followed.

We actually have an Internet-era remake of the Philippe le Bel versus Knights Templar saga. It played out only a decade ago in China when the Communist regime clashed with the Falun Gong religious sect. Falun Gong – a quasi-Buddhist religious movement that combines mind–body mysticism, faith healing and millenarian visions – claims to capture the truth of the universe through "Wheel of the Law" principles. In the West, Falun Gong's adherents are known mainly for their dedication to *tai chi* and *qigong* exercises that are often performed outdoors and look like slow-motion karate moves.

The sect's charismatic founder, Li Hongzhi, was born in China in 1951 and worked in a number of unremarkable jobs before founding Falun Gong in the early 1990s. Li's spiritual teachings throughout China quickly attracted a mass following by filling a void in a country lacking a robust civil society. By the end of the 1990s, Li was one of many *qigong* "masters" travelling throughout China and attracting huge crowds with his lectures and workshops.

In China, religion was officially discouraged by the Communist Party. Mao Zedong, the father of Chinese communism, had condemned Confucianism as "feudal superstition" and the regime had long repressed Buddhist dissent in regions like Tibet. China's regime was no less hostile to Roman Catholicism, especially after the Vatican opened old wounds by beatifying some 120 martyrs in China over four centuries. While China counts some 12 million Catholics, the regime controls the Catholic Church and bans any connection to the Pope – not surprising, given that the Vatican maintains diplomatic ties with Taiwan.[7] In the 1990s, however, the Chinese regime was ushering in reforms and therefore was relatively indulgent towards Falun Gong. At first, the spiritual movement seemed more like a harmless *tai chi* exercise club than a dangerous religious cult.

It didn't take long, however for Chinese rulers to realize that Falun Gong was more than a popular karate club. A first sign was Falun Gong's extraordinary claims of supernatural powers and miracle healing. More troubling, the religious sect had become, in less than a decade, a powerful organization throughout the country, mobilizing millions of people around ancient Chinese doctrines. Some estimates put Falun Gong membership in China at a staggering 70 million.[8] If the movement continued to grow, Falun Gong followers threatened to outnumber membership in the Communist Party.

A confrontation between China's communist state and the Falun Gong religious network was inevitable. It came in early 1999, when a single incident triggered a fateful showdown. In the city of Tianjin, police had scattered a Falun Gong meeting where followers were boisterously reacting to a published report criticizing the movement as dangerous. This clash prompted Falun Gong followers to stage a non-violent sit-in in Beijing to protest what they considered to be official harassment. In late April 1999, some 10 000 Falun Gong followers descended or Beijing's Temple of Heaven park and surrounded the communist leaders' compound at Zhongnanhai. Circling China's epicentre of state power, Falun Gong protesters appealed directly to the regime for official status in Chinese society.

The country's rulers were not listening. China's president, Jiang Zemin, vowed to crush Falun Gong, claiming it was more pernicious than Japan's infamous Aum cult whose adherents had released deadly gas in the city's underground train system. Four days after the Beijing demonstration, the regime denounced Falun Gong as an "evil cult" that was "damaging social stability under the pretext of practising martial arts". The regime claimed, specifically, that Falun Gong was an elaborate pyramid scheme that was financially scamming its own members. This is the same kind of accusation that, in the West, is frequently levelled against the Church of Scientology and other alleged religious cults. Shortly afterwards, Falun Gong leaders were arrested and jailed, while followers of lesser status were forced into "re-education" programmes. Falun Gong claimed that 35000 members had been arrested, 5000 imprisoned and 15 had died in custody.[9]

Falun Gong's leader Li Hongzhi, meanwhile, had defected to the United States in 1995 to run his global spiritual empire from a safer, and more lucrative, territorial base.[10] His self-imposed exile to the United States was fortuitous because the Internet was exploding in the mid-1990s. Li shrewdly understood that the Internet – a horizontally structured global network – was a powerful platform for a religious movement. Li set up a website (www.falundafa.com) not only to control his Chinese organization while in exile, but also to extend Falun Gong's influence outside China.

Li put in place a highly effective social network that linked some 40 different sites in countries from Canada and Australia to Russia, Germany and Taiwan. He was also communicating with his followers via an underground website available in China. It was believed Li had orchestrated the anti-regime Falun Gong protests in China – including the Beijing sit-in in 1999 – via the Internet from his base in New York. Li confirmed this indirectly when asked how the protests had happened so spontaneously in a country with secret police everywhere.

"They found out on the Internet," he said. "Also, the practitioners in different regions were friends, and relayed this information to others."

When the Chinese government discovered Li's online network, it moved quickly to shut it down in China. Numerous websites and more than a million free email services were switched off as part of the crackdown. On Google, any search in China for "Falun Gong" caused the results page to be blocked (though "FLG movement" evidently worked).[11] Bill Clinton described China's efforts to restrict Web communication as "trying to nail Jell-O to the wall", but the regime's web-filtering technology grew increasingly sophisticated and effective. The Chinese regime used the Web – notably on official sites like *People's Daily* – to discredit Falun Gong as an organization and attack Li personally (claiming, for example, that he was guilty of tax evasion and linked to the CIA). As one observer following the Falun Gong saga concluded: "It is clear that, for the first time in history, a movement and counter-movement occurred in cyberspace, apparently with dramatic effect." [12]

The Chinese regime itself is now harnessing the positive power of the Web to connect with its own citizens. In June 2008, Chinese President Hu Jintao conducted a "netizen" online forum with ordinary Chinese who posted questions for the leader to answer. While the questions were carefully hand-picked, the Chinese leader fielded queries such as "how much do you earn a month?" and "when are you going to root out corruption?". Hu told his online audience that he believed the Web was a powerful tool for keeping in touch with the Chinese people.

"Although I am too busy to browse the Internet everyday," he said. "I try to spend some time on the Web. First, I read domestic and international news on the Web. Through the Web I also want to know what netizens are thinking about and what their opinions are. Thirdly, I hope to get some suggestions and advice proposed by our netizens to the Government and the Party." [13]

Our purpose here, with this example of China, is not to present a Good Guy-versus-Bad Guy morality play. What interests us are the power dynamics between vertical top-down institutional structures and socially based horizontal networks. The Falun Gong saga, whatever it may reveal about religious sects in modern society, reveals something about the power of social networks in the Internet Age.

One key insight is that it's increasingly difficult for states, with their rigid bureaucratic structures, to control Web-based social movements which have been spontaneously organized by their own members. There are two reasons for this. First, online social networks transcend the time/space logic of states. And second, online social networks diffuse power to the periphery of society, making centralized state control less coercively effective.

Interestingly, the modern-day descendants of the Knights Templar seem to understand the dynamics of these e-ruptions. The

Freemasons, who have been criticized in many countries for their allegedly clandestine behaviour as a "secret society", have leveraged the social power of the Internet to reinforce internal solidarity. In Britain, the government has openly accused the Freemasons of infiltrating the criminal justice system with crony networks and, in some cases, thwarting due process to protect their own brethren. The Freemasons, for their part, have insisted that their activities are motivated by three principles: brotherly love, truth and charity. Unconvinced, in 1998 a parliamentary Home Affairs Committee accused the organization of operating as a secret network motivated by "mutual advancement and favour-swapping". The UK Home Secretary even took the extraordinary step of ordering all judges to declare, in a public register, any affiliations with the Freemasons.[14] In France, too, the Freemasons have long been accused of forming a secretive network – allegedly dominated by Protestants and Jews – at the highest ranks of the state. In Catholic France, it has never been forgotten that Freemasons – perhaps exacting historical revenge against Philippe le Bel – were instrumental in the "Enlightenment" movement that ignited the French Revolution and led to the execution of the French king, Louis XVI.

The UK Grand Lodge, under pressure from the British government, decided in 2000 to embrace the Internet as a gesture of openness aimed at lifting the alleged shroud of mystery about the organization's internal activities. "Over the past 20 to 30 years, perceptions have been changing," said Nava Navaratnarajah when announcing a United Grand Lodge-approved website. "We are trying to change the image Mr Joe Public has that we are some kind of secret society. It is far from it. It is only the rituals that we like to keep secret. As far as what freemasonry does and is about, that information is all publicly available. This is what we are trying to promote through the website." [15]

In 2006, two Freemasons published a book, *The Temple that Never Sleeps*, in which they called for a "new paradigm" shifting the organization towards "e-Masonry". And in an article called "Freemasonry and the Internet", American lodge member Brother Francis Vicente states that "the reach of the Internet (blogs, YouTube, Google, etc.) as a vehicle to promote Freemasonry and to blunt/counter anti-Masonic attacks is a must tool for the Fraternity in the new century". Vicente, a member of a lodge in Philadelphia, called on his Masonic brethren to embrace Internet blogging to spread a positive message about the Freemasons. "It should be noted that political dictatorships function the same way as ecclesiastical ones," he added. "This is the main reason that dictatorships close down lodges as they come to power. It is a fear of freedom being given to the masses which endangers their rule." [16]

Are we witnessing a resurgence of networked social power that, thanks to the horizontal dynamics of the Web, is challenging the archaic logic of vertical power structures? Has power really shifted from top-down vertical forms of *coercion* to horizontal systems of *cooperation* and *collaboration*? Or is this yet another naïve, techno-optimist vision that confuses *democracy* with *anarchy* and consequently is doomed to encounter the implacable reassertion of authoritative, intensive power? These are the questions we propose to explore in this final part of the book.

Since cooperation requires *collective action*, the best way to set the stage for the next four chapters is by examining the concept itself. Or to formulate it as a question: what motivates people to engage in strategies of collective action to achieve goals? Are we *coerced* into working together? Do we cooperate merely because we are *compensated* to do so? Are we *co-opted* into joining collective endeavours? Or are we driven by other motivations?

Fortunately, there's a classic book on the subject: *The Logic of Collective Action* by American economist Mancur Olson. [17] Published nearly a half-century ago, Olson's book is rich in insights about the costs and benefits of collective action and its implications for organizations and states. Olson's main goal was to challenge two familiar assumptions: first, that when members of a group have common interests, they will act collectively to advance those interests; and second, that in democracies, there is an ever-present danger (as Tocqueville warned) of a tyranny of the majority that will prejudice the interests of minorities.

Olson argued that, in both instances, the opposite is true. First, he demonstrated that individuals in groups have a rational interest to do nothing and benefit – as "free riders" – from the public goods produced by the whole group. He added, however, that rational individuals will actively participate in collective action if there are *specific incentives* in the form of private benefits. Second, Olson demonstrated that it's hard for groups, due to the rational calculations (high costs and low benefits) of their individual members, to organize collective action. Individuals in small groups, on the other hand, face lower costs and reap greater benefits, thus making collective action more effective. This explains, argued Olson, why special-interest lobbies whose members have specific interests (big business, unions, single-issue groups) are generally more effective than widely organized common-good organizations (consumer and citizen groups). Consequently, the real danger to democracy, argued Olson, is not tyranny of the majority – but tyranny of the *minority*.

Olson's theory of collective action has obvious consequences for the themes we are exploring in these pages. Since online social networks are, by definition, large and horizontally organized, the cost–benefit calculation does not, in theory, favour participation, cooperation and collaboration. Secondly, the high cost of socially organizing large groups would appear to be an obstacle to the mass collaboration benefits vaunted by Web 2.0 evangelists. If collective action is biased in favour of small groups, how can horizontal networks, complex organizations and democratic societies harness "collective smarts"?

Olson's notion of *specific incentives* is the key to answering this question. Rational individuals appear to need an incentive to participate in collective action. We therefore need to explore what kinds of incentives motivate people to collaborate and cooperate.

Some specific incentives are rational. People collaborate if they have a material interest to do so – in other words, if they are *compensated*. Don Tapscott illustrates this in his book, *Wikinomics*, which features an interesting anecdote about a large Canadian mining company, Goldcorp.[18] Seeking the optimal way of finding gold deposits in an area of 55 000 acres, Goldcorp decided to post geological data on its website and offer $575 000 in prizes for anyone who could come up with the most efficient way of finding and extracting the mineral. Goldcorp discovered that, thanks to the logic of collective smarts – or wisdom of crowds – about 80% of its crowdsourced proposals hit pay dirt, helping reduce the company's production costs by about 600%. For the mass collaborators who participated, there was a *specific incentive* to get involved in the project – money.

Political scientist Robert Axelrod, in his insightful book *The Evolution of Cooperation*, also argues that we have rational motivations to collaborate with others. Axelrod, a game theory expert, based his theory on the familiar "Prisoner's Dilemma": when two accomplices are incarcerated, each has a rational interest to provide the same alibi, because if they stick together both will walk free; whereas if one defects by snitching on the other, the fingered prisoner does hard time; and if both snitch on each other, they're both up the creek. The two prisoners, therefore, have a rational interest to mutually cooperate so they both benefit.

Axelrod illustrates the rational option of mutual cooperation with historical accounts of trench warfare during the First World War. Contrary to the common image we have of gruesome battlefield combat during World War I, Axelrod discovered that a so-called "live-and-let-live" syndrome prevailed over instincts to wipe out the enemy. German and Allied trenches were so close to each other that soldiers could make out the faces of the enemy troops. This injected a human dimension into trench warfare that was reinforced by the fact that enemy soldiers remained in the same trenches for long periods. Their sustained interaction at close range created a mutual familiarity that led to "tacit truces" – in other words, reciprocally understood cooperation based on not killing enemy soldiers in facing trenches. Mutual cooperation, and survival, was deemed rationally preferable to mutual destruction and certain death. As Axelrod put it: "The cooperative exchanges of mutual restraint actually changed the nature of the interaction. They tended to make the two sides care about each other's welfare".

Even more interesting, the two sides pursued their tacit cooperation despite commands from military headquarters to kill enemy soldiers. "The live-and-let-live system was endemic in trench warfare", noted Axelrod. "It flourished despite the best efforts of senior officers to stop it, despite the passions aroused by combat, despite the military logic of kill or be killed and despite the ease with which the high command was able to repress any local efforts to arrange a direct truce."[19] In other words, the social impulse to cooperate prevailed, even in conditions of war, over the dictates of a vertical, top-down command structure that ordered soldiers to attack and kill the enemy. Axelrod's conclusion could be called the Kindness of Strangers: "The live-and-let-live system that emerged in the bitter trench warfare of World War I demonstrates that friendship is hardly necessary for cooperation based on reciprocity to get started. Under suitable circumstances, cooperation can develop even between antagonists."

It might reasonably be argued that soldiers caught in First World War trench warfare cooperated in order to avoid certain death – in other words, they were obeying a rational survival instinct. While undoubtedly true, that still wouldn't explain why individuals cooperate and collaborate in other, non-life-threatening circumstances – for example, as we saw at the outset of this chapter, in transmitting information about natural disasters and tragic crimes. Why bother making the effort? There are other examples of spontaneous collaboration that similarly seem to defy rational explanation. Why, for example, do some people devote so much time and effort to contributing long and well-considered entries in Wikipedia? And why, in the US Congress and other legislatures, do politicians from opposing parties mutually cooperate through tacit understanding, and even vote-swapping, when they are supposed to be bitter adversaries? And why are people willing to participate in mass collaboration projects inside corporations despite the absence of any specific financial incentive?

We believe that the nonrational nature of cooperation can be explained, like other phenomena explored in this book, by the *exit/voice/loyalty* theory. People cooperate with one another – even when they are ascriptively assigned to adversarial roles – because they share common *loyalties* to their social settings – neighbourhood, corporation, legislature, democracy and so on. When social interaction among people is continuous over time, it reinforces a basic need for cooperation. In social networks, familiarity does not breed contempt, it reinforces loyalties – especially if we believe that we'll continue interacting with these same people. Axelrod calls this phenomenon the long "shadow of the future".

"For cooperation to prove stable, the future must have a sufficiently large shadow," observes Axelrod. "This means that the importance of the next encounter between the same two individuals must be great enough to make defection an unprofitable strategy when the other player is provocable. It requires that players have a large enough chance of meeting again, and that they do not discount the significance of their next meeting too greatly." In short, we cooperate when we have a reasonable anticipation of future social interaction with others – unless, of course, we choose *voice* or *exit* to mark dissent and disloyalty.

Sometimes the explanation is even simpler. People contribute to Wikipedia and participate in collaboration projects because cooperation validates their values and reinforces their self-esteem. Frequently they get involved simply because it's fun. True, social capital rewards like status are sometimes motivating factors. But in many cases, people participate in collective forms of action because it makes them feel good, especially when everyone places a high value on cooperation. In other words, when there is general buy-in to the conviction that cooperation and collaboration are positive values. To cite an insightful study on the organizational implications of voluntary collaboration: "Generalized reciprocity emerges when people have positive regard for the social system in which requests for help are embedded and show respect for it through offering help."[20]

If these insights are valid, do we need to reformulate the definition of *power* for the Web 2.0 era? If power has indeed been diffused, moving from vertical organizational structures towards horizontal social networks, perhaps a new definition should place less emphasis on its *coercive* dynamic and focus more on its potential to foster *cooperation*.

We will test this hypothesis in the following four chapters, focusing on specific examples of cooperation and collaboration in the marketplace, in corporations and in democratic institutions. In the final analysis, if the diffused power dynamics of Markets 2.0, Enterprise 2.0 and Democracy 2.0 succeed in getting things done, it may constitute the most powerful argument for the Web 2.0 revolution.

12

Davids and Goliaths: the revenge of the amateur

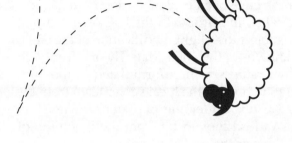

The 19th century historian Thomas Carlyle famously asserted that "the history of the world is but the biography of great men". Carlyle expanded on his Great Man Theory in an ambitious work published in 1840, *On Heroes, Hero-Worship and the Heroic in History*. In that book, Carlyle identified a number of remarkable figures – among them Dante, Shakespeare, Luther, Rousseau and Napoleon – whose place in the Pantheon of human achievement is beyond dispute.

The Great Man Theory has fallen on hard times. Its demise may one day be dated to 2006. That year, *Time* magazine – a longstanding proponent of Carlyle's theory through its "Man of the Year" covers stretching back to Charles Lindbergh in 1927 – made a momentous decision. Over the years, *Time* had selected for its annual distinction a fairly predictable roster of statesmen, peacemakers and powerful businessmen for its portrait gallery: John F. Kennedy, Mikhail Gorbachev, Anwar Sadat, Bill Clinton, George Bush (both of them), Ted Turner, Pope John Paul II, Bill Gates and so on. Henceforth, however, current events were no longer driven by powerful men in high places. In 2006, *Time*'s "Person of the Year" was somebody entirely unexpected: *You*. Yes, you. As in, you, me and everybody else on the planet. Each and every one of us.

"Look at 2006 through a different lens and you'll see another story, one that isn't about conflict or great men," *Time* noted in justifying its radically democratic selection. "It's a story about community and collaboration on a scale never seen before. It's about the cosmic compendium of knowledge Wikipedia and the million-channel people's network YouTube and the online metropolis MySpace. It's about the many wresting power from the few and helping one another for nothing and how that will not only change the world, but also change the way the world changes . . . Who has that time and that energy and that passion? The answer is, you do. And for seizing the reins of the global media, for founding and framing the new digital democracy, for working for nothing and beating the pros at their own game, *Time*'s Person of the Year for 2006 is you."[1]

One sphere where the pros have been beaten at their own game is soccer – or football, as it's called in Europe. In the UK, ownership of football clubs is frequently subject to a slight modification of the Great Man Theory, commonly known as the Rich Man Theory. The Rich Man Theory of football ownership was first formulated in the mid-1970s when pop star Elton John bought the local soccer team from his boyhood, Watford Football Club. Under the pop star's ownership, and thanks to his money, Watford moved up from the ignominy of the fourth division to the glory of the FA Cup final.

Elton John eventually stepped down as chairman of Watford, but his withdrawal from the front ranks of British football had no negative impact on the Rich Man Theory.[2] On the contrary, several British football clubs would later be purchased by high-profile billionaires. The Russian oil tycoon Roman Abramovich bought Chelsea Football Club and Indian-born steel magnate Lakshmi Mittal acquired Queens Park Rangers. The list of fabulously rich men who own professional soccer teams, especially in Europe, is very long indeed.[3]

The Rich Man Theory of football, like the Great Man Theory of history, has been challenged by the Internet. As the purchase of Ebbsfleet United Football Club in late 2007 demonstrated, sometimes wide support is better than deep pockets to rescue a languishing soccer team. Ebbsfleet's owner is not a rich man. The team is owned by thousands of ordinary Ebbsfleet supporters. The fans of Ebbsfleet – formerly known as Gravesend & Northfleet – leveraged the power of Internet-based mass collaboration to storm the Kent-based football club's boardroom. Organized on the website MyFootballClub.co.uk, roughly 27 000 fans paid £35 each (about $70) to buy – and manage – the underperforming team. As London's *Times* described this unexpected twist in British football management: "Democracy gatecrashed the autocratic world of football yesterday."

Today the team's new owners – in the spirit of the club's motto "Own The Club, Pick The Team" – not only vote via the Internet on top management, but also select players and decide on transfers. It's pure wisdom of crowds – but in this case, a specialized football crowd. As *The Times* noted: "At most clubs it is considered daring if a supporters' representative is let anywhere near the boardroom; at Ebbsfleet, power will rest with the people, not profit-hungry billionaires."[4]

Launched by a former soccer journalist Will Brooks, MyFootball-Club.co.uk operates like an investment fund that prefers majority positions (it owns 51% of Ebbsfleet), voting control and takes a hand's-on approach to management. One of the first decisions taken by the team's virtual owners was to demote manager Liam Daish to head coach, thus making him subject to their online votes on team selection, formation and tactics. Critics quickly dismissed the new Ebbsfleet as "fantasy football", saying the experiment wouldn't last.[5] And yet, despite the naysayers, mass online ownership hasn't hurt the club's fortunes. In May 2008, Ebbsfleet won the FA Trophy – the first Kentish team ever to take this honour – after defeating Torquay United 1-0 at London's Wembley Stadium. MyFootballClub.co.uk has since been kicking the tyres of other takeover prospects, including clubs like Leeds United, Nottingham Forest, Cambridge United, Accrington Stanley and Halifax Town.[6]

Whether Ebbsfleet might one day stand alongside Chelsea, Arsenal and Manchester United among Britain's top football clubs is a long shot. But those who say to hell with mass online ownership of professional soccer clubs clearly have not grasped the e-ruptive dynamics of crowdsourcing – namely, that power is no longer located in centralized bureaucratic structures, but *diffused* democratically throughout society. Conservative attitudes towards these e-ruptions, as we shall see, are invariably motivated by entrenched values that defer to ascriptively defined roles of "professionals" and assign a lower status to "amateurs".

This chapter is about the revenge of the amateur. The tension between professionals and amateurs is arguably the fiercest war raging on the Web 2.0 battlefield. It's an uneven conflict between Davids and Goliaths, but as in the Bible, the power of clumsy Philistine giants is being toppled by smaller and smarter rivals.

As Glenn Reynolds, a former law professor who writes the InstaPundit blog, argues in his book *An Army of Davids:* "We're accustomed to thinking that big organizations are the important organizations because that's how it's been in recent centuries. Starting around 1700, big organizations became the most efficient way to do a lot of things. The main source of power, steam engines and the like, had to be big and to be efficient. And keeping track of information required armies of clerks, secretaries, etc., who needed a big organization to support them. These concepts – which economists call 'economies of scope and scale' – favoured big organizations. Big companies, big governments, whatever. Mass production. Bigger was better. *Goliath rules*."[7] Reynolds, needless to say, is a believer in David's sling. The subtitle of his book makes that clear: *How Markets and Technology Empower Ordinary People to Beat Big Media, Big Government and other Goliaths*. Reynolds is a Web 2.0 revolutionary who sings the body electric and celebrates the Do-It-Yourself diffusion of power to the common man.

Critics of the Internet's "amateur" culture counter that Web-inspired zealotry is little more than digital utopia. They claim that, in the real world, power legitimately resides with professional experts working in established institutions. They dismiss terms like "crowdsourcing" and "mass collaboration" as Web 2.0 slogans for online *collectivism*, with all the negative connotations that word suggests.

Jaron Lanier, in a widely discussed essay criticizing the hazards of online collectivism, referred disapprovingly to this phenomenon as "digital Maoism". While acknowledging that large groups may well be able to guess with remarkable accuracy the number of jellybeans in a large glass jar, Lanier remains sceptical about the wisdom of crowds in matters of greater importance. He reminds us, correctly, that collective "wisdom" can be astoundingly stupid: Tulipmania in the 17th century, stock market bubbles, hysteria over fictitious satanic child abductions, false alarms about the "Y2K" threat and so on. "What we are witnessing today," notes Lanier, "is the alarming rise of the fallacy of the infallible collective."[8]

Lanier's analysis is undeniably intriguing – and highly contestable. For one thing, his definition of terms appears to have been distorted to reinforce the bias of his argument. Collectivism is a rigid economic system that failed first in the Soviet Union, then in communist China. Collective action, on the other hand, is not communist; it is essentially liberal and democratic. The Internet is not collectivist, it's a platform for collective action. Blurring this distinction can only be considered specious. As Web 2.0 evangelist Howard Rheingold noted in a rebuttal of Lanier's essay, if the Internet is a Maoist collective, it has produced an astounding number of capitalist billionaires who have profited handsomely from launching communist companies like Amazon, Yahoo! and Google.[9]

A more serious critique of the Web 2.0 revolution takes aim at its *cultural* consequences. In a nutshell, it's this: the Web is dangerous because it is unleashing upon the world a passionate contagion of *amateurism*.

The most articulate voice in this school is Andrew Keen, author of the polemical book, *The Cult of the Amateur*. Following its publication in 2007, Keen's book was received by Web 2.0 evangelists as a frontal attack on their techno-social revolution headquartered somewhere in Silicon Valley.[10] Keen's critique is fascinating for two reasons – one quasi-religious, the other quasi-ideological.

First, Keen is an apostate. He's a Silicon Valley insider and former New Economy entrepreneur who, in 2004, was among the faithful at the O'Reilly Media conference where the term "Web 2.0" was coined. But Keen quickly became disillusioned, he says, by the self-interested opportunism of Web 2.0 evangelists selling digital snakeskin oil with promises of a phony Internet utopia. He candidly describes *The Cult of the Amateur* in a way that leaves no doubt about his status in Silicon Valley: "It's the work of an apostate, an insider now on the outside who has poured out his cup of Kool-Aid and resigned his membership in the cult."

Second, Keen is hostile to democracy. Or as he puts it, the danger of Web 2.0's democratic promise is that it quickly degenerates into an "intellectually corrosive radical egalitarianism". Keen argues that the Web 2.0 revolution's democratic pretensions have led to the emergence of a "noble amateur" who is destroying the quality of established culture. "Democratisation, despite its lofty idealisation," he argues, "is undermining truth, souring civic discourse and belittling expertise, experience and talent."

Keen's polemical discourse is situated in a clearly recognizable ideological tradition: reactionary radicalism. Like the Luddites who feared the disruptive effects of the Industrial Revolution, Keen is hostile to the technologically driven Web 2.0 revolution because he resents its destabilizing effects on the established order. After spitting out his Kool-Aid and tossing away the cup, Keen has seized the poisoned chalice of grumpy conservatism. He has become a stout defender of the old oligarchies and cultural gatekeepers that the Web 2.0 revolution is sweeping away.

"Our cultural standards and moral values are not all that are at stake," argues Keen. "Gravest of all, the very traditional institutions that have helped foster and create our news, our music, our literature, our television shows and our movies are under assault as well."

There it is, Keen's *casus belli* boldly stated in two words. He is hostile to the Web 2.0 revolution because it threatens *traditional institutions*.

Any serious argument against democracy commands attention. Yet upon closer inspection, Keen's critique of "amateur" culture is obviously based on a conceptual fallacy. He assigns the rank of *professional* status to classes of cultural producers – critics, journalists, editors, filmmakers, musicians – whose work he qualifies as *expert*. Yet, ironically, cultural production is the one sphere where the traditional distinction between amateur and professional is the hardest to defend.

The status designation of "professional" stretches back to pre-industrial societies in which expert craftsmen – stonemasons, carpenters, glasscutters and so on – were organized in confraternities that possessed monopoly knowledge about the secrets of their arts. Craft organizations existed in virtually every civilization – China, India, Egypt, Greece, Rome. By the Middle Ages, craftsmen were organized into guilds that enjoyed monopoly privileges formalized by letters patent granted by kings and local authorities. Guilds were strictly ranked according to skill level – *apprentice, journeyman* and *master craftsman.* Throughout medieval Europe, guilds exercised an economic stranglehold on many cities and – like labour unions in modern economies – enjoyed considerable political power. Cities where guilds held no sway were called "free". The term "cottage industry" comes from efforts to organize weaving skills in networks of cottages in rural areas where guild power was absent. In some countries, such as France, the power of guilds was encouraged and institutionalized because it centralized – and thus facilitated – tax collection.[11]

While guilds survived the emergence of capitalism, they had lost considerable status by the early 19th century due to their resistance to industrialization and free trade. Adam Smith, the intellectual father of capitalism, criticized the guild system. So did Karl Marx. While Marx argued that capitalism ultimately had to destroy the guild system in its overthrow of the feudal economy, he acknowledged that guilds had fettered workers with rigid regulations and impediments. Guilds were, in modern parlance, closed shops – not unlike regulated professions today.

In truth, the historical distinction between professional and amateur wasn't clearly demarcated until the 20th century. This was particularly so in the natural sciences. We have only to think of Leonardo da Vinci and Francis Bacon, two classic Renaissance figures whose brilliant scientific investigations were purely amateur. In Britain, amateur botanists had become so expert by the 19th century that professionals in the field were resentful of their activities.[12] The history of photography provides a more compelling example of the power of amateurs. At its origins in the mid-19th century, photography was entirely amateur, dominated by the same genteel class that was devoting itself to other amateur pursuits like botany and astronomy. We owe to the efforts of amateur photographers a rich treasure trove of visual social history of the 19th century. If novelist Lewis Carroll – the *nom de plume* for the eccentric Oxford don Charles Dodgson – hadn't taken photographs of a little girl called Alice Liddell, we would not have a photographic record of the inspiration for *Alice in Wonderland*. Early photographers were, like Dodgson, mainly gentlemen with the financial means to purchase photographic equipment. By the 1880s, American bank clerk George Eastman had invented his Kodak camera featuring a 100-exposure roll of film. When Kodak cameras hit the market shortly before the turn of the century, it heralded the mass popularity of photography. Anybody who could afford a camera became a shutterbug.

In the early 20th century, amateurism suffered a status setback due to the exigencies of modernity – namely, the social organization of professions into powerful institutional structures. As Charles Leadbeater, author of *We-think*, has described it: "In one field after another, amateurs and their ramshackle organizations were driven out by people who knew what they were doing and had certificates to prove it."[13] Whereas in previous eras amateur activities had been motivated largely by genteel altruism and were pursued in an independent manner, the rise of professionalism asserted monopoly control over knowledge and assigned social status based on ascriptive titles and credentials (Doctor, Professor, etc.). Also, whereas amateurism had been largely self-financed by wealthy gentlemen, or supported by aristocratic patrons, modern professions were organized and regulated by states.

The professionalization of certain fields brought definite social benefits, especially in areas – medicine, pharmacy, accounting – that had been tarnished by widespread quackery. Certain professions indeed urgently needed to be certified and governed. Thanks to the professionalization of medicine, patients wheeled into operating rooms had the assurance that the person holding the scalpel was a certified surgeon. It was said, indeed, that the core professional classes were those that healed our bodies and measured our profits. Given the importance of these functions, professional organizations were able to extract significant rewards and privileges for their efforts, not least of which were rich emoluments. Among other privileges that accrued to professions were monopoly entitlements, restrictive arrangements, self-regulatory powers and high social status. The time-honoured attraction of professions like medicine and law, especially to the middle classes, is indeed based on the expectation of these material and status rewards.[14] It also explains why professionals organize themselves to protect and promote their specific interests. Professions, whatever benefits their expertise brings to society, are structurally organized to preserve their monopoly power.[15]

Professional status is highly satisfactory, needless to say, if you are a doctor, lawyer, professor, pharmacist or even a journalist. But as Mancur Olson argued in his classic book, *The Rise and Decline of Nations*, the proliferation of professional associations, organized as interest groups, works against the overall social good and leads to economic decline. Why? Because special interest groups – say, a doctors' lobby – are motivated by self-interest and thus seek to obtain disproportionately large benefits for themselves that impose higher burdens on society as a whole. When this form of economic clientelism gets out of control, argues Olson, it produces negative externalities that, in the long term, as more and more interest groups' demands are appeased, leads inexorably to economic decline.[16]

Shortly after Olson published his book in 1982, the knowledge economy started to break apart the organizational rigidities that he blamed for economic decline. In an enlightening essay on "expert power", Michael Reed draws a typology based on a distinction between *professionals* and *knowledge workers*. Whereas organized professions used their technical expertise to pursue power strategies based on credentialism within closed institutional bureaucracies, knowledge workers have leveraged their analytical capacities in open networked markets. Here is Reed's major insight: because knowledge workers operate in horizontal networks rather than in administrative structures, their activities threaten professionals because they tend to *liberalize* and *commodify* services and products offered by organizationally structured experts. In a nutshell, knowledge workers are usurping the credentials-based monopoly power of professional experts.

We can say, therefore, that the monopoly privileges of professional organizations were already being challenged long before the Web 2.0 revolution. Professionalism was being demystified, and even discredited, by the advent of knowledge-based workers empowered by new technologies decades ago.

Let's now return to specific examples of expert power in the cultural sphere. We shall attempt to ascertain whether cultural gatekeepers possess indispensible expertise that produces social benefits; or whether they exploit the values of credentialism to protect monopoly privileges and status rewards. We will examine three different segments of publishing: literature, encyclopaedias and journalism.

In literature, editors working for major publishing houses select which novels get published, and which get rejected. For aspiring writers of fiction, these editors are powerful cultural gatekeepers. And yet their expertise can't be demonstrated according to any rational criteria. Even the top fiction editors in publishing, whatever the depth of their experience, can make no claim to professional status. In truth, nobody really knows how to recognize a great work of literature when it lands on their desk. We could fill these pages with stories about great writers whose works were flatly rejected by experienced editors at the world's most reputable publishing houses. When George Orwell submitted *Animal Farm* to a publisher, he received the following rejection notice: "It is impossible to sell animal stories in the USA." Ayn Rand, for her part, received the following rejection upon submission of her masterpiece *The Fountainhead*: "It is badly written and the hero is unsympathetic." And William Faulkner, arguably America's greatest novelist, got this snub when trying to get his first novel published: "My chief objection is that you don't have any story to tell."[17]

A more recent, and highly publicized, indictment of literary expertise at major UK publishing houses was the Jane Austen hoax. In 2007, David Lassman, director of the Jane Austen Festival in Bath, had a hunch about the level of literary expertise at publishing houses obsessed with blockbuster thrillers and How-To books. To confirm his suspicion, he took Austen's fiction – from lesser-known works like *Northanger Abbey* to *Persuasion* and *Pride and Prejudice* – and changed the titles and made other slight alterations before sending them off as the work of a first-time novelist. To his astonishment, most publishers – all but one – didn't even recognize that it was Jane Austen. Even more astounding, they rejected the work on the grounds that it was not up to their literary standards.

When Lassman circulated a slightly modified version of *Pride and Prejudice* he even cheekily kept the novel's famous opening line: "It is a truth universally acknowledged that a single man in possession of a good fortune must be in want of a wife." When the rejection slips started falling into his mailbox, he quickly discovered another universally acknowledged truth: literary experts, suffering from pride and prejudice themselves, don't know how to recognize a literary classic when it's staring them in the face. Only one publisher spotted it. "I was staggered," said Lassman. "Here is one of the greatest writers that has lived, with her *oeuvre* securely fixed in the English canon, and yet only one recipient recognized them as Austen's work."[18] Lassman learned that literary publishing isn't an open talent search, it's a closed cultural fortress. Though as we saw in Chapter 10 after Penguin paid $900 000 to Catherine Sanderson for two books based on her Petite Anglaise blog, the drawbridge is gradually creaking open.

Now let's look at encyclopaedias. Few can dispute that Wikipedia is the Internet's most successful example of a spontaneous mass collaboration project. Wikipedia provides a perfect illustration of the *diffusion of power* away from cultural gatekeepers ensconced in centralized institutions towards democratic, horizontally organized, collective intelligence. Wikipedia was originally an offshoot of another free encyclopaedia, Nupedia, written and monitored by experts. Then founder Jimmy Wales decided to take a revolutionary approach: flinging open the doors and letting everybody write and edit the articles.[19] True, an oversight function is performed by so-called "administrators" (about 1500 in English) who have the power to delete pages, lock articles so no further changes can be made, and arbitrate editorial disputes among contributors. On the whole, however, anybody is free to contribute to Wikipedia.

In mid-2008, Wikipedia – featuring some ten million articles in the world's major languages – was being consulted by nearly 700 million visitors annually. The English version counted more than two million articles. Less than a decade following its launched in 2001, Wikipedia ranks among the top 10 websites worldwide – along with sites such as Yahoo!, Google, YouTube, MSN, Facebook, Live.com, MySpace, Blogger.com and Orkut and is one of the most recognized brands on the planet.[20] This achievement is, by any standard, an astonishing success story.

Beyond its success based on a global plebiscite, Wikipedia also established itself as a legitimate source of information on virtually any subject. As American economist Tyler Cowen put it: "If I had to guess whether Wikipedia or the median refereed journal article on economics was more likely to be true, after a not so long think I would opt for Wikipedia." Wikipedia has gained so much credibility as a source of factual information, in fact, that it has been favourably compared with the venerable *Encyclopaedia Britannica*, founded in 1768.

In 2005, a study published in the British journal, *Nature*, compared Wikipedia and *Britannica* using a sample of articles on a wide range of subjects. Based on reviews from a field of 42 experts, the *Nature* study concluded that Wikipedia and *Britannica* were largely comparable when assessed by accuracy and reliability. Eight serious errors had been discovered – four from each encyclopaedia. On average, Wikipedia produced 3.86 mistakes per article, while *Britannica* averaged 2.92 errors per article.[21] What was surprising for many observers was not so much that Wikipedia contained some errors, but rather that *Britannica* had so many. In Wikipedia, moreover, factual errors can be corrected instantly through the power of crowdsourcing. In published encyclopaedias, on the other hand, errors and biases linger for years, sometimes generations.

Britannica, like all self-respecting monopolists, reacted indignantly to the *Nature* study, denouncing its findings as biased. As the *Wall Street Journal* reported in a front-page story: "The venerable *Encyclopaedia Britannica* is launching an unusual public war to defend itself against a scientific article that argued it's scarcely better than a free-for-all Web upstart." *Britannica* was so incensed, in fact, that it took out half-page adverts in the London *Times* and *New York Times* calling on *Nature*, in a 7000-word rebuttal, to retract its study. *Britannica* also sent off the same rebuttal to some 5000 librarians, school administrators and curriculum coordinators.[22] In the end, however, *Britannica* caved and, in June 2008, decided to launch a "collaborative" online dictionary itself. While the revered encyclopaedia was obviously getting on the wiki bandwagon, it was careful to emphasize that "there are significant differences between our approach and what is popularly termed 'Web 2.0'." The main difference, said *Britannica*, is that "we believe that the creation and documentation of knowledge is a collaborative process but not a democratic one."

Note a recurrent theme: the rejection of democracy. *Britannica* clearly had self-interested motives for its compromise approach to online collaboration. First, the time-honoured encyclopaedia evoked the principle of "responsibility" to insist that it would own copyright to its content no matter who contributes. "We are not abdicating our responsibility as publishers or burying it under the now-fashionable 'wisdom of the crowds'," it said in an online statement. Second, *Britannica*'s self-styled "collaborative-but-not-democratic" approach is based on experts – or a widened "community of scholars" – who will be given "incentives" (presumably payment) to contribute articles. Finally, *Britannica* would allow nonexperts to contribute, but only through making "suggestions" to its expert editors deemed more "objective" than laymen contributors.

Britannica, making a grudging confession that it was late to recognize the power of mass collaboration, was announcing an incremental concession as a boldly innovative change of approach. Yet its new policy was not only conservative, it was condescending towards the democratic power of mass collaboration. "We believe that to provide lively and intelligent coverage of complex subjects requires experts and knowledgeable editors who can make astute judgments that cut through the cacophony of competing and often confusing viewpoints on a topic," noted *Britannica*. "In contrast to our approach, democratic systems settle for something bland and less informative, what is sometimes termed a 'neutral point of view'."[23]

Wikipedia is rarely bland. But it has been accused of offering a global platform for egregious bias, even shocking malice. Many critics cite a defamatory Wikipedia biographical entry about John Seigenthaler Sr., a former aide to Robert F. Kennedy, that remained undetected for months in 2005. Several sentences in the article suggested that Seigenthaler had played a role in the assassinations of both John F. Kennedy and Robert F. Kennedy. While this article was indeed a grievous mistake, it was, in fact, posted as a malicious hoax. Wikipedia nonetheless took steps to ensure that this kind of error was never repeated. Wikipedia's self-correcting mechanism – while this time late – swung into action.[24]

Negative reaction to Wikipedia has been particularly vehement in universities where the professional advancement of academics depends on status conferred by "peer reviews" by other professors. Academia is not a horizontal democracy, it's a vertical hierarchy. Andrew Keen reported with satisfaction in *Cult of the Amateur* that Wikipedia was banned by the history department at Middlebury College in New England. And yet at Harvard University, the *Harvard Crimson* newspaper reported in 2007 that some professors were including Wikipedia in their course syllabi.[25]

Wikipedia, it seems, has become a victim of its own success. As an upstart David slaying established Goliaths, is has become a convenient target for those who resent, and fear, the e-ruptive consequences of the Web 2.0 revolution. Charles Leadbeater argues that the power of Wikipedia is not in its content, but rather in the way it diffuses power: "As Wikipedia spreads around the world not only does it carry knowledge, it teaches habits of participation, responsibility and sharing. Wikipedia is not based on a naïve faith in collectivism but on the collaborative exercise of individual responsibility."[26]

Now let's look at another gatekeeper fortress that critics of Web 2.0 say needs to be protected from the online onslaught of amateurism: journalism. The rise of Web-based "citizen" journalism is driven by the same dynamics as blogging writers of fiction and amateur contributors to Wikipedia. Newsgathering sites like Slashdot, Wikinews, Agoravox and Indymedia have shifted power from "professional" journalists towards anyone who wishes to participate in the dissemination of information.[27] In South Korea, the OhMyNews site – whose motto is "Every Citizen is a Reporter" – has had a major impact on national politics. News has also been transformed by collaborative social media like Digg, which virally transmits, and ranks, news stories selected by others on a "check this out" basis. Traditional news gatekeepers are thus replaced with *gatewatchers*.[28]

This Web 2.0 e-ruption is profoundly democratic and distributes social capital through broad citizen engagement. Not surprisingly, established journalists and media organizations regard these bottom-up forms of newsgathering as a threat. The source of their hostility is not difficult to ascertain. As Glenn Reynolds puts it in his book *Army of Davids*: "Millions of Americans who were once in awe of the punditocracy now realize that anyone can do this stuff – and that many unknowns can do it better than the lords of the profession". Traditional journalists, who work in vertical corporate bureaucracies, feel threatened by the horizontal, network dynamics of the citizen journalism movement. They regard citizen journalism as an amateur usurpation of their professional monopoly and the status benefits it confers. Journalists argue that, since they are educated and trained, they possess *professional credentials*.

Support for this view, not surprisingly, can be found in the Ivory Tower of journalism education. At Columbia University's prestigious School of Journalism, the school's dean Nicholas Lemann published a column in *The New Yorker* magazine entitled "Amateur Hour: Journalism Without Journalists".[29] "To live up to its billing," argues Lemann, "Internet journalism has to meet high standards both conceptually and practically: the medium has to be revolutionary, and the journalism has to be good. The quality of Internet journalism is bound to improve over time, especially if more of the virtues of traditional journalism migrate to the Internet. But, although the medium has great capabilities, especially the way it opens out and speeds up the discourse, it is not quite as different from what has gone before as its advocates are saying." No one should be surprised that the dean of a well-known American journalism school that serves as a gatekeeper into the highest ranks of the "profession" is sceptical about the rise of citizen journalism.

Vincent Maher, a South African journalism professor at Rhodes University, is less subtle in his denunciation of citizen journalism. He has resolutely declared that it's already dead. "In fact, citizen journalism never lived," he wrote in 2005. "It was the hardening of a momentary ideal, puffed up with self-importance and glazed with a sweet optimism that kept us interested beyond its shelf life. But let me repeat, for the sake of clarity: Citizen Journalism as a concept is dead, a dry bone to be tossed over the back fence."[30]

Maher's thesis is based on what he calls the "Three Es" of journalism – ethics, economics and epistemology. Maher asserts that "professional" journalists derive their legitimacy from the following factors: first, they are trained and work according to a code of ethics; second, they are not subject to direct economic pressures by advertisers because they are employed by large organizations; and third, they can strive to seek the "truth" because they work within a hierarchical structure of knowledge. Amateur "citizen" journalists, on the other hand, are self-taught, not bound by any code of ethics, devoid of any accountability, subject to economic pressures because they seek advertizing on their blog sites and uninterested in the "truth" because they deal mainly in opinions.

On the question of *ethics*, the truth is that traditional journalism, from its origins, has been plagued by ethical scandals involving venality, corruption, plagiarism, fabrication and other dubious practices. These issues have persisted despite sincere efforts to infuse more professionalism into journalism. In the United States, the *New York Times* – a newspaper which considers itself among the best in the world – has been shaken by a series of ethical scandals over the past several years.[31] In many cases, traditional media organizations have been reluctant to police unethical conduct in their ranks. The reason for this is not a mystery: journalism has been organized institutionally with quasi-professional pretensions and, consequently, misconduct is frequently concealed for fear of bringing the entire "profession" into disrepute. Even when newspapers make factual errors, they frequently resist – unlike bloggers and Wikipedia – the ethical reflex to acknowledge the mistake in a prompt, open and transparent manner. As we saw in Chapter 9 with our example of the ethical scandals at British television networks, sometimes an arrogant professional culture, and disdain for the public at large, is at the origin of appalling professional misconduct. Meanwhile, over at Columbia's School of Journalism, the university has been shaken by an ethical scandal of its own. At the centre of this controversy: students cheating on an exam for a required course on, of all subjects, "Journalism Ethics". When students at America's top journalism school are cheating even before they get real jobs, it's little wonder journalism has such a poor reputation with the public.

On the *economics* of journalism, any suggestion that citizen journalists are more susceptible to influence than mainstream media because their sites depend on Google AdSense and other forms of micropayment can only be described as specious. An enduring doctrine at journalism schools is that capitalist ownership of media is the greatest danger to freedom of the press. Indeed, the hostility of journalists towards media magnates like Rupert Murdoch – as his takeover of the *Wall Street Journal* amply demonstrated – invariably finds justification in the need to protect the independence of the profession from the economic pressures and political interference exerted by powerful capitalists.[32] Any argument that citizen journalists and bloggers, whose activities require virtually no capital investment, are at greater risk of control by economic pressures is highly implausible at best. But for the sake of argument, let's look at the economic model of one of the most successful citizen journalists in the blogosphere: Jeff Jarvis. By his own account, Jarvis's BuzzMachine blog generated a grand total of $13 855 in revenue in 2007.[33] At most major newspapers, that's roughly the value of the corporate freebies that land in the newsroom in any given week.

The *epistemological* question about journalism's access to the "truth" invites a vast philosophical debate. Critics of citizen journalism argue that traditional journalists, thanks to their values of "objectivity", are more likely to get to the "truth" when reporting the news. This journalistic claim on "objective truth" is, in fact, a historically recent pretension. It is, what's more, culturally specific to journalism in the United States and Canada. In Britain, journalism has never made any claim on "objectivity", much less in continental Europe and elsewhere. In the UK, journalism isn't even considered a profession. In Britain, with its long cultural tradition of genteel amateurism, top-tier journalists have long been recruited straight out of the best universities, mainly from Oxford and Cambridge. There were no journalism schools in Britain until very recently. The uncomfortable truth, for journalists, is that they are not professionals. Journalism does not, by any formal definition, constitute a profession.[34] What is true, however, is that journalists – especially in North America – have appropriated the *status attributes* of professionalism. In the United States, the professional pretensions of journalism gained momentum following the Watergate scandal when the *Washington Post* brought down President Richard Nixon. The collapse of the Nixon administration was a great triumph for American journalism. Following the Watergate scandal, enrolment in American and Canadian J-Schools soared. Journalism was now the "fourth estate", a player in the system, a powerful force in American public life. That was undoubtedly true. But what journalism was not – and still is not – was a profession. The notion that journalism is a high-minded profession devoted to "objective truth" is a self-serving myth that doesn't stand up to serious scrutiny.

We can conclude, therefore, that the status tension between *professional* and *citizen* journalism has little to do with ethics, economics or epistemology. This distinction is a fallacy. The real issue is power. The Web is diffusing power away from bureaucratically organized forms of journalism that, traditionally, have required massive capital investment. Power is shifting towards spontaneously organized journalists who can newsgather and disseminate with no barriers to entry. This e-ruptive power shift has created resentment among established "professional" journalists who, like *Encyclopaedia Britannica*, are asserting what they consider to be their traditional monopoly privileges and prerogatives. And yet it's a safe bet that, a generation from now, bound encyclopedias and printed newspapers will no longer exist.

A good indicator of who's winning this power struggle came in early 2008 when an unknown American journalist, Joshua Micah Marshall, won a prestigious George Polk Award for legal reporting. Marshall was not a salaried investigative reporter with the *New York Times*, *Washington Post* or *Los Angeles Times*. He had published his tenacious citizen journalism on his own website, TalkingPointsMemo. Marshall has never attended journalism school; he holds a PhD in history.[35] These struggles over status and power aren't likely to subside until the final edition of the last newspaper comes off the press. If you are taking bets, you may wish to refer to a *New Yorker* article published in the spring of 2008, predicting that the world's last printed newspaper will drop on somebody's doorstep in the year 2043.[36]

In the meantime, a fascinating enigma remains unsolved: why do ordinary citizens contribute to journalistic websites? Why do so many amateur experts voluntarily contribute to Wikipedia? And why do so many people devote so much time to writing blogs, making videos and creating all kinds of content to be posted on user-generated sites? None of the traditional forms of power – coercion, compensation, cooptation – appears to explain the basic question of *motivation*. Put simply, why do people even bother making the effort?

Fortunately, an American academic, Oded Nov, asked precisely that question and conducted an empirical study on Wikipedia contributors to find the answer. In a paper entitled "What Motivates Wikipedians?", Nov first examined the motivations behind traditional "volunteer" behaviour. Most people who engage in volunteer activity are motivated by a combination of rational and nonrational factors, such as values, social capital, learning, career benefits, guilt-reduction and personal enhancement. Some critics have warned about the "risk" of using Wikipedia as a source of authoritative information due to the uncertain motivation of its contributors. While motivation can be altruistic, others motives can be opportunistic. There is also the risk of practical jokers and malicious intention. In his study of Wikipedian motivations, Nov discovered something else: the top motivation for Wikipedia participation, unexpectedly, is "fun". Despite the risk of factual error, or even vandalism, most people spend time and devote diligent effort contributing to Wikipedia because they enjoy it.[37]

Another American academic, Clay Shirky, tested this same question on himself. Shirky, author of *Here Comes Everybody: The Power of Organizing Without Organizations*, found an answer to the "why bother" question after contributing to a Wikipedia entry on the Koch snowflake. When he asked himself why he had bothered to refine and build upon the definition of the Koch snowflake for the benefit of the entire planet, Shirky came up with three answers. His first motivation was intellectual challenge. The second reason, he confessed, was pure vanity – the egotistical desire to put his own stamp on something. It's Shirky's third motivation, however, that's the most revealing: he simply wanted to "do a good thing".[38] He was motivated, in other words, by something intangible that defies rational explanation. He was paying it forward.

"The genius of wikis," says Shirky, "and the coming change in group effort in general, is the part predicated on the ability to make nonfinancial motivations add up to something of global significance."

If Clay Shirky is right, perhaps the revenge of the amateur, a century after being pushed aside by status-seeking professionals, will force us to think in a radically different way about the nature of power. It may now be possible to possess genuine expertise and wish to share it, altruistically, with the whole world.

13

Markets 2.0: why MyMusic calls the tune

The days when we walked into bricks-and-mortar retail stores to buy music on vinyl discs are rapidly fading into our collective memory. The record shop seems destined to find its place in history's cultural museum alongside the drive-in movie theatre. When we can download songs on Apple's iTunes, why bother to make a trip to HMV, Best Buy or Wal-Mart?

The record store as cultural relic is happening faster than you think. iTunes, which launched its service in 2003, is already the biggest music retailer on the planet, with total sales of more than 4 billion songs and a 70% market share of the music download market. iTunes, in a word, *is* the market.[1]

Powered by its iTunes/iPod/iPhone techno-triumvirate, Apple has – with a little help from pirate download sites – crushed once-invincible music retailers in its unstoppable march towards monopoly power. In the United States, iTunes outsells even major retail giants. One victim is Musicland, once a retail powerhouse that boasted more than 1300 stores. In early 2006, less than three years after iTunes hit the market, Musicland filed for bankruptcy in the United States. Another market loser is Tower Records, one of the world's biggest store music retailers. Like Musicland, Tower declared bankruptcy, liquidated its assets and went out of business in 2006. In London, Tower had been famous for its flagship store in Piccadilly Circus and another outlet in fashionable Kensington. Both outlets have been shut down. In Piccadilly, Richard Branson's Virgin MegaStore brand (rebranded as Zavvi in the UK and Ireland) is now making a go of it. Tower Records, like the Sam Goody music chain, packed up and left the UK market altogether.[2]

"The future looks particularly grim for all land-based music retailers", said music industry consultant Burt Flickinger following the Tower Records collapse, adding that bricks-and-mortar music retailers "literally have a toe-tag on them and they're boxed up for the proverbial boneyard." Another industry observer said that, going forward, the biggest challenge for music retailers will be "to get customers into the stores and to get them to carry the product out of the stores."[3]

That's easier said than done. The global music business has been going through a painful – and exhilarating – period of creative destruction over the past several years. And it's not over yet.

Now iTunes is looking over its shoulder. There's good reason to be paranoid. Here comes MySpace.

In April 2008, MySpace announced a deal with the major music labels to offer a one-stop online music service to its members worldwide. It's a no-brainer when you think about it. In a business driven by word-of-mouth, shared tastes and communities of fans formed around favourite bands, pop music has finally discovered the power of social networking.

Now here's the big news: MySpace Music is offering its music *free*. No cost, zip, zilch. MySpace members can stream music free-of-charge and share customized playlists with online "friends". The music is free because revenues are generated by advertising and selling concert tickets, cell phone ringtones and band merchandise like T-shirts. For MySpace, which had started off as a website for indie bands in California, its foray into the music big leagues is a logical return to its origins.

"This is really a mega-music experience that is transformative in a lot of ways," said MySpace chief executive Chris DeWolfe. "It's the first service that offers a full catalogue of music to be streamed for free, with full community features, to be shared with all of your friends."[4]

Sounds like a great deal for MySpace members. It's also a great deal – in the short term, at least – for the world's major record labels. They've been struggling to find their way out of a severe crisis that has seen their global revenues dramatically plummet over the past decade. At the end of the 1990s global music sales were declining by only about 1% annually. That was a major crisis at the time. By 2007, however, the drop was a steep 8%.[5] On a topline revenue basis, the major labels grossed $36.9 billion in 2000, but only $29.9 billion in 2007. This negative trendline continues to head south today.

Against this backdrop, the so-called "Big Four" music labels – EMI, Universal Music Group, Warner Music Group and Sony BMG – need all the help they can get. It's not just fed-up consumers who are turning to the Web to avoid paying high-markup retail prices for music. The pop stars who make the music are also getting their acts together online by connecting directly with their fans through innovative channels. Pop bands have realized that, thanks to the Internet, they no longer need the Big Four labels to produce and market their music.

Peter Gabriel was on the avant garde of this trend more than a decade ago. In the late 1990s, Gabriel invested in OD2, one of the world's first music downloading services, later purchased by Nokia for $38.6 million. "Never before has an artist been able to reach out and build an audience so easily – without needing record companies and their marketing departments," says Gabriel, who began his career in the early 1970s as frontman for the group Genesis. "Equally, you've never been able to explore all kinds of new music in the instant way the Internet allows."[6]

Since Peter Gabriel's pioneering foray into digital music, other pop stars have exploited pervasive uncertainty in the music business to cut their labels out of the action. Signing deals that would have been unthinkable only a decade ago, pop stars are partnering with unexpected retailers in return for lucrative payouts.

Pop icon Prince, in a marketing move that perplexed many, gave away his album *Planet Earth* as a free covermount CD in the British newspaper *Mail on Sunday*. Prince was one of the first pop superstars to rebel against a Big Four label by writing the word "slave" on his cheek during his bitter legal battles with Warner Music. His direct-to-retail manoeuvre was quickly followed by other superstars fed up with the Big Four. In early 2007, Paul McCartney walked away from EMI after 43 years to release his new album through a curiously unexpected, if not entirely unlikely, brand: Starbucks. The ex-Beatle said he was impressed by Starbucks's capacity to leverage its 13 500 retail outlets to sell his new album, *Memory Almost Full*, directly to its 44 million customers every week. McCartney added that he'd left EMI because the label was "jaded". Meanwhile, 1970s supergroup The Eagles left Warner Music to release a new album, *Long Road Out of Eden*, in an exclusive distribution deal with Wal-Mart. The deal guaranteed the band up-front revenues of $50 million. Madonna, too, left her label, Warner Music, to cut a stunning $120 million ten-year, record-and-tour deal with concert promoter Live Nation.[7]

Other pop bands have pursued an even more e-ruptive commercial strategy: cutting out both their music label and retailers by marketing directly to their fans. Bands like Coldplay and Nine Inch Nails have put songs on websites for free. As Nine Inch Nails frontman Trent Reznor put it: "I have been under recording contracts for 18 years and have watched the business radically mutate from one thing to something inherently very different, and it gives me great pleasure to be able to finally have a direct relationship with the audience as I see fit and appropriate."[8] REM meanwhile premiered its new album, *Accelerate*, on the social site iLike even before its commercial release in retail outlets. Other stars – from David Byrne and Moby to Kanye West and 50 Cent – are connecting directly with fans via blogs powered by social networking software. The pop e-ruption that created the most buzz, however, was British band Radiohead's decision to leave EMI and, in late 2007, put out their new record, *In Rainbows*, directly on the Web, asking fans to "pay what you want". The move shook the record industry because it was the first time that a globally successful pop band – Radiohead had sold 23 million albums worldwide – decided to go "off-label" and hand over market power directly to consumers.

"I like the people at our record company, but the time is at hand when you have to ask why anyone needs one," Radiohead's singer Thom Yorke told *Time* magazine. "And, yes, it probably would give us some perverse pleasure to say 'f – you' to this decaying business model."[9]

Radiohead pushed the envelope even further. In early 2008, the band asked fans online to make the first *In Rainbows* videoclip to be released on YouTube. Radiohead was, in effect, crowdsourcing a creative part of its latest record to its fans. The group also let fans do a remix of the second single from *In Rainbows*, a song entitled "Nude". Fans were asked to remix the song and upload their creations to the site Radioheadremix.com. Pop icon David Bowie had already pioneered this artist-driven market e-ruption in 2004, when he called on his fans to use his songs for mashups.[10]

These market e-ruptions aren't benefiting only famous pop stars. Emerging pop artists are no longer at the mercy of so-called "A&R" (for "artist and repertoire") music executives who scout for talent and decide which artists are signed to recording contracts. In the past, the Big Four's battalions of A&R gatekeepers were, ironically, remarkably conservative, and often dead wrong, about musical trends. They missed the punk movement during the 1970s disco craze, then later dismissed rap music as a passing fad. Most music trends, including rock 'n' roll, have spontaneously emerged bottom-up. The big music labels, driven by "hits", have frequently been late to the party. This entrenched conservative bias has made it difficult, and often frustrating, for emerging pop artists with a new and original sound to get a break in the business.

Thanks to the Web, however, direct interaction with fans can accelerate the emergence of authentic musical trends and virally spread them worldwide. Emerging pop artists can launch their own careers, and collaborate with other artists, on sites like iLike and OpenMusicFactory. No agents needed. No record label needed either. Musicians can also go directly to the Web to "crowd-fund" the financial resources necessary to market their work. Dedicated websites like Slicethepie and Sellaband serve as talent Meccas for bands in search of financing. By mid-2008, Slicethepie had attracted more than 9000 unsigned artists only a year after its launch.[11] It may one day be said of pop superstars, in tribute to Prince, that they were "formerly known as the audience".

"There's a prevailing wisdom that many established acts don't need a record label anymore," says Bruce Flohr, a music executive with Red Light Management which has managed pop artists including Alanis Morissette. "This is the new frontier. This is the beginning of a new era for the music business. The game used to be really simple. You get your record played on radio, you get your face on *Rolling Stone*, and you get on *Saturday Night Live*. Now, it's you put your video on YouTube, you get your MySpace page happening, you do your deal with Facebook, you tour . . . all these things add up, hopefully, to a successful record."[12]

We call this phenomenon Markets 2.0. Our definition of Markets 2.0 is based on the well-known, and widely discussed, dynamics of the digital economy: low barriers to entry, low distribution costs and unlimited inventory capacity which, combined, favour the entry of new market belligerents and disrupt established business models. Specifically, we define Markets 2.0 according to two key characteristics: first, *disintermediation of traditional gatekeepers* throughout the value chain; and second, *transformation of consumers into producers* who create new value-added business models driven by collaborative user-generated content.

A definition of "disintermediation" requires little further elaboration here as it is generally understood. In simple language, it signifies "cutting out the middleman" – namely, intermediaries in the value chain. The term first appeared more than forty years ago in the financial services sector, when consumers attracted by high interest rates bypassed banks to invest directly in money markets with higher yields. Since then, disintermediation has disrupted many markets – from stock trading and travel agencies to books, movies and music.

Traditionally, retail distributors have added value in the supply chain by monopolizing key components of the customer relationship such as information, transaction costs and service. Consumers used to go to book stores, for example, because retailers were sources of helpful information about products and, if a book was unavailable, they could put in a special order with suppliers. But Amazon disintermediated this retail market by moving transactions online and providing huge amounts of useful information (including reviews, ratings and rankings) about a vast array of products. Out-of-stock books, moreover, could be ordered instantly, and effortlessly, by the customer. In short, Amazon disintermediated bricks-and-mortar book retailers by seizing control of the customer relationship.

Amazon's market model is sometimes called "clicks-and-mortar" because, while transactions have moved online, it still has to stock inventory physically in warehouses. When the product is digital, however, disintermediation becomes powerfully e-ruptive because inventory and distribution costs are virtually zero. If Amazon's Kindle e-book takes off as a consumer product, there will be less reason for "mortar". Everything will be clicks. Consumers will download books for convenient portability like tunes on an iPod.[13] If e-books ever reach a tipping point, book retailers may one day be queuing up behind music stores in the bankruptcy courts. Amazon meanwhile is taking a social networking approach to marketing – or "social shopping" – by moving from a one-to-many to a many-to-many business model that leverages *network effects* on sites like Facebook.[14]

The second component of our Markets 2.0 definition – consumer-as-producer – is not a novel concept. Alvin Toffler coined the term "prosumer" three decades ago to describe what he predicted would be the merging of consumer and producer. The same idea was later reformulated by management consultant Don Tapscott, who employed the term "prosumption" in his 1995 book, *The Digital Economy*.[15] By that time, the exploding Web-based economy had inspired a new ideology of digital evangelism that championed consumer sovereignty, decentralized creativity and a new culture of sharing. The ethos of these trends was captured by the *Cluetrain Manifesto* and its Web 2.0 disciples in Silicon Valley. Consumers indeed have been engaged in collaborative innovation for years, creating new products as diverse as Linux and Lego and including, unexpectedly, the mountain bike.[16]

The pop music industry provides a textbook case study demonstrating how the e-ruptive impact of Markets 2.0 can turn an entire industry on its head. In Chapter 7 on the fame game, we examined how the blockbuster-driven logic of the entertainment industries distributes material and status rewards (namely, fame) in an arbitrary fashion. In the previous chapter on the revenge of the amateur, we analysed the tensions between established "professionals" and a new wave of amateurs who have recaptured power shifting away from vertically organized expertise. In this chapter, we propose to look specifically at another consequence of power diffusion – namely, the economic e-ruption that has literally blown the global music industry's business model to bits.

The music industry has been a blockbuster business since the explosion of rock n' roll music in the 1950s. Pop music produced huge cash flows because it was a highly scalable, low-marginal cost business catering to a global mass-consumption market. So long as the industry was dominated by a small clutch of oligopolistic suppliers that controlled most of the value chain, the music business enjoyed a high level of stability and predictability. The major labels carefully managed talent, maintained tight controls over supply chains and colluded in retail markets to maximize profits from a highly lucrative business selling "hit" songs.

The music industry achieved fantastic and largely uninterrupted growth from 1955 until the end of the 1970s. After a brief slump, the industry resurged in the 1980s thanks to the switch from LPs to CDs, which gave consumers an incentive to renew their entire music collections. It was the 1970s, however, that marked the apogee of the music labels' market power. Rock superstars like Led Zeppelin, Pink Floyd, The Who and Elton John were paid colossal sums and pampered like royalty. There was so much money sloshing about in pop music that self-destructive rock stars were indulged in the hope that they'd keep churning out blockbuster records.

The industry's enemy at the time was so-called "home taping", or copying of vinyl LPs onto cassette tapes to play music in cars. The major labels – whose slogan was "Home Taping is Killing Music" – fought vinyl-to-cassette copying with all their power, including so-called "spoiler signals" encoded directly onto LP records so they couldn't be taped without irritating listeners with a high-pitched sound. That backfired when some pop stars, including Elvis Costello, openly criticized this anti-consumer tactic. The big labels also lobbied governments to penalize consumers by imposing levies on retail purchases of blank cassette tapes.[17]

Today, the home-taping debate seems as remote as Ned Ludd's combat against mechanical weaving looms. At the time, however, the music industry lobby fought private copying as a matter of life and death. The major labels had fought the introduction of cassette recorders as a new technology, only to realize later that they could make billions by selling their music on cassettes. Two decades later, their reaction to the Internet would be no different. The battle against cassette tapes, in fact, was only a dress rehearsal for the industry's war against file-sharing and downloading. For the major labels, the issue was control.

As Wharton business professor Richard Shell has noted, the behaviour of the music labels was not unlike the war waged a century ago by an oligopoly of car manufacturers against a new player who had the audacity to manufacture and market an automobile at much lower prices. The new player was named Henry Ford. At the outset of the 20th century, the established auto makers in the United States – who called themselves the Association of Licensed Automobile Manufacturers – were hellbent on destroying Ford. They cleverly used copyright patents on auto parts to block Ford's attempt to make an affordable car for the mass market. Frustrated by the market power of the big incumbents, newcomer Ford was forced to fight the auto cartel in the courts from 1903 to 1907. Meanwhile, as Shell notes, the auto oligopoly "launched hundreds of lawsuits against Ford's customers to scare them away from his showrooms for buying 'unlicensed vehicles'." Shell argues that these failed attempts to keep Ford out of the car market should have been a cautionary tale for the Big Four music labels. Specifically, the major labels should have learned three lessons: first, you will never win in the marketplace by suing your own customers; second, no legal victory is strong enough to defeat a disruptive technical innovation; and third, innovation always drives the price of yesterday's technology into the dirt.

"The way to respond to the demise of the commercial CD is not to sue Internet-users," concluded Shell. "It is to figure out new ways to make money on music."[18]

When digital music files first started flying around the Internet in the 1990s, the major labels were in no mood to learn lessons from the past. Millions of teenagers were searching for, and finding, music on websites like MP3.com and Scour, provoking alarm in the industry about the consequences of a loudly proclaimed "digital culture".[19] The labels' reaction was three-pronged: consolidate their market strength, tighten their costs, and wage legal war on their customers in the courts.

To consolidate their market clout the industry underwent a rash of large-scale mergers and acquisitions which, by the end of the 1990s, left only four major players – Warner, EMI, Universal and Sony BMG. Together they controlled roughly 75% of the global music market. At the same time, the Big Four protected their cash flows with oligopolistic commercial practices, notably price fixing. In the United States, the Federal Trade Commission was investigating the major labels for CD price fixing – estimating the damage to consumers to be nearly $500 million. A coalition of 28 states meanwhile filed a lawsuit claiming that the Big Four and music retailers Musicland and Tower Records, among others, were in violation of US antitrust laws.[20] While the suit was settled out of court, the Big Four agreed to refund $67.4 million to purchasers of CDs between 1995 and 2000 and donate 5.5 million CDs to charities.[21]

The Big Four were also becoming more disciplined about costs, and thus started getting tough with their rosters of pampered pop stars. In the past, it had been difficult to fight pop stars in public because, at the end of the day, the stars had the fans (i.e. the major labels' customers) on their side. Sony's battle with pop singer George Michael had been particularly bitter. The pop singer finally left Sony in 1995 after five years of bitter legal battles with the label during which he accused the company of imposing conditions of "professional slavery".[22] With the digital downloading threat, however, the party was over. The Big Four were determined to move underperforming pop stars off their books. One particularly high-profile divorce was the split between EMI and Mariah Carey. EMI, which was unhappy with sales for Carey's most recent album *Glitter* – it had sold only two million units – dumped the pop diva from an expensive contract, paying her $49 million on her way out. Other pop stars who had once sold millions of records – Rod Stewart, Sinead O'Connor, Van Halen – were similarly dropped by their labels.[23]

The Big Four's biggest problem, however, was Napster. In 1998, an 18-year-old university student from Boston called Shawn Fanning had invented a peer-to-peer software application for finding – and sharing – music on the Internet. Kids could copy and share songs on a global scale without paying a cent for the music. Not surprisingly, Napster caught on worldwide like a viral contagion. Only a few months after Napster launched in 1999, some five million people had downloaded its software. Within two years, more than 80 million people had used Napster to download three billion songs. Napster's success also made Shawn Fanning a global media celebrity. Still only 19, Fanning was featured on the cover of *Business Week*, which portrayed the teenager as an upstart David taking on the Goliaths of the global music industry.[24] Napster had not only e-rupted the music industry's business model, it triggered a revolution that placed no commercial value on music and tremendous social value on sharing. Napster emerged at precisely the same moment as the *Cluetrain Manifesto* and its early Silicon Valley evangelists were declaring "the end of business as usual" and calling for a radical rethinking of intellectual property rights.[25]

The Big Four were having none of this evangelical techno-optimism. They convened their lawyers and declared war against their own customers. In the United States, the industry's powerful lobby, Recording Industry Association of America (RIAA), filed a lawsuit against Napster on 7 December 1999. The RIAA also sued a 12-year-old girl in New York City called Brianna LaHara, whose mother was forced to pay $2000 as compensation for her daughter's downloading. While that move did little to endear the billion-dollar music industry to the American public, the RIAA's chairman Mitch Bainwol declared victory. "We're trying to send a strong message that you are not anonymous when you participate in peer-to-peer file-sharing and that the illegal distribution of copyrighted music has consequences," he said. "And as this case illustrates, parents need to be aware of what their children are doing on their computers."[26]

You don't have to be an MBA graduate to know that a business strategy based on declaring war on your own customers is highly ill-advised. Yet it took the Big Four nearly a decade to figure this out.[27] In the final analysis, and to no one's surprise, the industry's arrogant legal belligerence backfired. Leaving aside the negative optics, the court cases aggravated the industry's problems by giving tremendous media publicity to Napster, encouraging millions of teenagers world-wide to download entire libraries of free songs. For many kids, it became a point of pride *not* to pay for music.

Pop artists were divided about the Napster threat. Some stars, like Eminem, joined their corporate masters and took a hard line against Napster and P2P file-sharing. The heavy metal band Metallica – who discovered that their song "I Disappear" had been circulating on the Internet even before its commercial release – launched their own lawsuit against Napster for copyright infringement. Metallica's drummer, Lars Ulrich, even showed up at Napster's headquarters with a list of more than 300000 names of people who had down-loaded the band's songs.

Other pop stars were delighted to see the Big Four taking a sling-shot in the eye. Bands like Limp Bizkit were outspoken supporters of Napster, and pop singer Alanis Morissette was an early investor in MP3.com. Superstar Elton John, who had little to fear from the Big Four's power over his career, denounced the major labels as "blatant out-and-out crooks" who had long been "laughing all the way to the bank". The legendary star added: "But they won't be laughing very soon, because when the music on the Internet comes in, the record companies will all be crying."[28]

The Big Four nonetheless won decisive legal victories against Internet-based P2P sites. In 2000, an RIAA lawsuit forced Scour out of business after investors were scared off. The same year, a US federal court found MP3.com guilty of copyright infringement, forcing settlements with the Big Four for a total of roughly $200 million.[29] The Big Four's biggest legal triumph came in 2001 when a US court issued a cease-and-desist injunction against Napster, forcing it to shut down. Hoping to stay in business, Napster held out a gold-plated olive branch to the major labels, offering them $1 billion over five years and a share of an estimated $150 million in annual revenue from a revamped subscription service. But the Big Four turned down the offer. They wanted Napster shut down. In the end, Napster was forced to pay a $26 million settlement with copyright owners plus a further $10 million as an advance against future licensing royalties.[30] But the Big Four's vindication in the courts was a Pyrrhic victory. The P2P revolution was only just beginning. No sooner had Napster closed its operations – temporarily – than its millions of followers were switch-ing to other P2P services like Gnutella, Kazaa and LimeWire.

Flush with these legal victories, the Big Four decided that the best battle plan going forward was to encourage digital music services that they could control. They had been attempting to impose a locked "Digital Rights Management" (DRM) system since 1998, but every effort had been foiled by clever hackers. Now they started pushing more aggressively for "legal" systems based on renting songs on monthy subscriptions. One early entrant into this tamed market was RealNetworks' Rhapsody, which launched in 2001 offering unlimited music at a flat monthly fee.

Services like Rhapsody might have stood a chance of taking off, but then something unexpected happened. A consumer electronics revolution exploded and quickly turned the entire music industry on its head. It was called the iPod.

When Apple first released the iPod, it seemed like a cool, ultra-light, consumer-friendly and beautifully designed device whose main function was the convenience of making music portable. Or as Apple called its first iPod: "1000 songs in your pocket". Apple wasn't selling the songs, it was only offering a high-tech fashion accessory to store and play music that had already been purchased.[31]

In 2003, however, Steve Jobs revealed his real ambitions. Jobs had shrewdly understood that, in the burgeoning digital download culture, people wanted to *own* their music, not rent it. "The sub-scription model of buying music is bankrupt," he said, referring to Rhapsody and other Big Four-friendly services. "I think you could make available the Second Coming in a subscription model and it might not be successful."

So in April 2003, Apple launched its own download retail service, iTunes, featuring a DRM protection system called FairPlay. Apple was no longer just selling the storage device, it was getting into music retailing. The scope of Jobs's e-ruptive ambitions was summed up by *Rolling Stone*, which in 2003 published an interview with the Apple boss. Its ominous headline was: "He changed the computer industry. Now he's after the music business".[32] That was an understatement.

In its first year, iTunes sold 85 million songs. At the same time, iPod sales were soaring around the world as a must-have consumer item – reaching 150 million units sold by 2007. With Apple's online retail store in the market, the iPod was no longer a fashion accessory. It had become a pocket-size, billion-dollar gatekeeper. So many people worldwide were buying songs on iTunes to play on their iPods – and later on iPhones – that Apple had effectively disintermediated the longstanding relationship between the major labels and their bricks-and-mortar retailers. The Big Four realized with mounting anxiety that Apple, while helping tame the out-of-control illegal download market, was now calling the shots.

"Never before in the history of content has the hardware been more valuable than the software," declared Warner Music president Edgar Bronfman, taking aim at the iPod. "You think about the VCR or the video cassette – the video cassette always had more value than the VCR that you shoved it into. Apple has been able to turn that model on its head."

What angered Bronfman most of all was that Steve Jobs, as the biggest music retailer on the planet, was dictating prices. It was Apple, for example, that set the retail price of iTunes songs – 99 cents in the United States and 79 pence in the UK. Bronfman and his fellow Big Four bosses were long used to telling retailers how much to charge for their music. But those days were over. Retailers had their own problems – including, like Musicland and Tower Records, the unpleasant business of declaring bankruptcy and disposing of distressed bricks-and-mortar assets.

True, there were some consumer complaints against Apple, mainly due to its proprietary system restricting the transfer of songs purchased on iTunes. Overall, however, Apple was winning its PR war against the Big Four. It was in this climate that Steve Jobs, hoping to make his own customers even happier, decided to call the Big Four's bluff. He dared them to release DRM-free songs that could be played on any device.[33]

And, to everyone's surprise, that's precisely what they did.[34] The Big Four's move away from restrictive DRM locks on songs may have been a symptom of their desperation, but it also appeared to herald a new era of openness and recognition of consumer sovereignty. Finally, it seemed, the Big Four were starting to think outside the box. In early 2008 when the labels signed their deal with MySpace to launch MySpace Music, it was an astounding about-face. They previously had been suing MySpace for copyright infringement. MySpace only agreed to launch its new one-stop music service on the condition that Universal Music drop its copyright lawsuit against the site.

MySpace Music should have been a no-brainer for the Big Four many years earlier. MySpace had been launched in 2003 as a platform for indie bands in California and within two years the site was rapidly becoming a must-go-to place for aspiring bands seeking recognition by uploading their music. In a profile of MySpace in 2005, *Wired* noted: "The real economic beneficiaries of MySpace are the ambitious young musicians in Pomona (California) and around the country who are creating a new, life-size kind of stardom. Over the past couple years, MySpace and other community sites, like Purevolume.com, have launched a number of acts: Fall Out Boy, My Chemical Romance, Relient K and Silverstein, among others." [35]

While late again, the Big Four were happy to appease MySpace if only because they had another agenda. They were hoping to turn social networking sites into powerful distribution outlets that would recapture value, boost flagging revenues and – most of all – loosen Apple's stranglehold on their business. In short, MySpace Music was the commercial product of a corporate truce. Making virtue of necessity, old enemies were suddenly best "friends". It didn't take long before Facebook, paranoid about getting outmanoeuvred by MySpace, was negotiating its own deal with the major labels to offer free music to its members.[36] The major labels finally realized that social networking sites can leverage network effects through gossip, chatter and buzz. Sites like MySpace, Facebook and Bebo have the potential to become viral marketing powerhouses.

In a study entitled "Does Chatter Matter?" conducted at New York University's Stern Business School, researchers found that record sales can increase five-fold thanks to 40 blog posts. "The number of friends a band has displayed on its MySpace page is like a public badge of popularity," noted the Stern study, adding that increases in MySpace friends drive higher sales. Blog posts are even more powerful viral marketing tools. An album's sales can increase five-fold thanks to only 40 legitimate blog posts.[37] Given these market dynamics, the only enigma is why the Big Four didn't figure out much earlier that MySpace might help boost their sales.

Apple, meanwhile, was quick to react to the MySpace Music challenge. Steve Jobs proposed a new business model: instead of selling music downloads via iTunes on a unit-pricing basis, customers could enjoy free access to its entire library and Apple would pay music labels a fixed sum for each iPod and iPhone device sold. This model wasn't actually new. Nokia was already paying Universal Music $80 per device to finance its "Comes With Music" downloading service.[38] Apple was now prepared, in like manner, to reach deeper into its pockets and offer music labels a cut of its hardware sales.

Edgar Bronfman could scarcely conceal his satisfaction now that Steve Jobs was knocking at his door. Asked about MySpace Music, Bronfman told the *Financial Times*: "I'm very hopeful. It's obviously a place where lots of people aggregate and lots of them aggregate around music and it will be a great experience for consumers where they can get everything from soup to nuts. They can experience music, they can share music, they can discuss music – just as they're currently doing. They can buy tickets, they can buy music, they can buy merchandise, they can create play lists. They can do anything and everything around music and the artist and the artist experience. If we can pull that off, it's a great opportunity."

Bronfman also acknowledged that, in retrospect, the Big Four had spent too much time and energy fighting the Internet instead of accepting that the industry needed a new business model. "The music industry was slow to recognize that ultimately this is an opportunity," he said, "but in fairness, when your house is burning down, it's hard to see that the foundation may ultimately support a better house."[39]

While inking deals with MySpace and Facebook, the Big Four were also vertically integrating into music-oriented social networking sites. In 2007, Universal Music took a stake in the urban social networking site, Loud.com, which features mainly rap music, and made a strategic investment in another music site, Mog.com.[40] The other three big labels (Sony BMG, EMI and Warner Music) meanwhile have partnered with Imeem.com, which offers music to its members in exchange for a cut of advertising revenue. More of these deals can be expected in the future as the Big Four bet heavily on the websites they once sued.

The Big Four's problems are far from over. British-based EMI, after an aborted merger with Warner Music, declared war on its stable of pop stars. Gary Hands, EMI's new chief executive, declared that he was more interested in "selling" music than nurturing musical talent. Henceforth, he said, he would flatten EMI's organizational structure. No more power for the A&R talent managers who blow EMI's money pampering egomaniacal pop stars. Hands wasn't pushing power down to consumers, though. He was pushing it up towards EMI executive suites.

"The power and the decision has sat with the A&R man, who is someone who gets up late in the day, listens to lots of music, goes to clubs, spends his time with artists and has a knack of knowing what would sell," said Hands. "What we are doing is taking the power away from the A&R guys and putting it with the suits – the guys who have to work out how to sell music."[41] Hands's tough-talk, take-charge style did little to endear him to the pop stars working for EMI. Almost immediately, The Rolling Stones and Paul McCartney left the label, while others like Robbie Williams and Coldplay were threatening to exit.

It's not inconceivable, given the market valuations of sites like MySpace and Facebook, that one of these sites might end up buying a music giant like EMI. If the Big Four are buying into social networking sites, why not takeovers in the opposite direction? Given that MySpace's corporate parent is News Corp, one of the world's biggest media conglomerates, integrating backwards into the music business might make sense. MySpace is already getting into the television business with *Roommates*, while Bebo has come out with its own television series, *Kate Modern*. These forms of disintermediation signal that the process of creative destruction is not over yet.

Will MySpace do a deal with Google to put social networking and music inside the new GooglePhone? Google and MySpace, remember, are already in bed through a $900 million advertising deal that expires in 2010. And surely Yahoo! and Microsoft want a piece of the music market. When America Online paid $850 million for Bebo in early 2008, it must have had music on its mind given the British social site's youth demo. And will Facebook and Blackberry do a deal including music downloading in the handset as a move against Apple's iTunes-iPhone combo?[42] Anything is possible. No deal can be ruled out.

Pop stars meanwhile are celebrating their new-found freedom that allows them to connect directly with their fans. One of them is Bryan Adams, who has sold more than 60 million records worldwide. "I really recommend it to most artists to take control of their music if they can," said Adams in 2008. "It's really time for artists to take control of what they're doing and appreciate what it takes to move forward. I really didn't understand how much went on behind the scenes in promoting a record. I know already that we're better off here doing it myself than when I was with a label. There's four times the interest just by doing it ourselves because we're creating our own buzz."[43]

If this message were a song title, it would undoubtedly be John Lennon's pop anthem, "Power to the People".

14

Enterprise 2.0: wiki while you work

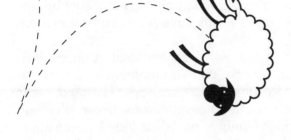

The Web 2.0 revolution has been frustrated by a powerful irony. The one place where Web 2.0 tools hold out the most promise to transform social organization is precisely the location where there has been the most resistance to change. That place is the corporation.

Social media, as we have seen, are revolutionizing the way we interact with others, build social capital, even achieve fame and riches. Yet when Web 2.0 social tools permeate corporate bureaucracies, they are often resisted as invasive and potentially threatening. If there is widespread agreement that Web 2.0 tools can have a tremendous upside for businesses, the reality is that, inside many companies, reactions to online social networking have been fixated on the downside.

This should not be surprising. Social networking is essentially a horizontal dynamic. The human need to connect socially is powerful, irrepressible and indispensible for getting things done. Markets, in like manner, operate according to inexorable laws that connect sellers and buyers. Market dynamics relentlessly seek to maximize efficiency to create surplus value. Markets work best when they are free, open, unfettered, unencumbered by monopolies, oligopolies, conspiracies and obnoxious practices. The classic design of corporate bureaucracies, by contrast, is based on the opposite dynamic. Traditionally, the social architecture of corporations has been vertical and closed. Corporate cultures are shaped by rigid hierarchies and ascriptive values of position, title and rank. Corporations are managed as top-down organizations that wield tremendous powers of compensatory coercion over their employees. Office environments are not cocktail parties; nor are they Greenwich Village streetscapes.

Let's face it, most employees working in corporate bureaucracies are, at present, not invited to engage in collaborative projects, contribute to company blogs and wikis or network online with colleagues and customers. The idea of "Facebook Fridays" for employees would be a non-starter in most corporate environments. Indeed some employees, as we have seen, are getting sacked when caught logged onto social networking sites at the office. The centralizing power of Philippe le Bel casts a long shadow over the executive suites at most modern corporations.

Despite the obstacle of status quo organizational cultures, Web 2.0 evangelists persist in their belief that an imminent social revolution is about to transform corporate bureaucracies. The buzzwords employed to describe this e-ruption are numerous: mass collaboration, self-organization, open innovation, distributed co-creation, bottom-up management, networked organization, virtual corporation. When Web 2.0 adoption reaches a tipping point, the major impact in corporations will be a diffusion of power towards employees and consumers. And corporate executives who don't exit the echo chamber to listen to what their staffs and customers are saying will suffer the consequences. Capitalism is no longer about the production and provision of goods and services. Capitalism, say Web 2.0 evangelists, is now a "conversation".

C.K. Prahalad, arguably the world's most prominent management guru, wrote a decade ago about this New Economy power shift towards consumers. "Thanks largely to the Internet, consumers have been increasingly engaging themselves in an active and explicit dialogue with manufacturers of products and services," wrote Prahalad in the *Harvard Business Review*. "What's more, that dialogue is no longer being controlled by corporations. Individual consumers can address and learn about businesses either on their own or through the collective knowledge of other customers. Consumers can now initiate the dialogue; they have moved out of the audience and onto the stage."[1]

We saw in the last chapter, with our music industry case study, how this power shift e-rupted a multi-billion-dollar business in only a few years. In pop music, the audience literally took control of the stage and created a dialogue among themselves, as artists and fans, while cutting out traditional gatekeepers. The lesson for corporations is that market dynamics have been fundamentally transformed by this power shift. Consumers are not only seeking value as customers, they are now *creating* and *competing* for value. Corporations, argues Prahalad, should see consumers as a new source of "competence".

The companies that understand the basic dynamics of this market e-ruption, and are adapting their organizational behaviour accordingly, are frequently called "Enterprise 2.0" firms. The generally accepted definition of Enterprise 2.0 is a corporation that – thanks to Web 2.0 software tools like wikis and blogs – encourages horizontal collaboration and harnesses the power of collective intelligence to boost productivity, foster innovation and create enhanced value.[2] That's a strictly organizational definition of Enterprise 2.0. In its broader definition, Enterprise 2.0 encompasses a vision advocating new modes of capitalist production and social organization.

Charles Leadbeater, an associate at the UK-based think tank Demos, is a notable thought leader for this broader vision of social transformation. "The developed world in the 20th century was preoccupied by organizing and reorganizing the mass-production system, its factories, industrial relations systems, working practices, supply chains," notes Leadbeater in his book/blog *We-think*. "Our preoccupation in the century to come will be how to create and sustain a mass innovation economy in which the central issue will be how more people can collaborate more effectively in creating new ideas."[3]

Living at the dawn of a new social order is an exhilarating prospect. For corporate executives, however, it signifies an urgent necessity to profoundly rethink how they structure, organize and manage their companies. And for many executives, that challenge is potentially too destabilizing, not to mention threatening.

Many CEOs, it is true, are intrigued by the business case for Enterprise 2.0. Surveys conducted by consulting firms like McKinsey and Forrester Research reveal that executives are showing more openness to Web-based collaboration and social networking tools.[4] Until recently, however, companies had invested mainly in "back-end" technologies that enable Web-based automation, while remaining paranoid about losing control if social networking tools like wikis and blogs become standard work tools. Forrester nonetheless forecasts robust corporate spending on Web 2.0 software – including blogs, mashups, podcasts, RSS, widgets and wikis. It projects consolidated Web 2.0 spending growth at 43% annually – from $764 million in 2008 to $4.6 billion in 2013.[5] Still, it can hardly be claimed that Fortune 500 companies – with the exception of a small clutch of leading-edge giants like IBM – are stampeding to join a Web 2.0 juggernaut. Moreover, while $4.6 billion looks like a big number, it's only a tiny fraction

– less than 1% – of global corporate spending on enterprise software. That's not an Enterprise 2.0 revolution. At best, it's cautious evolution.

How can we explain the lag between the bold ambition of the Enterprise 2.0 vision and the slow pace of its adoption by corporations? Dennis Howlett, a corporate software specialist who writes about Enterprise 2.0, puts the same question this way: "CEOs instinctively know that internal collaboration, whether through rudimentary technologies like blogs and wikis, hold significant efficiency promise. They know the technology is relatively inexpensive compared to other types of enterprise technology and that implementation can be rapid. They also get that, in the longer term, these technologies could hold incredible promise for business effectiveness across their entire value chain in releasing huge amounts of resource back into the business. None of that is disputed. What is disputed are two things: social media and social networking as applied internally. Why?"[6]

Good question. Let's try to answer it.

One possible explanation is that corporate executives simply don't understand Enterprise 2.0. In other words, it's fear of the unknown. Another theory is that executives consider Enterprise 2.0 to be little more than a trendy buzzword. They regard Web 2.0 tools like blogs and wikis as a distraction, if not a complete waste of time, whose downside risk is not worth betting on. A third explanation is that executives understand Enterprise 2.0 only too well – and that's precisely why they fear it. We can call these possible hypotheses *conceptual resistance, risk management* and the *fear factor*.

First, the *conceptual resistance* hypothesis. Some Enterprise 2.0 evangelists argue that corporate executives, blinkered by Old Think, just don't "get it". Many senior managers mistakenly believe Enterprise 2.0 is a product, like the latest Microsoft Office suite. They don't understand that Enterprise 2.0 is not a cost centre, but rather a "state of mind" – a revolutionary new way of managing companies and conducting business. Or as *Cluetrain Manifesto* put it, the "end of business as usual". Enterprise 2.0 evangelists believe that old-style, hierarchical corporations have a "DNA" problem with Web 2.0. Most corporate executives aren't even aware that a social revolution is about to sweep them with tsunami force from their C-suites.[7]

Andrew McAfee, a Harvard business professor who has written extensively about Enterprise 2.0 issues, has assessed this conceptual blockage. "We need to keep in mind that most Enterprise 2.0 tools are new, and that their acceptance depends on shifts in perspective on the part of business leaders and decision makers, shifts for which the word 'seismic' might not be an overstatement," notes McAfee. "Enterprise 2.0 tools have no inherent respect for organizational boundaries, hierarchies or job titles. They facilitate self-organization and emergent rather than imposed structure . . . They require, in short, the re-examination and often the reversal of many longstanding assumptions and practices."[8] That's a diplomatic way of saying what Web 2.0 evangelists put more bluntly: corporate executives just can't get their heads around the Enterprise 2.0 revolution.

Marc Smith, a senior research sociologist at Microsoft Research, says that many corporate executives, tied to traditional knowledge-management reflexes, fail to appreciate the potential of social networking in creating "architectures of cooperation". Noting that "the biggest asset of any enterprise is what your people know", Smith believes that socially oriented platforms like wikis allow corporations to identify and reward internal expertise on the basis of performance.

"Often enterprises spend a lot of effort incentivizing the wrong behaviour," argues Smith. "They don't see themselves as a group – and a group that doesn't know itself is not even a group. Software can make businesses visible to themselves; social networks are often the real structure of a company. Making all this visible will mean that what should have been rewarded all along gets rewarded – and once you reward the right thing, you probably get more of it. In the world of Sarbanes–Oxley, we're talking about helping people who want to help each other by making their help of one another visible and accountable to their management."[9]

Smith is undoubtedly right. But he wouldn't be making these arguments if Web 2.0 tools were massively deployed in most major corporations. His views betray an unmistakable level of disappointment that so many corporate executives don't yet grasp the Enterprise 2.0 model's potential to boost efficiency, productivity and shareholder value.

Second, the *risk management* hypothesis. Whatever the promise of Web 2.0 tools, many corporate managers regard blogs, wikis and social networks as an intriguing distraction at best, and a serious security risk at worst. Employee dismissals for spending work time on sites like Facebook are, as noted, becoming disturbingly frequent. In Britain, a survey of 3500 firms revealed that using Facebook and other social networking sites costs the national economy roughly $255 million *per day* in "wasted time". "Why should employers allow their workers to waste two hours a day on Facebook when they are being paid to do a job?" says Mike Huss from the employment law firm

Peninsula, which conducted the survey.[10] It's not difficult to find an Internet security firm that, hoping to boost sales of their Web 2.0 blocking software, strongly urges corporations to crack down on online social networking. The list of potential downside risks is indeed alarming: virus and spyware infections, data leaks, illegal activities, reputational damage, to name only a few. Web security specialists have made a business from playing on the worst fears of corporate managers.[11]

Beyond concerns about time-wasting and security risks, corporate executives tend to underestimate Web 2.0 tools because they are intangible assets. And like all intangible assets, it's difficult to assign a *value* to Web 2.0 software. As we noted in Chapter 3, corporations tend to have conservative attitudes towards IT software in general when calculating valuations. It shouldn't be surprising, then, that Web 2.0 software is regarded not as an asset that enhances value, but as a cost with an unproven upside.[12]

Many executives regard Web 2.0 tools as a passing fad and dismiss them with a "we've seen all this before" attitude. This scepticism is not entirely unjustified. Bold techno-revolutions have been trumpeted before – from Alvin Toffler's "adhocracy" to Shoshana Zuboff's "smart machine" vision – with the exhilarating promise of revolutionizing corporate bureaucracies.[13] Yet none of these Delphic techno-visions ever materialized. So why now believe this latest hype about Enterprise 2.0?

Third, the *fear factor* hypothesis. This theory interests us most here, since we are examining the Web 2.0 e-ruption's implications for power relationships – specifically, the *diffusion of power* from vertical hierarchies towards horizontal networks. From a strictly structural point of view, corporate executives accustomed to managing top-down hierarchies naturally distrust horizontal networks because they are difficult to *control*. As Harvard's Andrew McAfee observes, Web 2.0 tools have no regard for "organizational boundaries hierarchies or job titles". Try telling a senior executive that, going forward, there will be no more job titles, reporting lines and organizational boundaries in the company.

There is evidence, however, that resistance to Web 2.0 tools doesn't come from top executive suites, but rather from middle managers and especially from corporate IT departments. In a paper entitled "Enterprise 2.0: Fad or Future?", Gary Matuszak of KPMG International cited the familiar obstacles to Web 2.0 adoption such as security risk. But he also noted that in many bureaucratic settings the real problem is corporate culture. "Just as damaging are institutional cultures or norms that work against sharing information, either because of concerns about confidentiality or because of hierarchical structures," noted Matuszak. Providing a concrete example, he noted that when the US Defense Intelligence Agency introduced Intellipedia, senior and junior officers embraced the wiki. Mid-level bureaucrats, on the other hand, actively resisted Intellipedia. One reason middle managers oppose information sharing and open collaboration is because these innovations usurp their traditional role as information gatekeepers and drafters of internal reports.[14] It's interesting to note that, as we outlined in Chapter 8, virtual corporations often have flat organizational structures that eliminate middle management layers.

Don't count on Web 2.0 buy-in from IT departments either. In late 2007, *Information Week* noted that while social media are being deployed innovatively in some companies, in many corporations IT departments feel profoundly threatened by Enterprise 2.0. Why? Because like middle managers, they fear that Web 2.0 tools will threaten their monopoly over specific functions. When information flows are democratically diffused, the monopoly "expertise" of IT managers is effectively disintermediated. As *Information Week* put it: "Forget outsourcing, the real threat to IT pros could be Web 2.0." No wonder IT managers have worked hard to find persuasive arguments to alarm their corporate bosses about the downside risks of Web 2.0 – productivity losses, security threats, liability issues and so forth.

Given these three factors, it shouldn't be surprising that, at many large-scale corporations, Web 2.0 is still an intriguing concept to study, not a business strategy to execute. *Information Week* concluded that, bottom line, Enterprise 2.0 will be more enthusiastically embraced by young companies "without legacy systems to integrate". Enterprise 2.0 transformation isn't likely to be embraced in established organizations with entrenched power structures and conservative corporate cultures that can easily thwart Web 2.0 adoption in order to neutralize its threat.[15] Even if a networked Enterprise 2.0 model guarantees to improve productivity, foster innovation and boost profitability, it still runs up against basic laws of human nature. Corporate bureaucracies are not designed as bottom-up democracies, and consequently any push for radical reform is bound to meet determined resistance. Any impetus in favour of overhauling existing hierarchies threatens the authority and power of managers who have a vested interest in the status quo. For most corporate managers, there is just too much to lose – especially *power*.

The status quo, as banal as it may seem, includes daily corporate rituals like the "meeting". Most people who work in bureaucracies give it little thought, but it's worth asking: why do so many managers spend so much time in meetings? The meeting has become so pervasive in the modern corporate bureaucracy that it's a standard subterfuge used by protective secretaries ("he's in a meeting") to keep intrusive telephone inquirers at bay, even when the boss is not in a meeting. And yet when we give serious consideration to the real value of meetings, most of us would concur that they frequently don't serve much obvious purpose at all.[16] In truth, many meetings are an utter waste of time.

Cali Ressler and Jody Thompson, in their book *Why Work Sucks and How to Fix It*, addressed the issue of meetings head-on. As they put it, too many employees "sit through overlong, overstaffed meetings to talk about the next overlong, overstaffed meeting".[17] And yet meetings stubbornly persist as an indispensable form of professional interaction in corporate bureaucracies. Imagine an office empowered by Web 2.0 collaboration tools. The meeting becomes largely redundant – or, at a minimum, reduced to as-needed status. Sounds like a no-brainer. But don't count on it happening any time soon.

The inefficiency of the office meeting highlights a further irony. As management consultant Richard Donkin noted in his *Financial Times* column, the managers who dismiss MySpace and Facebook as a waste of time are frequently the same people who themselves waste valuable corporate time with pointless meetings. "There are important meetings and there are other meetings where everything you need to know or say is covered in the first five minutes and the rest of the time is wasted," says Donkin. "But I hear far fewer objections to time wasted in meetings than I do about time wasted on social networking sites. The reason for this is wholly to do with custom and practice. The meeting has become embedded within the fabric of organizations, while social networking and other forms of online communication continue to be viewed with suspicion."[18]

There is another possible explanation. While all meetings have an officially scripted agenda, their tacit agenda is *power*. Meetings establish who is in charge. When someone calls a meeting, he or she is asserting authority over those who are called on to attend. Meetings are exclusive and closed. In most corporations, who gets invited to a meeting – and who does not – sends a signal about who's "in the loop". Meetings are a form of social grooming inside organizations. Meetings impose vertical authority. They establish status hierarchies. The Enterprise 2.0 model is feared in corporations because it threatens status hierarchies. When power is diffused and distributed more democratically, meetings are no longer necessary. But corporations are not democracies.

Corporate strategy guru Gary Hamel has analysed this democratic deficit and where it inevitably leads. "In an autocratic system, there are few mechanisms for bottom-up renewal," noted Hamel in his book *The Future of Management*. "As a result, change tends to come in belated, convulsive spasms, via revolutions and insurrections. In democracies, change usually starts at the grass roots, and compounds upwards as interest groups and political activists amass support for their policies. With change constantly bubbling up from below, democracies are able to avoid the periodic rebellions that typify political life in totalitarian regimes. The same, unfortunately, can't be said for most large companies, where it usually takes a financial crisis and a shareholder revolt to provoke a change in leadership and strategy reboot."

Making a provocative analogy, Hamel compares large corporations to "poorly governed third-world dictatorships" where the only way to effect meaningful reform is to "depose the despots". He remains sceptical however about the effectiveness of board-led coups because they usually happen when it's already too late to save the company.[19] Hamel's solution is entrenching the *values* of democracy in corporate DNA – namely, mechanisms for accountability, a right of dissent and distributed leadership. In a nutshell, *diffusion of power*.

Hamel calls this revolution a Democracy of Ideas – or *thoughtocracy*. He notes regretfully that Web-based diffusion of power, which has transformed the media industries by fostering the emergence of "citizenship" journalism, has not occurred inside corporations. "While the Web was founded on the principle of openness," he notes, "the most honoured virtue among senior executives seems to be control. Most companies have elaborate programmes for top-down communication, including newsletters, CEO blogs, webcasts and broadcast emails; yet few, if any, companies have opened the floodgates to grassroots opinion on critical issues."[20]

Hamel's *thoughtocracy* seems like a variation of Enterprise 2.0. His Democracy of Ideas, however, is based on *values*, not software systems. The question, therefore, is whether Web 2.0 software tools can empower an essentially *value-based* democratic revolution.

Web 2.0 sceptics caution us against excessive optimism about the likelihood of a value-based e-ruption in corporations. They argue that Enterprise 2.0, while a noble organizational vision, fails to grasp the raw dynamics of power. Management thinker Tom Davenport makes this point while discounting the wishful thinking of Web 2.0 evangelists. Davenport, author of *Thinking for a Living*, praises Enterprise 2.0 as an admirable vision founded in democratic beliefs, but argues that it's fundamentally naïve.

"Such a utopian vision can hardly be achieved through new technology alone," he says. "The absence of participative technologies in the past is not the only reason that organizations and expertise are hierarchical. Enterprise 2.0 software and the Internet won't make organizational hierarchy and politics go away. They won't make the ideas of the front-line worker in corporations as influential as those of the CEO. Most of the barriers that prevent knowledge from flowing freely in organizations – power differentials, lack of trust, missing incentives, unsupportive cultures and the general busyness of employees today – won't be addressed or substantially changed by technology alone. For a set of technologies to bring about such changes, they would have to be truly magical, and Enterprise 2.0 tools fall short of magic."[21]

Interestingly, the most powerful pressures for Enterprise 2.0 transformation are coming from outside corporations. Enterprise 2.0 thought leadership stretches back at least a decade to *Cluetrain Manifesto*. The *Cluetrain* authors were clearly conscious of the quasi-religious passion they were bringing to their revolution, if only because their "95 Theses" was an allusion to Martin Luther's document that triggered the Protestant Reformation. *Cluetrain* celebrated the death of Organizational Man, Scientific Management, Taylorism, the Power Elite and the other dysfunctions of modern corporations. The book denounced the Holy Trinity of modern capitalism (mass production, mass marketing, mass media) as a false god that held sway for a century only because "the payoffs were so huge". *Cluetrain's* recommended exorcism was: "Burn down business-as-usual. Bulldoze it. Cordon off the area. Set up barricades. Cripple the tanks. Topple the statues of heroes too long dead into the streets."[22] Other early Web 2.0 evangelists were associated with Xerox's R&D brain trust in Silicon Valley known as PARC (Palo Alto Research Center). One was Howard Rheingold, who in the early 1990s wrote *The Virtual Community* and a decade later published *Smart Mobs*.[23] More recently, Web 2.0 evangelists have been leading the crusade in the blogosphere, notably Robert Scoble (Scobleizer) and Glenn Reynolds (Instapundit).

For corporate executives outside Silicon Valley, the first wave of Web 2.0 evangelism was radical and threatening. Web 2.0 discourse subsequently took on a less alarming tone when management consultants picked up its main ideas and transformed them into marketable concepts that could be communicated to Corporate America. Most Web 2.0 crusaders in management consulting played down the apocalyptical vision of radical change in favour of a more pragmatic, evolutionary approach based on hard empirical experience. Most notable among them is Don Tapscott, whose book *Wikinomics* – co-authored with Anthony Williams – is a classic tome of Web 2.0 evangelism focusing on mass collaboration. While careful not to sound too radical, Tapscott nonetheless is realistic about the potential threat of Web 2.0, which he says threatens to bring "great upheaval, dislocation and danger for societies, corporations and individuals that fail to keep up with relentless change." Another book in this genre is *Groundswell*, published in 2008 by two Forrester Research analysts, Charlene Li and Josh Bernoff. While sounding the same alarm bell, *Groundswell's* authors offer a How-To toolkit along with case studies that help readers grasp Web 2.0's real-world impact on corporations.[24]

Management consultants have also brought "marketing" into the picture. This approach is doubtless a heresy in the eyes of early Web 2.0 purists, who generally express disdain for the marketing and PR hucksters attempting to appropriate their revolution by transforming its élan into handy buzzwords and management concepts that help companies target consumers.[25] The marketing approach to Web 2.0 can be fraught with dangers. As we described in Chapter 10, Wal-Mart's ill-fated phony blog quickly backfired and caused serious reputational damage to the retailer and its PR consultant, Edelman. Procter & Gamble, for its part, uses social sites for marketing and product promotion. One P&G online creation is a virtual character called "Miss Irresistible", who launched her own MySpace page to promote the company's Crest brand of toothpaste. P&G also has a product-related social site for girls called BeingGirl, which encourages girls to express themselves in a product-related (Tampax, Always) marketing environment. But as Facebook learned after its disastrous Beacon initiative, the MySpace generation is savvy about salesmen and pedlars and generally resents commercial intrusions.

A third category of Web 2.0 thought leadership is located in think tanks and universities. Some of these authors, like Gary Hamel, focus specifically on change management in large-scale corporations, while others take a broader perspective about the wider implications of social media. Some, like Harvard's Andrew McAfee, are clearly in the evangelist camp. So are academics like Clay Shirky, a New York University professor whose book *Here Comes Everybody* analyses the phenomenon of self-organization. Charles Leadbeater, a British journalist-turned-consultant who was an advisor to former British Prime Minister Tony Blair, is an expert on bottom-up collective creativity whose recent work, *We-think*, was written as a wiki collaboration project.[26]

There are, to be sure, a number of articulate voices who take pains to debunk the entire Web 2.0 evangelist movement. As we saw in Chapter 12, critics like Jaron Lanier have described the Web 2.0 revolution as "digital Maoism", while *Cult of the Amateur* author Andrew Keen has blamed it for destroying traditional culture and institutions. Less polemical sceptics, like Tom Davenport, have offered measured critiques about Enterprise 2.0, focusing, as noted, on its failure to grasp the bottom-line realities about power. Others claim that mass collaboration, despite enthusiasm expressed by Web 2.0 management consultants, is "achieved far less often than it is invoked". Enterprise 2.0 advocates, they point out, confuse collaboration with information sharing. Genuine collaboration is the result of deep human solidarities in the workplace, not trendy software tools.[27]

The naysayers notwithstanding, Web 2.0 evangelists appear to have accumulated more thought-leadership momentum than their contradictors. Their arguments, moreover, find support in a big push by major software giants rolling out Web 2.0 applications for corporations. Among them are Microsoft's SharePoint Server, Intel's SuiteTwo, and IBM's Lotus Connections (dubbed "MySpace-for-the-Workplace"). Other players in the Enterprise 2.0 software market include SAP's Enterprise Portal, Oracle's Visible Path, Contact Networks and Leveraged Software. Google meanwhile has launched OpenSocial, which brings open-source social networking tools to the enterprise market. As Matt Glotzbach, Google's enterprise director for the United States, put it: "We are really just trying to bring good solutions to the business market. One of the benefits we have of being in Google is the constant innovation. It used to be that enterprise technology was at the cutting edge. Now the consumer market leads and we follow. All of our current applications are candidates [for corporations], and we get asked all the time about enterprise versions of tools such as Blogger and YouTube."[28]

The open-source movement – once considered a marginal cause led by Linux enthusiasts against Microsoft – has come a long way since its chief evangelist, Eric Raymond, wrote *The Cathedral and the Bazaar* in the late 1990s. With powerful proprietary players dominating the software market, it was difficult finding converts to the idea of enterprise software that operated according to the three rules, "nobody owns it, everybody uses it, anybody can improve it". Today, the open-source movement, remarkably, has gone mainstream with buy-in from IBM – and even from Microsoft itself. Open-source software, to be sure, has its critics. *New York Times* journalist Thomas L. Friedman, in his bestselling book *The World is Flat*, describes open-source software, wikis, blogs and other social media as one of the ten "flatteners" which, he argues, are producing dangerously disruptive impacts on the global economy.[29]

Google's OpenSocial gambit in late 2007 – joined by MySpace, Yahoo!, America Online, Oracle, Friendster, hi5, LinkedIn, Ning, Bebo and Google-owned Orkut – was a direct challenge to Facebook which was still operating closed, proprietary social networking software. For corporations, OpenSocial holds out the attraction of using Web 2.0 tools with no need to make major investments in knowledge-management systems. At the same time, it presents the risk of information flows on wide-open software systems. The dilemma is between the efficiency advantages of sharing and the impulse to maintain tight organizational controls.[30]

Concrete examples of Enterprise 2.0 strategies indicate that CEOs, despite resistance deeper down in their organizations, are gradually overcoming the fear factor. Many corporations, facing growing pressures to innovate to remain competitive, actually have no choice. Pressures in favour of organizational change are coming not only from thought leaders and software vendors, but from markets – investors, shareholders and stock prices. CEOs are starting to move past the techno-hype about social media to focus on bottom-line issues like performance and shareholder value. If shareholders push for *profitability*, management pushes for *productivity* and employees push for *participation*, the convergence of these three Ps may create the conditions for the Enterprise 2.0 revolution.

Many corporations, it is true, are interested in Web 2.0 tools mainly for "communications" functions (executive blogging, marketing, advertising and PR) that don't necessitate profound organizational change. Still, the Enterprise 2.0 model is starting to acquire legitimacy. In December 2007, McKinsey published a forward-looking prediction of "Eight Business Technology Trends to Watch". Five of them – more than half – were Web 2.0 trends: distributed co-creation, consumers as innovators, online mass collaboration, extracting more value from interactions and making businesses from information.[31]

Let's look at two areas where Web 2.0 tools are already proving that social media can make a strong bottom-line case for growth, profitability and shareholder value: *peer production* and *open innovation*.

Peer production is a form of mass collaboration popularized by Wikipedia. The underlying logic of peer production finds its origins in the theory of *transaction costs* that govern industrial organization. Nobel laureate Ronald Coase, in his classic work on the emergence of firms, pondered the question: why do we need organizations for economic production? The answer is that markets are more efficient than firms only when gains (minus transaction costs) are lower. Conversely, firms emerge and hire people to work for them as employees when transaction costs of organized production are lower.[32] Web 2.0 evangelists argue that Enterprise 2.0 reasserts the logic of self-organized markets. By diffusing power downwards and outwards (even beyond the firm), Enterprise 2.0 no longer needs managed hierarchies to organize production. As Harvard professor Yochai Benkler has noted, production in the networked firm is "radically decentralized, collaborative and nonproprietary connected individuals who cooperate with each other without relying on either market signals or managerial commands". Benkler calls this new mode of production "commons-based peer production".[33]

In the corporate world, the most widespread form of peer production is the wiki. Wikis harness the wisdom of crowds to solve problems and foster creativity to come up with new ideas. They are, in a word, a form of *crowdsourcing*. Wikis therefore require *network effects* to work: their value increases with the number of people participating. Otherwise, you might as well go back to face-to-face meetings.

Wikis can be valuable as a mass collaboration tool because they are highly effective at seeking out the best expertise to solve problems. Harvard's Andrew McAfee has aptly called this advantage "ties that *find*". As McAfee puts it: "Companies that rely heavily on innovation have always spent a great deal of time, money and effort on ways to help knowledge workers interact better with their close colleagues. These companies obsess about office and lab layouts, trying to ensure that people flow past each other often and feel drawn to common work areas. They assemble cross-functional teams and try to make sure that these groups have enough of the right kinds of diversity (whatever that is). They hold brainstorming sessions and off-sites where co-workers can interact with the same set of colleagues, but differently." The problem, however, is that managers tend to call on people they know and like to help solve problems. Most managers like the familiar sound of the echo chamber, and have more affection for Loveable Fools than Competitive Jerks. Wikis open up the process beyond the usual cronies, favourites and in-the-loopers who regularly get invited to closed-door meetings. Wikis network horizontally, blowing through corporate silos, to find those who can bring real expertise to a problem – even if he's a Competent Jerk. Wikis reject closed echo chambers and promote the brainpower of collective smarts.

Wikis are increasingly being deployed both internally and externally to improve productivity and build social capital. IBM launched its "WikiCentral" in 2005 as a vehicle for internal expertise. A year later the Big Blue organized a brainstorming platform called InnovationJam which was soon attracting more than 150000 participants inside and outside the company to help identify emerging business opportunities. SAP is promoting SAP Wiki to become part of the SAP Corporate Portal and has introduced the enterprise social network pilot Harmony as a platform for connecting people across the organization. General Motors uses its internal blog, FastLane, as a corporate "focus group" that attracts some 5000 visits daily, including from consumers. The television channel Discovery launched a wiki called "Wetpaint" to bring its customers – viewers – into the conversation. Through Wetpaint, Discovery not only got feedback from viewers, but also user-generated video content.[34]

Peer production can offer tremendous competitive advantages to firms in sectors where *innovation* produces winners and losers. Corporate executives are becoming increasingly aware that innovation should not be conceived as restricted to walled-off R&D departments, but promoted as a dynamic social process – or open innovation.[35] Procter & Gamble famously outsourced its R&D through sites like InnoCentive, which crowdsources product development and problem-solving for its clients. InnoCentive, an R&D braintrust spinoff from drug maker Eli Lilly, demonstrates that, more often than not, the best brains are somewhere outside the corporation. A.G. Lafley, P&G's chief executive, has said he wants 50% of the company's product development crowdsourced outside the company.[36]

As a *McKinsey Quarterly* report published in June 2008 noted: "Executives in a number of companies are now considering the next step in this trend towards more open innovation. For one thing, they are looking at ways to delegate more of the management of innovation to networks of suppliers and independent specialists that interact with each other to cocreate products and services. They also hope to get their customers in to the act." McKinsey cited the well-known example of Lego, which invited its customers to come up with new product models and paid for the best ideas.[37]

Perhaps the best-known example of a Fortune 500 company converted to open innovation is IBM. After the Big Blue chip business had lost $1 billion in 2002, the company was desperate for a new strategy. Crisis forced IBM to take drastic measures. The solution was a new "open ecosystem" that opened up its chip R&D to outside partners. And it worked. IBM's chip division quickly turned the corner and began booming. As Samuel Palmisano, the company's CEO, told *Business Week*: "We are the most innovative when we collaborate". IBM today is on the leading edge of major corporations that have embraced social media.[38] Other global corporations that have integrated social networking into their organizational strategies include FedEx, Shell Oil, Motorola, General Electric, Kodak, British Telecom, Kraft Foods, McDonald's and Lockheed Martin.

That's an impressive list. So why has Enterprise not yet reached a tipping point? One reason is that, as noted, in most companies Web 2.0 tools are still being used mainly for communications, marketing and HR purposes. These functions, while useful, don't drive radical organizational transformation. When a CEO is blogging and an HR vice-president is using Facebook as a recruitment tool, the optics are cool but, in truth, nobody's power base is threatened. That kind of change is *evolution*, not revolution.

Revolution, as Gary Hamel noted, comes only when crisis hits and a radical rethink of corporate strategy is imperative. Hamel nonetheless believes that corporate management will change radically over the next few decades due to the combined impacts of technology, competitive pressures to innovate and what he calls a "revolution in expectations" by younger generations.

"Take a look at our kids – the first generation that has grown up on the Web," notes Hamel. "Their basic assumption is that your contribution should be judged simply on the merits of what you do rather than on the basis of your title or your credentials or providence or anything else. This is the lesson they've drawn from the experience with what I call the 'thoughtocracy' of cyberspace."[39] Tom Davenport agrees that demographics may be the key driver to the Web 2.0 revolution. Having expressed doubts about the utopian evangelism about Enterprise 2.0, Davenport nonetheless believes that young people may see things differently. "It's going to be very interesting to see what happens when the young bucks and buckettes of today's wired world hit the adult work force," he says. "Will they freely submit to such structured information environments as those provided by SAP and Oracle, content and knowledge management systems and communication by email? Or will they overthrow the computational and communicational status quo with MySpace, MyBlog and MyWiki?"[40]

So we're back to our 40th-level half-elf in *World of Warcraft* who, one day, might be CEO of your company. While we are waiting for that demographic tipping point, we can say that Enterprise 2.0 has succeeded in gaining legitimacy on one key front: openness.

Empowered by open-source software, open collaboration and open innovation, Enterprise 2.0 may soon be open for business.

15

Democracy 2.0: friends in low places

The American presidential election of 2008 will go down in history for a symbolic reason that should inspire all liberal democracies. It's now possible, thanks to the shining examples of Barack Obama and Hillary Clinton, for African-Americans and women to seek the most powerful elected office in the world: President of the United States.

The same election was a watershed event for another, less publicized reason. It was the first time the Web was used by US presidential candidates to connect directly with voters via social networking sites like MySpace and Facebook.

The Internet had already been deployed in previous political campaigns in the United States and other countries, but before 2008 its role had largely been limited to nuts-and-bolts "Web 1.0" tasks – especially fundraising. In the run up to the US presidential election in 2004, for example, Howard Dean took an early lead for the Democratic nomination due to his campaign's pioneering Internet blitzkrieg that drummed up a staggering $50 million in grassroots donations. The Internet proved to be a formidable electoral money-pump.

Following the 2004 presidential vote in America, politicians seized on the electoral potential of sites like Facebook and MySpace to connect on an informal *social* level with voters. In the run up to the 2008 election, every major candidate kept a personal MySpace and Facebook page and accumulated "friends" during the campaign. For the first time, democratic politics leveraged on a massive scale the social power of the Web. From now on, a personal page on a social networking site will an indispensible part of every politician's campaign – not only in America but undoubtedly in many other countries too. Facebook pages not only create the impression that a political candidate is in touch with the latest trends popular with young people, they also allow politicians to reach out to voters on a platform that benefits from viral-marketing network effects.

Jeff Merritt, president of a US non-profit organization called Grassroots Initiative which helps political novices run for office, believes the Web has transformed American politics. "It used to be you stuck with direct mail, phone banking and door-to-door canvassing," he said. "Now it's clear you get more bang for your buck if you take advantage of pre-established networks and tap into online networks that are usually free."[1]

Consider this number. In 2008, more than 500 American politicians had their own page on Facebook, which at present is regarded as the most effective site for voter mobilization. American politicians court MySpace members and any online constituency where votes can be found. But Facebook is favoured by political candidates because its members tend to be older, wealthier and more likely to vote than MySpace members. *Reader's Digest* called the 2008 US presidential campaign the "Facebook Election."[2]

Facebook was not unaware of its powerful role in electoral politics. During the 2008 US presidential campaign, the site launched its own political forum to encourage online debates about voter issues. In the heat of the presidential nomination battles, some 300 000 Facebook users were participating in online forum debates. Facebook also teamed up with ABC News for election coverage and forums. For ABC, the old media/new media initiative brought Facebook's vast membership to its newsgathering. And Facebook, for its part, gained journalistic credentials thanks to the mainstream TV network's news coverage.

"There is a special connection among the people who use Facebook," said ABC News president David Westin. "They interact with one another and that provides a very special and different environment for political discourse and debate among people who know each other and follow one another."[3]

For John McCain, in his early seventies when he declared his candidacy for the White House, getting in tune with young Web-savvy voters on MySpace and Facebook was a challenge. But McCain couldn't afford to shun the Internet. He launched personal pages on both MySpace and Facebook and, in keeping with online values based on total openness and transparency, revealed his personal predilections. On Facebook, the former war hero listed his pastimes (sports, hiking, fishing, history); favourite movies (*Viva Zapata, Letters from Iwo Jima, Some Like It Hot*); top TV shows ("24" and "Seinfeld"); and favourite novel (Hemingway's *For Whom the Bell Tolls*). After McCain won the Republican nomination in April 2008, his campaign team launched a "John McCain Facebook Challenge" to promote the candidate virally through "friend" networks.[4] McCain's campaign managers quickly learned something about the funky, rebellious culture of the virtual world when an Internet prankster hacked the candidate's MySpace page and inserted the following message under the conservative Republican's profile photo: "Dear supporters, today I announce that I have reversed my position and come out in full support of gay marriage . . . particularly marriage between two passionate females."[5] The prank doubtless elicited lots of laughs on Facebook. But the McCain campaign frantically yanked it from the candidate's page.

Hillary Clinton, just turned sixty, also played along and opened up on Facebook. While her hobbies were decidedly less exciting (speedwalking, crossword puzzles), her tastes in music were passably hip (Rolling Stones, U2, Carly Simon, Aretha Franklin), and her favourite movie (*The Wizard of Oz*) was located squarely in America's social mythology about the importance of family, home and fulfilling personal dreams. On her MySpace page, Clinton revealed that her worst habit was "chocolate". And her home task needing the most tending was "organizing my closets". In politics, it always helps to add a human touch.

It was Barack Obama, a much younger candidate than his rivals, who most impressively leveraged the so-called "Facebook effect". On his Facebook page, which featured the motto "Our Moment is Now", Obama listed his favourite musicians as Miles Davis, Stevie Wonder and Bob Dylan. His pastimes, he said, were basketball, writing and "loafing w/kids" (using hip shorthand aimed at appealing to young voters). His favourite movies were hard to argue with: *Casablanca, Godfather I and II, Lawrence of Arabia* and *One Flew Over the Cuckoo's Nest*. And his favourite books seemed selected for political effect: The Bible, Abraham's Lincoln's Collected Writings, and Toni Morrison's *Song of Solomon*. Obama was a big hit on Facebook: some 200000 members signed up as supporters.[6]

But Obama's greatest electoral advantage came from another Web 2.0 platform: YouTube. After his 38-minute speech on race was posted on the video site, within two days it had attracted more than two million views. The "Yes We Can" videoclip was an even bigger YouTube hit: it was watched more than four million times in only four days, and 20 million times before Obama won the Democratic nomination. What's more, the Obama campaign team hadn't even produced the viral video. It was made organically by hip hop star Will. i.am from the group Black Eyed Peas. And yet it proved more effective than any official messaging produced by the Obama campaign's communication strategy. In fact, the compelling "Yes We Can" video marked a crucial turning point for the black candidate's momentum with white voters in Middle America.

It was thanks to the effectiveness of Obama's social networking campaign on the Internet that, long before his Democratic nomination victory, political strategists with their ear to the ground were already picking up signs that he'd defeat Hillary Clinton. Obama beat Clinton on the Web 2.0 battlefield. In early 2007, more than a year before he won his party's nomination, Obama had attracted a massive following on Facebook while Hillary Clinton was struggling with the negative fallout of a Facebook movement called "Stop Hillary Clinton". Both candidates boasted user-generated "One Million Strong" supporter pages on Facebook. But while Obama's page attracted 259 647 members, Hillary Clinton's page counted only 3251.[7]

"I'll tell you something about Barack Obama that the media has not picked up on," said David Kravitz, co-founder of a partisan Democratic website called BlueMass Group, when the campaign was in full swing. "He has got a very, very powerful presence on Facebook, on MySpace, on a lot of these sort of below-the-radar social networking sites on the Internet. It's way ahead of any other candidate."[8] Democratic Party delegates, it seemed, finally caught up with the political momentum Obama had already generated online.

There can be no doubt that, for political candidates, the 2008 presidential vote was a "Facebook election". But did social networking sites genuinely empower American voters? If the Web 2.0 e-ruption has revolutionized social interaction, turned business models on their head and transformed organizational behaviour, has its impact on the political process in liberal democracies been equally powerful?

It's not our intention here to revisit the entire history of political philosophy. It's worth reminding ourselves, though, that in the long march of human civilization, democracy has emerged for fleetingly short periods. Plato, the greatest of all philosophers, included democracy among his list of undesirable forms of government along with oligarchy and despotism. The ancient Greek philosopher advocated rule by an incorruptible class of wise and courageous "guardians". Democracy, asserted Plato, is dangerously susceptible to demagoguery that invariably degenerates into tyranny.

Democracy certainly has no claim on virtue or perfection. Even in the world's greatest modern liberal democracies – United States, Britain, France – it can hardly be argued that the electoral process encourages purely democratic outcomes. In Britain, the so-called "deferential" vote was a time-honoured tradition that coerced lower classes to vote for their betters, usually high-born Conservatives. The United Kingdom is also, needless to say, a monarchy that maintains a parliamentary system featuring a House of Lords whose membership is determined by two wholly undemocratic principles: hereditary entitlement and arbitrary appointment. In the United States, the electoral process was long dominated by so-called party "bosses" who controlled both voters and, in many cases, the politicians they voted for. The role of political "machines" in American politics does not evoke – at least semantically – high-minded democratic principles of open citizenship participation. In France, the Fifth Republic is effectively an elected monarchy with a parliament – including a non-elected Senate – that is virtually powerless. In these three countries, grassroots citizen movements rarely make themselves heard, unless from the streets, and in any case cannot match the power of vertically organized interest groups.

As Winston Churchill famously remarked, democracy is the worst imaginable political system – except for all the others. Fortunately, modern history has provided examples of robust democracies that, however imperfect, have striven to live up to the noble ideals of ancient Greece. The most powerful nation over the past century, America, is a strong democracy. So are the most prosperous nations in the world. That democracy is the best of all possible forms of government cannot be doubted. The question we pose here is whether, thanks to the Internet, we can herald the emergence of a new citizen-empowered Democracy 2.0.

Web 2.0 evangelists, as we have seen, have tended to focus on the transformation of the capitalist corporation. Less attention has been paid to techno-optimists who advocate a powerful role for the Internet in fostering more effective citizenship engagement. Many have been inspired by German philosopher Jurgen Habermas's notions about "rational consensus" in public debate and how it can be achieved through online activism.[9] *Wired* magazine, in keeping with its techno-optimist spirit , strongly endorses this vision: "The ideal democratic process is participatory and the Web 2.0 phenomenon is about democratizing digital technology. There's never been a better time to tap that technological ethic to redemocratize our democracy."[10]

In Chapter 6, we concurred with *Wired* about the promise of the Web to reinvigorate civic engagement.[11] Since Web 2.0 *diffuses* power away from institutions and towards people, social networking sites should provide effective platforms for promoting a genuinely bottom-up expression of citizen sovereignty. If so, the robust civic ethos of voluntary association that Alexis de Tocqueville observed in the young American republic in the 1830s may well make a spectacular comeback in the 21st century thanks to the Internet.[12] And beyond America, Web-based citizen empowerment can potentially strengthen liberal democracies and, more importantly, bring democracy to countries currently living under tyranny and despotism in its many forms.

One measure of the Web's role in providing a political voice to citizens is, paradoxically, the reactionary hostility it provokes by authoritarian regimes that oppose democracy. That dictatorships resent the power of the Web is no secret. They particularly fear the potentially destabilizing impact of websites like MySpace, Facebook and YouTube. Syria's autocratic state has jailed bloggers and blocks websites deemed a security threat. On Syria's black list are both Facebook and YouTube. Even in Egypt, an Arab country that enjoys open diplomatic relations with the West, the government takes a hard line towards online criticism of the state. Reporters Without Frontiers, the human rights media watchdog, has accused Egypt's state of "harsh repression" against online dissent, including jailing bloggers. The Chinese regime has also imprisoned "cyber-dissidents" and, in March 2008, shut down 25 websites including YouTube.[13] Indonesia meanwhile has banned both YouTube and MySpace. Other states that have banned websites or imprisoned cyber-dissidents include Iran, Saudi Arabia, Libya, Belarus, Burma, North Korea, Tunisia, Turkmenistan, Uzbekistan and Vietnam. An OpenNet Initiative survey published in 2007 reported that 25 of 41 countries surveyed were engaging in some form of Internet censorship.[14] Clearly, there is something about free and open sites like MySpace, Facebook and YouTube that nondemocratic regimes find threatening.

Some contend, it must be noted, that Web 2.0 social media are actually antidemocratic. They warn that, even in Western countries including the United States, there is an ever-present danger that states will succumb to "Big Brother" temptations and pry into social networking sites to spy on their citizens. There are even conspiracy theories that claim Facebook was started by the CIA through alleged links between the site's original venture capital backers and the American spy agency.[15] While CIA admits openly that it uses Facebook for recruitment purposes, there doesn't appear to be any operational linkage between the two organizations. The CIA's seemingly innocuous use of Facebook nonetheless has raised concerns among civil libertarians. Facebook's privacy policy, for example, states that it does not share personal information with third-party companies – but adds that, in order to comply with the law, it may give personal information to "government agencies". Nicole Ozer from the American Civil Liberties Union notes that, given that the CIA has a page on Facebook and is actively mining the site, "it would be surprising if they weren't using it in other ways."[16]

More disturbing are the findings of a "Dark Web" research project at the University of Arizona which tracked Jihadist extremist groups using Web 2.0 media. The study, published in 2008, came across an alarming number of Jihadist blogs, including one posting news updates about so-called "occupied Islamic countries". Jihadist bloggers were also active on YouTube, uploading videos featuring explosives, attacks, bombings and hostage-taking. "Although YouTube has made efforts to control video content, the site is still heavily used by extremists for video sharing," noted the study. On Second Life, meanwhile, a "Terrorist of SL" attracted 228 members and another group called "Liberation Front" counted 65 followers. The Dark Web study concluded: "Many of the Web 2.0 content providers may only act as Jihadist sympathisers or information dissemination agents for radical extremist materials. Most of them may not be the original content creators, i.e., the groups who performed the violent acts. However, their role and importance as online information dissemination agents or resource hubs cannot be underestimated."[17]

These troubling findings became eerily real for Americans in 2007 when a 21-year-old extremist, Samir Khan, was caught blogging from his quiet middle-class neighbourhood in North Carolina on a radical Islamic site called Inshallahshaheed (a.k.a Revolution). When Khan – born in Saudi Arabia but raised in the United States – was tracked down and exposed by the *New York Times*, he was online praising Osama bin Laden, calling on Allah to "curse more American soldiers", and posting videos of US Army vehicles being blown up by roadside bombs in Iraq. Khan has never been arrested or charged. While he has been feeling the wrath of local opinion in North Carolina, Khan has been careful to keep his activities legal. "I've never told anybody to build bombs," he insisted, defiantly.[18]

Critics of Web 2.0 claim that, even within the parameters of democratic debate, blogs and social networking sites tend to create communities of bias that polarize opinion. A notable proponent of this view is Harvard law professor Cass Sunstein, author of *Republic.com 2.0.*[19] For Sunstein, the paradox of the Web is that, while it has provided unprecedented access to information that stimulates debate and discussion, it has also reinforced entrenched opinion because people search for, and easily find, information that comforts their own biases. Conservatives go to the Web and plug into right-wing websites and blogs, while people with left-wing values seek similar reinforcement of their world view on the Internet. As Sunstein puts it, the Web "squelches diversity". Web 2.0 platforms, in short, are ideological echo chambers.

"For example, 80 per cent of readers of the leftwing blog Daily Kos are Democrats and fewer than 1 per cent are Republicans," notes Sunstein, who has worked as an adviser to Barack Obama. "Many popular bloggers link frequently to those who agree with them and to contrary views, if at all, only to ridicule them. To a significant extent, people are learning about supposed facts from narrow niches and like-minded others. This matters for the electoral process. A high degree of self-sorting leads to more confidence, extremism and increased contempt for those with contrary views."[20] In the first edition of his book *Republic.com*, Sunstein described an online "Boston Tea Party" whose members gradually radicalize and, because they have been mutually reinforcing their hostility towards government, start advocating violent action. The echo chamber is dangerous, he argues, because it pushes opinions to the dangerous extremes.

This theory can find support from certain Web 2.0 platforms used by far-right political movements, notably in Europe. As we saw in Chapter 5, France's far-right Front National party established a headquarters in Second Life; and Italy's extreme right-wing political factions similarly have been using the Internet to propagate their ideology.[21] But Sunstein's theory is about two centuries too late. From the earliest days of modern media – from 18th century pamphleteering to mass-audience newspapers a century later – public opinion was mobilized around entrenched values and strong ideological positions. Even today in Europe, newspapers are highly partisan, frequently right across the political spectrum. In Britain, there are "Labour" and "Tory" papers, and in France opinion on the far right and left of the political spectrum are served by their own newspapers.

Sunstein's argument is uniquely American not only in its conceptual perspective, but also in its normative bias. Only in the United

States have the media, especially newspaper journalists, elevated the principle of "objectivity" to the level of a professional credo. And only in the United States is mainstream media opinion situated in the broad centre. Sunstein, it seems, likes his omelettes cut off at both ends. He appears to believe that political debate should be located in the amorphous centre and exclude "niche" opinions, even on the margins of public debate, on the grounds that they are potentially dangerous. Some opinions are indeed contemptible, but pluralism in a free marketplace of ideas provides for their contradiction. Sunstein's bulging omelette is a recipe for squelching diversity, not promoting it.

The virtue of Web 2.0 tools like collaborative filtering and social networking is precisely that they encourage niches to proliferate – not only in the provision of goods and services to consumers, but also in the ideas arena of public debate. There is evidence, in fact, that – contrary to dire warnings about the polarization of opinion – the Web actively promotes a healthy respect for diversity of opinion. A study conducted by Jennifer Stromer-Gallery at the State University of New York in 2003 explicitly debunked Sunstein's "Boston Tea Party" theory through empirical research based on surveys of political conversations on the Internet. Stromer-Gallery discovered that most people engaged in online political debates were not reinforcing their biases in an echo chamber, but "expressly enjoyed the ability to encounter perspectives *other than their own.*"[22]

The American political system nonetheless remains, to use the language of economics, a de facto *duopoly* in which the two principal belligerents (Republicans and Democrats) are not differentiated by sharp ideological divisions. In other liberal democracies, like Britain and Canada, political systems are *oligopolies* that allow for a slightly broader spectrum of difference, but not significantly wider. In France, political debate has been opened considerably further to include political parties (communists, Trotskyites, right-wing nationalists) that would never be accorded a legitimate political voice in America. France, for all its dysfunctions, can claim to offer a comparatively diverse spectrum of legitimate political debate, including in electoral politics.

Albert Hirschman's exit/voice/loyalty theory provides insights into these distinctions.[23] Voters tend to behave like consumers when confronted with monopolies, duopolies and market pluralism. When voters are faced with no choice, they can protest through *voice* or opt to *exit*. In liberal democracies, *exit* is frequently expressed as apathy and low voter turnout. In theory, when the spectrum of political choice is wider, voter turnout should be higher. Cross-country comparisons confirm this. France, with its wider political offering, enjoys much higher levels of voter participation than countries like the United States where the electoral system is dominated by political duopolies.

Those who value a more diversified marketplace of ideas, therefore, should celebrate the "niche" orientation of Web 2.0 in the civic arena. If Web 2.0 platforms can be used to stimulate political debate and foster civic engagement, self-organizing grassroots movements should emerge and bring more voices to public debate. As American billionaire Ross Perot's presidential campaign in 1992 demonstrated, it's possible in America to challenge the established political duopoly. Web 2.0 holds out the same promise to reinvigorate political debate by mobilizing opinion beyond existing cleavages – and, what's more, without the prerequisite of a billion-dollar personal fortune. Some argue, it is true, that too many voices in democratic debate create a "cacophony" effect that's hard to manage. It's difficult to argue against democratic pluralism, however, on the flimsy grounds that public debate is cacophonous – unless, of course, it threatens to end in tyranny. The philosophical cornerstone of democracy is pluralism. When you evacuate pluralism, you no longer have democracy. Only despots ruling over one-party states in Africa would attempt to argue otherwise.

While we wait for the Web 2.0 revolution to usher in Democracy 2.0 – or "e-democracy" – we can test the effectiveness of the Internet in the public sphere by examining the nuts-and-bolts provision of so-called "e-government". If Democracy 2.0 is fundamentally about *values* (choosing what kind of society in which we wish to live), e-government is largely a *pragmatic* matter involving the management of public institutions to serve citizens more efficiently, effectively and equitably.

When the Internet first emerged, governments, following the trend already under way in business, seized on the Web as a conduit for "pushing" information at citizens in a top-down dissemination model. Thus, early e-government efforts mainly involved managing the websites of state agencies, making documents available online, publicizing public sector services, providing practical information, posting press releases and so forth. A great deal of government information was put online. Much of it, however, had an unmistakable "PR" spin, such as biographical details about elected officials and positive accounts of their many good deeds. Citizen feedback or input was rarely, if ever, actively solicited. This "Web 1.0" e-government phase nonetheless gave citizens unprecedented access to vast amounts of information that previously had been virtually impossible to obtain.

The United States, triggered by the *Government Paperwork Elimination Act* in 1998, was on the leading edge of this push for greater efficiency through e-government. President Bill Clinton's *Memorandum on E-Government*, issued in 1999, decreed that the 500 forms most used by American citizens be put online. In 2002, the US Congress passed the *E-Government Act* whose ambition was "establishing a broad framework of measures that require using Internet-based information technology to enhance citizen access to Government information and services, and for other purposes". The same year, President George W. Bush announced an e-government initiative based on three principles: citizen-centred, not bureaucracy-centred; results-oriented; and market-based, actively promoting innovation.[24]

Early thought leadership on e-government was coming from the private sector, too, especially big management consulting firms. Accenture, for example, started publishing e-government reports in 2000 and was soon issuing country rankings based on performance benchmarks in the provision of online services to citizens. Accenture's annual e-government ranking was topped annually – with the exception of high-performing Singapore – largely by industrialized liberal democracies like Canada, the United States, Denmark, Sweden, Finland, the United Kingdom and Japan.[25] The tiny Baltic country of Estonia, with a population of only 1.4 million, deserves special mention for its commitment to e-government. Estonia, in fact, has elevated e-government to the more ambitious goals of "e-democracy" and "e-society". In 2000, the Estonian parliament entrenched free and universal Internet access as a constitutional right. The same year, government cabinet meetings switched to a paperless system using a Web-based document system. As a joint INSEAD/World Economic Forum case study on Estonia's e-government initiative noted: "E-leadership has proven to be instrumental in helping Estonia through the painful transition from centralized planning to the model of modern governance it is today . . . This is especially remarkable when one notes that the nation was ruled by foreign powers – Denmark, Germany, Sweden and Russia – for centuries. The merger of e-leadership and political vision has been one of the critical factors in its economic growth, the spreading of democracy and its resulting accession to the European Union."[26]

While e-government policy fashion produced some outstanding examples like Estonia, most state-sponsored initiatives were focused on improving efficiency of *service provision* – mainly in bureaucratic

procedures like car registration, passport applications, birth certificates, building permits and the like. Many of these e-government
initiatives were remarkably successful. The US government site, Gov.
com, was – and remains – a model of open-access information policy
for an entire citizenry. Still, government websites were mainly posting
and processing information, not empowering citizen participation.
They were stuck in Web 1.0 think.

It didn't take long, however, for Web 2.0 evangelism in the corporate world to bring the public sector into the picture. In the United
States, the most articulate e-government vision came not from the
public sector, but from a Silicon Valley brain trust inside Cisco Systems.
In 2004, the Cisco Internet Business Solutions Group published an e-
government manifesto entitled *The Connected Republic: Changing the
Way We Govern*. The authors confidently stated that virtual networked
organizations promised to take government back to pure forms of
democracy known in ancient Greek city-states so that citizens can
"reconnect with each other, with their elected leaders and with their
public institutions."[27] *The Connected Republic* described its guiding
principle as *small pieces, loosely joined*, a reference to *Cluetrain Manifesto*
co-author David Weinberger's book of the same title.[28] The *Connected
Republic* authors shared Weinberger's vision of "a world in which
meaning and value increasingly derive from the ability to connect
people, ideas and organizations in new patterns of communication
and collaboration. This implies a radical shift away from hierarchy
and centralized control." The *Cluetrain* inspiration suggested that
the Cisco manifesto's tacit slogan was "the end of government as
usual".

The pragmatic dimension of the *Connected Republic* vision was pure
Web 2.0. Its action plan was based on constructing government as a
"Networked Virtual Organization" operating according to three
imperatives: using networks as platforms for collaboration and creativity; making the best use of expertise by "empowering the edge";
and harnessing the "power of us" to create knowledge, solve problems and deliver better services. The models for networked platforms
were GoogleMaps, YouTube, MySpace and Flickr. The authors were
realistic enough to grasp that, since these e-ruptions were regarded
as threatening in corporations, the powers of resistance in state
bureaucracies would be even more formidable. "Grasping these
opportunities is not going to be easy," acknowledged the *Connected
Republic* authors. "The scale of the transformation is huge. Furthermore, it involves not just organizational change, but the development
of new and different cultures. As the e-government project has illus-

trated, there are limitations to the speed with which major change programmes within government agencies can be carried out."

There are many good reasons to be sceptical about government's capacity to self-reform. As *The Economist* asked in a special report on e-government: "Why is government unable to reap the same benefits as business, which uses technology to lower costs, please customers and raise profits?" The answer: no competition, a tendency to reinvent the wheel and a government bias in favour of technology rather than organization. *The Economist* added: "Governments have few direct rivals. Amazon.com must outdo other online booksellers to win readers' money. Google must beat Yahoo!. Unless every inch of such companies' websites offers stellar clarity and convenience, customers go elsewhere. But if your country's tax-collection online offering is slow, clunky or just plain dull, then tough."[29]

In Britain, former Prime Minister Tony Blair put technology at the centre of his boldly announced "transformational government" policy. The initiative claimed to put citizens, not bureaucracy, at the centre of an IT technology-driven reform aimed at improving efficiency. In announcing his vision in 2002, Blair called for "a new relationship between citizen and state". Yet when the UK e-government initiative was finally spelled out in a Cabinet Office report in 2005, it was hardly a revolutionary e-government vision. It was a nuts-and-bolts approach based on harnessing IT tools to maximize the efficiency of what Blair called the "business of government".[30]

The UK's technology approach to e-government came with the usual hype, spin and window-dressing. The centrepiece was the government website DirectGov, launched in 2004 as a portal to all UK government information and services. The Blair government also created a new cabinet portfolio held by a Minister for Transformational Government. In 2008 the minister, Tom Watson, favourably compared Google to the Great Library of Alexandria in 300 BC. He even confided approvingly that his wife was a member of Netmums.com.

"It's a great site," declared Watson in a speech. "Parents chat, and offer, I've been there, advice on everything from baby whispering to school admissions. Except it's not just a handful of mums and dads, it's thousands of them, available in your living room, 24 hours a day. Sounds like hell well, it's a lifeline when your baby's screaming at four in the morning, you have no idea why and you just need to know you're not alone. But my point is, imagine if quarter of a million mums decided to meet at Wembley Stadium to discuss the best way to bring up their kids. Midwives would be there dispensing advice. Health visitors, nursery teachers, welfare rights advisers would be there. Even politicians would try and get in on the act. But when twice this number chooses to meet together in the same place online, we just ignore them. That's going to have to change."[31]

The UK e-government initiative, despite some successes, has been given a mixed report card. The DirectGov portal was mocked by e-government activists for its poor search engine capacities, and they even launched their own site, dubbed "DirectionlessGov", powered by Google. The criticism appeared to confirm the belief that governments are notorious for overspending on underperforming software. As *The Economist* noted in early 2008: "The story of e-government has been one of quantity, not quality. It has provided plenty of reason for scepticism and not much cause for enthusiasm. Whereas e-commerce has been a spectacular success, transforming industries as diverse as travel and book retailing, e-government has yet to transform public administration. Indeed, its most conspicuous feature has been a colossal waste of taxpayers' money on big computer systems, poorly thought out and overpriced." The British government, added the magazine, had wasted $4 billion over the previous seven years on e-government projects that were later cancelled and written off.[32]

Given these embarrassing setbacks, no wonder that the latest e-government push has focused, oddly enough, on the *nongovernment* voluntary sector for public services. In Britain, Charles Leadbeater – a former advisor to Tony Blair – has provided thought leadership on many of these initiatives for the UK government. Leadbeater has been an articulate evangelist for what he calls the "User-Generated State" and "Public Services 2.0". The main thrust of Leadbeater's vision is a power shift away from state bureaucracy and towards civil society – specifically, voluntary and community groups, social enterprises, charities and cooperatives. They would be empowered to create public goods in a collective, participatory bottom-up democratic process.

"Older forms of political engagement and campaigning are degenerating, new and energetic forms are emerging," wrote Leadbeater in a 2007 discussion paper entitled "Social Software for Social Change" commissioned by the British government. "The social Web will only revive the public domain by unsettling it and many of its inhabitants. That is because the incumbent players of the public domain – political parties and traditional civic organizations – are themselves creatures of the industrial media era – broadcast, print, newspapers – which are being disrupted by the rise of Web 2.0 . . . The social Web will create more ways for people to engage with causes, possibly bypassing established voluntary sector organizations."[33]

This vision of a networked, participatory, activist democracy is not techno-utopia. It's precisely what Tocqueville witnessed in America nearly two centuries ago – a robust civil society and egalitarian spirit that motivated citizens to engage in all manner of voluntary associations. Tocqueville put it this way: "Americans of all ages, all conditions, and all dispositions constantly form associations. They have not only commercial and manufacturing associations, in which all partake, but associations of a thousand other kinds – religions, moral, serious, futile, general or restricted, enormous or diminutive. Wherever at the head of some new undertaking you see the government in France, or a man of rank in England, in the United States you will be sure to find an association."[34]

The prospect, nearly two hundred years later, of harnessing these vigorous public-spirited energies not only in America but throughout the world, is surely a vision that should be encouraged. A Web-empowered political process that fosters mass participation, collaboration, deliberation and mobilization is what democracy is all about. It is already happening in the America of the 21st century with Web 2.0-mobilized political groups like PersonalDemocracy.com, whose slogan is "technology is changing politics". PersonalDemocracy. com, which is linked to the Democratic Party, features the following mission statement on its website: "Technology and the Internet are changing democracy in America. We envision this site as one hub for the conversation already underway between political practitioners and technologists, as well as anyone invigorated by the potential of all this to open up the process and engage more people in all the things that we can and must do together as citizens."

If Democracy 2.0 can leverage the collective intelligence of a sovereign people, maybe we can indeed reconnect with the values not only of the young American republic circa 1830, but with those that flourished during the high-flowering of democracy in ancient Greece. It sounds like a noble goal – and maybe it's possible. But let's remember that it was Tocqueville who warned us that the greatest danger facing America was an excess of democracy – namely, *tyranny of the majority*.

Most liberal democracies – including the United States – are, in fact, gentle oligarchies where voter turnout is alarmingly low and political life is the business of a small minority. The vast majority has opted for passive *exit* from the political process, resorting to *voice* only in times of crisis or momentous import. We know, however, that citizens show more *loyalty* to a political system, and feel more compelled to engage in civic activity, when they have confidence that their *voice* is heard and represented. When they don't feel they have a *voice*, they protest or retreat forlornly into empty bowling alleys.

Does that mean that citizens in liberal democracies should be empowered to vote directly via the Internet? What would the result have been if, in 2008, the US president had been elected not indirectly through an electoral college on a state-by-state basis, but directly through a Web-based e-voting system? Will this kind of direct democracy ever be a reality? It already is – in Estonia. That country adopted e-voting in 2005.

Would Democracy 2.0, diffusing power directly to the people, create a better society? Or would we find ourselves going back in time not to democratic Athens, but to ancient Rome whose leaders constantly feared the angry clamour of the mob? Is the danger of Democracy 2.0, indeed, that it may one day degenerate into Anarchy 1.0?

These questions are at the very heart of political philosophy. After three millennia of turbulent experience, humankind has learned – as Winston Churchill sagely noted – that democracy is the least imperfect of all known political systems. The question is not whether we want democracy, but rather what kind of democracy we wish to construct.

Given the power of Web 2.0 – socially, commercially and organizationally – there can be no doubt that it will, inevitably, produce an eruptive impact on our political institutions. And if the values of democracy prevail, we can be reassured that it will bring about a better world.

Conclusion

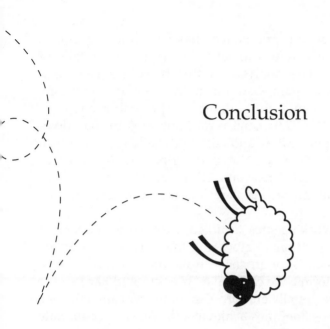

We began this book by heralding the Web 2.0 revolution and the profound social transformations it has triggered – how we interact with one another, how we behave in workplace environments and how we engage with the larger world around us. We, indeed, are living at a time of great change. The Internet has empowered us as individuals, consumers and citizens to take more control of our lives and organize ourselves spontaneously. Many core assumptions and received truths are being challenged. Old value systems shaped by long-established institutions are being overthrown. Some call this seismic social shift an emerging "do-it-yourself" culture. Others call it a new "power of us" ethos. Self-reliant and unfettered by the institutional biases of the past, we are increasingly putting faith in our instinctive feelings, sudden insights, intimate convictions and collective intelligence as we confront life's challenges.

The Web 2.0 revolution, as we have seen in the preceding chapters, has captured the social dynamic of this rupture. The phenomenal popularity of Web 2.0 platforms – from MySpace and Facebook to Flickr and Twitter – provides powerful examples of how our irrepressible social impulses are seeking spontaneous expression. We are embracing the infinite possibilities of social interaction and the exhilarating randomness of life in all its complexity. Accepting the practical limitations of rational calculations, we are realizing that the consequences of our social interactions can be surprisingly unintended, marvellously unexpected and sometimes unforeseeably tragic.

We believe that these e-ruptions will have far-reaching consequences. We have been careful, however, to avoid the pitfalls of passionate convictions. The analysis in this book has been animated neither by zealous evangelism nor by reactionary scepticism. One of the recurrent themes throughout the preceding chapters, indeed, has been that Web 2.0 social e-ruptions present, paradoxically, both exciting opportunities and difficult challenges. The profound social transformations we have described will not occur without confronting powerful resistance. Like all revolutions, Web 2.0 e-ruptions hold out great promise; but they are also fraught with great peril.

Thanks to social networking sites, as noted, we have been liberated from the burdens of institutional values and their pressures towards conformity. We can break through social isolation and reach out to the world on our own terms. We can make "friends" and harness the strength of weak ties, personally and professionally. We can seek fame and fortune online, and sometimes achieve both. We can accumulate social capital and gain recognition for our talents and efforts, individual and collective. In organizations, Web 2.0 tools are becoming powerful platforms for cooperation, collaboration and creativity. Consumers have been empowered in markets and citizens have become empowered in democratic participation.

This book has attempted to tell this story with illustrations and case studies which, we hope, have offered intriguing and instructive insights into these e-ruptions. What has interested us most is the Web 2.0 revolution's impact on the three social dynamics that gave this book its structure: identity, status and power. It will be recalled that we described our analytical approach to these themes as "3-D" – *disaggregation* of identities, *democratization* of status and *diffusion* of power.

Virtual identities, we have seen, are constructed as personal, multifaceted extensions of the self whose online expression can be tremendously liberating. Social interaction on sites like MySpace, Facebook, Bebo and Orkut is disarmingly open, candid and uninhibited. Secondly, few would argue that the democratization of status in the online world has not been a positive outcome. Once assigned according to the ascriptive values of rank and position, status is now attributed more democratically according to the measurable facts of performance and merit. Finally, power no longer resides exclusively in established institutions; it is being diffused towards the edges where individuals are spontaneously engaging in their own strategies of social interaction and collective action.

Yet there's also a dark underside to the Web 2.0 revolution. Never before have our identities been so exposed to danger – imposture, fraud, cyber-bullying, sexual predation and privacy invasion. When online identities are virtual avatars, the potential for deception is even greater. Parents are increasingly, and justifiably, concerned that their children have access to explicit sexual and violent content on social websites like YouTube. And as young people move into adulthood, they must now live with the realization that the traces of their lives left behind on sites like MySpace and Facebook are indelible and, like tattoos, last an entire lifetime. There is even reason to doubt the authenticity of some forms of social interaction in the online world. While maintaining online "friends" is undoubtedly a self-validating way of acquiring social capital and leveraging the strength of weak ties, it's possible to wonder whether the accumulation of hundreds, even thousands, of "friends" is a credible way of constituting a genuine social network. Life is not a masked ball where everybody's identity is a mystery. Social interactions, like financial transactions, must be founded on some basic notion of mutual recognition and trust. And when that trust breaks down, the consequences can be deeply troubling. As the heart-breaking story of young Megan Meier demonstrated, the capacity to manipulate identities and perniciously harass others on sites like MySpace can result in shocking tragedy. Sometimes identity fraud can be fatal.

The Web 2.0 revolution has also provided an outlet for questionable forms of social behaviour – like flaming, faming and shaming. And while social networking sites like YouTube have provided platforms for remarkable talents, they have also promoted the vacuous values of shallow notoriety and celebrity. Marketers and PR flaks meanwhile are insinuating themselves into social networking sites to flog and spam. Many seem to regard virtual reality not as a marketplace of ideas, but as a vast, soulless shopping mall in cyberspace. Political operators, too, are manipulating Web 2.0 sites to hype and spin. More disturbingly, extremists are exploiting the openness of Web 2.0 networks to spread hatred and incite violence. Meanwhile, corporations using Web 2.0 tools to promote collaboration and foster innovation must also worry about the dangers of security threats and reputational risks.

Make no mistake, the opportunities presented by the Web 2.0 revolution have been distorted and perverted by fraudsters, vandals, hucksters, sexual predators and even terrorists. The alarming trend towards abusive, violent, antisocial and criminal behaviour online will only strengthen the arguments of those who call for enforceable monitoring mechanisms, if not strict regulations, that draw the line between socially acceptable and invasive conduct. If these issues are not resolved, people doubtless will retreat back behind social fortresses, their virtual drawbridges pulled up and locked shut.

The values underpinning the Web 2.0 revolution indeed are still contested in many quarters. The diffusion of power triggered by Web 2.0 platforms, as we have seen, is meeting concerted resistance by those who feel threatened by change. Those who possess power rarely show willingness to surrender it. In corporate bureaucracies, managers can effectively resist and thwart – at least in the short term – the drive towards a Web 2.0 culture that proactively encourages open collaboration in horizontal networks. Enterprise 2.0 may be an elegant concept, but on the ground its open, horizontal social architecture collides with the raw dynamics of power politics. In most organizations, power is still a top-down system. The ghost of Philippe le Bel still looms ominously.

Web 2.0 evangelists understand this. They fear, in fact, that the Web 2.0 revolution is already being thwarted by powerful forces of centralization, consolidation and control. Even major corporate players that were once passionate Web 2.0 advocates – Google, Amazon, Facebook – now appear to be seizing control and bolt-locking the doors to capture the value they created. If they succeed, we could well witness the triumphant return of the same vertical top-down structures, monopoly business models and centralized command-and-control systems that the Web 2.0 revolution was supposed to sweep away. It wouldn't be the first time that a revolution has produced an unintended outcome that seems to betray the zealous idealism of its early proponents.

Tim O'Reilly, the Silicon Valley evangelist credited with coining the term "Web 2.0", has become a leading voice in this Cassandra chorus. "What we used to think of as a computer is really a device connected to a global computer," said O'Reilly in the spring of 2008. "It leads us again to large centralized players. It's a big part of Web 2.0 that we have to be aware of and worry about. Every Web 2.0 race is a race to grow that database. Bigger is better. Google, Amazon, eBay all want to get all these things in one place. The paradox in Web 2.0 is that applications built off open, decentralized networks lead to concentrations of power." [1]

Oxford professor Jonathan Zittrain also sounds this alarm in a book whose title clearly states his position: *The Future of the Internet and How to Stop It*. Zittrain describes the Web's imminent takeover by monopoly commercial players who value control more than freedom.

"The pieces are in place for a wholesale shift away from the original chaotic design that has given rise to the modern information revolution," contends Zittrain.[2] He argues that the open-ended "generative" Internet – from the Linux operating system to Web 2.0 platforms like Wikipedia – is being usurped by what he calls "tethered appliances" like the iPod, iPhone and Xbox. We're returning, in other words, to Apple and Microsoft locking everything down with proprietary systems and bundled software.

These warnings command our attention. And yet we should remind ourselves that the tensions described in this book – between the dynamics of horizontal networks and vertical institutions – are, in fact, not new. They are part of an inexorable cycle that has been playing out in human history since the Christian religion emerged from the ruins of the Roman Empire and extended its influence throughout medieval Europe and into the modern era. As we've recounted in these pages, once the Catholic Church was established as a highly centralized institution, it was challenged by the bottom-up Protestant Reformation triggered by Martin Luther and spread by new technologies like the printing press. Horizontal and decentralized medieval power was, in like manner, overthrown by the emergence of vertically constructed states. Today, we are witnessing the same dynamic at play. The Web 2.0 revolution represents another shift towards horizontally networked power. And it is bound to be countered by vertical forces of reaction. Web 2.0 social media may indeed empower individuals as consumers and citizens; but they give commercial players the capacity to build massive scale, capture value and reassert monopoly power. They also give states powerful instruments of control and coercion, including the means to monitor and spy on their own citizens.[3]

We have argued that the Web 2.0 revolution has reasserted, for better or for worse, essentially neomedieval forms of social organization. While the linkage of MySpace and global geopolitics may seem preposterous, we believe that this Web-driven trend towards neomedievalism is not a coincidence. The same dynamics are operating in the sphere of international affairs. The centralized state power that has dominated world diplomacy for the past three centuries is increasingly being challenged by the emergence of powerful networks. We are living in a world where, as in the Middle Ages, power is diffused, overlapping and multilayered.

In an essay in the prestigious *Foreign Affairs* journal, Richard Haass argues that the world is entering what he calls a "nonpolar" phase. Nineteenth-century diplomacy was based on a multipolar system characterised by a balance of power, followed by a bipolar system in the 20th century with the Cold War and superpower rivalry between the United States and Soviet Union. Following the collapse of the Soviet system in the early 1990s, an American-led world became essentially unipolar. Today, no single state dominates the world system. Global geopolitics is nonpolar – a concerted form of neomedievalism.

"International affairs in the twenty-first century will be defined by nonpolarity," says Haass, a former White House advisor and currently president of the Council on Foreign Relations. "Power will be diffuse rather than concentrated, and the influence of nation-states will decline as that of non-state actors increases."[4]

Web 2.0 evangelists remain optimistic about the Internet's second coming. They claim the Web 2.0 revolution will foster a new ethos of "cosmopoliteness" among citizens of a global civil society unburdened by the baggage of national identities, cultural constructions and state controls.[5] There is already techno-optimist talk about a "Web 3.0" revolution whose primary feature will be a so-called "semantic Web". If Web 2.0 is a networked platform, Web 3.0 will transform the Internet into a form of human intelligence capable of thinking with its own "brain" and answering complex questions.[6]

Religion and spirituality meanwhile have leveraged the power of horizontal networks to bring evangelism back to its historical roots. In early 2008, the London-based Fellowship of World Christians launched a social networking site called "Faith Book". Another religious movement calling itself "Faithbook" has opened its own Facebook page to combat extremism. But this Faithbook group isn't an online Christian movement, it's Jewish. It was organized by the UK-based Movement for Reform Judaism. In June 2008, the movement's executive director, Rabbi Shoshana Boyd Gelfand, told the London *Times*: "So much of what has happened with new media is that it has become a place where extremists can construct messages of hate and intolerance. We have got to combat that and create a space where people who may not meet face to face can have a constructive debate."[7]

Perhaps most intriguing of all, given our historical saga about the tension between kings and popes, is the Catholic Church's recent conversion to social networking sites. In May 2008, the Pontiff announced that the Church was launching a social networking site described as a "Catholic Facebook". *Wired* magazine jocularly invited readers to vote on the site's new name – placing bets on Popebook, Facemass and GraceSpace.[8] On World Youth Day held in Australia in

July 2008, Pope Benedict XVI sent an SMS text message to hundreds of thousands of Catholic youths. Perhaps Google is God after all. Or if not, a Google search may be the best way to find the pearly gates of cyberspace.

If the Web 2.0 revolution has validated the spiritual values of faith, it should be hoped that it will also reinforce the humanist values of reason, justice and truth. If the Internet is ushering in a new Society 2.0 in which the values of identity, status and power have been pro-foundly e-rupted, perhaps it's time for a new online social contract founded on *trust*. This is all the more urgent given that the dangers associated with the Web – from online imposture and cyber-bullying to fraud and cyber-terrorism – are based on justified feelings of distrust.

Francis Fukuyama, in his book entitled *Trust*, argues that the values of trust are not only at the basis of ethical social behaviour, but form the cornerstone of modern capitalist societies. "Economic activity represents a crucial part of social life and is knit together by a wide variety of norms, rules, moral obligations and other habits that together shape a society," noted Fukuyama. He added that "we can learn from an examination of economic life that a nation's wellbeing, as well as its ability to compete, is conditioned by a single, pervasive cultural characteristic: the level of trust inherent in the society."[9]

Trust is based not on rational calculation, but on deeply entrenched habits of ethical behaviour. Trust is based on reciprocal moral obliga-tions which embed stability into social relations through the values of cooperation. We would argue that the virtual world – online social interaction, commercial transaction, professional collaboration, civic participation – needs more trust.

There are, to be sure, practical housekeeping matters that can enhance trust in the online world. Open software, identity portability, interoperable platforms, distributed networks – the general move-ment towards openness and transparency will significantly reinforce the level of trust in the virtual world. But technology is not the only solution. Trust is an ethical matter of human conduct. It we truly wish to build a worldwide virtual republic rich in social capital and civic engagement, cyberspace must be founded on the values of trust.

In that respect, the success of the Web 2.0 revolution may depend on the capacity to find the proper balance between loosening controls and losing control – between self-regulation and legal constraints. Few would argue that chaos is an acceptable outcome of freedom. Even the most strident advocates of free market forces concede that markets need basic rules of conduct in order to function properly.

From the earliest days of capitalism, the values of trust have been essential to allow markets to produce value. But in markets, as in state diplomacy, trust is contingent upon the need to verify. We trust others because we have verified, informally or formally, that they are honest brokers. When virtual vandals and fraudsters, sexual predators and cyber-terrorists are loosed upon the online world, the resulting erosion of trust will inevitably lead to calls for stricter forms of control.

Trust must therefore be embedded into social interaction, into markets and into civic participation. Trust inspires *loyalty*. Loyalty to others. Loyalty to markets. Loyalty to community. Loyalty to life.

If the Web 2.0 revolution can accomplish that, it will have made the world a better place.

Notes

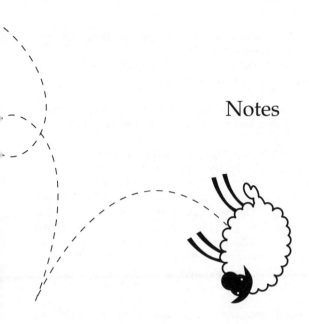

Preface

1. Survey of New Media: "What Sort of Revolution?", *The Economist*, 20 April 2006.

Introduction

1. The O'Reilly Media conference took place at San Francisco's Hotel Nikko from 5–7 October in 2004. For Tim O'Reilly's definition of Web 2.0, see: http://www.oreillynet.com/pub/a/oreilly/tim/news/2005/09/30/what-is-web-20.html.
2. See Rick Levine, Christopher Locke, Doc Searls and David Weinberger, *The Cluetrain Manifesto: The End of Business As Usual*, Basic Books, 2000. See also the Cluetrain Manifesto website: http://www.cluetrain.com/book.html.
3. This term "prosumer" was originally coined by Alvin Toffler in his book *The Third Wave*, Bantam, 1980.
4. See "The Power of Us: Mass Collaboration on the Internet is Shaking Up Business", *Business Week*, 20 June 2005, available at: http://www.businessweek.com/magazine/content/05_25/b3938601.htm.
5. "Oxford students fined over Facebook photos", *Daily Telegraph*, 18 July 2007, available at: http://www.telegraph.co.uk/news/main.jhtml?xml=/news/2007/07/17/nface117.xml; "Oxford University Fines Students with the Aid of Facebook", *The Times*, 18 April 2008, available at: http://www.timesonline.co.uk/tol/life_and_style/education/article3768282.ece; and "Students Warned that Officials at Oxford University are Using Facebook to Snoop", *International Herald Tribune*, 17 July 2007. See also "MySpace Profiles Mock St Hugo", *Detroit News*, 27 March 2007.
6. "Facebook posts could threaten your career", *Daily Telegraph*, 23 November 2007, available at: http://www.telegraph.co.uk/connected/main.jhtml?xml=/connected/2007/11/22/dblog122.xml; and "Facebook ban for hospital staff",

BBC News, 21 November 2007, available at: http://www.news.bbc.co.uk/go/pr/fr/-/1/hi/England/Nottinghamshire/7105733.stm.

7. "Facebook banned by City firms", *Daily Telegraph*, 28 July 2007, available at: http://www.telegraph.co.uk/news/main.jhtml?xml=/news/2007/07/27/nface127.xml.

8. "Facebook Fridays Enrich Internet Software Firm", Internetnews.com, 9 November 2007, available at: http://www.internetnews.com/bus-news/article.php/3710336.

9. For a history of the Knights Templar, see Malcolm Barber, *The New Knighthood: A History of the Order of the Temple*, Cambridge University Press, 1994.

10. Manual Castells, *The Rise of Network Society*, Volume I in trilogy *Information Age*, Blackwell, 1996. See also Castells's paper "Towards a Sociology of the Network Society", Contemporary Sociology, **29**(5), September 2000, pp. 693–699. For other themes mentioned in this paragraph, see, in particular, Yochai Benkler, *The Wealth of Networks*, Yale University Press, 2006; Bertrand Badie, *La Fin des Territoires*, Fayard, 1997; Lawrence Friedman, *The Horizontal Society*, Yale University Press, 1999; James Dale Davidson and William Rees Mogg, *The Sovereign Individual*, Simon & Schuster, 1997; and Kenichi Ohmae, *The End of the Nation State*, Free Press, 1995.

11. On the general subject of these transformations, see notably David Held *et al.*, *Global Transformations: Politics, Economics, Culture*, Polity Press, 1999; and David Held and Anthony McGrew, *The Global Transformation Reader*, Polity Press, 2000.

12. "Neomedieval" theories emerged in the 1970s with Hedley Bull's *The Anarchical Society*, originally published in 1977 and republished by Columbia University Press in 1995. For more recent works on the same theme, see Alain Minc, *The New Middle Ages*, Friedman, 1994; Stephen Kobrin, "Neomedievalism and the Postmodern Digital World Economy", in A. Prakash and J.A. Hart, *Globalization and Governance*, Routledge, 1999; Robert D. Kaplan, *The Coming Anarchy*, Random House, 2000; Jorg Friedrichs, "The Meaning of New Medievalism", *European Journal of International Relations*, **7**(4), 2001; and John Rapley, "The New Middle Ages", *Foreign Affairs*, May/June 2006.

13. Stephen Kobrin, "Neomedievalism and the Postmodern Digital World Economy", *Journal of International Affairs*, Spring 1998. Alain Minc's *The New Middle Ages* is a translation of his original book in French, *Le Nouveau Moyen Age*, Gallimard, 1993.

14. See Margaret Wertheim, *The Pearly Gates of Cyberspace: A History of Space from Dante to the Internet*, W.W. Norton, 1999. See also Tom Beaudoin, *Virtual Faith: The Irreverent Spiritual Quest of Generation X*, Jossey-Bass, 1998; Margaret Wertheim, "Is Cyberspace a Spiritual Place?", *Cybersociology*, **7**, September 1999; Morten Hojsgaard and Margit Warburg (Eds) *Religion and Cyberspace*, Routledge, 2005; and Anastasia Karaflogka, *e-religion: A Critical Appraisal of Religious Discourse on the World Wide Web*, Equinox, 2006.

15. "Is Google God?" *Time*, 16 May 2006, available at: http://www.time.com/time/arts/article/0,8599,1194830,00.html.

16. Michael Mann, *The Sources of Social Power*, Volume I, Cambridge University Press, 1986, p. 19.

17. See *Serious Business: Web 2.0 Goes Corporate*, Economist Intelligence Unit, 2007.

18. We define Generation V as the "digital" generation born since the advent of the Web in the 1990s. In the year 2010, the oldest members of Gen V will be approach-

ing age 20. The generally accepted definition of Generation Y is those born between 1983 and 1994, succeeding Generation X defined as those born between 1965 and 1983. While the precise sociographic boundaries separating these generations are not always clear, we can say generally that Generation X is composed mainly of those born in the 1970s, and Generation Y is mainly people born in the 1980s. We use the term Gen V loosely, since many young people in Gen Y, born in the late 1980s, can be considered Gen V because they grew up from their earliest childhood familiar with the Internet. Don Tapscott, adopting a broad definition, has called this demographic the "Net Generation", which he defines as the "Baby-boom echo" born between 1977 and 1996. See Don Tapscott, *Growing Up Digital: The Rise of the Net Generation*, McGraw Hill, 1998.

Chapter 1

1. For a dissection of how the international media got duped by the Facebook prankster, see the following item on the *New York Times* blog, The Lede: Notes on the News: "Prankster Playing Bhutto's Son on Facebook Fools News Outlets", *New York Times*, 2 January 2008, available at: http://www.thelede.blogs.nytimes.com/2008/01/02/prankster-playing-bhuttos-son-on-facebook-fools-news-outlets/.

2. For AFP's original story, see "Online support grows for 'hot' Bhutto son", Agence France Presse, 1 January 2008, available at: http://www.afp.google.com/article/ALeqM5j5-bAFVQF1CIJUBaNWn7ZSUPq6Qg. For AFP's follow-up correction two days later, see "Facebook disables Bhutto profile, says not genuine", Agence France Presse, 3 January 2008, available at: http://www.afp.google.com/article/ALeqM5iK1NCBG-EIO3siDfNq1vZ9FiUCQA.

3. "Facebook apologizes for suspending British Member of Parliament as fake", *International Herald Tribune*, 19 December 2007.

4. "Facebook Denies Role in Morocco Arrest", *Wall Street Journal*, 29 February 2008, available at: http://www.online.wsj.com/public/article/SB120424448908501345-RDbhXLEEdOSA4O6eRP_4PS_aCLE_20090228.html.

5. "Morocco: Man Held in Alleged Royal Identity Theft", *New York Times*, 7 February 2008, available at: http://www.nytimes.com/2008/02/07/world/Africa/07briefs-identity.html. On the Moroccan king's royal pardon, see "Morocco's Facebook 'prince' given royal pardon", *Daily Telegraph*, 20 March 2008, available at: http://www.telegraph.co.uk/news/main.jhtml?xml=/news/2008/03/20/wmorocco120.xml.

6. See "Woman branded prostitute on Facebook scam", *Daily Telegraph*, 2 July 2008, available at: http://www.telegraph.co.uk/news/uknews/2230058/Woman-branded-prostitute-in-Facebook-scam.html.

7. "Facebook: More Popular than Porn", *Time*, 31 October 2007; and "Sex on the Internet: Devices and Desires", *The Economist*, 19 April 2007.

8. "Websites to be studied after Bridgend suicides", *Daily Telegraph*, 24 January 2008, available at: http://www.telegraph.co.uk/news/main.jhtml?xml=/news/2008/01/24/nsuicide124.xml; and "The lethal 'glamour' factor", *The Times*, 24 January 2008, available at: http://www.women.timesonline.co.uk/tol/life_and_style/women/families/article3245864.ece.

9. See the classic work by Peter Berger and Thomas Luckmann, *The Social Construction of Reality: A Treatise on the Sociology of Knowledge*, Anchor Books, 1966.

10. See Benedict Anderson, *Imagined Communities*, Verso, 1983; Eric Hobsbawn and Terence Ranger, *The Invention of Tradition*, Cambridge University Press, 1983; and José Miguel Salazar, "Social Identity and National Identity", in Stephen Worchel *et al.* (Eds), *Social Identity: International Perspectives*, Sage, 1998.

11. For an analysis of the distinction between social and personal identity, see Stephen Worchel *et al.* (Eds) *Social Identity: International Perspectives*, Sage, 1998, Ch. 1.

12. On personal identity, see Steven Hitlin "Values as the Core of Personal Identity: Drawing Lines Between Two Theories of Self", *Social Psychology Quarterly*, **66**(2), 2003.

13. See Danah M. Boyd and Nicole B. Ellison "Social Network Sites: Definition, History, and Scholarship", *Journal of Computer-Mediated Communication*, **13**(1), 2007.

14. "The Cut-and-Paste Personality: Lacking inspiration and a moral compass, some online daters are borrowing other people's witty Web profiles", *Wall Street Journal*, 15 February 2008, available at: http://www.online.wsj.com/public/article/SB120303234117369959.html?mod=blog.

15. "Too Few Friends? A Web Site Lets You Buy Some (and They're Hot)", *New York Times*, 26 February 2007, available at: http://www.nytimes.com/2007/02/26/technology/26fake.html?_r=1&oref=slogin.

16. For more on the notion of control, see Danah Boyd, "Why Youth (Heart) Social Network Sites: The Role of Networked Publics in Teenage Social Life", in David Buckingham (Ed.), Macarthur Foundation Series on Digital Learning: *Youth, Identity, and Digital Media*, MIT Press, 2007.

17. Erving Goffman, *The Presentation of Self in Everyday Life*, Doubleday, 1959; and Erving Goffman, *The Interaction Ritual*, Pantheon, 1967.

18. See Christine Rosen, "Virtual Friendship and the New Narcissism", *The New Atlantis*, number 17, Summer 2007.

Chapter 2

1. For more on the *friending* phenomenon, see "Online networkers who click with 1,000 'friends'", *The Times*, 11 September 2007, available at: http://www.timesonline.co.uk/tol/news/uk/science/article2426229.ece. See also D. Fono and K. Raynes-Goldie, "Hyperfriends and Beyond: Friendship and Social Norms on LiveJournal", in M. Consalvo and C. Haythornthwaite (Eds), *Internet Research Annual Volume 4: Selected Papers from the Association of Internet Researchers Conference*, Peter Lang, 2006.

2. See "Facebook accused Michael Hurst found not guilty", *The Mirror* (UK), 27 March 2008, available at: http://www.mirror.co.uk/news/topstories/2008/03/27/facebook-accused-michael-hurst-found-not-guilty-89520-20364282/; and "Facebook friends not real friends: judge", *Sydney Morning Herald*, 27 March 2008, available at: http://www.smh.com.au/news/technology/facebook-friends-not-real-judge/2008/03/27/1206207279597.html. See also "Confessions of 'Facebook stalkers'", *USA Today*, 7 March 2007, available at: http://www.usatoday.com/tech/webguide/internetlife/2007-03-07-facebook-stalking_N.htm. For the Urban Dictionary definition of "Facebook stalker", see http://www.urbandictionary.com/define.php?term=facebook+stalker.

3. See "Jilted husband attacked love rival after 'Facebook affair'", *Daily Telegraph*, 12 May 2008, available at: http://www.telegraph.co.uk/news/1949635/Jilted-husband-attacked-love-rival-after-'Facebook-affair'.html.

4. "Facebook gives Jérome Kerviel cult status", *Daily Telegraph*, 27 January 2008, available at: http://www.telegraph.co.uk/money/main.jhtml?xml=/money/2008/01/25/bcncult125.xml.

5. Saul Hansell, "He Didn't Want to be That Kind of Friend", *New York Times*, 13 July 2007, available at: http://www.bits.blogs.nytimes.com/2007/07/13/he-didnt-want-to-be-that-kind-of-friend/.

6. See "Debrett's guide to online etiquette", *Daily Telegraph*, 13 July 2008, available at: http://www.telegraph.co.uk/connected/main.jhtml?xml=/connected/2008/06/12/dldebretts.xml.

7. See "Help! I'm Suffering Facebook Envy", *Daily Telegraph*, 2 November 2007, available at: http://www.telegraph.co.uk/connected/main.jhtml?xml=/connected/2007/11/02/ftface102.xml. On "friending" etiquette, see Reihan Salam, "The Facebook Commandments", *Slate*, 25 September 2007, available at: http://www.slate.com/id/2174439.

8. See Lauren Collins, "Friend Game", *The New Yorker*, 21 January 2008, available at: http://www.newyorker.com/reporting/2008/01/21/080121fa_fact_collins.

9. "Internet Hoax Turned Fatal Draws Anger But No Charges", *International Herald Tribune*, 28 November 2007, available at: http://www.iht.com/articles/2007/11/28/america/28hoax.php. For the Wikipedia entry, see http://www.en.wikipedia.org/wiki/Megan_meier.

10. See "Mom indicted in deadly MySpace hoax", Associated Press, 15 May 2008, available at: http://www.edition.cnn.com/2008/CRIME/05/15/internet.suicide.ap/.

11. See "MySpace Mom: 20-year Term Not Enough", ABC News, 16 May 2008, available at: http://www.abcnews.co.com/TheLaw/story?id=4861399&page=1.

12. "Facebook suicide: the end of a virtual life", *The Times*, 15 September 2007, available at: http://www.women.timesonline.co.uk/tol/life_and_style/women/body_and_soul/article2452928.ece.

13. See Andrew Leonard, "You Are Who You Know", Salon.com, 15 June 2004, available at: http://www.dir.salon.com/story/tech/feature/2004/06/15/social_software_one/.

14. See "Meet My 5,000 New Best Pals", *USA Today*, 19 September 2006, available at: http://www.usatoday.com/tech/news/2006-09-19-friending_x.htm; and Danah Boyd, "Friends, Friendsters and Top 8: Writing community into being on social network sites", *First Monday*, **11**(12), December 2006.

15. See Robin Dunbar's two essays, "Neocortex size as a constraint on group size in primates", *Journal of Human Evolution*, 22, 1992; and "Coevolution of neocortical size, group size and language in humans", *Behavioral and Brain Sciences*, **16**(4), 1993. See also Dunbar's book *Grooming, Gossip and the Evolution of Language*, Harvard University Press, 1998. Malcolm Gladwell popularized the Dunbar Number in his book *The Tipping Point: How Little Things Can Make a Big Difference*, Little Brown, 2000, in his insightful analysis of "context" in social groupings. See also Christopher Allen's blog, Life With Alacrity, for a discussion of Dunbar's Number and wikis and games: http://www.lifewithalacrity.com/2004/03/the_dunbar_numb.html; and Carl Bialik, "Sorry, You May Have Gone Over Your Limit of Network Friends", *Wall Street Journal*, 16 November 2007, available at:

http://www.online.wsj.com/article/SB119518271549595364.html?mod= googlenews_wsj.

16. Mark S. Granovetter, "The Strength of Weak Ties", *American Journal of Sociology*, **78**(6), May 1973. See also Mark S. Granovetter, "The Strength of Weak Ties: A Network Theory Revisited", in P. Marsden and N. Lin (Eds) *Social Structure and Network Analysis*, Sage Publications, 1982.

17. Mark Granovetter, *Getting a Job: A Study of Contacts and Careers*, University of Chicago, 1974.

18. James Surowiecki, *The Wisdom of Crowds: Why the Many are Smarter than the Few*, Abacus, 2004. See also John Meuller's insightful book, *Capitalism, Democracy and Ralph's Pretty Good Grocery*, Princeton University Press, 1999.

19. See Bonnie A. Nardi, Steve Whittaker and Heinrich Schwarz, "It's Not What You Know, It's Who You Know", *First Monday*, **5**(5), May 2000; and Rob Cross and Andrew Parker, *The Hidden Power of Networks: Understanding How Work Really Gets Done in Organizations*, Harvard Business School, 2004.

20. Steve Jobs interview, "The Seed of Apple's Innovation", *Business Week*, 12 October 2004, cited in Alexander Fliaster and Josef Spiess, "Knowledge Mobilization through Social Ties: The Cost–Benefit Analysis", *Schmalenbach Business Review*, January 2007.

21. See Don Tapscott and Anthony D. Williams, *Wikinomics: How Mass Collaboration Changes Everything*, Portfolio, 2006. The term prosumer, interestingly, was first coined by futurist Alvin Toffler in his 1980 book *The Third Wave*, Bantam Books, 1980.

22. See Andrew McAfee's blog on the Harvard Business School site for his thoughts on "The Ties that Find", 1 October 2007: http://www.blog.hbs.edu/faculty/ amcafee/.

23. "Not Losing Facebook in China", *The Economist*, 13 September 2007.

24. For more on *guanxi*, see Thomas Gold, Doug Guthrie and David Wank, *Social Connections in China: Institutions, Culture and the Changing Nature of Guanxi*, Cambridge University Press, 2002; and Karen Christensen and David Levinson, "Guanxi", in *Encyclopaedia of Community*, Sage, 2004.

25. Erika Pearson, "Digital gifts: Participation and gift exchange in LiveJournal communities", *First Monday*, **12**(5), May 2007; and Alan Smart, "Gifts, Bribes and Guanxi: A Reconsideration of Bourdieu's Social Capital", *Cultural Anthropology*, **8**(3), August 1993. See also Marcel Mauss's classic book on the gift-exchange economy first published in 1954, *The Gift: The Form and Reason for Exchange in Archaic Societies*, W.W. Norton, 2000.

26. Jeff Jarvis, "Friendship on the web will thrive and make a fortune", *The Guardian*, 3 December 2007, available at: http://www.guardian.co.uk/media/2007/ dec/03/mondaymediasection.facebook.

Chapter 3

1. See Jarvis's BuzzMachine blog entry, "Amazing Facebook", 29 May 2007, available at: http://www.buzzmachine.com/2007/05/29/amazing-facebook/. Jarvis also writes a column for Britain's *Guardian* newspaper.

2. "How Sticky is Membership on Facebook? Just Try Breaking Free", *New York Times*, 11 February 2008, available at: http://www.nytimes.com/2008/02/11/ technology/11facebook.html.

3. Albert O. Hirschman, *Exit, Voice and Loyalty: Responses to Decline in Firms, Organizations and States*, Harvard University Press, 1970.

4. See Danah Boyd, "Friendster lost steam. Is MySpace just a fad?" Apophenia Blog, 21 March 2006, available at: http://www.danah.org/papers/FriendsterMySpaceEssay.html; and Boyd, "Friendster and Publicly Articulated Social Networks", Conference on Human Factors and Computing Systems, Vienna, 24–29 April 2004, available at: http://www.danah.org/papers/CHI2004Friendster.pdf.

5. See Gary Rivlin, "Wallflower at the Web Party", *New York Times*, 15 October 2006, available at: http://www.nytimes.com/2006/10/15/business/yourmoney/15friend.html.

6. Danah Boyd, "Friendster lost steam. Is MySpace just a fad?" Apophenia Blog, 21 March 2006, available at: http://www.danah.org/papers/FriendsterMySpaceEssay.html.

7. See "Way Too Good for Facebook or MySpace", *Business Week*, 21 August 2007; "A Facebook for the few", *New York Times*, 6 September 2007, available at: http://www.nytimes.com/2007/09/06/fashion/06smallworld.html; and "MySpace for millionaires", *Wall Street Journal*, 30 November 2007, available at: http://www.blogs.wsj.com/wealth/2007/11/30/a-myspace-for-millionaires/.

8. "Innovative Voices", *Hollywood Reporter*, 13 November 2006.

9. The "six degrees" theory was developed in the 1960s by Stanley Milgram, and published in "The Small World Problem", *Psychology Today*, May 1967. See also Mark Buchanan, *Nexus: Small Worlds and the Groundbreaking Science of Networks*, W.W. Norton, 2002.

10. aSmallWorld's main investor is well-connected Hollywood producer Harvey Weinstein, who also owns the Halston fashion house. Other big names behind the site include MTV founder Bob Pittman and Alexander von Furstenberg, son of designer Diane von Furstenberg. See Thomas Langenberg and Alexander Schellong, "ASW – Monetizing Connectivity?", Program on Networked Governance working paper PNG07-004, Harvard University, 2007.

11. See David P. Reed, "That Sneaky Exponential: Beyond Metcalfe's Law to the Power of Community Building", *Context*, Spring 1999, available at: http://www.reed.com/gfn/docs/reedslaw.

12. While the term "social graph" has been used for decades, Facebook's Mark Zuckerberg revived it in a highly publicized speech. See "Social Graph-iti", *The Economist*, 18 October 2007.

13. See "A Facebook for the few", *New York Times*, 6 September 2007, available at: http://www.nytimes.com/2007/09/06/fashion/06smallworld.html; and "MySpace for millionaires", *Wall Street Journal*, 30 November 2007, available at: http://www.blogs.wsj.com/wealth/2007/11/30/a-myspace-for-millionaires/.

14. See "Way Too Good for Facebook or MySpace", *Business Week*, 21 August 2007, available at: http://www.businessweek.com/technology/content/aug2007/tc20070821_830716.htm; and "Social networking with the elite", *Business Week*, 15 November 2007, available at: http://www.businessweek.com/innovate/content/nov2007/id20071114_257766.htm.

15. "Modelshotel: The Gated Social Network", *New York Times*, 19 September 2007, available at: http://www.bits.blogs.nytimes.com/tag/modelshotel/.

16. "Beautiful website only skin deep", *USA Today*, 27 July 2005, available at: http://www.usatoday.com/life/lifestyle/2005-07-27-beautiful-people_x.htm.

17. "Can Models Find Bliss Behind a Digital Velvet Rope?" *Wall Street Journal*, 10 September 2007, available at: http://www.online.wsj.com/public/article/SB118938447913522114.html.

18. See "Mikhail Prokhorov plans invitation-only website – called Snob", *The Times*, 25 April 2008, available at: http://www.technology.timesonline.co.uk/tol/news/tech_and_web/article3671900.ece.

19. "Social networking goes professional", *Wall Street Journal*, 28 August 2007, available at: http://www.online.wsj.com/article/SB118825239984310205.html.

20. See "How Sticky is Membership on Facebook? Just Try Breaking Free", *New York Times*, 11 February 2008; and "Why won't they let me delete my Facebook page?" *The Independent*, 13 February 2008, available at: http://www.independent.co.uk/life-style/gadgets-and-tech/features/cyberclinic-why-wont-they-let-me-delete-my-facebook-page-781472.html.

21. For the conspiracy theory about Facebook's financial backers, see Tom Hodgkinson, "With friends like these . . .", *The Guardian*, 14 January 2008, available at: http://www.guardian.co.uk/technology/2008/jan/14/facebook.

22. "Zuckerberg Apologizes, Allows Facebook Users to Evade Beacon", *New York Times*, 5 December 2008, available at: http://www.bits.blogs.nytimes.com/2007/12/05/zuckerberg-apologizes-allows-facebook-users-to-evade-beacon/; and "After Stumbling, Facebook Finds a Working Eraser", *New York Times*, 18 February 2008, available at: http://www.nytimes.com/2008/02/18/business/18facebook.html.

23. On valuation of intangible software assets, see Soumitra Dutta, "Recognisng the True Value of Software Assets", INSEAD, November 2007. For a *Financial Times* article on the Dutta report, see "Study calls for a rethink on IT valuations", *Financial Times*, 5 November 2007, available at: http://www.serach.ft.com/ftArticle?queryText=Soumitra+Dutta&aje=true&id=071105000186&ct=0.

Chapter 4

1. See "For Some Online Persona Undermines a Résumé", *New York Times*, 11 June 2006, available at: http://www.nytimes.com/2006/06/11/us/11recruit.html. See also "Facebook can ruin your life. And so can MySpace, Bebo . . .", *The Independent*, 10 February 2008; and "What you say online could haunt you", *USA Today*, 3 August 2006, available at: http://www.usatoday.com/tech/news/internetprivacy/2006-03-08-facebook-myspace_x.htm.

2. See "Inspector loses promotion over Facebook", *Daily Telegraph*, 28 February 2008, available at: http://www.telegraph.co.uk/news/main.jhtml?xml=/news/2008/02/28/nfbook128.xml; and "PC's Facebook spanking", *The Sun*, 18 July 2007, available at: http://www.thesun.co.uk/sol/homepage/news/article246648.ece.

3. "Facebook posts could threaten your career", *Daily Telegraph*, 22 November 2007, available at: http://www.telegraph.co.uk/connected/main.jhtml?xml=/connected/2007/11/22/dlblog122.xml.

4. Sheldon Teitelbaum, "Privacy is History – Get Over It", *Wired*, February 1996, available at: http://www.wired.com/wired/archive/4.02/brin.html. For an academic book on the same subject, see Kieron O'Hara and Nigel Shadbolt, *The Spy in the Coffee Machine: The End of Privacy as We Know It*, One World, 2008.

5. See Privacy International's website at http://www.privacyinternational.org/.
6. Daniel J. Solove, *The Future of Reputation*, Yale University Press, 2007, p. 31.
7. "Friends Swap Twitters and Frustrations", *Wall Street Journal*, 16 March 2007, available at: http://www.online.wsj.com/public/article/SB117373145818634482-ZwdoPQ0PqPrcFMDHDZLz_P6osnI_20080315.html.
8. Jenny Sunden, *Material Virtualities: Approaching Online Textual Embodiment*, Peter Lang, 2003.
9. On the link between teenage girls and online narration, see "Girl-e-Power", *Sunday Times*, 9 March 2008.
10. "Steamy D.C. sex blog scandal heads to court", Associated Press, 27 December 2006, available at: http://www.msnbc.msn.com/id/16366256/. For an account of the Jessica Cutler story from a legal perspective, see Daniel Solove's *The Future of Reputation*, Yale University Press, 2007, Ch.3.
11. See Nick Emler, "A social psychology of reputations", *European Journal of Social Psychology*, 1, 1990; and N. Emler, "The Truth About Gossip", *Social Psychology Newsletter*, 27, 1992.
12. Robin Dunbar, *Grooming, Gossip and the Evolution of Language*, Harvard University Press, 1996, pp. 173–174.
13. See "States hope tax scofflaws will pay to avoid being outed on Web", *USA Today*, 27 April 2004, available at: http://www.usatoday.com/tech/webguide/internetlife/2004-04-27-tax-public-shaming_x.htm; and "Latest tax tool: 'Internet shaming'", *USA Today* 22 December 2005, available at: http://www.usatoday.com/tech/news/2005-12-22-tax-shaming-websites_x.htm.
14. Among shaming sites, see Baddriving.com, PlateWire.com, Caughtya.org. MyBikeLane.com, Flickr.com, YouTube.com, HollaBackNYC.com, LitterButt.com, RudePeople.com and Isawyournanny.blogspot.com. For a newspaper story on these sites, see "The Snoop Next Door", *Wall Street Journal*, 12 January 2007, available at: http://www.online.wsj.com/public/article/SB116855242776974364-OeszoAs0Sa3YsO80IOEwzj7Vfg8_20080112.html.
15. See "Wife takes divorce drama to YouTube", Associated Press, 16 April 2008, available at: http://news.aol.com/story/_a/wife-takes-divorce-drama-to-youtube/20080416063709990001?icid=100214839x1200054966x1200002215; and "Actress in YouTube rant at millionaire husband", *Daily Telegraph*, 14 April 2008, available at: http://www.telegraph.co.uk/news/main.jhtml?xml=/news/2008/04/14/ntube114.xml.
16. See "Smeared on the Internet? Then call in the cleaners", *Sunday Times*, 17 February 2008, available at: http://www.technology.timesonline.co.uk/tol/news/tech_and_web/the_web/article3382175.ece.
17. Diane Coutu, "We Googled You", *Harvard Business Review*, June 2007.
18. Neil Swidey, "A Nation of Voyeurs", *Boston Globe Magazine*, 2 February 2003, available at: http://www.faculty.fairfield.edu/mandrejevic/watching.html.
19. Beal's blog link for the ten points is http://www.marketingpilgrim.com/2007/10/google-reputation-management.html. See also Andy Beal and Judy Strauss, *Radically Transparent: Monitoring & Managing Reputations Online*, John Wiley & Sons, Inc., 2008.
20. "Google to Store Patients' Health Records", Associated Press, 21 February 2008, available at: http://www.cnbc.com/id/23272262; and "Google Goes to the Doc's Office", *Business Week*, 21 February 2008. On the British scandals, see "ID crisis deepens as 3m drivers' details lost", *Daily Telegraph*, 19 December 2007, available

at: http://www.telegraph.co.uk/news/main.jhtml?xml=/news/2007/12/17/ npols1117.xml; and "Data loss crisis spreads to the NHS", *Daily Telegraph*, 26 December 2007, available at: http://www.telegraph.co.uk/news/main. jhtml?xml=/news/2007/12/23/ndata223.xml.

21. "CIA Monitors YouTube for Intelligence", *Information Week*, 6 February 2008, available at: http://www.informationweek.com/news/showArticle.jhtml?articl eID=206106020; and "What do criminals know about you?", *The Guardian*, 18 October 2007, available at: http://www.guardian.co.uk/technology/2007/ oct/18/comment.internet.

22. Jeff Jarvis, "Friendship on the web will thrive and make a fortune", *The Guardian*, 3 December 2007, available at: http://www.guardian.co.uk/media/2007/ dec/03/mondaymediasection.facebook.

23. Sheldon Teitelbaum, "Privacy is History – Get Over It", *Wired*, February 1996, available at: http://www.wired.com/wired/archive/4.02/brin.html.

Chapter 5

1. "Sight Unseen: Firms Turn to Virtual-Life Site for Interviews", *New York Post*, 4 February 2008, available at: http://www.nypost.com/seven/02042008/jobs/ sight_unseen_289356.htm.

2. "A Job Interview You Don't Have to Show Up For", *Wall Street Journal*, 20 June 2007, available at: http://www.online.wsj.com/public/article/SB118229876637841321- NkCuEAak8wFXmvmPVWkALxqNS3M_20070719.html?mod=tff_main_tff_ top. See also "The Job Interview, Starring Your Avatar", *New York Times*, 10 February 2008, available at: http://www.nytimes.com/2008/02/10/jobs/10pre. html. On virtual fashion, see "Virtual Vogue: Second Life Wardrobes", *Daily Telegraph*, 16 March 2008, available at: http://www.telegraph.co.uk/fashion/ main.jhtml?xml=/fashion/2008/03/16/st_virtualfashion.xml.

3. See "Virtual World, Real Money", *Business Week* cover story, 1 May 2006; and "Living a Second Life", *The Economist*, 28 September 2006.

4. Geoffrey Norris, "For a new concert experience, get a second life", *Daily Telegraph*, 17 September 2007, available at: http://www.telegraph.co.uk/news/main. jhtml?xml=/news/2007/09/15/norch115.xml; and "Watching a Cyber Audience Watch a Real Orchestra Perform in a Virtual World", *New York Times*, 18 September 2007, available at: http://www.nytimes.com/2007/09/18/arts/music/ 18seco.html.

5. "Tiny island nation opens the first real embassy in virtual world", *The Times*, 24 May 2007, available at: http://www.technology.timesonline.co.uk/tol/news/ tech_and_web/article1832158.ece.

6. See "Gartner Says 80 Percent of Active Internet Users Will Have A 'Second Life' in the Virtual World by the End of 2011", Gartner press release, 24 April 2007, available at: http://www.gartner.com.

7. See Susan Wu, "Virtual Goods: The Next Business Model", TechCrunch, 20 June 2007, available at: http://www.techcrunch.com/2007/06/20/virtual-goods-the- next-big-business-model/.

8. See "Doing Real Good with Virtual Goods" on Ravi Mehta's blog, Virtual Goods Insider, 28 March 2008, available at: http://www.virtualgoodsinsider.com/ category/virtual-gifts/.

9. See Ravi Mehta's Virtual Goods Insider blog posting, "Goodbye Atoms, Hello Bits", 18 February 2008, available at: http://www.virtualgoodsinsider.com/2008/02/18/goodbye-atoms-hello-bits/.

10. Erika Pearson, "Digital gifts: Participation and gift exchange in LiveJournal communities", *First Monday*, **12**(5), May 2007; and Alan Smart, "Gifts, Bribes and Guanxi: A Reconsideration of Bourdieu's Social Capital", *Cultural Anthropology*, **8**(3), August 1993.

11. In March 2008, Second Life's money supply was $4.6 trillion (Linden dollars) at a currency exchange rate of L$270 = US$1. The site's economic statistics are available at: http://www.secondlife.com/whatis/economy_stats.php.

12. "Second Life world may be haven for terrorists", *Sunday Telegraph*, 14 May 2007, available at: http://www.telegraph.co.uk/news/main.jhtml?xml=/news/2007/05/13/internet13.xml.

13. See Randolph Harrison, "Second Life: Revolutionary Virtual Market or Ponzi Scheme?" Capitalism 2.0 blog, 23 January 2007, available at: http://www.randolfe.typepad.com/randolfe/2007/01/secondlife_revo.html. See also two articles by Matthew Beller of the Ludwig von Mises Institute: "The Coming Second Life Business Cycle", 2 August 2007; and "Wildcat Banking on the Virtual Frontier", 5 February 2008, available at: http://www.mises.org/story/2862.

14. See Reuters account of the Ginko meltdown, "Ginko Financial – Pioneer or Pyramid?", Reuters, 15 October 2006, available at: http://www.secondlife.reuters.com/stories/2006/10/15/ginko-financial-pioneer-or-pyramid/. See also *Wired* magazine's account: "Bank failure on Second Life leads to calls for regulation", *Wired*, 15 August 2007, available at: http://www.wired.com/gaming/virtualworlds/news/2007/08/virtual_bank.

15. See Robin Sidel, "Cheer Up, Ben: Your Economy Isn't as Bad as This One, In the Make-Believe World of 'Second Life' Banks Are Really Collapsing", *Wall Street Journal*, 23 January 2008, available at: http://www.online.wsj.com/public/article/SB120104351064608025.html.

16. See cover of *Business Week*, "Virtual World, Real Money", 1 May 2006, and Chung's Wikipedia biography at http://www.en.wikipedia.org/wiki/Anshe_Chung.

17. "Exploding pigs and volleys of gunfire as Le Pen opens HQ in virtual world", *The Guardian*, 20 January 2007, available at: http://www.guardian.co.uk/technology/2007/jan/20/news.france.

18. See "Sex, Pranks and Reality", *Forbes*, 2 July 2007, available at: http://www.forbes.com/home/free_forbes/2007/0702/048.html.

19. See "Sex, Pranks and Reality", *Forbes*, 2 July 2007, available at: http://www.forbes.com/home/free_forbes/2007/0702/048.html.

20. "How Madison Avenue Is Wasting Millions on a Deserted Second Life", *Wired*, 24 July 2007. For Chris Anderson's blog posting, see http://www.thelongtail.com/the_long_tail/2007/07/why-i-gave-up-o.html. For an analysis of advertising revenues on Second Life, see Eric K. Clemons, "The Future of Advertising and the Value of Social Networks", Wharton Information Strategy & Economics Blog 4, 27 May 2007.

21. See Nathalie Rothschild, "Second Life: A Virtual Nanny State", Spiked, 7 August 2007, available at: http://www.spiked-online.com/index.php?/site/article/3706/.

22. Axel Bruns, *Blogs, Wikipedia, Second Life and Beyond*, Peter Lang, 2008, p. 301.
23. See "Virtual theft leads to arrest", BBC News, 14 November 2007, available at: http://www.news.bbc.co.uk/2/hi/technology/7094764.stm.
24. See "Chinese gamer sentenced to life", BBC News, 8 June 2005, available at: http://www.news.bbc.co.uk/2/hi/technology/407204.stm.
25. See Julian Dibbell, "The Life of the Chinese Gold Farmer", *New York Times*, 17 June 2007, available at: http://www.juliandibbell.com/texts/goldfarmers.html.
26. See Edward Castronova, "Virtual Worlds: A First-Hand Account of Market and Society on the Cyberian Frontier", *The Gruter Institute Working Papers on Law, Economics and Evolutionary Biology*, **2**, Article 1, 2001, available at: http://www.bepress.com/giwp/default/vol2/iss1/art1.
27. See Richard Bartle, "The Pitfalls of Virtual Property", Themis Group, April 2004, available at: http://www.themis-group.com/uploads/Pitfalls%20of%20Virtual%20Property.pdf; and Erez Reuveni, "On Virtual Worlds: Copyright and Contract Law at the Dawn of the Virtual Age", *Indiana Law Journal*, **82**(261), 2007, available at: http://www.papers.ssrn.com/sol3/papers.cfm?abstract_id= 1113334. See also Ian MacInnes's two papers, "Property rights, legal issues and business models in virtual world communities", *Electronic Commerce Research*, January 2006; and "Business models and operational issues in the Chinese online game industry", *Telematics and Informatics*, May 2007.
28. For references to virtual charity walks, see "Walking for a good cause without ever leaving home", Reuters, 2 October 2007. On virtual pet rescue and adoption, see Angela Garcia, "Virtual Animal Shelters vs. the Dog Pound: How the Internet is Transforming Pet Adoption", paper presented at the annual meeting of the American Sociological Association, Marriott Hotel, Loews Philadelphia Hotel, Philadelphia, 12 August 2005, available at: http://www.allacademic.com/meta/ p22007_index.html. On virtual education, see "The Ultimate Distance Learning", *New York Times*, 7 January 2007. For an example of how MBA schools like INSEAD are using virtual environments, see "A second life for classrooms with vision", *Financial Times*, 29 February 2008; and "A leap into the virtual world", *Financial Times*, 29 February 2008. On virtual health care, see "Hospital Takes its Grand Opening to Second Life", *Information Week*, 25 February 2008, available at: http:// www.informationweek.com/internet/showArticle.jhtml?articleID=206801783; and "Virtual health care gets UK trial", BBC News, 31 January 2008, available at: http://www.news.bbc.co.uk/1/hi/Scotland/north_east/7219547.stm.
29. See Paul Jackson and Japp Favier, "Should You Be in Second Life?: The Real Business of Virtual Worlds", Forrester, 9 January 2008; and Erica Driver and Paul Jackson, "Getting Work Done in Virtual Worlds", Forrester, 7 January 2008.
30. See Tom T. Ahonen and Jim O'Reilly, *Digital Korea*, Futuretext, 2007, p. 42. See also "The Future is in South Korea", *Business 2.0*, 14 June 2006, available at: http://www.money.cnn.com/2006/06/08/technology/business2_future-boy0608/index.htm.
31. Kyung-Hee Kim and Haejin Yun, "Cying for Me, Cying for Us: Relational Dialectics in a Korean Social Network Site", *Journal of Computer-Mediated Communication*, **13**(1), 2007. See also Jaz Hee-jeong Choi, "Living in Cyworld: Contextualising Cy-Ties in South Korea", in A. Bruns and J. Jacobs (Eds) *Use of Blogs*, Peter Lang, 2006.
32. See Edward Castronova, "Virtual Worlds: A First-Hand Account of Market and Society on the Cyberian Frontier", *The Gruter Institute Working Papers on Law,*

Economics and Evolutionary Biology, **2**, Article 1, 2001, available at: http://www. bepress.com/giwp/default/vol2/iss1/art1.

33. Adam Reuters, "Congress to Second Life: No New Taxes?" Reuters, 8 October 2007, available at: http://www.secondlife.reuters.com/stories/2007/10/08/ congress-to-second-life-no-new-taxes/. See also Clive Thompson, "The Virtual Taxman Cometh", *Wired*, 18 December 2006, available at: http://www.wired. com/gaming/gamingreviews/commentary/games/2006/12/72317.

Chapter 6

1. France's serious news magazine, *L'Express*, was one of the many established media outlets that got duped by Derambarsh's scam. The linked story is available at: http://www.lexpress.fr/info/quotidian/actu.asp?id=463510. For newspaper stories, see "Facebook 'president' traps French media in web of deceit", *The Times*, 12 January 2008, available at: http://www.timesonline.co.uk/tol/ news/world/Europe/article3173279.ece; and "Le president Facebook Monde n'existe pas!", *Le Parisien*, 9 January 2008.

2. Thomas Keightley, *Secret Societies of the Middle Ages: The Assassins, the Templars and the Secret Tribunals of Westphalia*, Weiser Books, 2005, p. 221.

3. Robin Dunbar, *Grooming, Gossip and the Evolution of Language*, Harvard University Press, 1996.

4. For an essay on Veblen's ideas, see Peter Ritter, "Thorstein Veblen and the New Barbarians", *The Rake Magazine*, February 2005, available at: http:// www.rakemag.com/commentary/rakes-progress/thorstein-veblen-and-new-barbarians.

5. Thorstein Veblen, *Theory of the Leisure Class*, Macmillan, 1899. For a free online version of Veblen's classic book, see http://www.de.geocities.com/veblenite/ txt/tlc.txt.

6. See Pierre Bourdieu, *La Distinction: Critique Sociale du Jugement*, Editions de minuit, 1979, translated as *Distinction: A Social Critique of the Judgement of Taste*, Harvard University Press, 2007.

7. See "Prince Charles complains about people rising above their station", MSNBC News, 24 November 2004, available at: http://www.msnbc.msn.com/id/ 6519640/.

8. See Nan Lin, *Social Capital: A Theory of Social Structure and Action*, Cambridge University Press, 2001, Ch.2. For another discussion and definition of social capital, see Paul Adler and Seok-Woo Kwan, "Social Capital: The Good, the Bad and the Ugly", available at: http://www.papers.ssrn.com/sol3/papers.cfm? abstract_id=186928.

9. For a theory of closure, see Ronald S. Burt, *Brokerage and Closure: An Introduction to Social Capital*, Oxford University Press, 2005.

10. For an analysis of the "echo chamber" effect, see Ronald S. Burt, "Bandwidth and Echo: Trust, Information and Gossip in Social Networks", in Alessandra Casella and James E. Rauch (Eds) *Networks and Markets*, Russell Sage Foundation, 2001.

11. Much has been written on France's elitist production of bureaucratic and corporate leaders. See notably Mairi Maclean, Charles Harvey and Jon Press, *Business Elites and Corporate Governance in France and the UK*, Palgrave Macmillan, 2006.

For a journalistic account in *The Economist*, see "Fraternity: French boards are chummy affairs", *The Economist*, 27 March 2008.

12. See "Jerome Kerviel – In His Own Words", *Business Week*, 30 January 2008, available at: http://www.businessweek.com/globalbiz/content/jan2008/gb20080130_886902.htm.

13. See Paul Adler and Seok-Woo Kwon, "Social Capital: Prospects for a new concept", *Academy of Management Review*, **27**(1), 2002.

14. Alexis de Tocqueville, *Democracy in America*, Anchor Books, 1969, pp. 513–517.

15. Robert Putnam, *Bowling Alone: The Collapse and Revival of American Community*, Simon & Schuster, 2000. Also see Putnam's 1995 essay, "Bowling Alone: America's Declining Social Capital", *Journal of Democracy*, **6**(1), January 1995.

16. For a notable critique of *Bowling Alone*, see Noah Barish's paper, "*Bowling Alone* and the Virtual Community", Stanford University, 18 March 2003, available at: http://www.stanford.edu/class/symbsys205/Bowling_Alone_Barish.html. See also economist Steven N. Durlauf's paper, "*Bowling Alone*: A Review Essay", *Journal of Economic Behavior & Organization*, **47**(3), March 2002. An abridged version of the paper is available at: http://www.wellesley.edu/Polisci/Han/Pol199/Syllabus/Durlauf-Short.pdf.

17. Even before *Bowling Alone* was published, sociologists were predicting that Internet-based communities would produce social capital. See Barry Wellman and Milena Gulia, "Net-Surfers Don't Ride Alone: Virtual Communities as Communities", in Barry Wellman (Ed.) *Networks in the Global Village: Life in Contemporary Communities*, Westview, 1999.

18. Nan Lin *Social Capital: A Theory of Social Structure and Action*, Cambridge University Press, 2001, p. 216.

19. For a study of bridging social capital on Facebook, see Nicole B. Ellison, Charles Steinfeld and Cliff Lampe, "The Benefits of Facebook 'Friends': Social Capital and College Students' Use of Online Social Networks", *Journal of Computer-Mediated Communication*, **12**(4), 2007, available at: http://www.jcmc.indiana.edu/vol12/issue4/Ellison.html.

20. See Andrew Leonard, "The intellectual elite . . . my ass", Salon.com, 27 September 2006, available at: http://www.salon.com/src/pass/sitepass/spon/sitepass_website.html; and Andrew Leonard, "Social networking on the Subcontinent", Salon.com, 11 October 2006, available at: http://www.salon.com/tech/htww/2006/10/11/orkut_india/. On MySpace/Facebook class divisions in America, see Danah Boyd, "Viewing American class divisions through Facebook and MySapce", Apophenia blog, 24 June 2007, available at: http://www.danah.org/papers/essays/ClassDivisions.html. For the geek/glam distinction, see Brian Braiker, "A New World Order: MySpace Is Glam, Facebook Is Geek", *Newsweek*, 12 November 2007, available at: http://www.newsweek.com/id/67964.

21. See Courtenay Honeycutt, "Hazing as a Process of Boundary Maintenance in an Online Community", *Journal of Computer-Mediated Communication*, **10**(2), 2005.

22. "Reality-check or rip off? People spending millions on virtual gifts", Associated Press, 3 December 2007, available at: http://www.edition.cnn.com/2007/TECH/12/03/virtual.gifts.ap/index.html.

23. For further analysis of the digital scarcity principle, see a blog posting by the Lightspeed venture capital firm, "Three use cases for virtual goods", Lightspeed Venture Partners, 28 January 2008, available at: http://www.lsvp.wordpress.com/2008/01/28/three-use-cases-for-virtual-goods/.

Chapter 7

1. See article by YouTube co-founder Chad Hurley, "YouToo", Forbes, 7 May 2007, available at: http://www.forbes.com/free_forbes/2007/0507/068.html.
2. See Danah Boyd and Nicole Ellison, "Social Network Sites: Definition, History and Scholarship", *Journal of Computer-Mediated Communication*, **13**(1), 2007.
3. "British YouTube girl's big gig", *The Sun*, 18 January 2008, available at: http://www.thesun.co.uk/sol/homepage/news/article701058.ece.
4. See Lev Grossman, "Tila Tequila", *Time*, 16 December 2006, available at: http://www.time.com/time/magazine/article/0,9171,1570728,00.html; and Jonah Weiner, "Tila Tequila for President", *Slate*, 11 April 2006, available at: http://www.slate.com/id/2139691/.
5. See "ROFLCon: Welcome to the Fame Revolution", *Wired*, 25 April 2008, available at: http://www.blog.wired.com/underwire/2008/04/welcome-to-the.html; and "Web celebs consider their role", *Boston Globe*, 28 April 2008, available at: http://www.boston.com/business/technology/articles/2008/04/28/web_celebs_consider_their_role/. Weinberger is the author of *Everything Is Miscellaneous: The Power of the New Digital Disorder*, Times Books, 2007.
6. On celebrity worship, see notably Carlin Flora, "Seeing by Starlight: Celebrity Obsession", *Psychology Today*, July/August 2004; Diane Ashe, John Maltby and Lynn McCutcheon, "Are celebrity-worshippers more prone to narcissism?", *North American Journal of Psychology*, 6 January 2005; and John Maltby, Liza Day, Lynn McCutcheon, James Houran and Diane Ashe, "Extreme celebrity worship, fantasy proneness and dissociation", *Personality and Individual Differences*, 40, 2006. Also see Jake Halpern, *Fame Junkies: The Hidden Truths Behind America's Favorite Addiction*, Houghton Mifflin, 2006.
7. Adorno's essay "On Popular Music", jointly written with George Simpson, was first published in *Studies in Philosophy and Social Science*, Institute of Social Research, New York, 1941, **IX**, pp. 17–48, also available at: http://www.libcom.org/library/on-pop-music-theodor-adorno-george-simpson. In 1947, Adorno published, with Max Horkheimer, *The Cultural Industry: Enlightenment as Mass Deception*; and Adorno's *The Culture Industry Reconsidered* was published posthumously in 1975.
8. See Chuck Phillips, "Record Label Chorus: High Risk, Low Margin", *Los Angeles Times*, 31 May 2001, available at: http://www.anybodylisten.com/home/Record_Labels_respond.htm.
9. See Robert H. Frank and Philip J. Cook, *The Winner-Take-All Society: Why the Few at the Top Get so Much More than the Rest of Us*, Free Press, 1995, Ch.10.
10. Tyler Cowen, *What Price Fame?*, Harvard University Press, 2000.
11. See *Rolling Stone*'s Greatest Albums of All Time, available at: http://www.rollingstone.com/news/story/5938174/the_rs_500_greatest_albums_of_all_time/.
12. For a world's top-selling albums of all time list, see http://www.timefm.co.uk/bestselling-albums/.
13. Chris Anderson, *The Long Tail: How Endless Choice is Creating Unlimited Demand*, Random House, 2006.
14. Kartik Hosanagar and Daniel Fleder, "Blockbuster Culture's Next Rise or Fall: The Impact of Recommender Systems on Sales Diversity", NET Institute, Working Paper #07-10, September 2007, available at: http://www.netinst.org/Fleder-Hosanagar_07-10.pdf. See also Andres Hervas-Dran, "Word of Mouth and

Recommender Systems: A Theory of the Long Tail", NET Institute, Working Paper #07-41, November 2007, available at: http://www.netinst.org/Hervas_07-41.pdf.

15. "Star Wars Kid cuts a deal with his tormentors", *Globe and Mail* (Toronto), 7 April 2006, available at: http://www.theglobeandmail.com/servlet/story/RTGAM.20060407.wxstarwars07/BNStory/National/home.

16. See "Woman at the Center of Governor's Downfall", *International Herald Tribune*, 13 March 2008, available at: http://www.iht.com/articles/2008/03/13/America/12cndkristen.php.

17. "Can Spitzer Call Girl Cash In?", Associated Press, 13 March 2008, available at: http://www.news.moneycentral.msn.com/provider/providerarticle.aspx?feed=AP&date=20080313&id=8336858.

18. See Eric Schulman, "Can Fame Be Measured Quantitatively?" *Annals of Improbable Research*, May/June 1999; and Eric Schulman, "How Should Fame Be Measured Quantitatively?", *Annals of Improbable Research*, November 2001, available at: http://www.members.verizon.net/~vze3fs8i/air/fame2.html.

19. See Eric Schulman, "Measuring Fame Quantitatively III: What Does it Take to Make the A List?", *Journal of Improbable Research*, January/February 2006, available at: http://www.members.bellatlantic.net/~vze3fs8i/air/fame3.html.

20. See Leslie Lamport, "Measuring Celebrity", Microsoft Research, 15 November 2005, available at: http://www.research.microsoft.com/users/lamport/pubs/celebrity.pdf. It should be noted, of course, that this Microsoft paper measured the celebrity of Bill Gates, founder of Microsoft, which raises some questions about its deontology.

Chapter 8

1. See *Leadership in Games and at Work: Implications for the Enterprise of Massively Multiplayer Online Role-Playing Games*, IBM and Seriosity, 11 June 2007; *Virtual Worlds, Real Leaders*, IBM and Seriosity, 2007; and *Leadership in a Distributed World: Lessons from Online Gaming*, IBM Global Services, 2007. See also "Virtual World Gets Another Life", *Wall Street Journal*, 3 April 2008, available at: http://www.online.wsj.com/article/SB120719726445485981.html.

2. See "Gartner Says 'Generation Virtual' Will Have a Profound Influence on Culture, Society and Business", Gartner Group, 13 November 2007, available at: http://www.gartner.com/it/page.jsp?id=545108.

3. See Gary Hamel, *The Future of Management*, Harvard Business School Press, 2007, pp. 190–194.

4. In the original French, the first article of the 1780 Declaration of the Rights of Man states: "Les hommes naissent et demeurent libres et égaux en droits. Les distinctions sociales ne peuvent être fondées que sur l'utilité commune."

5. The classic book on the English aristocracy's resistance to the capitalist ethos is historian Martin Weiner's *English Culture and the Decline of the Industrial Spirit 1850–1980*, Penguin, 1981. For the counter-thesis to Weiner's "cultural critique", see W.D. Rubinstein, *Capitalism, Culture and Decline in Britain 1750–1990*, Routledge, 1993.

6. See Jennifer Oberbeck, Joshual Correll and Bernadette Park, "Internal Status Sorting in Groups: The Problem of Too Many Stars", in Melissa Thomas-Hunt (Ed.) *Research on Managing Groups and Teams Volume 7, Status and Groups*, Elsevier, 2005.

7. See Ronald Burt, Robin Hogarth and Claude Michaud, "The Social Capital of French and American Managers", *Organization Science*, March–April 2000.

8. See Melissa Thomas-Hunt, Tonya Ogden and Margaret Neale, "Who's Really Sharing? Effects of Social and Expert Status on Knowledge Exchange Within Groups", *Management Science*, **49**(4), April 2003.

9. See C. Morrill, E. Snyderman and E.J. Dawson, "It's Not What You Do, But Who You Are", *Sociological Forum*, **12**(4), December 1997; and Benedict Anderson, J. Berger, B.P. Cohen and M. Zelditch Jr, "Status Classes in Organizations", *Administrative Science Quarterly*, **11**(2), September 1966.

10. Melissa Thomas-Hunt, Tonya Ogden and Margaret Neale, "Who's Really Sharing? Effects of Social and Expert Status on Knowledge Exchange Within Groups", *Management Science*, **49**(4), April 2003.

11. Tiziana Casciaro and Miguel Sousa Lobo, "Competent Jerks, Lovable Fools, and the Formation of Social Networks", *Harvard Business Review*, June 2005.

12. See Nigel Nicolson, "How to Motivate Your Problem People", *Motivating People*, January 2003; Sarah Cliffe, "What a Star – What a Jerk", *Harvard Business Review*, September 2001; and Marsha Petrie Sue, *Toxic People: Decontaminate Difficult People at Work Without Using Weapons or Duct Tape*, John Wiley & Sons, Inc., 2007.

13. The concept of the self-interested *Homo œconomicus* is central to the liberal philosophical tradition, notably in the works of Adam Smith and John Stuart Mill. See Joseph Persky, "Retrospectives: The Ethology of Homo Economicus", *The Journal of Economic Perspectives*, Spring 1995.

14. See Oliver E. Williamson, "The Economics of Organization: The Transaction Cost Approach", *American Journal of Sociology*, **87**, 1981; and Francis Fukuyama and Abram N. Shulsky, *The "Virtual Corporation" and Army Organization*, RAND, 1997.

15. Francis Fukuyama and Abram N. Shulsky, *The "Virtual Corporation" ad Army Organization*, RAND, 1997, p. 17.

16. See Andrew McAfee, "Enterprise 2.0: The Dawn of Emergent Collaboration", *MIT Sloan Management Review*, **47**(3), Spring 2006, available at: http://www.sloanreview.mit.edu/smr/issue/2006/spring/06/; and McAfee's refinements to his analysis on his Harvard blog at http://www.blog.hbs.edu/faculty/amcafee/. See also Don Tapscott and Anthony D. Williams, *Wikinomics: How Mass Collaboration Changes Everything*, Portfolio, 2006.

17. Alvin Toffler, *Future Shock*, Random House, 1970.

18. See "Why Managers Resist Machines", *New York Times*, 7 February 1988, available at: http://www.query.nytimes.com/gst/fullpage.html?res=940DEEDE103 DF934A35751C0A96E948260.

19. Shoshana Zuboff, *In the Age of the Smart Machine: The Future of Work and Power*, Basic Books, 1988.

20. Malcolm Gladwell, "Designs for Working", *The New Yorker*, 11 December 2000, available at: http://www.gladwell.com/2000/2000_12_11_a_working.htm.

21. See "The Network Computer as the PC's Evil Twin", *New York Times*, 4 November 1996, available at: http://www.query.nytimes.com/gst/fullpage. html?res=9502E6DD1538F937A35752C1A960958260.

22. Shoshana Zuboff and James Maxmin, *The Support Economy: Why Corporations Are Failing Individuals and the Next Episode of Capitalism*, Viking, 2003.

23. See "The Capitalist Revolution" BBC News, 9 May 2003, available at: http://www.news.bbc.co.uk/2/hi/business/3003277.stm.

24. See Don Tapscott and Anthony D. Williams, *Wikinomics: How Mass Collaboration Changes Everything*, Portfolio, 2006, p. 15.

25. "UK companies see social networking as a threat", Datamonitor, 22 November 2007, available at: http://www.computerwire.com/industries/research/pid=5E8F37BA-8CBC-4DCF-A8AE-3DD66C2DA94B.

26. See *Serious Business: Web 2.0 Goes Corporate*, Economist Intelligence Unit, 2007.

27. David Constant, Lee Sproull and Sara Kiesler, "The Kindness of Strangers: The Usefulness of Electronic Weak Ties for Technical Advice", *Organizational Science*, 7(2), March–April 1996.

Chapter 9

1. See Google's technology page: http://www.google.com/technology/.

2. As an Anglo-Norman, Marshal was also known as Guillaume le Maréchel. He ruled as Regent under the boy-king Henry III and was also "Lord Marshal" of England. Marshal, regarded as one of the most powerful men in Europe, was invested into the Knights Tempar on his deathbed. See notably David Crouch, *William Marshal: Knighthood, War and Chivalry, 1147–1219*, Longman, 2002.

3. James Surowiecki, *The Wisdom of Crowds: Why the Many are Smarter than the Few*, Abacus, 2004. See also Howard Rheingold's earlier book *Smart Mobs: The Next Social Revolution*, Basic Books, 2002.

4. Kerry Bodine and Ross Popoff-Walker, *User Ratings Top Consumers' Online Wish Lists: Expectations For Consumer Electronics, Travel, Banking, And Media Sites*, Forrester Research, 6 February 2008.

5. See "Study: User-generated reviews are driving product sales", *Computerworld*, 1 October 2007, available at: http://www.computerworld.com/action/article.do?command=viewArticleBasic&articleId=9040158.

6. For Amazon's own account of how its recommendation algorithms work, see Greg Linden, Brent Smith and Jeremy York, "Amazon.com Recommendations: Item-to-Item Collaborative Filtering", *IEEE Internet Computing*, January/February 2003, available at: http://www.win.tue.nl/ laroyo/2L340/resources/Amazon-Recommendations.pdf.

7. For Malcolm Gladwell on Connectors, see his website: http://www.gladwell.com/tippingpoint/tp_excerpt2.html.

8. See "Amazon pushes social shopping", *Financial Times*, 13 March 2008, available at: http://www.ft.com/cms/s/0/bc5487dc-f129-11dc-a91a-0000779fd2ac.html.

9. See Daniel Fleder and Kartik Hosanagar, "Blockbuster Culture's Next Rise or Fall: The Impact of Recommender Systems on Sales Diversity", Wharton Business School, Working Paper #07-10, September 2007, available at: http://www.knowledge.wharton.upenn.edu/article.cfm?articleid=1818. See also Andres Hervas-Drane, "Word of Mouth and Recommender Systems: A Theory of the Long Tail", NET Institute Working Paper #07-41, available at SSRN: http://www.ssrn.com/abstract=1025123.

10. See "Ofcom asks ITV for X Factor information", *The Guardian*, 20 December 2007, available at: http://www.guardian.co.uk/media/2007/dec/20/itv.ofcom; "ITV admits X Factor vote mistake", BBC News, 28 February 2007, available at: http://www.news.bbc.co.uk/2/hi/entertainment/6405979.stm; and "ITV faces £70m fine after viewers cheated out of millions on premium phone-ins", *The Guardian*, 19 October 2007, available at: http://www.guardian.co.uk/media/2007/oct/19/1.

11. See "ITV admits fake phone-in scandal will cost £18m", *The Guardian*, 19 October 2007, available at: http://www.guardian.co.uk/business/2007/oct/19/5. For Michael Grade's full statement, see the ITV corporate site at: http://www.itvplc.com/itv/news/releases/pr2007/2007-10-18/.

12. See "BBC admits new breaches of trust", BBC News, 24 September 2007, available at: http://www.news.bbc.co.uk/2/hi/entertainment/7005053.stm; "BBC cleanup only just begun", BBC News, 21 September 2007, available at: http://www.news.bbc.co.uk/2/hi/uk_news/7007720.stm; and "BBC to lift lid on TV fakery", *The Guardian*, 20 September 2007, available at: http://www.guardian.co.uk/media/2007/sep/20/bbc.television1.

13. For BBC director general Mark Thompson's blog posting, see http://www.bbc.co.uk/blogs/theeditors/2007/09/trust_and_values.html.

14. See "At a glance: Show in TV scandal", BBC News, 5 October 2007, available at: http://www.news.bbc.co.uk/2/hi/entertainment/6915136.stm. For an academic paper analysing the UK television fakery scandals, see Yasmin Ibrahim, "The Emergence of Audience as Victims: The Issue of Trust in an Era of Phone Scandals", *Journal of Media & Culture*, **10**(5), October 2007, available at: http://www.journal.media-culture.org.au/0710/09-ibrahim.php.

15. See "ITV hit with record £5.68m fine", BBC News, 8 May 2008, available at: http://www.news.bbc.co.uk/2/hi/entertainment/7373131.stm; and "How Robbie Williams helped Ant and Dec swipe Catherine Tate's Prize", *The Times*, 8 May 2008, available at: http://www.business.timesonline.co.uk/tol/business/industry_sectors/media/article3895555.ece.

16. For the immediate impact on ITV, see "Phone-in confidence fall hits ITV", BBC News, 17 May 2007, available at: http://www.news.bbc.co.uk/2/hi/business/6664441.stm.

17. See Garth Risk Hallberg, "Who is Grady Harp? Amazon's Top Reviewers and the Fate of the Literary Amateur", *Slate*, 22 January 2008, available at: http://www.slate.com/id/2182002/pagenum/all/#page_start.

18. "Everyone's a Critic", *Time*, 19 August 2001, available at: http://www.time.com/time/magazine/article/0,9171,171811,00.html?iid=chix-sphere.

19. For Amazon's "Top 10 Reviewers", see http://www.amazon.com/gp/customer-reviews/top-reviewers.html/ref=cm_pdp_more_top_reviewers.

20. See "Everyone's a Critic: A Worthy Opinion Can Earn You Some Cash", *San Francisco Chronicle*, 22 January 2000, available at: http://www.sfgate.com/cgi-bin/article.cgi?f=/c/a/2000/01/22/BU40556.DTL&hw=epinions&sn=001&sc=1000.

21. See Jeannette Kindred and Shaheed N. Mohammed, "He Will Crush You Like an Academic Ninja! Exploring Teacher Ratings on RateMyProfessors.com", *Journal of Computer-Mediated Communication*, **10**(3), 2005, available at: http://www.jcmc.indiana.edu/vol10/issue3/kindred.html.

22. See "Soaring number of teachers say they are 'cyberbully' victims", *The Times*, 19 January 2008, available at: http://www.timesonline.co.uk/tol/life_and_style/education/article3213130.ece; and "Facebook and Bebo used to bully teachers", *Daily Telegraph*, 25 June 2008, available at: http://www.telegraph.co.uk/digital-life.amin.jhtml?xml=/connected/2008/06/25/dlfacebook125.xml.

23. See "Revisiting RateMyProfessors: Everyone's a Critic", *New York Times*, 23 April 2006, available at: http://www.nytimes.com/2006/04/23/education/edlife/revisit/html?scp=3&sq=RateMyProfessors&st=nyt.

24. See James Felton, Peter T. Koper, John B. Mitchell and Michael Stinson, "Attractiveness, Easiness, and Other Issues: Student Evaluations of Professors on RateMyProfessors.com", Central Michigan University, July 2006, available at: http://www.ssrn.com/abstract=918283.

25. Jeannette Kindred and Shaheed N. Mohammed, "He Will Crush You Like an Academic Ninja! Exploring Teacher Ratings on RateMyProfessors.com", *Journal of Computer-Mediated Communication*, **10**(3), 2005, available at: http://www.jcmc.indiana.edu/vol10/issue3/kindred.html. See also James Otto, Douglas Sanford Jr and Douglas Ross, "Does RateMyProfessors.com really rate my professor?", *Assessment & Evaluation in Higher Education*, 9 October 2007, available at: http://www.informaworld.com/smpp/section?content=a782926822&fulltext=7132409 28; and Jeffrey Hoopes and Steve Halbrecht, "An Empirical Evaluation of RateMyProfessors.com", Brigham Young University, Working Paper Series, 21 August 2007, available at: http://www.papers.ssrn.com/sol3/papers.cfm?abstract_id=1019271.

26. See "Turning the Tables on Students", *New York Times*, 23 April 2006, available at: http://www.nytimes.com/2006/04/23/education/edlife/ratestudents.html?scp=2&sq=RateMyProfessors&st=nyt.

27. See "Must try harder – teachers get ticking off on pupils' website", *The Times*, 28 February 2008, available at: http://www.timesonline.co.uk/tol/news/world/Europe/article3448128.ece.

28. See "Send Your Boss a Performance Review – Via the Web", *Business Week*, 11 May 2000, available at: http://www.businessweek.com/bwdaily/dnflash/may2000/nf00511f.htm; and "Workers of the World, Rate your Boss!", *Fortune*, 18 September 2000, available at: http://www.money.cnn.com/magazines/fortune/fortune_archive/2000/09/18/287707/index.htm.

29. For more on Glassdoor, see "Looking for a big salary? See what this startup has to say", CNET News.com, 10 June 2008, available at: http://www.news.cnet.com/8301-10784_3-9965353-7.html. On Criticat, see its site at http://www.criticat.com/.

30. See Web 2.0 analyst Jeremiah Owyang's Forrester blog posting at http://www.webstrategist.com/blog/2008/06/11/dangers-and-opportunities-of-the-crowdsourced-company/.

Chapter 10

1. For Anne Conti's story, see http://www.bigcrow.com/anna/ebay_fraud/evidence.htm. For the eBay art scams, see "Seven charged in 'eBay art scam' ", BBC News, 20 March 2008, available at: http://www.news.bbc.co.uk/2/hi/Americas/7306366.stm.

2. To review the petition online, see http://www.petitiononline.com/jkrebay1/petition.html.

3. See "Potter author sues eBay over pirate books", *The Times*, 26 February 2007, available at: http://www.timesonline.co.uk/tol/news/uk/article1437673.ece; and "J.K. Rowling badmouths eBay", *The Register*, 8 June 2007, available at: http://www.theregister.co.uk/2007/06/08/rowling_badmouth_ebay/.

4. See "eBay fights its toughest legal battle: Tiffany lawsuit puts 'hands off' approach to the test", MSNBC, 21 September 2004, available at: http://www.msnbc.msn.

com/id/6030048/; and "Tiffany and eBay clash over fakes", *International Herald Tribune*, 27 November 2007, available at: http://www.iht.com/articles/2007/11/27/business/ebay.php. For the Louis Vuitton and Dior lawsuits, see: http://www.louis-vuitton-news.newslib.com/story/7516-240/. For the L'Oreal suit see a Reuters story at http://www.in.reuters.com/article/businessNews/idinindia-29441820070910.

5. See "eBay fined $63m over fake goods", CNN.com, 1 July 2008, available at: http://www.edition.cnn.com/2008/BUSINESS/06/30/louis.vuitton/index.html.

6. See "College killer bought bullet clips on eBay", *The Times*, 23 April 2007, available at: http://www.timesonline.co.uk/tol/news/world/us_and_americas/article1690352.ece; "Securitas robbers bought uniforms on eBay", *The Times*, 27 July 2007, available at: http://www.timesonline.co.uk/tol/news/uk/crime/article1994265.ece; "Sporting memorabilia were worthless fakes, court is told", *The Times*, 8 February 2008, available at: http://www.timesonline.co.uk/tol/news/uk/crime/article3330547.ece; "Cyber-savvy town gets rich on eBay frauds", *The Times*, 3 February 2008, available at: http://www.timesonline.co.uk/tol/news/world/Europe/article3295468.ece; "Revealed: How eBay sellers fix auctions", *The Times*, 28 January 2007, available at: http://www.technology.timesonline.co.uk/tol/news/tech_and_web/the_web/article1267565.ece; and "Not a Whole Lotta Love for eBay", *Forbes*, 9 October 2007, available at http://www.forbes.com/2007/10/09/led-zeppelin-ebay-face-cx_ll_1008autofaces-can02.html?partner=msn.

7. See Josh Boyd, "In Community We Trust: Online Security Communication At eBay", *Journal of Computer-Mediated Communication*, April 2002; and Paul Resnick and Richard Zeckhauser, "Trust Among Strangers in Internet Transactions: Empirical Analysis of eBay's Reputation System", in Michael R. Baye (Ed.) *The Economics of the Internet and e-Commerce*, Elsevier Science, 2002, available at: http://www.si.umich.edu/~presnick/papers/ebayNBER/index.html.

8. "The Most Trusted Companies in e-Business", *E-Commerce Times*, 22 December 2003, available at: http://www.technewsworld.com/story/32435.html; and "What Makes eBay Invincible", *E-Commerce Times*, 4 March 2003, available at: http://www.technewsworld.com/story/20900.html.

9. Al Golin, *Trust or Consequences: Build Trust Today or Lose Your Market Tomorrow*, Amacom, 2003.

10. See Kim Peterson, "eBay Tries to Wash Away Mistakes with New Service", MSN Money Blog TopStocks, MSN Money, 10 October 2007, available at: http://www.blogs.moneycentral.msn.com/topstocks/archive/2007/10/10/ebay-tries-to-wash-away-mistakes-with-new-service.aspx; "The Depth of eBay's Problems 1: Disappointed Buyers", *New York Times*, 17 December 2007, available at: http://www.bits.blogs.nytimes.com/2007/12/17/the-depth-of-ebays-problems-1-disappointed-buyers/; Gary Sattler, "Meg Whitman and Mitt Romney: Oh, the gut-wrenching horror of it", 27 December 2007, BloggingStocks, available at: http://www.bloggingstocks.com/2007/12/27/meg-whitman-and-mitt-romney-oh-the-gut-wrenching-horror-of-it/; and Henry Blodget, "eBay: Time for CEO Meg Whitman to go?", Silicon Alley, 6 December 2007, available at: http://www.alleyinsider.com/2007/12/ebay-time-for-CEO-meg-whitman-to-go.html.

11. See Kim Peterson, "Did the eBay Boycott Work?", MSN Money Blog TopStocks, 25 February 2008, available at: http://www.blogs.moneycentral.msn.com/topstocks/archive/2008/02/25/did-the-ebay-boycott-work.aspx.

12. See "eBay's CEO Whitman preparing to retire: report", Reuters, 22 January 2008, available at: http://www.news.moneycentral.msn.com/ticker/article.aspx?Ffeed=OBR&Date=20080122&ID=8072939&Symbol=EBAY.

13. For a discussion of trust in bloggers, see Forrester analyst Jeremiah Owyang's blog, Web Strategy, at: http://www.web-strategist.com/blog/2008/04/29/who-do-people-trust-it-aint-bloggers. For the Edelman Trust Barometer, see http://www.edelman.com/trust/2008/. And for the Pollara study, see: http://www.pollara.ca.Library/News/04032008-study.htm.

14. See Elihu Katz and Paul Lazarsfeld, *Personal Influence*, Glencoe, 1955; and Ed Keller and Jon Berry, *The Influentials*, Free Press, 2003.

15. For the article on Duncan Watts's contradiction of Gladwell's *Tipping Point* theories, and Gladwell's reply, see "Is The Tipping Point Toast?", *Fast Company*, 28 January 2008, available at: http://www.fastcompany.com/magazine/122/is-the-tipping-point-toast.html. See also Watts's book, *Six Degrees: The Science of a Connected Age*, W.W. Norton, 2004; and for Watts's 'small world' experiments at Columbia University, see http://www.smallworld.columbia.edu/watts.html.

16. For Forrester analyst Josh Bernoff's blog posting on this issue, see http://www.blogs.forrester.com/charleneli/2008/04/data-chart-of-1.html. See also "Bloggers Influence on Consumers Continues to Rise", Forrester Research, 26 June 2008, available at: http://www.researchrecap.com/index.php/2008/06/26/bloggers-influence-on-consumers-continues-to-rise/.

17. For Jeff Jarvis's "Dell Lies, Dell Sucks" blog posting, see http://www.buzzmachine.com/archives/2005_06_21.html; and for his open letter to Michael Dell, see http://www.buzzmachine.com/2005/08/17/dear-mr-dell/.

18. See Jeff Jarvis, "My Dell Hell", *The Guardian*, 29 August 2005, available at: http://www.guardian.co.uk/technology/2005/aug/29/mondaymediasection.blogging.

19. See "Dell Learns to Listen", *Business Week*, 17 October 2007, available at: http://www.businessweek.com/bwdaily/dnflash/content/oct2007/db20071017_277576.htm?chan=top+news_top+news+index_top+story.

20. See Jeff Jarvis's blog post "Dell's progress" at http://www.buzzmachine.com/2007/06/12/dells-progress/. See also Dell's corporate blog at http://www.direct2dell.com/one2one/default.aspx, and IdeaStorm at http://www.dellideastorm.com/.

21. See Charlene Li, "Blogging: Bubble or Big Deal?" Forrester Research, 5 November 2004; and "How to make the most of a corporate blog", *The Times*, 6 March 2008, available at: http://www.timesonline.co.uk/tol/life_and_style/career_and_jobs/article3489399.ece.

22. See Robert Scoble and Shel Israel, *Naked Conversations: How Blogs are Changing the Way Businesses Talk with Customers*, John Wiley & Sons, Inc., 2006.

23. For Serena Software's "Facebook Fridays", see http://www.serena.com/company/news/pr/sPR_11022007.html.

24. See Rohit Aggarwal, Ram Gopal and Ramesh Sankaranarayanan, "Blog, Blogger and the Firm: An Analysis of Firm Policies", SSRN, 23 March 2007, available at: http://www.papers.ssrn.com/sol3/papers.cfm?abstract_id=976121.

25. See "Fired Flight Attendant Finds Blogs Can Backfire", *New York Times*, 16 November 2004, available at: http://www.nytimes.com/2004/11/16/business/16pose.html.

26. See "Blogs May Be a Wealth Hazard", *Wired*, 6 December 2004, available at: http://www.wired.com/culture/lifestyle/news/2004/12/65912; and Simonetti's Wikipedia entry, http://www.en.wikipedia.org/wiki/Ellen_Simonetti.

27. See "Bridget Jones blogger fire fury", CNN.com, 19 July 2006, available at: http://www.edition.cnn.com/2006/WORLD/Europe/07/19/france.blog/index.html?section=cnn_tech.

28. See Catherine Sanderson, "The Blog, the Frog and the Petite Anglaise", *Daily Telegraph*, 6 March 2008, available at: http://www.telegraph.co.uk/arts/main.jhtml?xml=/arts/2008/03/06/boblog106.xml; "Petite Anglaise moves from blog to book", *Daily Telegraph*, 21 February 2007, available at: http://www.telegraph.co.uk/news/main.jhtml?xml=/news/2007/02/21/nbook21.xml; and "La Petite Anglaise is sweeping the world", *Daily Telegraph*, 22 July 2006, available at: http://www.telegraph.co.uk/news/main.jhtml?xml=/news/2006/07/22/nblogs222.xml.

29. See Jeff Jarvis's blog post on the Blog Council at http://www.buzzmachine.com/2007/12/09/its-not-the-blog/; and Dave Taylor's post at http://www.intuitive.com/blog/blogcouncil_created_business_world_yawns.html. See also "The Blog Council, Bad or Inspired Idea?", TechCrunch, 6 December 2007, available at: http://www.techcrunch.com/2007/12/06/the-blog-council-bad-or-inspired-idea/.

30. For an article on Jonathan Schwartz's blogging, see "All the Internet's a Stage: Why Don't CEOs Use It?", *New York Times*, 30 July 2006, available at: http://www.nytimes.com/2006/07/30/business/yourmoney/30digi.html?_r=4&oref=slogin&pagewanted=print. See also Charlene Li, "Blogging: Bubble or Big Deal?", Forrester Research, 5 November 2004.

31. For a list of "billionaire bloggers" and billionaires who don't blog, see http://www.readwriteweb.com/archives/a_guide_to_billionaire_bloggers.php.

32. See "PR firm admits it's behind Wal-Mart blogs", CNN Money.com, 20 October 2006, available at: http://www.money.cnn.com/2006/10/20/news/companies/walmart_blogs/index.htm; and "Corporate blogging: Wal-Mart's fumbles", CNN Money, 18 October 2006, available at: http://www.money.cnn.com/2006/10/17/technology/pluggedin_gunther_blog.fortune/index.htm.

33. See "Wal-Mart's Jim and Laura: The Real Story", *Business Week*, 9 October 2006, available at: http://www.businessweek.com/bwdaily/dnflash/content/oct2006/db20061009_579137.htm and "Wal-Mart vs. the Blogosphere", *Business Week*, 17 October 2006, available at: http://www.businessweek.com/bwdaily/dnflash/content/oct2006/db20061018_445917.htm. See also "Pro-Wal-Mart Travel Blog Screeches To a Halt", *Online Media Daily*, 12 October 2006, available at: http://www.publications.mediapost.com/index.cfm?fuseaction=Articles.san&s=49505&Nid=24192&p=82937.

34. See Scoble's posting "Blog integrity is important" on his Scobleizer blog; and the TechMeme blog, 15 October 2006 at http://www.techmeme.com/061015/p16#a061015p16. For Richard Edelman's clarifications, see http://www.edelman.com/speak_up/blog/archives/2006/10/what_is_edelman.html.

35. For a discussion of Wal-Mart's Checkout blog, see Forrester analyst Jeremiah Owyang's blog post at http://www.web-strategist.com/blog/2007/12/06/

will-wal-marts-newest-blogging-initiative-succeed-an-interview-with-one-of-the-bloggers/.

36. See the Consumerist blog posting : http://www.consumerist.com/consumer/all-i-want-for-xmas-is-a-psp/meet-the-douchebags-behind-the-sony-psp-flog-221617.php.

37. See the BoingBoing blog for "Whole Foods CEO caught bashing Wild Oats on Yahoo forums", 12 July 2007, available at: http://www.boingboing.net/2007/07/12/whole-foods-ceo-caug.html.

38. See "Mr Mackey's Offense", *Wall Street Journal*, 16 July 2007, available at: http://www.online.wsj.com/article/SB118454129429667079.html?mod=opinion_main_review_and_outlooks. See also "Whole Foods CEO: Busted!" on the Marketing Profs Daily Fix blog at http://www.mpdailyfix.com/2007/07/busted.html.

39. See the Consumerist blog posting at http://www.consumerist.com/385304/burger-king-exec-hides-behind-daughters-email-account-to-trash-talk-opponents.

40. See Seth Godin's blog post at http://www.sethgodin.typepad.com/seths_blog/2004/10/beware_the_ceo_.html.

41. See Dave Taylor, "Why CEOs Shouldn't Blog", Global PR Blog Week 2.0, 19 September 2005, available at: http://www.globalprblogweek.com/2005/09/19/taylor-why-ceos-should-not-blog/. For the opposing view, in favour of CEO blogging, see Jeneane Sessum's column "Adding Your Voice to the Conversation: Why CEOs Should Blog", available at: http://www.globalprblogweek.com/2005/09/19/sessum-why-ceos-should-blog/.

42. See Jonathan Schwartz, "If You Want to Lead, Blog", *Harvard Business Review*, 1 November 2005; and for Schwartz's blog, see http://www.blogs.sun.com/jonathan/. See also "All the Internet's a Stage: Why Don't CEOs Use It?", *New York Times*, 30 July 2006, available at: http://www.nytimes.com/2006/07/30/business/yourmoney/30digi.html?_r=4&oref=slogin&pagewanted=print.

43. See Bob Lutz, "Nothing to Fear From Executive Blogging", *Information Week*, 11 July 2005, available at: http://www.informationweek.com/news/software/crm/show/Article.jhtml?articleID=165700961.

Chapter 11

1. See "Facebook has a new role – fighting crime in Manchester", TechCrunch UK, 18 April 2008, available at: http://www.uk.techcrunch.com/2008/04/18/facebook-has-a-new-role-fighting-crime-in-manchester/; and "Facebook program to fight crime", BBC News, 15 April 2008, available at: http://www.news.bbc.co.uk/2/hi/uk_news/England/Manchester/7349422.stm. See also the Greater Manchester Police website at http://www.gmp.police.uk/mainsite/pages/1591DCCE9694D4B48025742D004CDE8D.htm.

2. For the study conducted at the University of Colorado, see "Emergency 2.0 is coming to a website near you", *New Scientist*, 2 May 2008, available at: http://www.technology.newscientist.com/channel/tech/mg19826545.900-emergency-20-is-coming-to-a-website-near-you.html.

3. For Robert Scoble's blog posting on the Chinese earthquake, see http://www.scobleizer.com/2008/05/12/quake-in-china/.

4. See "Facebook 'more effective than emergency services in disaster'", *Daily Telegraph*, 30 April 2008, available at: http://www.telegraph.co.uk/news/1914750/Facebook-'more-effective-than-emergency-services-in-a-disaster'.html.

5. See the book *1,000 Years, 1,000 People: Ranking Men and Women Who Shaped the Millennium*, available at: http://www.pirate.shu.edu/ gottlitr/mil_site/milhome.html.

6. Michael Mann, *The Sources of Social Power*, Vol I, Cambridge University Press, 1986, p. 8.

7. See "A day of saints and sinners", *The Economist*, 5 October 2000.

8. See "The real enemy within", *The Economist*, 29 April 1999. *The Economist* noted that the state-controlled Chinese Academy of Sciences put Falun Gong membership at 20 million.

9. See "Gong but not forgotten", *The Economist*, 27 April 2000; and "Jiang almost meets Falun Gong", *The Economist*, 10 May 2001. See also "In Beijing: A Roar of Silent Protesters", *New York Times*, 27 April 1999, available at: http://www.partners.nytimes.com/library/world/asia/042799china-protest.html.

10. See "The Man with the Qi", *Time*, 2 May 1999, available at: http://www.time.com/time/magazine/article/0,9171,1101990510-23878,00.html.

11. See "The party, the people and the power of cyber-talk", *The Economist*, 27 April 2006, available at: http://www.economist.com/world/displaystory.cfm?story_id=6850080.

12. See the section on Falun Gong in the book by Nan Lin, *Social Capital: A Theory of Social Structure and Action*, Cambridge University Press, 2001, pp. 217–226.

13. See "Elder brother Hu Jintao makes Internet debut", *The Times*, 24 June 2008, available at: http://www.timesonline.co.uk/tol/news/world/asia/article4198310.ece.

14. See "New judges must declare Masonic membership", BBC News, 5 March 1998, available at: http://www.news.bbc.co.uk/2/hi/uk/politics/57381.stm; and "Masons under pressure to name names", BBC News, 5 March 1998, available at: http://www.news.bbc.co.uk/2/hi/uk_news/58188.stm.

15. See "From Freemasonry to e-Masonry", BBC News, 22 May 2000, available at: http://www.news.bbc.co.uk/2/hi/uk_news/wales/759413.stm.

16. See Josh Heller and Gerald Reilly, *The Temple that Never Sleeps: Freemasons and E-Masons, Towards a New Paradigm*, Cornerstone Publishers, 2006; and Francis Vicente, "Freemasonry and the Internet", Grand Lodge of Pennsylvania, available at: http://www.freemasons-freemasonry.com/freemasonry_internet.html.

17. Mancur Olson, *The Logic of Collective Action: Public Goods and the Theory of Groups*, Harvard University Press, 1965.

18. See Don Tapscott and Anthony D. Williams, *Wikinomics: How Mass Collaboration Changes Everything*, Portfolio, 2006, Ch.1. See also "Wikinomics could change everything as concept of sharing spreads", *USA Today*, 2 February 2007, available at: http://www.usatoday.com/money/books/reviews/2007-01-02-wikinomics_x.htm.

19. Robert Axelrod, *The Evolution of Cooperation*, Basic Books, 1984, Ch. 4.

20. David Constant, Lee Sproull and Sara Kiesler, "The Kindness of Strangers: The Usefulness of Electronic Weak Ties for Technical Advice", *Organizational Science*, 7(2), March–April 1996.

Chapter 12

1. See "Time's Person of the Year: You", *Time*, 13 December 2006, available at: http://www.time.com/time/magazine/article/0,9171,1569514,00.html.

2. See "Elton John quits Watford", BBC Sport, 28 May 2002, available at: http://www.news.bbc.co.uk/sport2/hi/football/teams/w/Watford/2013086.stm.
3. See "The Soccer Billionaires", *Forbes*, 5 February 2008, available at: http://www.forbes.com/2008/02/04/soccer-billionaires-abramovich-biz-sports-cx_af_0205soccerbillies.html.
4. "Ebbsfleet offer total power to the people", *The Times*, 14 November 2007, available at: http://www.timesonline.co.uk/tol/sport/football/football_league/article2866156.ece.
5. See "MyFootballClub agree takeover of Ebbsfleet", *The Times*, 13 November 2007, available at: http://www.timesonline.co.uk/tol/sport/football/article2862403.ece.
6. See "Web fans log on to Ebbsfleet FA Trophy glory", *Daily Telegraph*, 5 May 2008, available at: http://www.telegraph.co.uk/sport/main.jhtml?xml=/sport/2008/05/11/sfgebb111.xml. For a more critical view, see "Fantasy Football", *Sunday Times*, 18 November 2007, available at: http://www.timesonline.co.uk/tol/sport/football/article2891038.ece.
7. See Glenn Reynolds, *An Army of Davids: How Markets and Technology Empower Ordinary People to Beat Big Media, Big Government and Other Goliaths*, Nelson Current, 2006, p. xii.
8. The term "digital Maoism" was coined by Jaron Lanier in an online essay in *Edge* entitled "Digital Maoism: The Hazards of the New Online Collectivism", available at: http://www.edge.org/3rd_culture/lanier06/lanier06_index.html. See also "Digital Maoism", *The Guardian*, 26 August 2006, available at: http://www.guardian.co.uk/commentisfree/story/0,1858773,00.html.
9. Rheingold's comments were included in a number of responses to Lanier's "Digital Maoism" essay. Other responses came from Douglas Rushkoff, Quentin Hardy, Yochai Benkler, Clay Shirky, Cory Doctorow, Kevin Kelly, Esther Dyson, Larry Sanger, Fernanda Viegas and Martin Wattenberg, Jimmy Wales, George Dyson and Dan Gillmor. See link at http://www.edge.org/discourse/digital_maoism.html.
10. Andrew Keen, *The Cult of the Amateur: How Today's Internet is Killing Our Culture*, Doubleday, 2007.
11. See Fernand Braudel, *The Wheels of Commerce, Civilization and Capitalism*, Volume 2, University of California, 1992; and Mancur Olson, *The Rise and Decline of Nations*, Yale, 1982, Ch. 6.
12. For an interesting historical account of the "Rise of the Amateur", see Jeff Howe's Crowdsourcing blog at http://www.crowdsourcing.typepad.com/cs/2008/02/chapter-two-ris.html.
13. See Charles Leadbeater, "Amateur Revolution", *Fast Company*, 19 December 2007, available at: http://www.fastcompany.com/node/51040/print. Leadbeater, a British policy consultant from the think tank Demos, which was Prime Minister Tony Blair's brain trust, crowdsourced his book *We-think*, available at: http://www.wethinkthebook.net/book/home.aspx.
14. See Magali Sarfatti Larson, *The Rise of Professionalism: A Sociological Analysis*, University of California, 1979.
15. See Michael Reed, "Expert Power and Control in Late Modernity: An Empirical Review and Theoretical Synthesis", *Organization Studies*, **17**(4), 1996.
16. See Mancur Olson, *The Rise and Decline of Nations: Economic Growth, Stagflation and Social Rigidities*, Yale University Press, 1982.

17. See Elizabeth Rose, "Famous Rejections" on the Scribesworld website at http://www.scribesworld.com/writersniche/articles/FamousRejections.htm.

18. See "The author and the Austen plot that exposed publishers' pride and prejudice", *The Guardian*, 19 July 2007, available at: http://www.guardian.co.uk/uk/2007/jul/19/books.booknews.

19. See Harvard professor Andrew McAfee's case study on Wikipedia at: http://www.courseware.hbs.edu/public/cases/wikipedia/. It should be noted that former Wikipedia employee Larry Sanger has since launched a new online encyclopaedia called Citizendium that claims to remedy complaints about Wikipedia through a greater role of "expert oversight" and transparent identification of authors. The launch of Citizendium has been interpreted as a direct challenge to Wikipedia's open-ended model. For more on Citizendium, see http://www.en.wikipedia.org/wiki/Citizendium and the site at http://www.en.citizendium.org/wiki/Main_Page.

20. See the Alexa rankings at http://www.alexa.com/site/ds/top_sites?ts_mode=global&lang=none.

21. See Jim Giles, "Internet encyclopaedias go head to head", *Nature*, 15 December 2005, available at: http://www.nature.com/nature/journal/v438/n7070/full/438900a.html. See also "Wikipedia survives research test", BBC News, 15 December 2005, available at: http://www.news.bbc.co.uk/2/hi/technology/4530930.stm.

22. See "In a War of Words, Famed Encyclopaedia Defends its Turf", *Wall Street Journal*, 24 March 2006, available at: http://www.online.wsj.com/public/article/SB11431713988907191-5LS6K_sRtG_8dVOe9tDO_Ps8JRc_20070324.html.

23. See "Collaboration and the Voice of Experts", *Encyclopaedia Brittanica*, 3 June 2008, available at: http://www.brittanicanet.com/?p=88.

24. See Wikipedia's entry on the "Seigenthaler Incident" at http://www.en.wikipedia.org/wiki/Seigenthaler_incident.

25. For a viewpoint of one Middlebury professor, see Neil Waters, "Why You Can't Cite Wikipedia in My Class", *Communications of the ACM*, **50**(9), September 2007. For the Harvard issue, see "Professors Split on Wiki Debate", *Harvard Crimson*, 26 February 2007, available at: http://www.thecrimson.com/article.aspx?ref=517305.

26. For Charles Leadbeater's quote, see his book *We-think* at: http://www.wethinkthebook.net/book/home.aspx.

27. On "citizen" journalism, see Dan Gillmor, *We the Media: Grassroots Journalism By the People, For the People*, O'Reilly Media, 2004; and Shayne Bowman and Chris Willis, *We Media: How Audiences are Shaping the Future of News and Information*, 2003, at: http://www.hypergene.net/wemedia/weblog.php.

28. See Axel Bruns, *Gatewatching: Collaborative Online News Production*, Peter Lang, 2005.

29. See Nicholas Lemann, "Amateur House: Journalism Without Journalists", *The New Yorker*, 7 August 2006, available at: http://www.newyorker.com/archive/2006/08/07/060807fa_fact1.

30. See Vincent Maher, "Citizen Journalism is Dead" at http://www.vincentmaher.com/?p=400. It should be noted that some journalism professors are active advocates of citizen journalism, notably Jay Rosen and Jeff Jarvis, who both teach at New York universities. For Jay Rosen's commentary on Nicholas Lemann's "Amateur Hour", see his PressThink blog posting at http://www.journalism.

nyu.edu/pubzone/weblogs/pressthink/2006/08/04/nicl_am.html. For Jarvis's response to the Lemann article, see http://www.buzzmachine.com/2006/07/31/talk-of-the-town/.

31. For a book on the ethical controversies at *The New York Times*, see Seth Mnookin, *Hard News: The Scandals at the New York Times and Their Meaning for American Media*, Random House, 2004. See also Glenn Greenwald, "The ongoing journalistic scandal at the *New York Times*", Salon.com, 9 July 2007, available at: http://www.salon.com/opinion/greenwald/2007/07/09/hoyt/. For a comprehensive list of journalism scandals in the United States, see http://www.en.wikipedia.org/wiki/United_States_journalism_scandals. On the Columbia Journalism School cheating controversy, see http://www.ethicsscoreboard.com/list/Columbia.html.

32. See "Wall Street Journal workers protest over Murdoch takeover", *The Independent*, 29 June 2007, available at: http://www.independent.co.uk/news/business/news/wall-street-journal-workers-protest-over-murdoch-takeover-455216.html.

33. See Jarvis's valuation of his blog, "Guardian: Value of this blog", BuzzMachine, 14 April 2008, available at: http://www.buzzmachine.com/2008/04/14/guardian-the-value-of-this-blog/.

34. See Jennifer Roberts and Michael Dietrich, "Conceptualizing Professionalism: Why Economics Needs Sociology", *American Journal of Economics and Sociology*, October 1999, available at: http://www.findarticles.com/p/articles/mi_m0254/is_4_58/ai_58496769.

35. See "Blogger, Sans Pyjamas, Rakes Muck and a Prize", *New York Times*, 25 February 2008, available at: http://www.nytimes.com/2008/02/25/business/media/25marshall.html.

36. See Eric Alterman, "Out of Print: the Death and Life of the American Newspaper", *The New Yorker*, 31 March 2008, available at: http://www.newyorker.com/reporting/2008/03/31/080331fa_fact_alterman.

37. See Oded Nov, "What Motivates Wikipedians?", *Communications of the ACM*, **50**(11), November 2007. For the risks of Wikipedia, see Peter Denning, Jim Horning, David Parnas and Lauren Weinstein, "Wikipedia Risks", *Communications of the ACM*, **48**, November/December 2005.

38. See Clay Shirky, *Here Comes Everybody: The Power of Organizing Without Organizations*, Penguin Press, 2008, Ch. 5.

Chapter 13

1. See "Music's New Gatekeeper", *Wall Street Journal*, 9 March 2007, available at: http://www.online.wsj.com/public/article/SB117340340327331757-OZTwdOgBiRz0flPHET_MBcnOfmc_20080308.html.

2. See "Dealwatch: Music Stores and Bankruptcies", TheDeal.com, 23 February 2007, available at: http://www.thedeal.com/dealscape/2007/02/dealwatch_music_stores_and_ban.php.

3. See "Big Music Retailer Is Seeking Bankruptcy Protection", *New York Times*, 10 February 2004, available at: http://www.query.nytimes.com/gst/fullpage.html?res=940E3DB143AF933A25751C0A9629C8B63.

4. See "MySpace and Record Companies Create Music Site", *New York Times*, 3 April 2008, available at: http://www.nytimes.com/2008/04/03/technology/

03cnd-myspace.html?_r=1&hp&oref=slogin; and "MySpace Seeks Venture for Online Music Service", *Wall Street Journal*, 20 February 2008.

5. For global music sales stats, see the IFPI website at: http://www.ifpi.org/content/section_statistics/index.html.

6. See "Peter Gabriel on the future of music", *MacWorld*, 7 November 2007, available at: http://www.macworld.co.uk/ipod-itunes/news/index.cfm?newsid=19611; and "Peter Gabriel on the digital revolution", CNN.com, 22 July 2004, available at: http://www.edition.cnn.com/2004/TECH/07/20/peter.gabriel/.

7. On the Paul McCartney deal with Starbucks, see "McCartney joins Starbucks label", BBC News, 22 March 2007, available at: http://www.news.bbc.co.uk/2/hi/entertainment/6476843.stm. On the Eagles deal with Wal-Mart, see "Marketing Music: Who Needs a Label?", *Advertising Age*, 19 May 2008, available at: http://www.adage.com/print?article_id=127077. On Madonna's deal with Live Nation, see "Madonna, Live Nation make music: $120 million pact would be for 10 years", *Variety*, 10 October 2007, available at http://www.variety.com/article/VR1117973815.html?categoryid=16&cs=1.

8. See "Are record labels dead?", Associated Press, 12 October 2007, available on the CNN site at http://www.edition.cnn.com/2007/SHOWBIZ/Music/10/12/irrelevantrecordlabels.ap/.

9. See "Radiohead challenges labels with free album", *Daily Telegraph*, 8 November 2007, available at: http://www.telegraph.co.uk/money/main.jhtml?xml=/money/2007/10/02/cnradio102.xml; and "Radiohead says; Pay What You Want", *Time*, 1 October 2007, available at: http://www.time.com/time/arts/article/0,8599,1666973,00.html. Other bands that have crowdsourced videos include Decemberists, Modest Mouse, Junior Boys, Willie Nelson, Bjork, Jonathon Coulton and The Hold Steady. See "Radiohead Looks to Fans for Music Video Production" at http://www.readwriteweb.com/archives/radiohead_music_video_contest.php.

10. See "Mashup Artists Face the Music", *Wired*, 4 May 2004, available at: http://www.wired.com/entertainment/music/news/2004/05/63314.

11. See "Slicethepie puts bands on track to success", *Sunday Telegraph*, 25 May 2008, available at: http://www.telegraph.co.uk/money/main.jhtml?xml=/money/2008/05/25/ccslice125.xml.

12. See "Are record labels dead?" Associated Press, 12 October 2007, available on the CNN.com site at: http://www.edition.cnn.com/2007/SHOWBIZ/Music/10/12/irrelevantrecordlabels.ap/.

13. See "Publishers are braced for the slow death of the book", *The Times*, 13 February 2008, available at: http://www.business.timesonline.co.uk/tol/business/columnists/article3359899.ece; and "Amazon Kindle: buyers rush for the iPod of books", *Sunday Times*, 8 June 2008, available at: http://www.technology.timesonline.co.uk/tol/news/tech_and_web/article4087306.ece.

14. See "Amazon pushes social shopping", *Financial Times*, 13 March 2008, available at: http://www.ft.com/cms/s/0/bc5487dc-f129-11dc-a91a-0000779fd2ac.html. For an analysis of Amazon's customer-relationship management, see Soumitra Dutta, Theodore Evgeniou and Vasiliki Anyfioti, "Making Sense of Customer Relationship Management Strategies in a Technology-Driven World", in H. Tsoukas and N. Mylonopolous (Eds) *Organizations as Knowledge Systems, Learning and Dynamic Capabilities*, Palgrave Macmillan, 2004.

15. See Alvin Toffler, *The Third Wave*, Bantam, 1980; and Don Tapscott *The Digital Economy: Promise and Peril in The Age of Networked Intelligence*, McGraw Hill, 1995. Axel Bruns has slightly modified Toffler's original neologism, describing the consumer-as-producer phenomenon as "produsage", thus incorporating the notion of user-generated content. See Axel Bruns, *Blogs, Wikipedia, Second Life and Beyond: From Production to Produsage*, Peter Lang, 2008.

16. Charles Leadbeater has used the invention of the mountain bike as an illustration of bottom-up mass collaboration. See Leadbeater's *We-think* at http://www. wethinkthebook.net/home.aspx; and "Co-opting the creative revolution", BBC News, 15 July 2005, available at: http://www.news.bbc.co.uk/2/hi/technology/4683385.stm.

17. See Matthew Fraser, "Home taping has record industry reeling", *Globe and Mail*, 20 August 1983; and "How home taping fuels the record industry", *Forbes*, 11 July 1997, available at: http://www.forbes.com/1997/07/11/taping.html.

18. See Richard Shell, "Suing Your Customers: A Winning Business Strategy?", Wharton Business School, 23 October 2003, available at: http://www.knowledge. wharton.upenn.edu/article.cfm?articleid=863.

19. See Charles C. Mann, "Digital Culture: the MP3 Revolution", *Atlantic Monthly*, 8 April 1999, available at: http://www.theatlantic.com/unbound/digicult/dc990408.htm.

20. See "States target record labels with price-fixing suits", CNET News.com, 8 August 2000, available at: http://www.news.cnet.com/States-target-record-labels-with-price-fixing-suit/2100-1023_3-244195.html; and "EMI dismisses price-fixing claim", BBC News, 9 August 2000, available at: http://www.news. bbc.co.uk/2/hi/business/871769.stm.

21. See "Suit settled over pricing of music CDs at 3 chains", *New York Times*, 1 February 2002, available at: http://www.query.nytimes.com/gst/fullpage.html?res=9C05E5D91238F932A35753C1A9649C8B63.

22. See "George Michael Severs Sony Tie to Join Dreamworks and Virgin", *New York Times*, 14 July 1995, available at: http://www.query.nytimes.com/gst/fullpage. html?res=990CE7D8163BF937A25754C0A963958260.

23. See Matthew Fraser, "Pop go the rock stars as tech rules", *National Post*, 28 January 2002; and "EMI drops Mariah Carey", BBC News, 23 January 2002, available at: http://www.news.bbc.co.uk/2/hi/entertainment/1777172.stm.

24. For the *Business Week* cover story, see "Inside Napster", *Business Week*, 14 August 2000, available at: http://www.businessweek.com/2000/00_33/b3694001.htm.

25. See Steve Lohr, "The Sharing Society: In the Age of the Internet, Whatever Will Be, Will Be Free", *New York Times*, 14 September 2003, available at: http://www. query.nytimes.com/gst/fullpage.html?res=990DE2DF1E3BF937A2575AC0A9659C8B63.

26. See "12-year-old settles music-swap lawsuit", CNN.com, 18 February 2004, available at: http://www.edition.cnn.com/2003/TECH/internet/09/09/music. swap.settlement/.

27. See Richard Shell, "Suing Your Customers: A Winning Business Strategy?", Wharton Business School, 23 October 2003, available at: http://www.knowledge. wharton.upenn.edu/article.cfm?articleid=863.

28. For Elton John's comments and a critique of the Big Four reaction to Napster, see Charles C. Mann, "The Heavenly Jukebox", *Atlantic Monthly*, September 2000, available at: http://www.theatlantic.com/issues/2000/09/mann.htm.

29. Universal Music, then controlled by Vivendi Universal, later bought MP3.com for $372 million and divested it to CNET.

30. The following year, the German media giant Bertelsmann bought Napster for $85 million, but US courts prevented the deal by forcing Napster to declare bankruptcy and liquidate its assets. Napster's downfall was a stunning victory for the vertical power of multinational corporations. See Patrick Burkhart and Tom McCourt, *Digital Music Wars: Ownership and Control of the Celestial Jukebox*, Rowman & Littlefield, 2006, Ch.3.

31. For a case study on Apple's e-ruptive impact on the music industry, see Soumitra Dutta, "Online Music, Case (B): Whistling a new (i)Tune?", Case 11/2004-5236, INSEAD, 2004, available at: http://www.knowledge.insead.edu/abstract.cfm?ct=14384.

32. See "Steve Jobs: He changed the computer industry. Now he's after the music business", *Rolling Stone*, 3 Decmber 2003.

33. For Steve Jobs's public statement on Digital Rights Management, see http://www.apple.com/hotnews/thoughtsonmusic/.

34. See "Amazon to offer DRM-free music downloads", CNET News.com, 16 May 2007, available at: http://www.news.cnet.com/Amazon-to-offer-DRM-free-music-downloads/2100-1025_3-6184178.html; and "Like Amazon's DRM-Free Music Downloads? Thank Apple", *Wired*, 25 September 2007, available at: http://www.wired.com/entertainment/music/news/2007/09/drm_part_one.

35. See Jeff Howe, "The Hit Factory", *Wired*, 25 November 2005, available at: http://www.wired.com/wired/archive/13.11/myspace.html.

36. See "Facebook asks big labels about music service", *Financial Times*, 5 March 2008, available at: http://www.ft.com/cms/s/0/4dc3ea28-ea54-11dc-b3c9-0000779fd2ac.html.

37. See "Blog, social network buzz correlates to better album sales", Ars Technica, 9 February 2008, available at: http://www.arstechnica.com/news.ars/post/20080209-blog-social-network-buzz-correlates-to-better-album-sales.html. For the Stern study, see Vasant Dhar and Elaine Change, "Does Chatter Matter?: The Impact of User-Generated Content on Music Sales", Leonard N. Stern School of Business, New York University, February 2008, available at: http://www.ssrn.com/abstract=1113536.

38. See "Apple in talks with music companies", *Financial Times*, 19 March 2008, available at: http://www.ft.com/cms/s/0/e35a7404-f557-11dc-a21b-000077b07658.html.

39. See "View from the Top: Edgar Bronfman, chief executive of Warner Music", *Financial Times*, 30 May 2008, available at: http://www.ft.com/cms/s/0/ed013f78-2de3-11dd-b92a-000077b07658.html.

40. See "Universal Music bets on social-networking site", Associated Press, 8 August 2007, available on the MSNBC site at http://www.msnbc.msn.com/id/20187126/.

41. See "Leave talent spotting to the suits says EMI boss", *The Guardian*, 28 February 2008, available at: http://www.music.guardian.co.uk/news/story/0,2260355,00.html/

42. See "Why Would Google Want a Phone?", *Washington Post*, 19 March 2007, available at: http://www.washingtonpost.com/wp-dyn/content/article/2007/03/19/AR2007031900964.html; and "Facebook music service: the rumours continue", CNET News.com, 6 March 2008, available at: http://www.cnet.com.au/software/music/0,239025669,339286534,00.htm.

43. See "Bryan Adams goes indie in the U.S.: Singer says artists should take control", *Calgary Herald*, 5 May 2008, available at: http://www.canada.com/calgaryherald/news/entertainment/story.html?id=d6ab1cb5-19f1-4be2-9a3c-184c978d6cd2.

Chapter 14

1. See C.K. Prahalad and Venkatram Ramaswamy, "Co-opting Customer Competence", *Harvard Business Review*, January–February 2000.
2. For a definition of Enterprise 2.0, see Andrew McAfee's Harvard blog at http://www.blog.hbs.edu/faculty/amcafee/index.php/faculty_amcafee_v3/enterprise_20_version_20/.
3. See Charles Leadbeater's online version of *We-think*, available at: http://www.wethink.wikia.com/wiki/Main_Page.
4. See "How Businesses are using Web 2.0", *McKinsey Quarterly*, 2007, available at: http://www.mckinseyquarterly.com/How_businesses_are_using_Web_20_A_McKinsey_Global_Survey_1913_abstract.
5. "Global Enterprise Web 2.0 Market Forecast: 2007 To 2013", Forrester Research, April 2008, available at: http://www.forrester.com/Research/Document/Excerpt/0,7211,43850,00.html; and "Forrester: Consolidated Web 2.0 Market to Reach $4.6 Billion by 2013", CIO.com, 21 April 2008, available at: http://www.cio.com/article/338617/Forrester_Consolidated_Web_._Market_to_Reach_._Billion_By_.
6. See Dennis Howlett, "The Poverty of Enterprise 2.0 and Social Media", ZDNet, 16 April 2008, available at: http://www.blogs.zdnet.com/Howlett/?p=370.
7. See Rick Levine, Christopher Locke, Doc Searls and David Weinberger, *The Cluetrain Manifesto: The End of Business as Usual*, Basic Books, 2000. See also Dion Hinchcliffe, "The state of Enterprise 2.0", ZDNet, 22 October 2007, available at: http://www.blogs.zdnet.com/Hinchcliffe/?p=143.
8. See Andrew McAfee's Harvard blog posting, "Enterprise 2.0 May be Fine for the Business, But What About the IT Department?", 14 November 2007, available at: http://www.blog.hbs.edu/faculty/amcafee/index.php/faculty_amcafee_v3/enterprise_20_may_be_fine_for_the_business_but_what_about_the_it_department/. See also Andrew McAfee, "Enterprise 2.0: The Dawn of Emergent Collaboration", *MIT Sloan Management Review*, **47**(3), Spring 2006.
9. See "Social skills that confer a business advantage", *Financial Times*, 3 October 2007.
10. See "Facebook 'costs businesses dear' ", BBC News, 11 September 2007, available at: http://www.news.bbc.co.uk/2/hi/technology/6989100.stm.
11. See "Social Networking Sites Cost UK plc £6.5 Billion In Lost Productivity", Global Secure Systems, 21 January 2008, available at: http://www.gss.co.uk/press/?&id=17; and "Employers Shunning MySpace, Facebook", CNET News.com, 7 November 2007, available at: http://www.news.cnet.com/8301-10784_3-9812520-7.html.
12. On valuation of intangible software assets, see Soumitra Dutta, "Recognising the True Value of Software Assets", INSEAD, November 2007. For a *Financial Times* article on the Dutta report, see "Study calls for a rethink on IT valuations", *Financial Times*, 5 November 2007, available at: http://www.search.ft.

com/ftArticle?queryText=Soumitra+Dutta&aje=true&id=071105000186&
ct=0.

13. See Alvin Toffler, *Future Shock*, Random House, 1970; and Shoshana Zuboff, *In the Age of the Smart Machine: The Future of Work and Power*, Basic Books, 1988.

14. See Gary Matuszak, "Enterprise 2.0: Fad or Future?", KPMG International, 2007, available at: http://www.kpmg.fi/Binary.aspx?Section=174&Item=3885. See also Victoria Furness, "Web 2.0 and the Enterprise", Business Insights, 2008, available at: http://www.globalbusinessinsights.com/rbi/content/rbtc0108t. pdf.

15. See "Growing Pains: Can Web 2.0 Evolve Into and Enterprise Technology?" *Information Week*, 27 October 2007, available at: http://www.informationweek. com/shared/printableArticle.jhtml?articleID=202601956; see also Dennis Howlett, "The problem with Forrester's $4.6 billion prediction", ZDNet, 21 April 2008, available at: http://www.blogs.zdnet.com/Howlett/?p=375.

16. For an analysis of face-to-face meetings versus networked collaboration, see Ilan Oshri, Julia Kotlarsky and Leslie Willcocks, "Missing Links: Building Critical Social Ties for Global Collaborative Teamwork", *Communications of the ACM*, **51**(4), April 2008.

17. See Cali Ressler and Jody Thompson, *Why Work Sucks and How to Fix It*, Portfolio, 2008. See a reference to the book in Richard Donkin, "What matters most is that the job is done well", *Financial Times*, 15 May 2008, available at: http://www.ft. com/cms/s/0/ac49cc0e-2215-11dd-a50a-000077b07658.html.

18. See Richard Donkin, "A bright idea for 2008: be nice to your staff", *Financial Times*, 10 January 2008, available at: http://www.search.ft.com/ftArticle?queryText= Donkin+and+meetings&aje=true&id+080110000139&ct=0.

19. See Gary Hamel, *The Future of Management*, Harvard Business School Press, 2007, pp. 164–169. In 2008, Hamel was ranked by *The Wall Street Journal* as the world's top management guru.

20. Gary Hamel, *The Future of Management*, Harvard Business School Press, 2007, pp. 190–194.

21. See Tom Davenport, "Why Enterprise 2.0 Won't Transform Organizations", Harvard Business School, 21 March 2007, available at: http:// www.discussionleader.hbsp.com/davenport/2007/03/why_enterprise_20_ wont_transfo.html. For Davenport's numerous books on knowledge management, see his website at: http://www.tomdavenport.com/books.html.

22. Rick Levine, Christopher Locke, Doc Searls and David Weinberger, *The Cluetrain Manifesto: The End of Business as Usual*, Basic Books, 2000, Ch.1.

23. Howard Rheingold's *Virtual Community* is available online at: http://www.rheingold.com/vc/book/intro.html. See also Rheingold's *Smart Mobs: The Next Social Revolution*, Basic Books, 2002. *Smart Mobs* laid the groundwork for James Surowiecki's later book, *The Wisdom of Crowds*.

24. See Don Tapscott and Anthony D. Williams *Wikinomics: How Mass Collaboration Changes Everything*, Portfolio, 2006; and Charlene Li and Josh Bernoff, *Groundswell: Winning in a World Transformed by Social Technologies*, Harvard Business School Press, 2008.

25. For a Forrester report aimed at marketers, see Charlene Li, "How Consumers Use Social Networks", Forrester Research, 21 June 2007, available at: http:// www.blogs.forrester.com/charleneli/2007/06/how-consumers-u.html.

26. See Gary Hamel, *The Future of Management*, Harvard Business School Press, 2007; and Clay Shirky, *Here Comes Everybody: The Power of Organizing Without Organizations*, Penguin Press, 2008. See Andrew McAfee's Harvard blog at http://www.blog.hbs.edu/faculty/amcafee/; and Charles Leadbeater's site at http://www.charlesleadbeater.net/home.aspx.

27. See Peter Denning and Peter Yaholkovsky, "Getting to 'We': Solidarity, not software, generates collaboration", *Communications of the ACM*, **51**(4), April 2008.

28. See "Social networking gears up for business", *IT Week*, 12 November 2007, available at: http://www.itweek.co.uk/itweek/analysis/2203217/social-networking-gears-3632723.

29. For an online version of Raymond's *The Cathedral and the Bazaar*, see: http://www.catb.org/ esr/writings/cathedral-bazaar/. For the "flattening" impact of open source, see Thomas L. Friedman, *The World is Flat: A Brief History of the Twenty-First Century*, Farrar, Straus and Giroux, 2005, updated and expanded in a 2007 edition.

30. See "Yahoo and MySpace join with Google", Reuters, 25 March 2008, available on the *International Herald Tribune* website at: http://www.iht.com/articles/2008/03/25/technology/google.php. On open-source enterprise software, see Don Tapscott in *Wikinomics*, Ch. 3.

31. See "Eight Business Technology Trends to Watch", *McKinsey Quarterly*, December 2007, available at: http://www.mckinseyquarterly.com/Eight_business_technology_trends_to_watch_2080_abstract.

32. For Ronald Coase's classic 1937 essay on the *Nature of the Firm*, see http://www.cerna.ensmp.fr/Enseignement/CoursEcoIndus/SupportsdeCours/COASE.pdf.

33. See Yochai Benkler, *The Wealth of Networks: How Social Production Transforms Markets and Freedom*, Yale University Press, 2006, p. 60. See also Yochai Benkler, "Coase's Penguin, or, Linux and The Nature of the Firm", *Yale Law Journal*, December 2002, available at: http://www.benkler.org/CoasesPenguin.pdf.

34. See *Serious Business: Web 2.0 Goes Corporate*, Economist Intelligence Unit, 2007; and "Wikis While You Work: Using the Technology in the Enterprise Requires a Careful Balance of Freedom and Control", *eWeek*, 21 November 2007, available at: http://www.eweek.com/c/a/Content-Creation/Wikis-While_You_Work/.

35. See Henry Chesbrough, *Open Innovation: The New Imperative for Creating and Profiting from Technology*, Harvard Business School Press, 2003. On Open innovation's implications for corporate strategy, see Henry Chesbrough and Melissa Appleyard, "Open Innovation and Strategy", *California Management Review*, Fall 2007, available at: http://www.openinnovation.haas.berkele.edu/readingroom.html. See also John Seely Brown and John Hagel, "Creation Nets: Getting the Most from Open Innovation", *McKinsey Quarterly*, **2**, 2006, available at: http://www.mckinseyquarterly.com/Creation_nets_Getting_the_most_from_open_innovation_1766_abstract.

36. On InnoCentive, see "Prizes for Solutions to Problems Play Valuable Role in Innovation", *Wall Street Journal*, 25 January 2007, available at: http://www.online.wsj.com/public/article_print/SB116968486074286927-7z_a6JoHM_hf4kdePUFZEdJpAMI_20070201.html.

37. See Jacques Bughin, Michael Chui and Brad Johnson, "The next step to open innovation", *McKinsey Quarterly*, June 2008.

38. See "Radical Collaboration", *Business Week*, 30 August 2007, available at: http://www.businessweek.com/innovate/content/aug2007/id20070830_258824.htm;

and "Big Blue Embraces Social Media", *Business Week*, 22 May 2008, available at: http://www.businessweek.com/magazine/content/08_22/b4086056643442. htm?chan=search.

39. See "Innovative management: A conversation between Gary Hamel and Lowell Bryan", *McKinsey Quarterly*, November 2007, available at: http://www. mckinseyquarterly.com/Innovative_management_A_conversation_ between_Gary_Hamel_and_Lowell_Bryan_2065_abstract.

40. See Tom Davenport, "Why Enterprise 2.0 Won't Transform Organizations", Harvard Business School, 21 March 2007, available at: http://www. discussionleader.hbsp.com/davenport/2007/03/why_enterprise_20_wont_ transfo.html.

Chapter 15

1. See "Social networks key to '08 race", IDG News, 22 February 2007, available at: http://www.networkworld.com/news/2007/022207-worldbeat-social-networks-key-to.html?page=1.

2. See "The Facebook Election", *Reader's Digest*, available at: http://www.rd.com/ your-america-inspiring-people-and-stories/facebook-influences-2008-election/ article57845.html.

3. See "ABC Joins Forces with Facebook", ABC News, 18 December 2007, available at: http://www.abcnews.go.com/Technology/story?id=3899006.

4. For the "John McCain Facebook Challenge" site, see http://www.blog.clickz. com/080403-143619.html.

5. See "Oops, John McCain's MySpace Page Gets Pranked", CNET News.com, 27 March 2007, available at: http://www.news.cnet.com/8301-10784_3-6170883-7. html.

6. See "Facebook rides wave of US election interest", *Daily Telegraph*, 8 January 2008, available at: http://www.telegraph.co.uk/money/main.jhtml?xml=/ money/2008/01/07/bcnface107.xml.

7. See "Clinton Haters Outpace Obama Backers on Facebook", *Wired*, 28 September 2007, available at: http://www.wired.com/politics/law/news/2007/09/ facebook_hillary; and "Young Voters Find Voice on Facebook", *Washington Post*, 17 February 2007, available at: http://www.washingtonpost.com/wp-dyn/ content/article/2007/02/16/AR2007021602084.html.

8. See Seth Gitell, "Obama's Facebook", *New York Sun*, 13 February 2007, available at: http://www.nysun.com/opinion/obamas-facebook/48560/; and "Internet key to Obama victories", BBC News, 22 May 2008, available at: http://www. news.bbc.co.uk/2/hi/technology/7412045.stm.

9. For more on Habermas's theory and the Internet, see Michael S.H. Heng and Aldo de Moor, "From Habermas's communicative theory to practice on the Internet", *Information Systems Journal*, **13**(4), 2003. See also a Wikipedia entry on Habermas's notion of "ideal speech" at: http://www.en.wikipedia.org/wiki/ Ideal_speech_situation.

10. See "Saving Democracy with Web 2.0", *Wired*, 25 October 2006, available at: http:// www.wired.com/software/webservices/commentary/circuitcourt/2006/10/72001.

11. On the Internet and social capital, see Nan Lin, *Social Capital: A Theory of Social Structure and Action*, Cambridge University Press, 2001, p. 216.

12. See Alexis de Tocqueville, *Democracy in America*, Anchor Books, 1969.

13. See "China shuts down 25 websites", Associated Press, 21 March 2008, available at: http://www.usatoday.com/news/world/2008-03-21-china-internet-shutdown_ N.htm; and "China blocks YouTube over Tibet riots", *Daily Telegraph*, 18 March 2008,availableat:http://www.telegraph.co.uk/news/worldnews/asia/1581879/ China-blocks-YouTube-over-Tibet-riots.html.

14. See "Syria tightens monitoring of Internet use, jails bloggers, blocks Web sites as security threat", *International Herald Tribune*, 25 March 2008; "Rights group names 'Enemies of the Internet'", CNET News.com, 8 November 2006, available at: http://www.news.cnet.com/Rights-group-names-Enemies-of-the-Internet/2100-1028_3-6133645.html; and "Dictatorships catching up with Web 2.0", CNET News.com, 2 February 2007, available at: http://www.news.cnet.com/Dictatorships-catching-up-with-Web-2.0/2010-1028_3-6155582.html. The OpenNet Initiative is a joint programme involving centres at four universities: Harvard, Oxford, Cambridge and the University of Toronto. For its reports, see http://www.opennet.net/reports.

15. For the Facebook/CIA conspiracy theory, see the Question Everything blog at http://www.qwstnevrythg.blog-city.com/was_facebook_started_by_the_cia.htm.

16. For the CIA using Facebook as a recruitment tool, see "CIA Gets In Your Face(book)", *Wired*, 24 January 2007, available at: http://www.wired.com/techbiz/it/news/2007/01/72545; and "CIA Turns to Facebook for New Talent", ABC News, 27 January 2007, available at: http://www.abcnews.go.com/Technology/story?id=2829253.

17. See Hsinchun Chen, Sven Thoms and T.J. Fu, "Cyber Extremism in Web 2.0: An Exploratory Study of International Jihadist Groups", IEEE International Conference on Intelligence and Security Informatics, 2008, available at: http://www.ai.arizona.edu/research/terror/publications/ISI2008-Sven-WEB2.pdf.

18. See "An Internet Jihad Aims at U.S. Viewers", *New York Times*, 15 October 2007, available at: http://www.nytimes.com/2007/10/15/us/15net.html?_r=1&hp&oref=slogin; and "Muslim Extremist's Website Stirs Mixed Emotions in Charlotte, N.C.", Fox News, 9 June 2008, available at: http://www.foxnews.com/story/0,2933,363821,00.html. Kahn's website is www.Revolution.Muslimpad.com.

19. Cass Sunstein, *Republic.com 2.0*, Princeton University Press, 2007.

20. See Cass Sunstein, "The rise of the Daily Me threatens democracy", *Financial Times*, 10 January 2008, available at: http://www.ft.com/cms/s/0/3e2ee254-bf96-11dc-8052-0000779fd2ac.html; and "The Internet is making us stupid", Salon.com, 7 November 2007, available at: http://www.salon.com/news/feature/2007/11/07/sunstein/.

21. On France's Front National in Second Life, see "Exploding pigs and volleys of gunfire as Le Pen opens HQ in virtual world", *The Guardian*, 20 January 2007, available at: http://www.guardian.co.uk/technology/2007/jan/20/news.france. For a case study of Italian right-wing movements on the Web, see Luca Tateo, "The Italian extreme right on-line network: An exploratory study using an integrated social network analysis and content analysis approach", *Journal of Computer-Mediated Communication*, **10**(2), 2005, available at: http://www.jcmc.indiana.edu/vol10/issue2/tateo.html.

22. See Jennifer Stromer-Galley, "Diversity of Political Conversation on the Internet: Users' Perspectives", *Journal of Computer-Mediated Comunication*, **8**(3), April 2003, available at: http://www.jcmc.indiana.edu/vol8/issue3/stromergalley.html.

23. See Albert O. Hirschman, *Exit, Voice and Loyalty: Responses to Decline in Firms, Organizations and States*, Harvard University Press, 1970.

24. See "Implementing the President's Management Agenda for E-Government", White House, 27 February 2002, available at: http://www.whitehouse.gov/omb/inforeg/egovstrategy.pdf. See also Maria Elena Murru "E-Government: From Real to Virtual Democracy", Boston University, 11 April 2003, available at: http://www.unpan1.un.org/intradoc/groups/public/documents/UNPAN/UNPAN011094.pdf.

25. For more on the Accenture e-government reports, see http://www.accenture.com/Global/Services/By_Industry/Government_and_Public_Services/PS_Global/. See also "Technology and Government: The Good, The Bad and the Inevitable", *The Economist*, 14 February 2008.

26. See Soumitra Dutta, "Estonia: A Sustainable Success in Networked Readiness?", in Soumitra Dutta and Irene Mia (Eds) *The Global Information Technology Report 2006–07: Connecting to the Networked Economy*, INSEAD/World Economic Forum, Palgrave Macmillan, 2007.

27. See Mark Badger, Paul Johnston, Martin Stewart-Weeks and Simon Willis, *The Connected Republic: Changing the Way We Govern*, Cisco Internet Business Solutions Group, 2004. This report was updated by Johnston and Stewart-Weeks in September 2007 under the title *The Connected Republic 2.0: New Possibilities and New Value for the Public Sector*, available at: http://www.theconnectedrepublic.org/.

28. See David Weinberger, *Small Pieces, Loosely Joined: A Unified Theory of the Web*, Basic Books, 2002.

29. See "Government offline: Why business succeeds on the Web and government mostly fails", in *The Economist* special report, *Technology and Government*, 14 February 2008.

30. For the UK Cabinet Office's *Transformational Government* report, see http://www.cio.gov.uk/transformational_government/strategy/.

31. "Power of Information: New Taskforce", speech by Tom Watson MP, Minister for Transformational Government, 31 March 2008, available at: http://www.cabinetoffice.gov.uk/about_the_cabinet_office/speeches/Watson/080331watson.aspx.

32. See "Technology and Government: The Good, the Bad and the Inevitable", *The Economist*, 14 February 2008. For examples of local e-government success stories in Britain, see "Politicians are using the Internet to harness your bright ideas," *Sunday Times*, 7 September 2008, available at http://www.technology.timesonline.co.uk/tol/news/tech_and_web/the_web/article4692454.ece.

33. See Charles Leadbeater, "Social Software for Social Change", a discussion paper for the Office of the Third Sector, July 2007, available at: http://www.charlesleadbeater.net/cms/xstandard/social_software.pdf; and Charles Leadbeater and Hilary Cottam, "The User Generated State: Public Services 2.0", available at: http://www.charlesleadbeater.net/archive/public-services-20.aspx.

34. See Book II, Chapter V "Of the Use Which Americans Make of Public Associations in Civil Life", in Alexis de Tocqueville's *Democracy in America*, Anchor Books, 1969, available at: http://www.xroads.virginia.edu/~HYPER/detoc/ch2_05.htm. For a critique of Tocqueville regarding American volunteerism, see Theda Skocpol, "What Tocqueville Missed: Government made all that

'volunteerism' possible", Slate.com, 15 November 1996, available at: http://www.slate.com/id/2081.

Conclusion

1. See "Web 2.0 Expo: Before centralized power", *San Francisco Chronicle*, 26 April 2008, available at: http://www.sfgate.com/cgi-bin/article.cgi?f=/c/a/2008/04/26/BU2V10C5G6.DTL&hw=tim+0%27reilly&sn=007&sc=553.
2. See Jonathan Zittrain, *The Future of the Internet and How to Stop It*, Allen Lane, 2008, p. 8.
3. See "Web 2.0 euphoria tempered by social problems", *Financial Times*, 26 May 2008; and "Caught in the net", *The Economist*, 23 January 2003.
4. See Richard Haass, "The Age of Nonpolarity: What Will Follow U.S. Dominance", *Foreign Affairs*, May/June 2008.
5. See Leo W. Jeffres, David J. Atkin, Cheryl Campanella Bracken and Kimberly A. Neuendorf, "Cosmopoliteness in the Internet Age", *Journal of Computer-Mediated Communication*, November 2004, available at: http://www.jcmc.indiana.edu/vol10/issue1/jeffres.html.
6. See "Web 3.0 and beyond: the next 20 years of Internet", *The Times*, 24 October 2007, available at: http://www.technology.timesonline.co.uk/tol/news/tech_and_web/the_web/article2726190.ece.
7. See "Faithbook launches on Facebook to tackle extremism", *The Times*, 3 June 2008, available at: http://www.timesonline.co.uk/tol/news/uk/article4057686.ece.
8. See "Pope goes digital to connect with youth", Reuters, 7 May 2008, available at: http://www.reuters.com/article/technologyNews/idUSSYD19071020080507?feedType=RSS&feedName=technologyNews; and "Pope readies text-message blitz, Catholic Facebook", *Wired*, 7 May 2008, available at: http://www.blog.wired.com/underwire/2008/05/pope-readies-te.html.
9. See Francis Fukuyama, *Trust: The Social Virtues and the Creation of Prosperity*, Free Press, 1995, p. 7. See also Barbara Misztal, *Trust in Modern Societies*, Polity Press, 1996.

Index

Index compiled by Indexing Specialists (UK) Ltd